PROGRAMMING WITH
PL/I

PROGRAMMING WITH PL/1

HENRY RUSTON

Polytechnic Institute of New York

McGRAW-HILL BOOK COMPANY

New York   St. Louis   San Francisco   Auckland   Bogotá
Düsseldorf   Johannesburg   London   Madrid   Mexico   Montreal   New Delhi
Panama   Paris   São Paulo   Singapore   Sydney   Tokyo   Toronto

PROGRAMMING WITH PL/I

Copyright © 1978 by McGraw-Hill, Inc.
All rights reserved.
Printed in the United States of America.
No part of this publication may be reproduced,
stored in a retrieval system, or transmitted,
in any form or by any means,
electronic, mechanical, photocopying, recording, or otherwise,
without the prior written permission of the publisher.

567890   DODO   832

This book was set in Times Roman by University Graphics, Inc.
The editors were Charles E. Stewart and Barbara Brooks;
the cover was designed by Nicholas Krenitsky;
the production supervisor was Dennis J. Conroy.
The drawings were done by Fine Line Illustrations, Inc.
R. R. Donnelley & Sons Company was printer and binder.

Library of Congress Cataloging in Publication Data

Ruston, Henry.
     Programming with PL/I.

     Includes index.
     1.   PL/I (Computer program language)   I.   Title.
QA76.73.P25R87   001.6′424   77-16407
ISBN 0-07-054350-X

To
JANET,
ANNE,
LILLIAN,
and
EILEEN

CONTENTS

PREFACE

ORGANIZATION

This material was prepared as a textbook for students who have had no previous exposure to programming. The organization is along tutorial lines, with the third chapter offering a first pass through the PL/I syntax. This early presentation of essentials enables students to write programs immediately. Later chapters provide more exposure and cover in detail other aspects of programming and of PL/I. They amplify and extend the material, thus fleshing out the previously introduced skeleton.

CONTENTS

The book is intended for a one-semester course. It contains more material than can be digested easily in a typical three-credit course. However, not all sections in every chapter need be covered, and sections which may be omitted with no loss in continuity have been identified.

The material is a mix of PL/I language and programming topics and has evolved through five years of class testing at the Polytechnic Institute of New York. The first three chapters form the introductory part and consist of a brief introduction, the elements of problem solving, and the essentials of PL/I. These chapters can be covered in approximately two weeks of class time, after which the student is able to program. In the next six chapters selection, looping, and program debugging are described. After students master those tools, structured programming and programming style are described in the following four chapters. This completes the first half of the course; the third quarter demonstrates in six chapters how to handle list- and data-directed input and output, character and bit strings, and arrays and structures. The last quarter of the text describes built-in functions (with material selected for scientific programming); procedures; edit-directed and record-oriented input and output; and program interrupts, as well as structured programming in large tasks.

In the appendixes, PL/I dialects such as PL/C and PLAGO are described, and enough details are given to allow the use of the book for these PL/I-like languages.

OBJECTIVES

The prime objective has centered on producing a readable book. In line with this objective, programming jargon is used infrequently. Topics are arranged in tutorial rather than "logical" order. The material on edit-directed and record-oriented input-output, for example, is covered in later chapters rather than immediately after the more elementary list- and data-directed input-output.

Another objective is the maintenance of balance. Rather than totally omitting certain constructs by dictum (the GO TO statement, for example), reasons for their avoidance are given at a point when these reasons are best able to be understood. This makes it possible to discuss at that point also the instances when such constructs are indeed to be preferred to other alternatives.

APPROACH

The book reflects my belief that it is better to present the essentials of the language initially and to teach good programming techniques only after some programming experience than to do so in reverse order. It has been my experience that too early an emphasis on good programming techniques frustrates students and decreases their motivation toward programming. As students learn the language, they wish to program immediately problems solved so tediously in high school. Placing constraints on program construction only inhibits this early enthusiasm. Furthermore, it is only after some programming work that good style and construction are appreciated.

OTHER FEATURES

The book contains 168 complete and tested illustrative programs and many additional examples illustrated with program segments. The topic of procedures, a source of difficulty for many students, is covered in detail with 44 illustrative programs. Over 260 problems appear in the text for practice, reinforcement, and extension of the material. An instructor's manual with a complete solution to each problem is available.

ACKNOWLEDGMENTS

I gratefully acknowledge the comments of my colleagues M. Adamowicz, D. Doucette, S. Habib, E. Lancevich, J. LaTourrette, P. McGregor, T. Parsons, and

M. Petrella. My special thanks go to Jerry Weiss for his many perceptive and most valuable suggestions. I also thank Frances Crowe, Elaine Cummings, and Ruth Drucker for their excellent typing, and both Myrna Singer and Maryon Fischetti for their help in the preparation of the manuscript. My admiration goes to Alice Goehring for her excellent work in the editing of this manuscript and to Barbara Brooks of McGraw-Hill Book Company for her advice, thoroughness, and cooperation.

Henry Ruston

INTRODUCTION

This is a book on programming with the PL/I language. *Programming* is the writing of instructions for a computer. A set of such instructions is called a *program*, and its writer a *programmer*. In this introductory chapter we shall describe the different types of programs and computer languages, as well as some gross features of the PL/I language.

1.1 THE DIFFERENT TYPES OF PROGRAMS

A program can be written in several ways. First, it can be written so that the computer can understand it. Such a program is written in the computer's own language, which is called a *machine language*. The program itself is called an *object program*. In the earlier computers all programs were written in machine language. Such programs contain very detailed instructions for each calculation and for the usual clerical chores accompanying each task. These instructions are written in a binary form; that is, each instruction consists of a string of characters containing a combination of 1s and 0s (for example, 01011010 for the instruction *add*). Thus numeric binary code words must be either memorized or looked up. Obviously, programming in machine language is tedious and time-consuming. However, it has the advantage, desired at times, that the programmer has full control over computer operations.

Second, a program can be written so that letters or words replace the binary code of the machine language. In such a program, the letter A would be employed for the code meaning *add*. This language is named *assembly language*, and the program so written, a *source program*. A computer does not understand the assembly language; hence, the words have to be translated into a code recognizable by the computer. This translation from assembly language into machine language (that is, from a source program into an object program) is performed by a program stored in the computer memory. Such a translation program is known as an *assembler;* it "assembles" a program into a language understandable to the computer. Programming in assembly language is simpler than in machine language. An assembly language program still exercises full control over computer operations, but it is still too tedious and time-consuming for the average computer programmer.

Third, a program can be written in a language close to the programmer's natural language (for example, English). Such a language is named a *high-level language*. A program in this language consists of *statements*, which constitute a source program. Each statement may correspond to many machine language instructions. Furthermore, the instructions for the clerical work accompanying each calculation—for example, the transfer of numbers to and from storage—no longer need be specified. As in the case of the assembly language, the source program in the high-level language has to be translated into an object program. This translation program is named a *compiler*; it "compiles" a set of detailed machine language instructions to execute the statement.

A program in a high-level language does not exercise the complete microscopic control over each instruction as the object program does. A high-level language statement is macroscopic and usually translates into several object program instructions, where the translation is dictated by the translating program (that is, compiler) rather than by the programmer. This is, however, rarely a disadvantage. For one, the compiler does a better job than an average machine language programmer. And now the programming is performed in a natural easy-to-learn, English-like language, freeing the programmer from all the clerical drudgery. It is this type of programming, the programming in a high-level language, that we shall study in this book.

1.2 THE LANGUAGES OF THE FIFTIES AND PL/I

A number of high-level languages have been introduced in the last 20 years. These are also known as *procedure-oriented*, or *P-O*, *languages*, for short. As the name implies, these languages are designed so that they are particularly convenient for describing a problem-solving procedure. Foremost among them are Fortran, Algol, Cobol, and PL/I.

Fortran (an acronym for FORmula TRANslation) has gained an eminent acceptance in the United States since its inception in 1954. As its name implies, it is an algebraically oriented language. Algol (ALGOrithmic Language), introduced in 1958, is a popular European algebraic language. Since 1959, Cobol (COmmon Business Oriented Language) has been the language used for nearly all business-type programs (for example, accounting). But despite the existence of all these and yet other languages, computer users still found problems for which no existing language was a satisfactory one. There are, for example, problems requiring both scientific and businesslike capabilities. Thus in 1963 the International Business Machines Corporation (that is, IBM, the major manufacturer of computers) established a committee consisting of personnel from IBM and major scientific and business users. Their recommendations resulted in the development of a new computer language, PL/I (Programming Language One), with the following features:

1. It is a single language useful for both scientific and business-type problems.
2. It is more "English-like," and thus easier to learn.
3. It is a "commonsense" language. If, for instance, the programmer fails to give explicit instructions, the compiler will make a reasonable decision on the programmer's intentions.
4. It is richer, more powerful, and better suited for solution of all types of problems than all the three previous languages combined.
5. It is modular. This means that a programmer can write useful programs knowing just a fraction (that is, small module) of the total language.
6. It is a forerunner of a new generation of languages: the PL/II, the PL/III, and other such languages.

In the following pages we will introduce a fraction of the PL/I language—a fraction sufficient for nearly all problems encountered in engineering and scientific practice.

1.3 SUMMARY

In this chapter we described the different types of programs, namely, object and source programs. The programs can be written in machine, assembly, and high-level languages. We also described some of the gross features of the PL/I language.

QUESTIONS

1.1 What is *(a)* an object program, *(b)* a source program, *(c)* machine language, *(d)* assembly language, *(e)* a compiler?

1.2 What are the differences between scientific problems and business problems?

1.3 What type of problems require a language with both scientific and business capabilities?

2 PROBLEM SOLVING, ALGORITHMS, AND FLOWCHARTS

In this chapter we will describe how we plan to solve a problem on a computer. We will introduce the symbols of the flowchart, and we will show that the flowchart is a convenient plan for the solution of a problem.

2.1 PROBLEM SOLVING

Problem solving is our main occupation in daily life, where the problems vary in scope from finding food and shelter to finding roots of an algebraic equation. As always, problem solving involves these four steps:[1]

1. Understanding the problem
2. Devising a plan of solution
3. Carrying out the plan
4. Examining the solution

Understanding the problem requires the selection of the unknowns (that is, the variables to be found), the selection of data needed for finding the unknowns, and the introduction of notation for the unknowns. The plan of solution calls for finding the connection between the given data and the unknowns, for example, finding equations for the unknowns. The carrying-out phase of the plan demands the actual calculation. The examination part principally checks the answers, and occasionally investigates the generality of the method for solving other related problems.

When the problem is solved with a computer, the first two steps still require human skills. It is the third step, usually the most time-consuming and the dullest, that utilizes the computer's skills. The computer carries out the human plan, and if this plan is faulty, the computer's answers are faulty too. The fourth step, the

---

[1]This formulation is due to Prof. G. Polya and is described in detail in his book "How to Solve It," 2d ed., Anchor Book A93, Doubleday, Garden City, NY, 1957.

examination of results, is performed by the human problem solver, although the computer with its diagnostic skills can help greatly here.

2.2 ALGORITHMS

The problem-solving plan for computer execution must be given in the form of detailed instructions for the computational and other tasks. For example, the plan for obtaining the sum of two numbers A and B may be specified as follows:

1. Start working on the problem.
2. Get A and B.
3. Obtain total = A + B.
4. Tell us what total is.
5. That's all.

In the above problem, our step-by-step plan for obtaining the sum of two numbers is in essence a set of instructions that we give to a moron. A computer requires just such detailed instructions. Instructions which tell how to solve a problem, that is, give a recipe or procedure for solving a problem, are named an *algorithm.*[1] Evidently, a computer requires a very detailed algorithm, allowing no ambiguity. An algorithm for a human being may contain some ambiguity (for example, the algorithm for calculating income taxes as given in the Internal Revenue Service instructions) and still be of use occasionally.

Algorithms are rarely as simple as the one in our addition problem. Often they require that a decision be made during the computational process. The answer, that is, the solution, depends then upon the outcome of the decision. For different outcomes there are different answers. As an example of such an algorithm, consider the problem of determining whether three positive numbers A, B, and C could be the sides of an equilateral triangle. A possible algorithm for this problem is as follows:

1. Start working on the problem.
2. Get A, B, and C.
3. If A ≠ B, then go to step 9.
4. If A = B, then continue downward.
5. If A ≠ C, then go to step 9.
6. If A = C, then continue downward.
7. Say: These three numbers can be the sides of an equilateral triangle.
8. That's all.
9. Say: These three numbers cannot be the sides of an equilateral triangle.
10. That's all.

---

[1] For a more precise definition of an algorithm listing its properties see D. E. Knuth, "The Art of Computer Programming," Vol. 1, 2d ed., pp 4–7, Addison-Wesley Publishing Co., Reading, Mass., 1973.

This algorithm leads to the following observations:

1. For specific values of A, B, and C, the problem solving consists of different steps as we jump from step to step following the instructions of the algorithm. For the case A = B = C, we perform steps 1,2,4,6,7, and 8. For A = B ≠ C, we perform steps 1,2,4,5,9, and 10. Similarly, for A ≠ B, we perform steps 1,2,3,9, and 10. Thus the actual computations as well as the final results depend upon the outcome of intermediate computations. These intermediate computations lead to a decision, which selects a particular sequence of steps of the algorithm.
2. The algorithm may end at different steps. Here the algorithm ends either at step 8 or at step 10. Note that if we wish a single end, we can replace the instruction "That's all" in step 8 by a "Go to step 10" instruction.
3. The algorithm is inconvenient, unnecessarily complicated, and rather clumsy for the simple problem considered here. This brings up the question: Is there a better way to represent an algorithm? Fortunately, the answer is an emphatic yes.

A better way to represent an algorithm is to do so pictorially, showing the flow of the computational process. Such a representation is provided through a diagram named a *flowchart*.

2.3 FLOWCHARTS

A flowchart is the most popular way of giving an algorithm for computer programming. There are good reasons for the flowchart's popularity. First, it shows pictorially both the computations themselves and the sequence of the computational process. Second, distinct flowchart symbols are used for different instructions. These distinct symbols, once learned, aid in visualizing the computational process.

We will introduce the flowchart symbols by means of the algorithm for the addition problem. The flowchart for this algorithm is shown in Fig. 2.1. The start of the algorithm (symbol 1) is represented by the *oval* with the word START inside it. Note that the end of the algorithm (symbol 5) is also represented by the same oval, but now with the word END inside it. Thus the *oval is the symbol* for both the *start and the end of the algorithm*.

Symbol 2 is the input symbol. It is used to show the input data needed for the calculations. The same symbol is used for the output (symbol 4), showing the result of the computation, Thus the *parallelogram symbol is used for both input and output,* and inside the parallelogram we write the word GET and the names of the input (that is, A,B) for input, or the word PUT and the name of the output (that is, TOTAL) for output.

Symbol 3 is a *rectangle and represents processing*. Here the numbers named A,B are processed into the number named TOTAL by the indicated addition.

Note that the flowchart symbols are connected by arrows. These arrows are named *flowlines* and indicate the sequence of the algorithm.

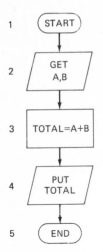

1 START

2 GET A,B

3 TOTAL=A+B

4 PUT TOTAL

5 END

Figure 2.1 Flowchart for the addition problem.

We still need a symbol for a decision, which some algorithms require. *The symbol for decision is the diamond,* shown in Fig. 2.2. Here, as an example, the question is asked: Does A=5? One flowline is followed if the answer is YES, another if the answer is NO.

Next, we shall draw a flowchart for the algorithm of the 10-step triangle problem given in Sec. 2.2. This flowchart is portrayed in Fig. 2.3. We will now interpret this flowchart.

In step 1 we start to work on the problem. The start is shown on the flowchart with the oval symbol (with START inside it). Step 2, "Get A,B and C," is the input data-acquiring step and is shown by the input parallelogram symbol (with GET A,B,C inside it). Steps 3 and 4 require only a single flowchart symbol—the decision diamond—because two flowlines lead out of the decision box, one if A≠B (that is, if the answer to A≠B? is YES) and the other if A=B (that is, if the answer to A≠B? is NO). Similarly, the decisions of steps 5 and 6 need only the single decision symbol. Step 7 gives the output for the condition that both A=B and A=C, and it is represented by the output symbol (that is, the parallelogram), putting out the appropriate message. Similarly, step 9, represented by the output symbol, gives the output for either of the two conditions (1) A≠B or (2) A=B, but A≠C. Finally, the algorithm comes to its end with the oval END symbol, representing steps 8 and 10.

It is evident that the flowchart of Fig. 2.1 allows an easier interpretation of the algorithm than the five-step text in Sec. 2.2. The advantage of the flowchart of Fig. 2.3 over the 10-step text in Sec. 2.2 is also obvious. This advantage of the flowchart

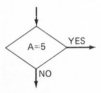

A=5 YES
NO

Figure 2.2 Symbol for decision.

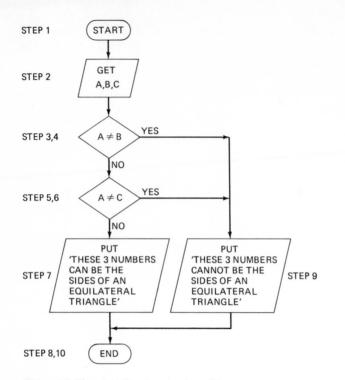

Figure 2.3 Flowchart for the triangle problem.

over English text becomes even greater as one learns the flowchart symbols and identifies at a glance the types of instructions (to the computer) which these symbols represent.

2.4 EXAMPLES

We will describe three more problems and illustrate their solutions with flowcharts.

Example 2.4.1 Obtain a flowchart for calculating the sum of four numbers.

Solution This problem is similar to the previous problem of obtaining the sum of two numbers. Thus the flowchart is analogous to the one of Fig. 2.1. Now we obtain four numbers, represented by the symbols A, B, C, and D, and form a quantity named TOTAL as the sum of these four numbers. The flowchart of Fig. 2.4 illustrates this approach.

A second approach to this problem consists of obtaining one number at a time and adding it to the running sum. Here we initially obtain the first number and let the quantity named TOTAL be equal to it. We then obtain the second number and add it to TOTAL. We continue until all four numbers are contained in TOTAL, and we tell (that is, put) the resulting the sum. The flowchart of Fig. 2.5 illustrates this approach.

As we inspect the last two flowcharts, we are thankful that we were asked to add just four numbers. If we were asked to add 1000 numbers we will need still a different approach. We will consider this problem next.

Example 2.4.2 Obtain a flowchart for calculating the sum of 1000 numbers.

Solution To construct a flowchart such as the one of Fig. 2.4 will require 1000 symbols for the 1000 numbers, in addition to the drudgery of writing these 1000 symbols. To construct a flowchart such as the one of Fig. 2.5 requires the drawing of 1000 input symbols and 1000 processing symbols, which is not an attractive proposition. A better approach is to view this problem as one in which we obtain a number and add it to the running sum, and then repeat the process.

Let us assume that there are exactly 1000 numbers in our input. Thus the last number is the 1000th number, and when it is added we complete the sum. With this assumption, we obtain the flowchart of Fig. 2.6. Observe the two features of this flowchart:

1. There is a decision box. The YES branch leads to the result and the end of the calculation. The NO branch leads to repetition of the calculation.
2. The calculation for the addition of the next number is the same as the one for the previous number. Because of this, we can return to the previous part of the flowchart and perform the same task as before. Such a repetition is named a *loop*. The use of loops simplifies the construction of a flowchart, because the same calculation does not have to be shown several times.

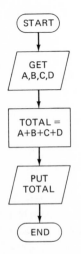

Figure 2.4 Flowchart for the solution to Example 2.4.1.

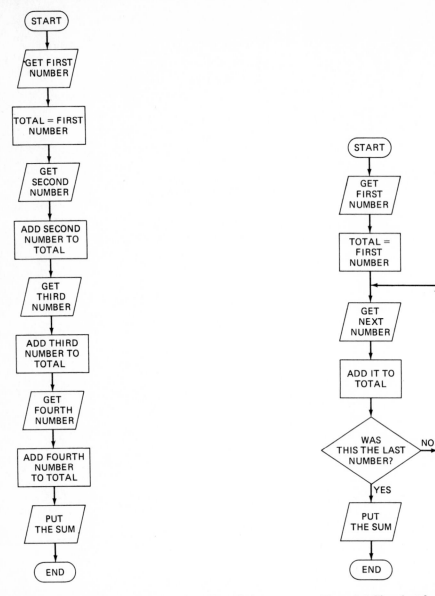

Figure 2.5 Flowchart portraying an alternative solution to Example 2.4.1.

Figure 2.6 Flowchart for the solution to Example 2.4.2.

As a further illustration, let us next assume that there are more than 1000 numbers in the input, but we still want the sum of just the first 1000 numbers. Now, we must count the numbers (rather than look for the last number), and when we add the 1000th number we will have the desired sum. This leads to the flowchart of Fig. 2.7, where we use a quantity named COUNT to count the added number. Note that whenever a number is added to the running sum,

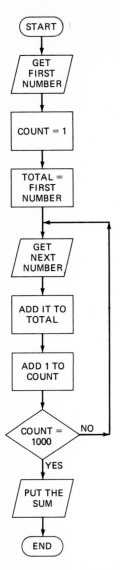

Figure 2.7 Flowchart for the alternative solution to Example 2.4.2.

COUNT is increased by 1. Eventually COUNT is 1000, leading to the YES branch of the decision box and completion of the calculation.

Example 2.4.3 Construct a flowchart for sorting a deck of cards into the four suits.

Solution The flowchart is shown in Fig. 2.8. We obtain a card and ask whether or not it is a club. If it is a club, we place it in the clubs pile. If it is not a club, we determine whether it is a diamond. If it is a diamond, we place it in the diamonds pile. Otherwise, we determine whether it is a heart. If it is a heart, we

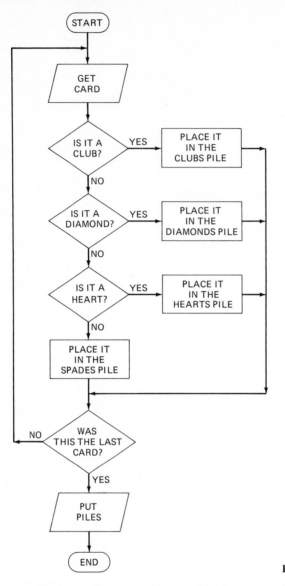

Figure 2.8 Flowchart for Example 2.4.3.

place it in the hearts pile. If it is not a heart (and it was not a club nor a diamond), it must be a spade, and it is placed in the spades pile. Now we determine whether this was the last card. If so, the sorting is completed; we give the piles (to whoever gave us the sorting job) and end the task. If it is not the last card, we return to the beginning (that is, loop to the GET CARD box) and repeat the process.

This last example illustrates that flowcharts are equally as useful for nonnumerical (for example, the sorting) as for numerical problems.

2.5 SUMMARY

In this chapter we described the problem-solving plan needed for computer execution. This plan, named an algorithm, must be in the form of detailed, unambiguous, step-by-step instructions. We introduced the flowchart symbols and illustrated the use of a flowchart for presenting an algorithm. As we saw the flowchart is useful for both numerical and nonnumerical algorithms.

PROBLEMS

2.1 There are two numbers on a data card. The first number represents resistance of an electric network; the second number represents current applied to this network. It is known that

$$\text{Voltage} = \text{resistance} * \text{current}$$

Draw a flowchart to acquire the two numbers and to calculate and print out the resulting voltage.

2.2 Construct a flowchart for purchasing a house. The input is the inspection report of a house, the output one of the two statements BUY HOUSE or DO NOT BUY HOUSE. Examples of the decisions that have to be made are

1. Does the house meet the requirements?
2. Are immediate major repairs needed?
3. Is the house worth the asking price and cost of repairs?
4. Can the purchaser afford the initial cost?
5. Can the purchaser afford the payments?

2.3 Construct a flowchart for repairing a chair. The input is the inspection of the chair, the output either the repaired chair or the statement DO NOT FIX THE CHAIR. Examples of some of the required decisions are

1. Is the chair worth repairing?
2. Are the tools available?
3. Are the parts available?

Here the decisions require extra processes such as

1. Listing of tools and parts
2. Purchasing or borrowing of tools
3. Obtaining or buying of parts.

2.4 Construct a flowchart for writing a check in payment for a bill. Here the bill is the input, and the writing of a check an output. Before a check is written, two decisions should be made: to ascertain whether the bill should be paid and whether there is enough money in the bank to cover the check.

2.5 There is a set of numbers on the data cards. It is desired to count the number of nonzeros in the first 100 numbers. Draw a flowchart to do so.

2.6. There are 100 non-negative numbers on the data cards. The last number is zero, and there are no other zeros in the set. Draw a flowchart to find and print out the largest number in the set.

2.7 There is a set of numbers on the data cards. It is desired to obtain the sum of consecutive numbers but to include only those numbers which exceed 10 and are smaller than 50. The sum should include as many numbers as possible but should not exceed 1000. Draw a flowchart for this problem.

2.8 Draw the flowchart for making a telephone call to someone whose name and address you know. The telephone number should preferably be obtained from the telephone directory, or if one is not available, from information. Make provisions for an unlisted number and try to take into account all possible conditions (for example, broken telephone, telephone in use, coin telephone, etc.).

3

SIMPLE PL/I PROGRAMS

In the preceding chapter we discussed the flowchart as a convenient first step in solving a problem on a computer. The next step requires the translation of the flowchart into a program, that is, the actual writing of a program. The writing of a program, or programming, is the topic of this chapter. We will describe how we begin and end the program, and how we instruct the computer to perform the desired tasks. In later chapters we will study additional instructions for the writing of more sophisticated programs.

3.1 PROGRAM FOR THE ADDITION PROBLEM

As our first example we will write a PL/I program for the addition problem. The flowchart for this problem appears in Fig. 2.1. Obviously, we first start the program. We do so with the statement

Label: PROCEDURE OPTIONS (MAIN);

The *label* is the name (or label) we give to the program. Here a suitable label is perhaps the word ADD. The label is followed by the colon, then the words PROCEDURE OPTIONS (MAIN), and finally a semicolon. Thus in our program the first statement reads

ADD: PROCEDURE OPTIONS (MAIN);

Note that the semicolon terminates the first statement. In fact, the semicolon terminates each program statement.

The second statement must instruct the computer to acquire two numbers represented by A and B. The instruction to do that is

GET LIST (A,B);

Note the parentheses around A and B.

The third statement must tell the computer to obtain TOTAL, this being the sum of A and B. The instruction to do so is

$$TOTAL = A + B;$$

Next we wish to print out the result, this being the number represented by TOTAL. The instruction for such a printout is

$$PUT\ LIST\ (TOTAL);$$

Again note the presence of parentheses around TOTAL.

Now we are done. Thus we terminate the program with the instruction

$$END\ ADD;$$

We generally terminate the program with

$$END\ label;$$

where *label* is the name (label) given to the program. In our program this label is ADD. Thus our entire program reads

```
ADD:    PROCEDURE OPTIONS(MAIN);
        GET LIST(A,B);
        TOTAL = A + B;
        PUT LIST(TOTAL);
        END ADD;
```

It is certain that this program raises a number of questions. We shall try to answer some of them.

1. How is this program given to the computer?

The two common ways are through punched cards or through a special typewriter. When a program is prepared on punched cards, blank cards are fed into a keypunch, which is a typewriterlike device that simultaneously types and punches holes (in the cards). As the statements of the program are typed on the cards, the keypunch makes appropriate holes in the cards. The cards are then stacked in order and brought (by the programmer) to the computer center. There the cards are read by a device named the *card reader* which interprets the punched holes into the desired computer instructions. Both the program and the results (in our program, the number represented by TOTAL is the single result) are printed on sheets of paper, and this paper (with the original cards) is returned to the customer. In some computer installations the program can be given to the computer directly through a special typewriter. Then the program is merely typed. Incidentally, the operation through the punched cards is known as *batch* operation (because a quantity of jobs are given to the computer at one time). The direct operation through a typewriter is known as a *timeshared* operation, because the computer is shared among customers. In the following, we will focus our attention on the punched-card operation, because it is more common and its programming is practically identical to the timeshared one.

2. What number would we obtain as a result of our addition program?

In our program, there would be no answer, because we have not told the computer what are the numbers for A and B. To do so, we must have an additional card (or cards) with numbers for A and B. Let us assume that A = 11.7 and B = 8.5. Then the card with numbers (that is, data card) reads

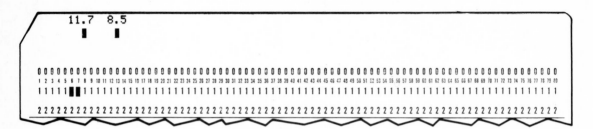

The numbers are separated by one or more spaces. Alternatively they can be separated by a comma (or a comma and spaces), as

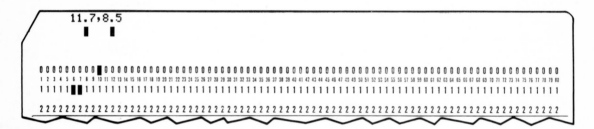

Note that there are no semicolons on the data part of the program.

3. Is the addition program with the data cards a complete program?

Not quite. The compiler needs further instructions. It must ascertain, for example, whether or not the customer is a valid user (that is, has a valid account). Also, a computer center executes programs in various languages—thus there must be some way to tell the system that our program is in the PL/I language and hence needs the PL/I compiler. All this is accomplished with additional cards: so-called control cards. In the jargon of programming, the five-statement program deck of cards is named the *source deck*. The data card or cards with numbers (for A and B) are named the *data deck* and are placed after the source deck. There is always one *job card,* which identifies the user's job, in front of the entire deck. Then there are typically two control cards in front of the source deck and one card at its end. These are followed by one card in front of the data deck and one at its end. Finally, there is a card signifying the end of a job. Thus there are typically seven extra cards (or statements in timeshared operation) accompanying our program. The contents of these cards are posted at each computer installation (prepunched cards are often available there). We have listed them in App. 6, and they need not concern us here.

4. Is it necessary to place just one statement on a card?

No. It is usually done so, however, because it makes program reading so much easier.

5. Why are programs written in capital letters?

Because the keypunch prints only capital letters.

6. Are there any restrictions on the words used for labels?

Yes. There are three restrictions. These are

a. A label must start with a *letter*. A letter is any one of the 26 letters of the alphabet from A to Z or the characters $, #, and @. Thus there are 29 letters that can be used for the first character of a label.
b. The second and subsequent characters of a label can be any of the 29 letters, any of the 10 digits (that is, 0 to 9), or the break (underscore) character. Note that the space is not an allowed character. If we want a label suggestive of two words, we use the break character for separation (for example, TOO___ MUCH)
c. A label contains at least 1 character and at most 31 characters.[1]

7. Are there any restrictions on the names given to the variables[2] in the programs?

Yes. The variables (for example, A, B, TOTAL) have the same three restrictions as the labels. The names given to variables and labels are known as *identifiers*.

8. What are the rules on the format of the program?

The IBM punch card has 80 columns. However, the PL/I compiler executes instructions only when they are in columns 2–72. Column 1 is used on control cards. Columns 73–80 are used for identification. Thus all PL/I source statements should appear[3] in columns 2–72. Data cards, however, are read in all 80 columns. Thus data numbers can be punched anywhere on the card without restrictions. Also the rules are very flexible on spaces. Spaces separate identifiers, and whenever one space is allowed, many spaces are also allowed. Similarly certain characters such as arithmetic signs (for example, + signs), parentheses, colons, or semicolons separate identifiers, and spaces are optional when these characters are used.

We can write, for example,

---

[1] This number applies for the IBM PL/I (F) compiler. Other compilers may have other permissible lengths of characters. Certain labels, to be discussed later on, are limited to seven characters.

[2] A variable name is a symbol for an unspecified quantity. This quantity may change during the execution of the program.

[3] It is possible to change these margins with control cards.

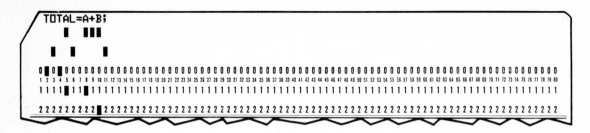

or

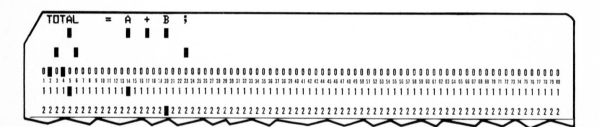

or

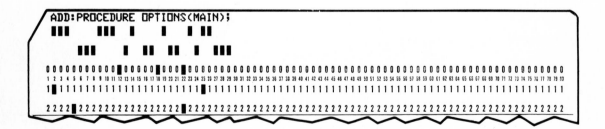

Similarly the statement

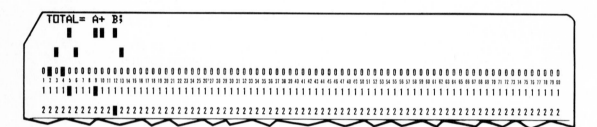

can be written as

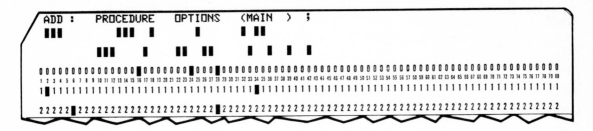

which shows the rules on spaces to be rather "free," as noted.

We are ready now to describe crudely the working of the compiler in executing our program. First, the program is scanned and the names of the variables (that is, A,B,TOTAL) are picked out. Then storage locations (in computer memory) are assigned to the variables. Therefore, when we call for an instruction involving an operation on A, the computer operates on the contents of the location assigned to A. Thus, in the execution of the statement

GET LIST (A,B);

the first data number (that is, 11.7 in our example) is transferred from the data list to the location reserved for A, and then the second data number (that is, 8.5) is transferred from the data list to the location reserved for B. Similarly, the statement

TOTAL = A + B;

causes the addition of the contents of A and the contents of B. The result is stored in the location allocated to TOTAL. Finally, the statement

PUT LIST (TOTAL);

causes the listing (printing) of the contents of the location allocated to TOTAL.

Consider now the meaning of the statement

J = J + 1;

In accordance with the above explanation, 1 is added to the number stored in location J, and the result is stored again in J. This leads to two observations:

1. An equationlike statement (for example, TOTAL = A + B) *is not* an equation. Because of that, such a statement is named an *assignment*. In such a statement the right side of the statement is executed, and the result is stored in the location of the variable of the left side. Thus the statement "assigns" a new value to the variable on the left side. Because of this, some authors employ the ← sign instead of the = sign. For example,

J ← J + 1;

would be written using this notation. We shall use the = sign as in program writing. Note further that the expression

$$A + B = TOTAL;$$

has no meaning. The computer interprets this statement as requiring the contents of TOTAL to be stored in the variable $A + B$, which has an illegal name (because the $+$ character is not allowed in an identifier).

2. The computer memory is such that if a number is stored, it erases (that is, destroys) the previous number in the storage location, and only the new number occupies the storage location. For example, in the two instructions (statements)

$$J = 16;$$
$$J = J+3;$$

first, the number 16 is stored in the J location. Second, the content of J (that is, the number 16) is added to 3; the result is stored in J. Thus after the execution of the second instruction the number 19 is stored in J.

We are just about done with this section. Let us now summarize the statements that were introduced here.

Summary

1. The first statement of a program is

Label: PROCEDURE OPTIONS (MAIN);

where *label* is the name of the program.

2. The statement commanding the acquiring of data (input) is

GET LIST (*name1, name2,* etc.);

where *name1, name2,* etc., are the names of variables, in whose locations the data is to be placed. For example, the statement

GET LIST (MOON, NUT, A, TOM);

will cause the acquiring of four successive numbers from the data cards. The first number will be placed in the MOON location (that is, location reserved for the variable MOON), the second number in the NUT location, and so on.

3. The statement requiring the printout is

PUT LIST (*name1, name2,* etc.);

where *name1, name2,* etc., are again the names of variables whose values are to be printed out. This statement can be generalized to contain a list of arithmetic expressions instead of a list of variables. For example, the statement

PUT LIST (A + B);

will cause the sum $A + B$ (a single number) to be formed and the result printed. Similarly,

PUT LIST (A + B, A− B, A);

will calculate and print out numbers for $A + B$, $A - B$, and A.

Incidentally, the PUT LIST statement does not affect the data being "read." This means that the statement

PUT LIST (A);

causes no changes in the contents of A. Here, the printing of the number stored in A requires that the number be "read" or copied from its storage location. The reading is nondestructive; hence, after the reading, there is still the same number in the storage location for A.

4. The assignment statement requires the operation on the right side of the equal sign to be performed, and the result (a single number) is stored in the location of the identifier on the left side of the equal sign. For example, in the instruction

D = A + B − D;

A + B − D is calculated (that is, the contents of location A are added to the contents of location B, and the contents of D are subtracted) and the result is stored in D. Incidentally, observe that after the instruction, D has a new value, and the old value of D is no longer stored.

5. The statement terminating each program is

END *label;*

where *label* is the name given to the program.

3.2 TRANSFER INSTRUCTIONS

In the addition program of the last section, the instructions were executed sequentially in the order of the program statements. Occasionally, we desire to "jump over" several statements. We do so with the statement

GO TO *label1;*

with the result that the statement labeled *labell* is executed next. The GO TO instruction can also be used to return to a previously executed program statement. We will now illustrate the use of this instruction with the following problem.

Given

A set of numbers.

Find

Its instantaneous and total sum.

Solution We shall first draw a flowchart for the solution of this problem. Such a flowchart appears in Fig. 3.1. This flowchart has several features that need explaining. First, the variable TOTAL (that is, the contents of the storage location reserved for TOTAL) is set to zero. We then obtain a number from the data list, store it in A, and form the sum of TOTAL and A. Since TOTAL is zero, the sum is the number stored in A. The sum (that is, A) is stored in TOTAL and printed out. We return to the data list (that is, data from cards),

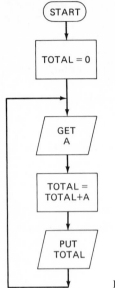

Figure 3.1 Flowchart for the summing problem.

read the next number in the data, and store it in A. Incidentally, the computer does this automatically. In executing the GET LIST (A); instruction (which implements the GET A box) for the second time, it will read the second number in the data list. Again we form the sum of TOTAL and A, store it in TOTAL, and print it out. Thus we print out the instantaneous sum, as required. We now return to the GET A box and repeat the process.

When would it end? When we run out of data! When there are no more data, the computer will stop automatically. Thus the final number printed out is the total sum, as desired.

We are ready now to write the program and do so below.

```
SUMMING:  PROCEDURE OPTIONS(MAIN);
          TOTAL = 0;
AGAIN:    GET LIST(A);
          TOTAL = TOTAL + A;
          PUT LIST(TOTAL);
          GO TO AGAIN;
          END SUMMING;
```

Observe that we named the program SUMMING. Note further that the GET LIST (A); statement is labeled AGAIN. We can label each statement if we so desire; however, it makes little sense to label statements unnecessarily. The statement GET LIST (A); is labeled because we wish to return to it after the PUT LIST (TOTAL); statement. The statement

GO TO AGAIN;

carries this out. As explained above, the statement GET LIST (A); is executed if there is a number on the data list. When the data list is exhausted, the computations will cease, thus ending the program (with a message that there are no more data to be handled). There are other ways to end the execution of a program, which will be discussed later on.

The GO TO statement just described provides a jump or transfer to another statement in the program. Since this jump does not depend upon any condition, it is known as an *unconditional jump*.

There is one other transfer instruction, the *conditional jump*. It can be used to implement a decision, such as the one portrayed in Fig. 2.2. This instruction has the form

IF *condition1* THEN GO TO *label1;*

As an example, the decision diamond of Fig. 2.2. can be programmed with the statement

IF A = 5 THEN GO TO YES;

Here, A = 5 is the condition. If this condition is true, we execute next the statement labeled YES. If it is false (that is, A $\neq$ 5), the next statement is executed. Thus this jump is conditional, depending upon meeting or failing of the condition.

To illustrate the use of the conditional jump consider the following problem:

Given

A set of numbers.

Find

The sum of the first 20 numbers.

Solution The first step is the drawing of the flowchart, shown in Fig. 3.2. Again, we start by "clearing" TOTAL, that is, setting it to zero. The identifier K, which will be used to count the numbers being added, is set to 1. We obtain A and add it to TOTAL. We now ask if K is 20. If YES, we are done, print out the result, and stop the program. If NO, we increase K by 1, return to the GET A box, and repeat the process. We are ready now for the program, this being

```
TWENTY:    PROCEDURE OPTIONS(MAIN);
           TOTAL = 0;
           K = 1;
REPEAT:    GET LIST(A);
           TOTAL = TOTAL + A;
           IF K=20 THEN GO TO FINISHED;
           K = K + 1;
           GO TO REPEAT;
FINISHED:  PUT LIST(TOTAL);
           END TWENTY;
```

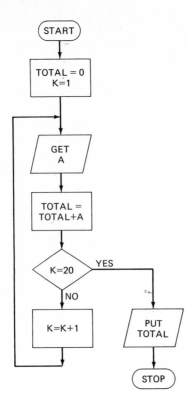

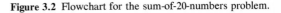

Figure 3.2 Flowchart for the sum-of-20-numbers problem.

We named the program TWENTY. Since we return to the GET LIST (A); statement, we must label it, and we choose REPEAT for the label. The K = 20 decision box is implemented by the statement

IF K = 20 THEN GO TO FINISHED;

If K = 20, we jump to the statement labeled FINISHED, print out the contents of TOTAL, and end the program. If K ≠ 20 (that is, K < 20), we execute the next statement, thus increment K by 1, return to the statement labeled REPEAT, and repeat the process.

Inspect the flowchart again. Note that the four boxes from GET A to K = K + 1 form a loop. This loop is executed 19 times. After that we get out of the loop to the PUT TOTAL box. Thus the part of the program between the statements REPEAT: GET LIST (A) ; and GO TO REPEAT ; is executed 19 times. This looping feature is one of the strengths of programming, in that a small group of instructions need be given only once, even though the computer executes it repeatedly a large number of times.

In passing note that we terminated our program on the flowchart with the word STOP rather than with END as earlier. The use of STOP is more common.

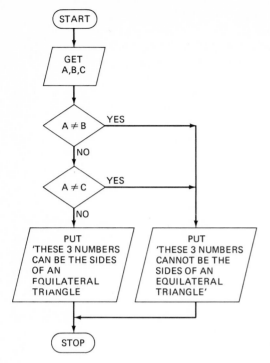

Figure 3.3 Flowchart for the triangle program.

3.3 PROGRAM FOR THE TRIANGLE PROBLEM

We know enough about programming now to write a program for the triangle problem of Sec. 2.2. The object was to determine whether three positive numbers assigned to the variables A,B, and C could be the sides of an equilateral triangle (that is, whether A=B=C).

The flowchart for this problem appears in Fig. 3.3. We will write a program first and then explain the statements.

```
STMT LEVEL NEST
  1              SIDES:     PROCEDURE OPTIONS(MAIN);
  2       1                 GET LIST(A,B,C);
  3       1                 IF A¬=B THEN GO TO FAIL;
  5       1                 IF A¬=C THEN GO TO FAIL;
  7       1                 PUT LIST
                   ('THESE 3 NUMBERS CAN BE THE SIDES OF AN EQUILATERAL TRIANGLE');
  8       1                 GO TO FINISHED;
  9       1      FAIL:      PUT LIST
                   ('THESE 3 NUMBERS CANNOT BE THE SIDES OF AN EQUILATERAL TRIANGLE');
 10       1      FINISHED: END SIDES;
```

In the following explanation of the program, numbered items correspond to statement numbers in the above program.

1. We labeled the program SIDES.
2. The GET LIST (A,B,C); statement acquires three numbers (from the data) and stores them in the locations named A,B, and C.
3. In PL/I the symbol ¬ means *not;* hence A ¬ = B means A ≠ B (there is no ≠ symbol). If A ≠ B, we jump to the statement labeled FAIL. If A = B, there is no jump, and the next statement in the sequence is executed.
5. If A ≠ C we jump to the statement labeled FAIL. If A = C, the next statement is executed.
7. We arrive at this statement only if A = B and A = C. Hence, we print the appropriate message. Observe that the message is enclosed in single quotation marks. Such enclosing causes a literal printout of the message.
8. We are done with testing of the three numbers. Thus we jump to the closing statement labeled FINISHED.
9. We arrive at the statement labeled FAIL only if A ≠ B or A ≠ C. Thus we wish to print out the message that these three numbers cannot be the sides of an equilateral triangle.
10. We arrive here either through a jump from statement 8 or after execution of statement 9. In either event, we end the program.

Note that this program implemented the flowchart of Fig. 3.3 and required eight statements to do so (PL/I counted statements 3 and 5 as double statements). The program works, but it is not a program that will bring pride to a skilled programmer. A skilled programmer will construct the program in a clearer fashion and with no more than five statements (we are not ready for that yet).

Consider again the IF statement. Recall that we introduced this statement as having the form

If *condition1* THEN GO TO *label;*

and *condition1* can be either an equality or an inequality expressed in correct PL/I form. Such valid conditions are shown in the accompanying table. Thus, for example, the statement

Mathematical form	PL/I form*
A = B	A = B
A ≠ B	A ¬ = B
A > B	A > B
A ≯ B	A ¬ > B
A ≥ B	A >= B
A < B	A < B
A ≮ B	A ¬ < B
A ≤ B	A <= B

*Note that if there are two symbols, the ¬ is always the first symbol and the = sign the last symbol. Note further that there must be no space between the two symbols.

IF A <= B THEN GO TO ANYWHERE;

is a valid statement.

Even at this early stage we can see that a long program with a jungle of GO TO statements will be difficult to debug or understand. Because of this fact skilled programmers avoid the use of these statements in large programs. Later on we will say more about this.

In the next chapter we will study the different forms of numbers that are stored or operated on. A little later on (in Chap. 6) we will return to our triangle problem and discuss it in light of our knowledge gained by then.

3.4 MORE EXAMPLES OF PL/I PROGRAMS

In the following we will give five examples of PL/I programs. To program the arithmetic operations we must know their symbols. These symbols are shown in the following table:

Symbol	Operation	Example
+	Addition	A + B
−	Subtraction	A − B
*	Multiplication	A * B
/	Division	A / B
**	Exponentiation	A ** B

We are now ready for our first problem.

Example 3.4.1 Generate a list of squares and cubes for all integers from 1 to 20. Print out each number, its square, and its cube.

Solution We start again with a flowchart, shown in Fig. 3.4. We set N = 0, then test N to determine whether or not N is 20. If N = 20, we are done and wish to stop. If N ≠ 20, then N < 20, and we increment N by 1. For the new N we calculate its square (named NSQUARE) and its cube (named NCUBE), and print out N, NSQUARE, and NCUBE. We return to the test box and repeat the process.

Note that we calculate NSQUARE as N*N rather than N**2. As a rule multiplication is faster than exponentiation; and thus we use a good programming practice. Similarly, the calculation of NCUBE from N*NSQUARE is faster than from N**3. The program listing our table (and named TABLE) is

```
TABLE:    PROCEDURE OPTIONS(MAIN);
          /* TABLE OF SQUARES AND CUBES FROM 1 TO 20 */
          N = 0;
```

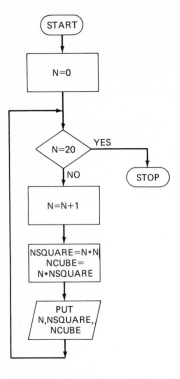

Figure 3.4 Flowchart for Example 3.4.1.

```
AGAIN:      IF N=20 THEN GO TO ALL_DONE;
            N = N+1;
            NSQUARE = N*N;
            NCUBE = N*NSQUARE;
            PUT LIST(N,NSQUARE,NCUBE);
            GO TO AGAIN;
ALL_DONE: END TABLE;
```

The above program should be self-explanatory. However, often we wish to explain the program to the reader of the program. We do so with comments, written on the program itself (that is, on the punched cards). To tell the compiler that the comment is to be ignored in the execution of the program, we use the symbols /* before the comment and the symbols */ after the comment. For example,

NCUBE = N* NSQUARE; /* THIS IS THE SAME AS N**3 */

illustrates the use of a comment.

There is one note to be made about comments. Comments are not executed; hence they can appear in all 80 columns of a punch card. However, the symbols /* and */, which must be read by the compiler, have to be placed in columns 2–72 only. Observe what happens if a comment ending (that is, */) occurs in columns 75 and 76. The compiler does not read these columns, and hence it does not know that the comment has ended. Thus the statements on the following cards are treated as a continuation of the comment and are ignored.

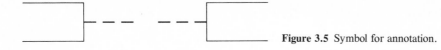

Figure 3.5 Symbol for annotation.

A comment can be placed whenever a space is permissible. Thus a comment can appear in front of, in the middle of, or at the end of a statement. Even though legal, it is not good practice to place a comment in the middle of a statement, because it causes an interruption in the reading of the statement.

Sometimes we desire to explain the operation at a point in a flowchart; that is, we wish to include a "comment" in a flowchart. The symbol for the explanatory material is a box, open on either the left or the right side, and connected by dotted lines to the point requiring the explanation. Figure 3.5 portrays the symbol, which is named the *annotation symbol.*

Example 3.4.2 Given a list of numbers, obtain (1) the count of positive numbers, (2) the count of negative numbers, and (3) the sum of all positive numbers. The program is to stop if either (1) we encounter the number 0 or (2) the sum of positive numbers exceeds 1000.

Solution The flowchart is shown in Fig. 3.6. Let K be the count for positive numbers, L the count for negative numbers, TOTAL the sum, and A the number from the list. With these the program is as shown below, with explanations of the program occurring as comments.

```
COUNTS: PROCEDURE OPTIONS(MAIN);
        /* THIS PROGRAM COUNTS POSITIVE NUMBERS,        */
        /* NEGATIVE NUMBERS, AND SUMS POSITIVE NUMBERS. */
        /* IT STOPS IF EITHER INPUT IS ZERO OR IF THE   */
        /* SUM EXCEEDS 1000.                            */
        K=0; L=0; TOTAL=0;                 /*K COUNTS POSITIVE NUMBERS*/
                                           /*L COUNTS NEGATIVE NUMBERS*/
REPEAT: GET LIST(A);
        IF A=0 THEN GO TO PRINT;           /*IF A=0 WE ARE FINISHED  */
        IF A>0 THEN GO TO UPDATE;          /*FOR POSITIVE A WE MUST  */
                                           /*INCREASE K AND TOTAL    */
        L = L+1;                           /*INCREASE NEGATIVE COUNT */
        GO TO REPEAT;
UPDATE: K = K+1;
        TOTAL = TOTAL+A;
        IF TOTAL<=1000 THEN GO TO REPEAT;/*REPEAT IF NOT DONE        */
PRINT:  PUT LIST(K,L,TOTAL);               /*RESULTS OF THE PROGRAM  */
        END COUNTS;
```

Note the placement of comments on the right side. Such positioning is the recommended practice. It allows the covering of the comments if one wants to read

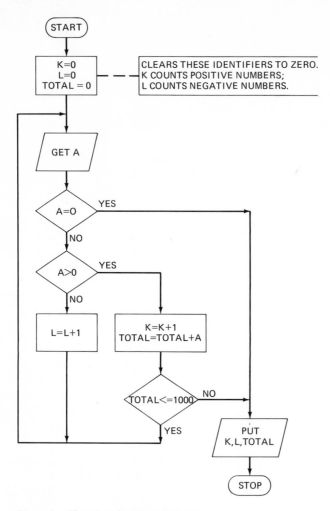

Figure 3.6 Flowchart for Example 3.4.2.

just the program. Also note that the additional comment marks are placed to increase the visibility of a comment.

Example 3.4.3 Write a program to calculate the interest payable on Series E U.S. Savings Bonds. Assume that the interest is compounded quarterly, as in a bank savings account.

Solution One such bond costs $18.75 and matures to $25 after 7 years and 9 months. If the yearly interest rate is P percent, the $18.75 grows after a year (4 quarters) into

$$18.75 \left(1 + \frac{P}{400} \right)^4$$

and after 7 years and 9 months (31 quarters) into

$$18.75 \left(1 + \frac{P}{400} \right)^{31}$$

Therefore

$$18.75 \left(1 + \frac{P}{400} \right)^{31} = 25$$

and

$$\left(1 + \frac{P}{400} \right)^{31} = \frac{25}{18.75}$$

or

$$1 + \frac{P}{400} = \left(\frac{25}{18.75} \right)^{1/31}$$

yielding

$$P = \left[\left(\frac{25}{18.75} \right)^{1/31} - 1 \right] 400$$

In PL/I language this expression has the form

$$P = ((25/18.75)**(1/31) - 1)*400$$

and the program here is simple enough and does not require a flowchart.

```
BOND:   PROCEDURE OPTIONS(MAIN);
        P = ((25/18.75)**(1/31) - 1)*400;
        PUT LIST(P);
        END BOND;
```

Observe the use of parentheses in the calculation of P. There are no brackets in PL/I symbols; hence, parentheses must be used exclusively. Parentheses remove ambiguity and tell the compiler that the expressions in parentheses must be calculated first. For example,

$$25/18.75**1/31$$

is ambiguous to read. It could mean, for example,

$$\frac{\left(\frac{25}{18.75^1} \right)}{31}$$

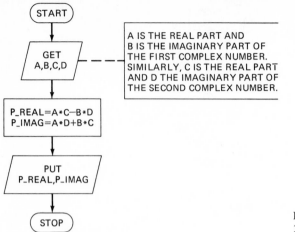

Figure 3.7 Flowchart for Example 3.4.4.

which is, in fact the interpretation that the compiler will give it. Incidentally, extra parentheses cause no harm. Thus, if we write the formula for P as

$$P = (((25/18.75)**(1/31)) - 1)*400$$

we will still calculate P correctly.

Example 3.4.4 Given two complex numbers as two pairs of real numbers. In each pair, the first number is the real part and the second number is the imaginary part of the complex number. Write a program to calculate the product of these two complex numbers.

Solution If the first number is represented by $A + jB$ and the second number by $C + jD$, then the product P is given by[1]

$$P = (A + jB)(C + jD) = (AC - BD) + j(AD + BC)$$

The flowchart for calculating P is shown in Fig. 3.7 and results in the program

```
PRODUCT: PROCEDURE OPTIONS(MAIN);
         GET LIST(A,B,C,D);           /* WE REALLY HAVE    */
         P_REAL = A*C - B*D;          /* A+JB AND C+JD.    */
         P_IMAG = A*D + B*C;          /* FROM THE FORMULA  */
         PUT LIST(P_REAL,P_IMAG);     /* FOR P, P_REAL IS  */
         END PRODUCT;                 /* THE REAL PART,    */
                                      /* P_IMAG THE IMA-   */
                                      /* GINARY PART OF P  */
```

Example 3.4.5 For the polynomial
$$Y = X^5 + 1.7X - 3.4$$

---

[1]The letter j is used in engineering and the letter i in mathematics as symbols for $\sqrt{-1}$.

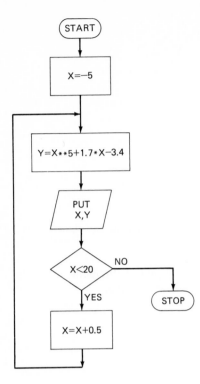

Figure 3.8 Flowchart for Example 3.4.5.

calculate the values of Y if X varies from −5 to 20 in steps of 0.5.

Solution The flowchart for the calculation of Y appears in Fig. 3.8. The program follows as

```
POL:      PROCEDURE OPTIONS(MAIN);
          X = -5;
AGAIN:    Y = X**5 + 1.7*X - 3.4;
          PUT LIST(X,Y);
          IF X¬<20 THEN GO TO DONE;
          X = X + 0.5;
          GO TO AGAIN;
DONE:     END POL;
```

Observe that we replaced the condition X<20 in the flowchart by X¬<20 in the program. Had we implemented the condition X<20, the program would read

```
POL2:     PROCEDURE OPTIONS(MAIN);
          X = -5;
AGAIN:    Y = X**5 + 1.7*X - 3.4;
          PUT LIST(X,Y);
          IF X<20 THEN GO TO REPEAT;
          GO TO DONE;
```

```
REPEAT:   X = X + 0.5;
          GO TO AGAIN;
DONE:     END POL2;
```

The POL2 program is one statement longer than the POL program. Note that an inversion of the condition in the IF statement in the program POL, resulted in a simpler (and shorter) program. This illustrates that we should loosely implement the flowchart and look for changes in the flowchart that improve the resulting program.

3.5 SUMMARY

In this chapter we introduced the writing of programs. We shall now summarize the chapter contents.

1. The program starts with the statement

   Label: PROCEDURE OPTIONS (MAIN);

   where *label* is the name given to the program.
2. Each statement ends with a semicolon.
3. We can label (that is, name) any statement. A label is followed by a colon and has at most 31 characters. The first character must be either a letter of the alphabet or one of the characters $, #, and @. The other characters are either the letters of the alphabet, or the characters $, #, @, or the 10 digits (that is, 0 to 9), or the break (underscore) character. No space is allowed in the label.
4. The names of variables have the same restriction on characters as labels. The names given to variables and labels are known as identifiers.
5. If we want to acquire numbers from the data cards, we do so with the statement

   GET LIST (*name1, name2, . . . , namek*);

   This will transfer k data items from data cards and store the first into storage locations assigned to the variable named *name1,* the second into storage location assigned to the variable named *name2,* and so on.
6. The statement

   PUT LIST (*name1, name2, . . . , namek*);

   will print out the contents of storage locations assigned to variables *name1, name2,* and so on. The statement

   PUT LIST ('ANYTHING');

   will print out the text between the single quotation marks, that is, the word ANYTHING here.
7. The statement

   name1 =expression;

will evaluate the expression on the right side and place the result into the storage location assigned to the variable named *name1*.

8. The program ends with the statement

END *label;*

where *label* is the name given to the program in the first statement that is,

label: PROCEDURE OPTIONS (MAIN);

9. The items on data cards are separated by either spaces or commas.
10. We can transfer to any statement in the program with the statement

GO TO *label1;*

with the result that the statement labeled *label1* is executed next.

11. The statement

IF *condition1* THEN GO TO *label1:*

will transfer to the statement labeled *label1* if *condition1* is true. If *condition1* is false, the next statement is executed. *Condition1* is either an equality or an inequality.

12. The PL/I symbols for inequalities are

Mathematical form	PL/I form
$A \neq B$	$A \neg = B$
$A > B$	$A > B$
$A \not> B$	$A \neg > B$
$A \geq B$	$A >= B$
$A < B$	$A < B$
$A \not< B$	$A \neg < B$
$A \leq B$	$A <= B$

13. The PL/I symbols for arithmetic operations are

PL/I symbol	Operation
+	Addition
−	Subtraction
*	Multiplication
/	Division
**	Exponentiation

14. A comment in the program starts with the symbols /* and ends with the symbols */. A comment is printed as it stands, but its contents are ignored by the compiler.

15. A PL/I program must appear in columns 2–72 of a punch card.[1] Data can appear in all 80 columns of a punch card. Delimiters of comments (that is, /* and */) must appear in columns 2–72 (to be read by the compiler), but contents of comments can appear in all 80 columns.

16. Parentheses are used to avoid ambiguity in calculating expressions. Redundant parentheses cause no harm.

PROBLEMS

3.1 Write a program for the algorithm described by the flowchart in Fig. P3.1.

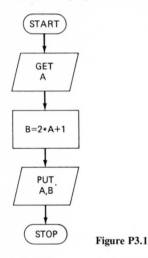

Figure P3.1

3.2. Write a program for Prob. 2.1.

3.3 Correct the errors in the following programs:

(*a*)
```
1STPROB. PROC. OPTION MAIN:
        */ FIND ROOTS OF QUAD. EQUATION /*
        GET LIST A,B, AND C;
        DISC = B**2 −4AC;
        IF DISC=> 0 THEN ROOT = −B+ − DISC**1/2;
        PRINT ROOTS
        END 1ST PROBLEM
```

(*b*)
```
JOE −  PROCEDURE OPTION MAIN.
    LABEL: GET LIST (A*B; A+B)
           C=A*B−(A+(B));
           IF C> 0 GO TO GET LIST;
           PUT C;
           GO TO GET LIST;
           END PROCEDUR E;
```

---

[1] It is possible to change these margins with control cards.

3.4 Write a program for Prob. 2.5.

3.5 Write a program for Prob. 2.6.

3.6 Write a program to calculate the squares of all integers between 1 and 100 that are divisible by 7 (that is, the squares of 7, 14, etc.). Print out your results.

3.7 It is desired to calculate the grade average for several students. The average is calculated with the formula

$$[(4 \times \text{credits with A grade}) + (3 \times \text{credits with B grade})$$
$$+ (2 \times \text{credits with C grade}) + (1 \times \text{credits with D grade})$$
$$+ (0 \times \text{credits with F grade})] / (\text{Total credits})$$

The input consists of cards, each with five numbers. The first number gives the number of credits with the A grade, the second number gives the number of credits with the B grade, etc. The last card has the number -10 on it and is to be used to stop execution. Calculate the averages by using a program. The input is

72	3	16	2	3	first card
3	18	35	12	4	
19	32	65	10	0	
21	18	38	0	3	
17	42	58	6	2	
-10					last card

(The program should work for other inputs.)

3.8 A saving bank pays 5 percent interest. To what amount would $10 grow in 10 years, if

(a) The interest is credited (that is, compounded) yearly.

(b) The interest is credited quarterly (that is, 1.25 percent is credited during each quarter).

Draw a flowchart for this problem on your computer printout.

3.9 Write a program which will test the first 20 numbers on the data cards and count the number of zeros. If there are N zeros, the output should be

THERE ARE N ZEROS IN THE FIRST 20 NUMBERS

Extra spaces are allowed in the output. The numbers on the data cards are

$$1, 1.3, 1.23, 12.3, 0, 0, 7, 13.2, 0.83, 0, 3.7, 102,$$
$$13.7, 0, 4.2, 0.03, 7.2, 123.12, 10.30, 0, 0.1, 0, 2, 0$$

Show a flowchart on your printout.

3.10 In the electric circuit shown in Fig. P3.10, write a single program to calculate and print out V_2 for

(a) $R_1 = 4 \text{ k}\Omega$, $R_2 = 3 \text{ k}\Omega$, $V_1 = 5(5)100 \text{ V}$

(b) $R_1 = 4 \text{ k}\Omega$, $R_2 = 2(2)10 \text{ k}\Omega$, $V_1 = 10 \text{ V}$

(c) $R_1 = 2(2)10 \text{ k}\Omega$, $R_2 = 3 \text{ k}\Omega$, $V_1 = 10 \text{ V}$

(*Note:* $n(m)k$ means n to k in steps of m.) Show a flowchart on your computer printout.

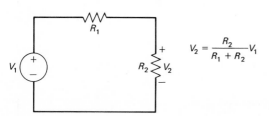

$$V_2 = \frac{R_2}{R_1 + R_2} V_1$$

Figure P3.10

3.11 There are four numbers on each data card. The first number represents a, the second b, the third c, and the fourth d in the expression

$$\frac{a + jb}{c + jd} = e + jf \qquad (j = \sqrt{-1})$$

Write a program to calculate e and f. The numbers on the data cards are

First card	1, 2, 3, 4
Second card	1.5, 2.6, 3.8, 1.2
Third card	3.78, 5.31, −16, −0.13
Fourth card	1, 3.7, −1.9, 2.889
Fifth card	13.77, −6.84, −17.92, 8.37

Print out your results so as to display just e and f on each line. Show the flowchart on your computer printout sheet.

3.12 On a daily interest account the Fat Cat Savings Bank credits at the rate of 5.25 percent per year. Joe College had $854.18 on Dec. 31, 1977. He made the transactions shown during the following quarter:

Date	Deposit, $	Withdrawal, $
1/10	295.32	
1/23	147.66	
2/15		800.00
2/28	151.35	
3/8	168.58	
3/22	155.11	

What interest is credited on March 31?

3.13 Write a program which will
(a) Obtain a sum of only the numbers on the data cards which are larger than 2 and smaller than 8.
(b) Obtain a count of how many numbers are included in the sum of part (a).
(c) Print out the results of (a) and (b) properly identified.
(d) Show the flowchart on your printout page. The numbers on the data cards are

$$3, 1, 712, 18.3, 2.92, 4.3, 5.7, 6.1, 4,$$
$$2, 31.2, 18, 3.7, 7.9, 32.3, 1.25, 0$$

It is known that the only zero occurs as the last number on the data card. The program should end when this zero is encountered.

3.14 There are several nonnegative numbers on data cards. Write a program which will print
(a) The sum of all numbers.
(b) The sum of all numbers exceeding 5.
(c) The count of all zeros.
The input data are

$$5, 6.3, 3.7, 17, 0, 8, 4, 0, 2.5, 0, -1$$

The last number of −1 is not in the data but is to be used for terminating the program.

3.15 (a) Calculate y and draw a flowchart for this problem on your printout sheet:

$$y = \sqrt[3]{x} + 7x - 3 \qquad \text{for } x = 1, 2, \text{ and } 3$$

(b) Indicate briefly (on your printout sheet) how you would calculate y for $x = 1, 2, \ldots, 100$.

3.16 Calculate

(a) $y = x^3 + 3x^2 - 7x + 1$

(b) $y = 1.3x^3 - 2.42x^2 + 0.83 - 1.7 \sqrt[5]{x}$

for three given values of x. Print out x and y for the following values of x: 1.37, 3, -7.2. Draw a flowchart for this problem on your printout sheet.

3.17 There are several positive integers on data card. Write a program which will print out on separate lines (a) an integer and 0 if the integer is even, or (b) an integer and 1 if the integer is odd. The input data are

$$5, 7, 8, 3, 6, 14$$

3.18 A sum of \$20,000 is to be saved through 240 monthly payments, invested at 6 percent/annum and compounded monthly. Find the monthly payment by using a program.

Hint: Recall that the geometric series can be summed; that is,

$$A + Ap + \cdots + Ap^N = A \frac{1 - p^{N+1}}{1 - p}$$

3.19 Joe Saver is saving for his retirement. He intends to save \$50/month during the first year and 10 percent more per month each following year (that is, \$55/month the second year, \$60.50/month the third year, and so on). The money is compounded monthly at 6 percent/annum and 240 payments will be made. After the last payment, the money would be left for 10 more years without any additional payments but still compounded monthly at 6 percent/annum. How much money would Joe receive at the end of the last 10 years?

3.20 Write a program that will calculate the amount due to the bank for maintaining a checking account for 1 month. The bank calculates its charges as follows:

(a) There is a fixed cost of \$1/month.

(b) It costs 6 cents to process each check, 3 cents to process each deposit.

(c) A credit is given at the rate of 3 percent/annum on the average balance.

(d) The average balance is calculated by taking the average of the largest balance and the smallest balance.

(e) Write the program as before, but change parts (c) and (d) to read:

(c) A credit is given at the rate of 3 percent/annum on the account's balance.

(d) The credit is calculated and compounded daily. For example, \$500 left in the account for a day will earn the credit

$$500 * 0.03 * \frac{1}{365} = \$0.041$$

hence, 4.1 cents.

Assume that the first item in the data is the balance at the first of the month. For the first part we are given positive and negative amounts for the deposits and checks, respectively. For the second part each amount is accompanied by the day of transaction. As an example, -162.13, 6 means that a check in the amount of 162.13 was cashed on the 6th day of the month.

The last data item is zero, indicating the termination of transactions. Select reasonable data to test your program.

4 ARITHMETIC ATTRIBUTES

When we solve a numerical problem, we perform various operations on the numbers. The numbers can be integers, decimal fractions, or rational numbers and can even be represented in different number systems. We have the same facility when working with the computer. We tell the compiler how we wish our numbers to be represented, be they integers, decimal fractions, or some other representations. If we do not tell the compiler explicitly what we want, we default our choice, and the compiler makes a unique selection in accordance with its *default rules*.

We will discuss here the various characteristics that numbers may possess, that is, their attributes. We will also describe the default rules, that is, the choices that will be made by the computer if there are no explicit descriptions of attributes of a number.

4.1 BASE

In general, a number can be represented in any number system. In our positional decimal system we interpret the number 123 as

$$1 \times 100 + 2 \times 10 + 3 = 1 \times 10^2 + 2 \times 10^1 + 3 \times 10^0$$

We could similarly use any other base and interpret a number in terms of powers of this base. Thus in the binary (base 2) number system, the number 1011 means

$$(1011)_{\text{base } 2} = 1 \times 2^3 + 0 \times 2^2 + 1 \times 2^1 + 1 \times 2^0 = 8 + 2 + 1 = (11)_{\text{base } 10}$$

In PL/I we can store the numbers internally in either decimal or binary forms. The arithmetic operations are then performed on either decimal or binary numbers. Thus the number base is either DECIMAL or BINARY. Externally, in the output printout, the numbers appear always in the familiar decimal form.

4.2 MODE

In many engineering problems we operate on complex numbers. In PL/I we can specify a number to be either REAL or COMPLEX. These are the two modes of a number.

4.3 SCALE

Often we operate with very small or very large numbers. Let us say that one of our numbers is 23,000,000,000. It is inefficient to write (or store) so many zeros. It is more efficient to represent this number in exponential form as, say, 23×10^9.

Observe the different representations of the number 123.456:

$$123.456 = 0.0123456 \times 10^4 = 1.23456 \times 10^2 = 12.3456 \times 10^1$$
$$= 123.456 \times 10^0 = 1234.56 \times 10^{-1} = 1,234,560.0 \times 10^{-4}$$

In the decimal fraction on the left, the decimal point is fixed—any change in its position will change the number. In the exponential form, the decimal point can be placed anywhere—it can float anywhere—with the exponent providing the necessary adjustment. Because of this feature, a number can be represented in either a FIXED form or in a FLOAT form. These two representations, FIXED and FLOAT, are named the scale of a number.

4.4 PRECISION

We can specify the precision of numbers used in our calculation. For fixed numbers the precision is given by two numbers p, q enclosed in parentheses, that is,

$$(p, q)$$

where p = total number of significant digits in the number
q = number of significant digits to the right of the decimal point
Several examples are shown in the table below.

Number	Precision
1.23	(3, 2)
12.3	(3, 1)
123	(3, 0)
1230	(3, −1) or* (4, 0)
1230000	(3, −4), (4, −3), (5, −2), (6, −1), or (7, 0), depending on the number of significant zeros
0.123	(3, 3)
0.0123	(3, 4)

*1230 is of precision (3, −1) if we are only certain about the first three digits and if 1230 is an approximation to a number such as 1234. If the last zero is significant the precision is (4, 0).

Observe that if $q \leqslant 0$, then the number is an integer. Note also that if $q < 0$, there are $p + |q|$ digits in the number, but only p are significant, and $|q|$ are zeros.

The same notation applies to fixed binary numbers. Thus

1.11 has precision (3,2)
0.011 has precision (2,3)
1100 has precision $(2,-2)$, $(3,-1)$, or $(4,0)$, depending upon the number of significant zeros

For floating-point numbers, a single precision number p suffices. Thus

1.23×10^2 has precision (3)
12.3×10^2 also has precision (3)

The floating-point binary number 1.101×2^6 has precision (4). Clearly, (p) denotes the number of digits in front of the exponential part, that is, the number of digits in the mantissa.

4.5 DEFAULT RULES

The four attributes just described allow us to choose the form in which the numbers are to be stored and used. If we do not exercise this choice, we default our prerogative and the computer will choose the attributes in accordance with its rules—the so-called default rules. These are

1. If the variable starts with the letters I,J,K,L,M,N (that is, the first character is one of the letters from I to N inclusive), then the attributes assigned to the variable by the default rules are

Base	BINARY
Mode	REAL
Scale	FIXED
Precision	(15, 0)—that is, an integer of 15 binary digits

   Thus the variable can represent without loss of digits integers not exceeding $2^{15}-1$, or 32767. The internal representation is binary; the external printout gives a decimal number.

2. If the variable starts with letters other than I through N, then its attributes are

Base	DECIMAL
Mode	REAL
Scale	FLOAT
Precision	(6)

Here the variable represents a number having the form

$$(\pm \text{ x.xxxxx}) \ 10^{\pm yy}$$

Note that the exponent part can have two digits. This seems to imply that as large a number as 99 can be used for the exponential part. In practice, however, the typical range is from 10^{-78} to 10^{75}, with the exact range depending upon the particular PL/I compiler.

Observe that we can choose integer operations by naming our variables with names starting with letters I through N. Similarly variables with names starting with other letters are floating-point numbers. As an example, in the addition problem of Sec. 3.1 the variables A and B represent by their names floating-point numbers. Even if data cards have integers for A and B, these integers will be converted to floating-point (that is, FLOAT) form and stored as floating-point numbers. Similarly, the variable A and the variable TOTAL in the program of Sec. 3.2 as well as the variables A,B, and C in the triangle program of Sec. 3.3 represent floating-point numbers. In Example 3.4.1, N, NSQUARE, and NCUBE are integer variables. In Example 3.4.2, K and L are integer variables and TOTAL is a floating-point variable.

All these choices were deliberate. A choice of an integer name for a number with a fractional part results in a loss of accuracy. The reason is that an integer is made out of the number by truncating the fractional part, when we assign the number to the variable. For example, the statement

GET LIST (N);

with the number 12.73 on the data card stores 12 for N since N is expressed (by default) to be an integer. Similarly, the statement

I = 12.73;

stores 12 (the integer part of the number) for I.

As a further example, the statements

GET LIST (N1,N2,N3);
ITOTAL = N1 + N2 + N3;
PUT LIST (ITOTAL);

with the numbers 5.21, 7.8, 6.41, on the data card result in the following operations:

The GET LIST statement acquires the data and stores 5,7, and 6 for N1, N2, and N3.
The ITOTAL statement obtains ITOTAL = 5 + 7 + 6 = 18.
The PUT LIST statement prints out 18 for ITOTAL.

The result is in error due to the integer truncation. If we had used the names A, B, C, and TOTAL, then the statements

GET LIST (A,B,C);
TOTAL = A + B + C;
PUT LIST (TOTAL);

with numbers as before result in the following:

The GET LIST statement stores 5.21000×10^0, 7.80000×10^0, and 6.41000×10^0 for A, B, and C.

The TOTAL statement obtains TOTAL = 1.94200×10^1.

The PUT LIST statement prints out 1.94200×10^1 (in a somewhat different form as discussed in the next paragraph) for TOTAL (observe that the mantissa of the output number is printed in the standard form x.xxxxx), thus giving the correct result in floating-point form.

Incidentally, the printer does not contain superscripts needed for the powers of floating-point numbers. It will in fact represent 1.94200×10^1 as

$$1.94200E + 01$$

with the sign and number to the right of E denoting the exponent. Similarly, if we wish to punch the above floating-point number on a card, we either use the above form or more simply eliminate the redundant zeros and write

0.1942E2   or   1.942E1   or   19.42E0   or   194.2E−1

Any one of these is satisfactory. Note that the + sign is optional for positive exponents. Observe further that the output of the printer has a uniform format for floating-point numbers, but the input format (for numbers punched on cards) is more flexible. This topic will be discussed further in Chaps. 14, 15, and 16.

4.6 SUMMARY

In this chapter we described the four attributes of a number, these being its base (BINARY or DECIMAL), mode (REAL or COMPLEX), scale (FIXED or FLOAT), and precision (given as two digits p, q for fixed-point numbers, and one digit p for floating-point numbers). We also saw that if we do not choose otherwise (and the next chapter describes how such a choice is made), a variable with names starting with letters I through N (the first two letters of INteger) represents an integer, and a variable with any other name represents a floating-point number.

PROBLEMS

4.1 Represent in base 2 number system
   (*a*) 1025
   (*b*) 432.432
   (*c*) .003

4.2

Represent the following numbers in floating-point form $\pm x.xxxxx\ 10^{\pm yy}$, choosing the correct sign.

(a) 1025

(b) 432.432

(c) .003

(d) $-512*10^{14}$

4.3 Obtain the precision of

(a) 1025

(b) 432.432

(c) 100

(d) -24.300

4.4 What is the output of the program

```
P44:   PROC OPTIONS (MAIN);
       I=1;
       A=1;
       PUT LIST (I,A);
       END P44;
```

4.5 Write a program which will obtain numbers from data cards and print

(a) The numbers having the decimal fraction 0.5 (for example, 13.5, -1.5, etc.).

(b) All integers divisible by 7.

All other numbers are to be ignored. The data consists of nonzero numbers, and an additional card with the zero is to be used for the termination of the program. The data are

$$7,\ -18.5,\ 17.3,\ 8.73,\ 49,\ 12,\ 17,\ 14,\ 1.5$$

4.6 Write a program that will

(a) Round off each number on the data cards to the nearest integer. Print out the result of your roundoff.

(b) Obtain and print out the count of even numbers and the count of odd numbers. Zero is to be counted as an even number. For these counts use the integers obtained through the roundoff. Only the final counts are to be printed.

(c) Stop when the third zero is encountered. Show the flowchart on your printout page. Identify the two counts through proper titles or headings. The numbers on the data cards are

3.15, 0, 13.67, 14.52, 1.23, -1.43, -2.73, 0, 18.6, 7.45, -8.62, 2, 4, -2, 7.83, 0.82, 0, 1.82, 1.28.

5 THE DECLARE STATEMENT

The DECLARE statement is a way of expressing our wishes on the handling of data. With the DECLARE statement we establish the precision of the numbers handled, their base, mode, and scale. We can override conventions (that is, default rules) and make, for example, the variable I a floating-point number and the variable A an integer.

5.1 USE OF THE DECLARE STATEMENT

The principal use of the DECLARE statement is for giving the attributes of a variable. This statement has the form

    DECLARE OHM DECIMAL REAL FIXED (6,3);

and tells the compiler that the variable named OHM is to be stored as a fixed, real, decimal number, with precision (6,3). Thus OHM has the form xxx.xxx. If OHM is defined by the statement

    OHM = 52.3;

then the number

    052.300

is stored in the location for OHM.[1]

The attributes can be given in any order, except that the precision attribute cannot be next to the variable (but must follow one of the other attributes). Thus the above DECLARE statement for OHM could also be given as

    DECLARE OHM FIXED (6,3) REAL DECIMAL;

or

    DECLARE OHM REAL (6,3) FIXED DECIMAL;

[1]In the printout the leading zeros are suppressed.

and so on. Several other examples of the DECLARE statement are

DECLARE A FIXED (4,1) COMPLEX BINARY;

[means that A is a complex variable, with both its real and imaginary parts being fixed, binary numbers of precision (4,1)]

DECLARE B FLOAT (12) BINARY REAL;
DECLARE C FIXED (12,0) DECIMAL REAL;

The DECLARE statement may be placed anywhere in the body of the program (that is, between the PROCEDURE and END statements), because the compiler scans the program for the DECLARE statement before the execution of the program. The DECLARE statement is not an executable statement but an instruction to the compiler, and thus its position in the card deck is of no consequence. It is, however, a common programming practice to place the DECLARE statement right after the PROCEDURE statement. Such a placement improves the readability of the program, since it tells the reader immediately about the attributes of the variables.

5.2 SHORTCUTS IN THE USE OF THE DECLARE STATEMENT

There are several shortcuts in the use of the DECLARE statement. These are:

A Abbreviations

The word DECLARE can be abbreviated to DCL. Similarly, the abbreviations of BIN for BINARY, DEC for DECIMAL, and CPLX for COMPLEX are valid. Thus the following DECLARE statements are valid:

DCL A FIXED BIN CPLX (4,1);
DCL B FLOAT (3) DEC REAL;

B One DCL Statement for Several Variables

There can be one DCL statement for each variable, as, for example,

DCL A FIXED (6,3) REAL BIN;
DCL B FIXED (6,3) REAL DEC;

or one DCL statement for several variables, such as

DCL A FIXED (6,3) REAL BIN, B FIXED (6,3) REAL DEC;

where a comma separates each variable and its attributes.

C Factoring of Attributes

Through the use of parentheses, one attribute can be specified for several variables. For example, the last statement can also be written as

$$\text{DCL (A BIN, B DEC) REAL FIXED (6,3);}$$

Here REAL FIXED (6,3) applies to both variables in the parentheses. We call this more compact form *factoring* of the attributes, because it parallels the algebraic factoring as in $(ab+cb) = (a+c)b$. There can be several parentheses in a DCL statement, that is, several factoring, as, for example,

$$\text{DCL(((A,B) FLOAT (3), C FIXED (3,1)) REAL, D CPLX FIXED (3,2)) DEC;}$$

which is the same as

$$\text{DCL A FLOAT (3) REAL DEC, B FLOAT (3) REAL DEC,}$$
$$\text{C FIXED (3,1) REAL DEC, D CPLX FIXED (3,2) DEC;}$$

The second version is longer but clearer, and hence preferable. Note that within parentheses the names of variables and their attributes are separated by commas from other variables (and their attributes).

5.3 DEFAULT RULES

In Sec. 4.5 we discussed default rules associated with the names of variables if there is no DCL statement specifying their attributes. Observe that these default rules are convenient, because when we desire numbers with attributes given by the default rules, just the choice of an appropriate name for the variable suffices. In such a case we save the writing of the DECLARE statement. Thus, if we wish a variable to be an integer, just the choice of the name for the variable such as JAK suffices. In other instances just a partial declaration of attributes suffices, with the attendant saving in program writing. The remaining attributes are selected by the default rules, which will be now described.

If no attributes are specified:

First letter of name	Default attributes are
is I through N	FIXED BIN REAL (15, 0)
First letter of name	Default attributes are
is not I through N	FLOAT DEC REAL (6)

If one or more attributes are specified, the compiler makes the following assumptions for the unspecified attributes:

Unspecified attribute	Default attribute
Base	DEC
Mode	REAL
Scale	FLOAT
Precision	(15, 0) for FIXED BIN
	(5, 0) for FIXED DEC
	(21) for FLOAT BIN
	(6) for FLOAT DEC

Thus in this case the first letter of the variable is immaterial. For example,

1. DCL A FLOAT;

   is equivalent to

   $$\text{DCL A FLOAT DEC REAL (6);}$$

2. DCL I FLOAT BIN;

   is equivalent to

   $$\text{DCL I FLOAT BIN REAL (21);}$$

3. DCL A FIXED;

   is equivalent to

   $$\text{DCL A FIXED DEC REAL (5,0);}$$

4. DCL J FLOAT (8);

   is equivalent to

   $$\text{DCL J FLOAT DEC REAL (8);}$$

5.4 ILLEGAL USES OF THE DECLARE STATEMENT

Obviously, no contradictory statements can be made in the DECLARE statement. Thus

$$\text{DCL A FIXED FLOAT;}$$

is clearly illegal, since A is either FIXED or FLOAT but not both. Incidentally,

$$\text{DCL FIXED FLOAT;}$$

is a valid statement. It defines a variable named FIXED as a FLOAT number. However, such a choice of a name is confusing and thus not recommended.

It is also invalid to use more than one DCL statement for a variable. Thus the statements

$$\text{DCL A FIXED (6,2);}$$
$$\text{DCL A DEC;}$$

are illegal. We must instead write

$$\text{DCL A FIXED (6,2) DEC;}$$

that is, a single statement.

5.5 OTHER USES OF THE DECLARE STATEMENT

There are several more uses of the DCL statement. These are

1. The DCL statement is often used for documentation and program readability.

For example, if we are not sure that the readers of the program know the default attribute of the precision, we include it in the DCL statement. Thus we may have the DCL statement

DCL A FLOAT BIN (21);

for better program documentation, even though the precision attribute could have been omitted.

2. An initial value can be given to the variable with the statement.

DLC A FIXED (6,0) INITIAL (62);

which is equivalent to the two statements

DCL A FIXED (6,0);
A = 62;

The word INITIAL can be abbreviated to INIT as, for example,

DCL A FIXED INIT (62), I FLOAT INIT (−12E−1);

3. The DCL statement has several more uses, in instances when it is necessary to tell the compiler that the variables require special treatment. One example of such is a nonnumerical variable. Another example is an array of many numbers. These uses will be described later on.

5.6 SUMMARY

We described the use of the DECLARE statement to override conventions and to establish attributes of variables. We described the default rules that apply when the DECLARE statement specifies attributes only partially. We also described the use of the DECLARE statement for documentation and initialization of variables. Still further uses of the DECLARE statements will be described in later chapters.

PROBLEMS

5.1 Write DECLARE statements declaring
    (a) VOLT as a variable holding a decimal number of the form xx.xxx
    (b) FREQ as an integer variable
    (c) NEWTON as a floating-point variable

5.2 What attributes are associated with variables ALPHA, GAUSS, and BERN through the declarations
    (a) DCL ALPHA FLOAT BIN;
    (b) DCL GAUSS CPLX (6,1);
    (c) DECLARE BERN FIXED (8,5);

5.3 Are the following declarations legal?
    (a) DCL A(2,5) DEC REAL;
    (b) DCL (A,B) REAL FLOAT (8,2);
    (c) DCL C CPLX BIN REAL (8,2);

5.4 What is the output of the program

```
P54: PROCEDURE OPTIONS (MAIN);
      DCL A FIXED (6,3), B FLOAT (4) INIT (3);
      A = B;
      PUT LIST (A,B);
      END P54;
```

5.5 The following data appear on data cards:

11.53	12.7	− 3.12	4.23	8.75
−6.9	8.33	7.63	13.09	10.71

Write a program

(*a*) To acquire each number.

(*b*) To print out each number and the integer corresponding to the roundoff of each number. For example, number $N + \alpha$, with N as the integer part, satisfying

$$N < N + \alpha < N + 0.5$$

rounds off to N, while a number $N + \beta$ satisfying

$$N + 0.5 \leqslant N + \beta < N + 1$$

rounds off to $N + 1$.

(*c*) To print out the sum of all numbers and the sum of all integers obtained by the roundoff. Identify both sums through descriptive headings.

6 THE IF STATEMENT

The conditional transfer form of the IF statement was introduced in Sec. 3.2. We are returning now to this topic and will consider it in more detail. We will see the power of this instruction for writing programs which require decisions during the carrying out of the computations. We will also study the extensions of the IF statement which further strengthen this valuable tool.

6.1 THE IF STATEMENT AS A CONDITIONAL TRANSFER

We introduced the IF statement as the conditional transfer statement in Sec. 3.2. This statement has the form

IF *condition1* THEN GO TO *label1;*

where *condition1* is any equality or inequality and *label1* is some statement label. We also used the transfer in examples. Recall that some of these examples were

IF A = 5 THEN GO TO YES;
IF A ¬ = B THEN GO TO FAIL;
IF A <= B THEN GO TO ANYWHERE;

These examples show the basic form of the conditional transfer.

6.2 A MORE GENERAL THEN CLAUSE

Note that the IF statement has two parts: the IF clause and the THEN clause. Up to now the THEN clause had the form

THEN GO TO *label1;*

However, it is also valid to write for the THEN part

THEN *statement1;*

where *statement1* is any executable PL/I statement[1] and not just a transfer statement. Thus the following are valid statements:

IF A = 5 THEN X = 7;
IF A < B+3 THEN PUT LIST (C,D);
IF 8 < B THEN I = I + 1;

As before, if the condition is true, we execute the THEN part of the statement. After that, the next statement is executed. If the condition is false, the THEN part is ignored, and again the next statement is executed.

To illustrate this use of the IF statement, consider the following example.

Example 6.2.1 Given a set of numbers, with only the last number being zero, find the sum of all positive numbers in the set.

Obviously, we wish to stop our summation when zero is encountered. The flowchart for this problem is as shown in Fig. 6.1. The program is thus

```
EXAMPLE:   PROCEDURE OPTIONS(MAIN);
           TOTAL = 0;
REPEAT:    GET LIST(A);
           IF A=0 THEN GO TO FINISHED;
           IF A>0 THEN TOTAL = TOTAL + A;
           GO TO REPEAT;
FINISHED:  PUT LIST(TOTAL);
           END EXAMPLE;
```

Note that if the condition $A > 0$ is satisfied, then we execute the statement TOTAL=TOTAL+A;. This leads to the observation that if the condition is met, we can execute a single statement. What do we do if we wish to execute several statements?

In such a case we wish to group several statements together and to execute the group only if the condition is met. There is a means for such a grouping, and it is provided by the so-called DO group. Here the statements have the form

IF *condition1* THEN DO;
statement1;
statement2;
. . . .
statementm;
END;
statementn;

As before, *condition1* is tested. If it is met then all the statements in the DO group (between the DO; and the END;) are executed. Afterward, the next state-

---

[1]An *executable* statement is one which causes some computer action. A statement such as the DECLARE is a *nonexecutable* statement because it requires no computer action—it just tells the compiler about the data.

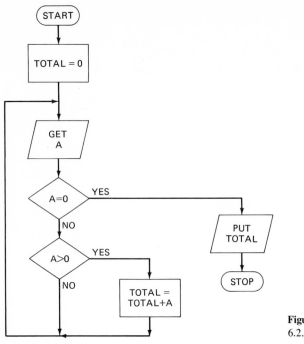

Figure 6.1 Flowchart for Example 6.2.1.

ment in the program, *statementn,* is executed. If *condition1* fails, the DO group is ignored, and just *statementn* is executed.

In the above program segment observe the following:

1. The THEN clause has the form

    THEN DO;

2. The DO group always ends with the statement

    END;

    which signifies the end of the DO group.
3. The DO group must be used whenever we wish to execute more than one statement following the THEN clause.
4. In the program segment above, the END; statement is aligned with the DO; statement. This is of course not necessary—the compiler can read it in any column—but it is a convenient program-writing practice which improves the readability of the program. The statements within the DO; and END; are also aligned. Another common format is

    IF *condition1* THEN
        DO;
            statement1;
            statement2;

            . . . .

statementm;
  END;
statementn;

To illustrate the use of the DO group, consider the following example:

Example 6.2.2 Given a set of numbers, with only the last one being zero, find the sum of all positive numbers in the set and the sum of their squares.

This example is similar to the previous one. The flowchart for this problem is as shown in Fig. 6.2, and the program is

```
EXAMPLE: PROCEDURE OPTIONS(MAIN);
         TOTAL = 0;
         SUM_SQUARE = 0;
REPEAT:  GET LIST(A);
         IF A=0 THEN GO TO DONE;
         IF A>0 THEN DO;
                    TOTAL = TOTAL + A;
                    SUM_SQUARE = SUM_SQUARE + A*A;
                END;
         GO TO REPEAT;
DONE:    PUT LIST(TOTAL,SUM_SQUARE);
         END EXAMPLE;
```

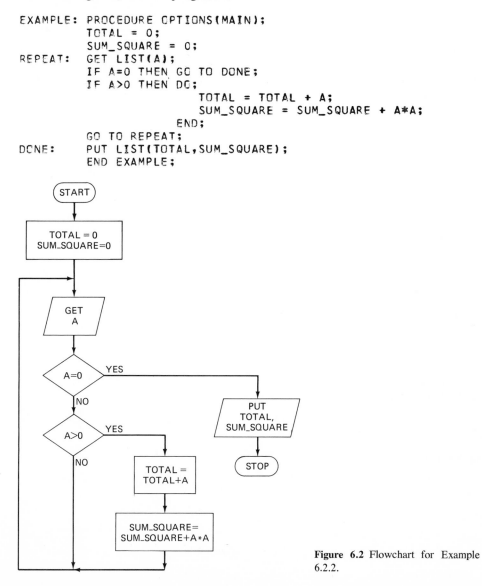

Figure 6.2 Flowchart for Example 6.2.2.

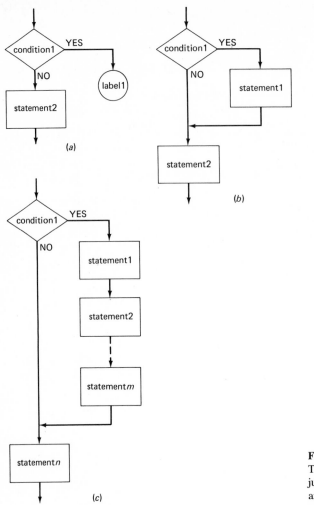

Figure 6.3 Three forms of the THEN clause: (*a*) the conditional jump, (*b*) the conditional statement, and (*c*) the conditional DO group.

Let us now pause and summarize the generalizations of the THEN clause. Initially, we introduced the IF statement as a conditional jump with

IF *condition1* THEN GO TO *label1;*
statement2;

which leads to the flowchart shown in Fig. 6.3*a*.

We then allowed the more general form, in which any statement (not necessarily a GO TO statement) is conditionally executed with

IF *condition1* THEN *statement1;*
statement2;

This is portrayed by the flowchart of Fig. 6.3*b*.

Finally, we generalized further to the conditional execution of a group of statements, that is, the DO group) with

IF *condition1* THEN DO;

statement1;

statement2;

$\cdots\cdots$

statementm;

END;

statementn;

which is pictured with the flowchart of Fig. 6.3*c.*

Observe that we have used in Fig. 6.3*a* a new symbol, the circle enclosing *label1*. The circle is named the *connector* symbol and is used to show the connection from one part of a flowchart to another. It is necessary to use the connector symbols if a flowchart is drawn on more than one page, but it is also convenient even in one-page flowcharts. In a complete flowchart, the connector symbols occur in pairs, with one connector showing the exit (as in Fig. 6.3*a*), and the other showing the entry. Since Fig. 6.3*a* portrays only a segment of a flowchart (that is, it corresponds to only a part of a program), it shows just the exit connector.

6.3 THE ELSE CLAUSE

Let us return to Fig. 6.3*b.* Just a glance at it reveals that there is another flowchart situation that can occur: when we wish to execute a statement after failing *condition1* but prior to reaching *statement2*. Such a situation is portrayed in Fig. 6.4, and its programming is achieved with the ELSE clause. Specifically, the program segment for the flowchart of Fig. 6.4 is

IF *condition1* THEN *statement1b;*

ELSE *statement1a;*

statement2;

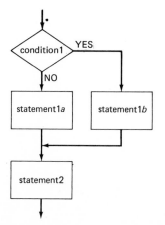

Figure 6.4 Flowchart illustrating the ELSE clause.

Again, the alignment of the THEN and ELSE above is just for improvement of program readability. To show how the ELSE clause streamlines our program, we will write the above program segment without it. One example is

> IF *condition1* THEN DO;
> > > *statement1b;*
> > > GO TO *label1;*
> > END;
>
> > *statement1a;*
> > *label1:* *statement2;*

which uses a DO group, and a GO TO statement to execute *statement1b* followed by *statement2* if *condition1* is satisfied, and *statement1a* followed by *statement2* if *condition1* fails. Observe that the program segment has now six statements instead of the three statement achieved with the ELSE clause. If we avoid the DO group the program segment becomes

> IF *condition1* THEN GO TO *label1;*
> *statement1a;*
> GO TO *label2;*
> *label1:statement1b;*
> *label2:statement2;*

Here we saved a statement, but the program is less clear because of the additional GO TO statement. Thus with the ELSE clause we can have the cake and eat it too—we have fewer statements and a more readable program.

We are ready now for an example illustrating the ELSE clause. To do so consider the following example.

Example 6.3.1 Given a set of numbers, with only the last number being zero, find the sum of all positive numbers and the sum of all negative numbers in the set.

(This example is a modification of Example 6.2.1.) The flowchart appears in Fig. 6.5, and the program is

```
EXAMPLE: PROCEDURE OPTIONS(MAIN);
         SUM_POS = 0;
         SUM_NEG = 0;
REPEAT:  GET LIST(A);
         IF A=0 THEN GO TO DONE;
         IF A>0 THEN SUM_POS = SUM_POS + A;
              ELSE SUM_NEG = SUM_NEG + A;
         GO TO REPEAT;
DONE:    PUT LIST(SUM_POS,SUM_NEG);
         END EXAMPLE;
```

As an aside, observe that the names chosen for the sums, namely, SUM_POS and SUM_NEG, ensure floating-point sums, and if such are desired, these sums do

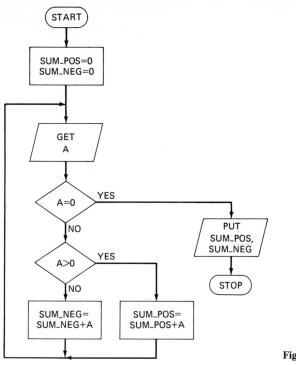

Figure 6.5 Flowchart for Example 6.3.1.

not require declarations (that is, a DECLARE statement). Had we chosen the names POS_SUM and NEG_SUM for the sums, then a declaration would be needed, because NEG_SUM by the default rules designates an integer. Obviously, no declaration is needed for POS_SUM, since it is by default already a floating-point variable. Of course, if some other form is desired such as FIXED DEC (6,2), we need a declaration for both sums, regardless of the names chosen for them. In such a case, we can use the INITIAL option and write our program as

```
EXAMPLE:   PROCEDURE OPTIONS (MAIN);
           DCL (SUM_POS, SUM_NEG) FIXED DEC (6,2) INITIAL (0);
           GET LIST (A);
           . . . . . . . . . . . . . . . . . . . . . . . . . . . . . . . . . . . . . . . . . . . . . . . . . . .
```

The remainder of the program is as above. Note the factoring of attributes—the precision and the initial value apply to both SUM_POS and SUM_NEG.

Returning to the discussion of the ELSE clause, consider again Fig. 6.4. Let us assume now that if we satisfy *condition1* we wish to execute not just *statement1b* but several statements prior to *statement2*. Similarly, if *condition1* fails, we wish to execute several statements before *statement2*. Thus we are speaking about the situation portrayed in Fig. 6.6. Its programming is easily accomplished with the use of DO groups both in the THEN clause and in the ELSE clause, as the following example illustrates.

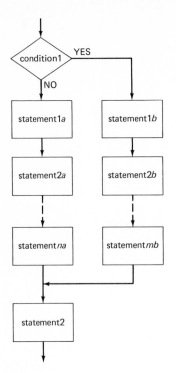

Figure 6.6 Flowchart illustrating the ELSE clause with the DO group.

```
IF condition1 THEN DO;
                    statement1b;
                    statement2b;
                    . . . . . . . . . . . .
                    statementmb;
               END;
           ELSE DO;
                    statement1a;
                    statement2a;
                    . . . . . . . . . . . .
                    statementna;
               END;
       statement2;
```

6.4 FURTHER EXTENSIONS OF THE IF STATEMENT

A Nested IF Statements

It is instructive to reconsider the THEN clause. This clause has the form

$$\text{THEN } statement1;$$

where *statement1* is any executable PL/I statement. Thus *statement1* can be another IF statement, resulting in the THEN clause.

> THEN IF *condition2* THEN *statement1a;*

The complete statement with the next statement reads

> IF *condition1* THEN IF *condition2* THEN *statement1a;*
> *statement2;*

and means

1. If both *condition1* and *condition2* are satisfied, then execute *statement1a*. Next, execute *statement2*.
2. If either *condition1* or *condition2* fails, execute the next statement *(statement2)*.

The flowchart for this program segment appears in Fig. 6.7. Note that *statement1a* can again be an IF statement, which can in turn contain another IF statement, and so on. As an example consider

> IF A>5 THEN IF B=C+2 THEN IF X<=2 THEN D=D+3;
> Z=D+1;

and as before, if all the three conditions (that is, A>5, B=C+2, X≤2) are satisfied, the statement D=D+3; is executed prior to the Z=D+1; statement. If any one of the conditions fails, the statement D=D+3; is ignored and just Z=D+1; is executed.

In the above statement, the IF statements are contained, or nested, within the original IF statement. Such a situation is known as "nested IF statements."

B Nested IF Statements with ELSE Clauses

Consider now the flowchart of Fig. 6.8. The program segment for this flowchart is

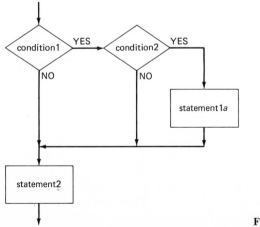

Figure 6.7 Flowchart for the program segment.

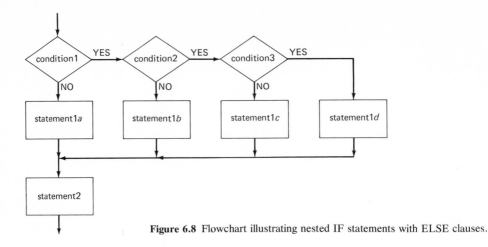

Figure 6.8 Flowchart illustrating nested IF statements with ELSE clauses.

IF *condition1* THEN IF *condition2* THEN IF *condition3* THEN *statement1d;*
ELSE *statement1c;*
ELSE *statement1b;*
ELSE *statement1a;*
statement2;

The alignment of THEN and ELSE clauses is made for convenience (the compiler does not need it) to illustrate the rule for their association. The rule is: *Each* ELSE *clause is matched with the last unmatched* THEN *clause* (that is, with the last THEN clause not having an associated ELSE clause). Thus the first ELSE clause—ELSE *statement1c;*—is matched with the last THEN clause and is executed only if *condition3* fails. The next ELSE statement—ELSE *statement1b;*—is matched with the second THEN clause and is executed if *condition2* fails. Finally, the statement ELSE *statement1a;* goes with the first THEN clause, and the ELSE clause is executed only if *condition1* fails. Observe that we execute either *statement1d,* or *statement1c,* or *statement1b,* or *statement1a.* Any one of these statements is then followed by *statement2.*

C The Null ELSE

Consider now the flowchart of Fig. 6.9. The program segment for this flowchart can be written as

IF *condition1* THEN IF *condition2* THEN IF *condition3* THEN *statement1c;*
ELSE *statement1b;*
ELSE GO TO *label1;*
ELSE *statement1a;*
label1: statement2;

Observe the ELSE clause for *condition2.* We need the ELSE clause, because without it, the next ELSE clause (for *condition1*) will be mismatched. But we really do not wish to execute any statement. Thus we simply jump to *statement2.*

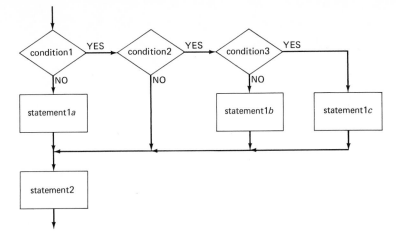

Figure 6.9 Flowchart illustrating the null ELSE.

There is another alternative for handling such situations—the null ELSE. This is simply the statement

ELSE;

which instructs the compiler to execute nothing but simply to jump to the next statement (*statement2* here). The null ELSE assures a correct match with its associated THEN clause. Using the null ELSE the last program segment modifies to

IF *condition1* THEN IF *condition2* THEN IF *condition3* THEN *statement1c;*
ELSE *statement1b;*
ELSE;
ELSE *statement1a;*
statement2;

which simplifies the ELSE clause (there is nothing simpler than the null ELSE) and obviates the need for labeling *statement2*.

D The Null THEN

Figure 6.10 pictures another twist. This time there is no statement after satisfaction of *condition3*. To write the program segment we can again use the GO TO statement, resulting in

IF *condition1* THEN IF *condition2* THEN IF *condition3* THEN GO TO *label1;*

ELSE;
ELSE *statement1a;*
label1: statement 2;

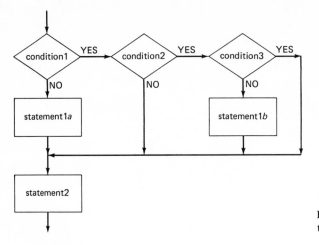

Figure 6.10 Flowchart illustrating the null THEN.

There is an alternative in the use of the null THEN. With the null THEN, the program segment reads

IF *condition1* THEN IF *condition2* THEN IF *condition3* THEN;
ELSE *statement1b;*
ELSE;
ELSE *statement1a;*
statement2;

Again, with the null THEN nothing is executed after satisfaction of *condition3*, and a jump to *statement2* takes place.

Incidentally, there is still another way of programming the flowchart of Fig. 6.10. We can negate *condition3* (that is, reverse or replace it by its opposite) so as to move *statement1b* into the last branch of the flowchart. For example, the program segment

IF A < B THEN IF C ¬=5 THEN IF D > 3 THEN;
ELSE X = 3;
ELSE;
ELSE X = 4;
Y = X + 1;

can be written as

IF A < B THEN IF C ¬=5 THEN IF D ¬> 3 THEN X = 3;
ELSE;
ELSE;
ELSE X = 4;
Y = X + 1;

where the replacement of the condition D>3 by the opposite condition D¬>3 (which can be written alternatively as D<=3) exchanges the null THEN for the null ELSE.

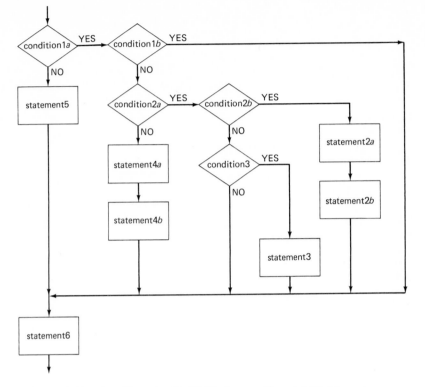

Figure 6.11 Flowchart illustrating the ELSE clauses with nested IF statements.

In fact, the last form is clearer to read. These many different ways of programming attest to the richness of the PL/I language.

E ELSE Clauses with Nested IF Statements

The statement in the ELSE clause can be an IF statement nesting other IF statements. These may in turn contain their own THEN and ELSE clauses, with or without DO groups. To illustrate such a complex situation, consider the monstrosity of Fig. 6.11. The program segment for this flowchart is

```
IF condition1a
    THEN IF condition1b
            THEN;
            ELSE IF condition2a
                    THEN IF condition2b
                            THEN DO;
                                    statement2a;
                                    statement2b;
                            END;
```

```
                                        ELSE IF condition3
                                            THEN statement3;
                                            ELSE;
                        ELSE DO;
                                statement4a;
                                statement4b;
                            END;
            ELSE statement5;
        statement6;
```

Observe the use of null THEN and null ELSE to provide an appropriate match for the IF statements. Note also how difficult it is to understand this program segment. Just as long sentences are unclear in English, so are long statements (that is, with the nested IF statements) unclear in PL/I. As a consequence, even though the nested IFs are legal, we try to avoid their use. Such avoidance is achieved by reversing the condition, as needed, and by using extra DOs. As an example, the program segment can be rewritten as

```
        IF ¬ condition1a
            THEN statement5;
            ELSE IF ¬ condition1b
                THEN DO;
                                IF ¬ condition2a
                                    THEN DO;
                                            statement4a;
                                            statement4b;
                                        END;
                                ELSE IF condition2b
                                    THEN DO;
                                            statement2a;
                                            statement2b;
                                        END;
                                ELSE IF condition3
                                    THEN statement3;
                                    ELSE;
                        END;
                    ELSE;
                statement6;
```

which is clearer than the previous one. Observe that the last two ELSEs are redundant but add to the clarity of the program segment. Note also the presence of the ¬ operator before the condition. Such use is allowed and reverses the condition. For example,

$$¬(A=1)$$

is equivalent to

$$A¬=1$$

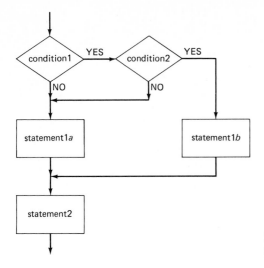

Figure 6.12 Flowchart illustrating the use of the & operator.

F IF Statement with Logical Operators

The so-called *logical* operators

         meaning *and*
      | meaning *or* (inclusive or)

can be used to simplify certain IF statements. To illustrate the use of the & operator, consider the flowchart of Fig. 6.12. A program segment for this flowchart is

    IF *condition1* THEN IF *condition2* THEN *statement1b;*
              ELSE *statement1a;*
      ELSE *statement1a;*
   statement2;

An alternate program segment with the & operator is

    IF *condition1* & *condition2* THEN *statement1b;*
           ELSE *statement1a;*
   statement2;

In the above, *statement1b* is executed if *condition1* and *condition2* are satisfied. The ELSE clause is executed if either *condition1* or *condition2* fails or if both conditions fail. Note that the use of the & operator simplifies the program, as asserted.

  To illustrate the use of the | operator, consider the flowchart of Fig. 6.13, which can be implemented with the program segment

    IF *condition1* THEN *statement1b;*
      ELSE IF *condition2* THEN *statement1b;*
          ELSE *statement1a;*
   statement2;

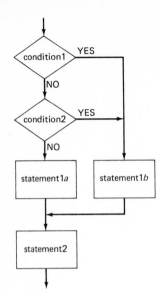

Figure 6.13 Flowchart illustrating the use of the   operator.

Using the   operator, the program becomes

IF *condition1*   *condition2*   THEN *statement1b;*
ELSE *statement 1a;*

statement2;

Here, *statement1b* is executed whenever *condition1* is satisfied, or *condition2* is satisfied, or both conditions are satisfied (that is why this is an inclusive OR). The ELSE clause is executed only if both conditions fail. Note again the simplification in the program.

Additional examples of IF statements with logical operators are

IF (A>5) | (7<= B+C) THEN X=Y+1;
IF ¬(A=1) & (B ¬ >C) THEN GO TO AGAIN;
IF ((A>B) | (A<C)) & (X<3) THEN Y=13.2E1;

As a preview to a later discussion (in Sec. 18.4) we shall now describe briefly how the PL/I compiler handles the decision process. The condition part is evaluated and if it is satisfied it receives the value of 1. If the condition fails, it receives the value of 0. Thus, a single bit, either 1 or 0, represents each decision. Because of the use of bits, the logical operators are also known as bit-string operators. We will discuss bit strings later on in Chap. 18.

6.5 LABELS

In Chap. 3 we discussed labels. We said that a statement can be labeled, resulting in the form *label1: statement1;*

This brings out a question regarding the labeling of an ELSE clause, that is,

ELSE *statement1;*

Should the label precede ELSE or *statement1?* PL/I syntax rules resolve this question by allowing the labeling of the statement only. Thus

ELSE *label1: statement1;*

is a legal statement, while

label1: ELSE *statement1;*

is an illegal one. Similarly, we can label the statement in the THEN clause, as in

IF A > B THEN AGAIN: X=Y+1;

where AGAIN is a label. As a second example, note that DO; is a statement and thus the following statement is legal:

IF C > D+1 THEN L1: DO;

with L1 being a label.

6.6 EXAMPLES

Example 6.6.1 Remember the triangle program of Sec. 3.3? The object was to determine whether A=B=C for positive A, B, and C. The program had eight statements, and we remarked that a skilled progammer could construct a five-statement program. Now we have these skills, so here is the five-statement program

```
SIDES_2: PROCEDURE OPTIONS(MAIN);
         GET LIST(A,B,C);
         IF (A=B) & (A=C) THEN PUT LIST
   ('THESE 3 NUMBERS CAN BE THE SIDES OF AN EQUILATERAL TRIANGLE');
                    ELSE PUT LIST
   ('THESE 3 NUMBERS CANNOT BE THE SIDES OF AN EQUILATERAL TRIANGLE');
         END SIDES_2;
```

This program is both shorter and clearer than the previous version.

Example 6.6.2 Given that

$$
y(t) = \begin{cases}
t & \text{for } 0 \le t < 1 \\
1 & \text{for } 1 \le t < 2 \\
t - 1 & \text{for } 2 \le t < 3 \\
-t + 5 & \text{for } 3 \le t < 5 \\
0 & \text{for } t \ge 5
\end{cases}
$$

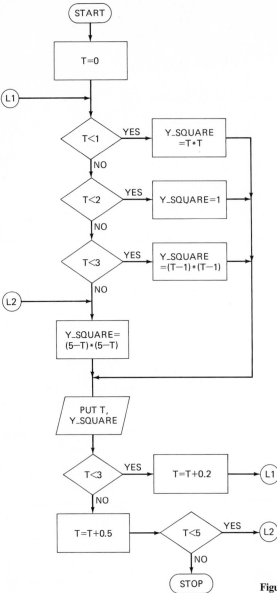

Figure 6.14 Flowchart for Example 6.6.2.

Obtain values of $y^2(t)$ in the interval $0 \leqslant t < 5$. Use steps of 0.2 for t in the interval $0 \leqslant t < 3$ and steps 0.5 for t in the interval $3 \leqslant t < 5$. Print out t and $y^2(t)$.

Solution The flowchart for the example appears in Fig. 6.14 (note the use of connector symbols). The program is then

```
VALUES:    PROCEDURE OPTIONS(MAIN);
           DCL T FIXED(2,1),Y_SQUARE FIXED(3,2);
           T = 0;
L1:        IF T<1 THEN Y_SQUARE=T*T;
               ELSE IF T<2 THEN Y_SQUARE=1;
                       ELSE IF T<3 THEN Y_SQUARE=(T-1)*(T-1);
                               ELSE L2: Y_SQUARE=(5-T)*(5-T);
           PUT LIST(T,Y_SQUARE);
           IF T<3 THEN DO;
                       T=T+0.2;
                       GO TO L1;
                   END;
               ELSE DO;
                       T=T+0.5;
                       IF T<5 THEN GO TO L2;
                   END;
           END VALUES;
```

Explanation of the program:

1. The clause ELSE IF T<2 THEN Y_SQUARE=1; is executed only if $T \geqslant 1$ (that is, if the condition $T < 1$ fails) and $T < 2$ (that is, if $1 \leqslant T < 2$).
2. The clause ELSE IF $T < 3$ THEN Y_SQUARE=$(T-1)*(T-1)$; is executed only if the two preceding statements fail. Thus Y_SQUARE has the value of $(T-1)*(T-1)$ for $2 \leqslant T < 3$.
3. The clause ELSE L2: Y_SQUARE=$(5-T)*(5-T)$; is reached only after failing the three earlier conditions. Thus $T \geqslant 3$, and Y_SQUARE has the value of $(5-T)*(5-T)$. Note the L2 label, to allow a transfer to the statement Y_SQUARE = $(5-T)*(5-T)$;
4. Should any of the conditions be met, the THEN clause following it is executed, the following ELSE clause is ignored, and the PUT LIST (T, Y_SQUARE); statement is executed next.
5. The next THEN clause requires a DO group, since we have two statements. The GO TO statement returns program execution to the statement labeled L1.
6. The associated ELSE clause also requires a DO group. If $T < 5$, we return to the statement labeled L2. We could also return to the statement labeled L1, but then we will perform the tests $T < 1$, $T < 2$, and $T < 3$, which are unnecessary and eat up computer time.
7. IF $T \geqslant 5$, the THEN clause statement GO TO L2; is ignored, the DO group ends, and the next statement (END VALUES;) is executed. We could have alternatively written the program segment from the last ELSE as

```
            ELSE DO;
                    T = T+0.5;
                    IF T < 5 THEN GO TO L2;
                            ELSE GO TO FINISHED;
                END;
      FINISHED: END VALUES;
```

This program segment is valid but one statement (and one label) longer, because the statement ELSE GO TO FINISHED; is redundant (the next statement is the END VALUES; statement even without the GO TO statement). This segment illustrates poor programming. Avoid using statements which clutter a program.

Example 6.6.3 The Fastbuck Real Estate Company is selling land by the following price schedule:
1. The basic price of land is $500/acre.
2. No land under ¼ acre is sold.
3. The land on the waterfront and the land near the highway costs more than the basic price. For such lots the basic price is multiplied by the number shown in the accompanying table.

Lot size	Near highway	Near water	Near highway and water
Less than 1 acre	1.5	1.8	2
1 acre or more, but less than 10 acres	1	1.2	1.5
10 acres or more	1	1	1.2

The input to the computer consists of three numbers. The first number gives the size of the lot desired by the customer. The second number is either 1 or 0, with 1 meaning that the lot should be near the highway, and 0 that it should not. The third number is also either 1 or 0, with 1 describing a waterfront lot, and 0 a nonwaterfront lot.

The output should be the price of the lot, given as a fixed number with two decimal places. No sale exceeding 100 acres is expected.

Solution A flowchart for the problem appears in Fig. 6.15. All the calculations can be performed in floating-point numbers, but the output must be fixed. Therefore, LOT has to be declared FLOAT and COST FIXED (7,2) (because the largest expected sale is $60,000). Thus the program is

```
LOTS:   PROC OPTIONS(MAIN);
        DCL LOT FLOAT, COST FIXED(7,2), (H,W)FIXED;
        GET LIST(LOT,H,W);
        IF LOT<0.25EO THEN DO;
                            PUT LIST('LOT TOO SMALL');
                            GO TO DONE;
                        END;
        F = 1;
        IF LOT<1 THEN IF H=1 THEN IF W=1 THEN F=2;
                                            ELSE F=1.5;
                            ELSE IF W=1 THEN F=1.8;
                                        ELSE;
                ELSE IF LOT<10 THEN IF H=1 THEN IF W=1 THEN F=1.5;
```

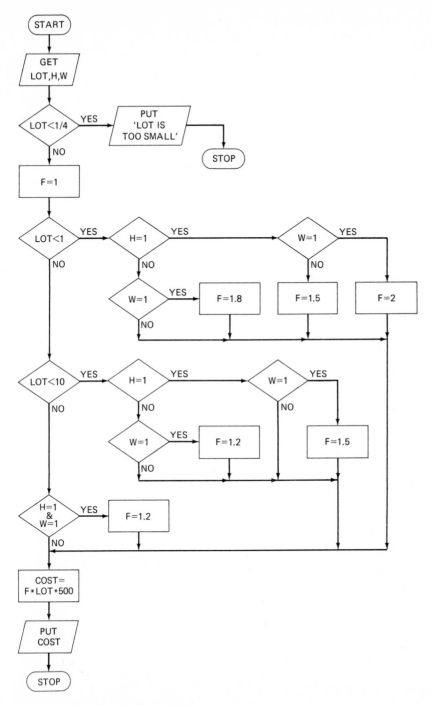

Figure 6.15 Flowchart for Example 6.6.3.

```
                                     ELSE;
                    ELSE IF W=1 THEN F=1.2;
                                     ELSE;
             ELSE IF H=1 & W=1 THEN F=1.2;
                                ELSE;
        COST = F*LOT*500;
        PUT LIST(COST);
DONE:   END LOTS;
```

Explanation of the program:

1. The DECLARE statement ensures that LOT is a FLOAT number. Without it, LOT would be an integer, and the fractional part of the number will be deleted (that is, 1.5 will be stored as 1). Also COST will be in the desired fixed-decimal form, and H and W will be integers.

2. We first test whether LOT is not smaller than $\frac{1}{4}$ acre. Note that we used 0.25E0, that is, the floating-point representation. 0.25 would also be satisfactory but would require conversion to floating-point; hence 0.25E0 saves a conversion and is thus a good programming practice. (We really should have represented all other numbers in floating-point form also, but we wished to make the program as readable as possible.)

3. We set F=1. This corresponds to the sale at the basic price.

4. If LOT <1, H=1, W=1, then F=2. Note that the first ELSE applies when the last condition fails; thus for LOT <1, H=1, W≠1. The second ELSE applies for LOT <1, but H ≠ 1. The third ELSE applies for LOT <1, H ≠ 1, W ≠ 1. Since this case requires no action (that is, no change in F), it is a null ELSE. It is needed to ensure the correct match between the THEN and ELSE clauses.

5. If LOT< 1, either the associated IF statement or one of the three following ELSE clauses are executed, and program control transfers to the "next statement," this being COST = F*LOT*500;. IF LOT ⩾ 1, none of these is executed and the fourth ELSE clause is tested. If 1 ⩽ LOT < 10, H= 1, W=1, then F=1.5 is executed. If 1⩽ LOT < 10, H= 1, but W≠ 1, the fifth ELSE applies, this being a null ELSE. The sixth ELSE pictures the conditions 1 ⩽ LOT < 10, H≠ 1, W=1. The seventh ELSE is a null ELSE for 1 ⩽ LOT < 10, H≠ 1, W≠ 1.

6. The eighth ELSE applies for LOT ⩾ 10. Note the use of the logical operator &. The ELSE associated with it (that is, the null ELSE) applies when the condition is not met; thus this ELSE is for either H ≠ 1, W=1, or H = 1, W≠ 1, or H ≠ 1, W ≠ 1. Observe that without the logical operator we will write

```
        ELSE IF H = 1 THEN IF W = 1 THEN F = 1.2;
                                     ELSE;
             ELSE;
```

Thus we will need one extra ELSE clause.

7. When we get to the statement calculating cost, the value of F will be either unchanged—if we reached the statement via a null ELSE—or will have the value arising from the appropriate conditions.

6.7 SUMMARY

In this chapter we discussed the IF statement and its use in writing programs which require a decision-making mechanism. We shall summarize now the contents of this chapter.

1. The IF statement has two parts: the IF clause and the THEN clause.
2. The IF statement has the basic form

IF condition1 THEN statement1;

 IF *condition1* is met then *statement1* is executed. If *condition1* is not met, *statement1* is ignored.
3. In the program segment

IF condition1 THEN DO;
statement1;
statement2;
. . . .
statementm;
END;

 the statements DO; and END; enclose a so-called DO group. The statements *statement1, statement2, . . . , statementm* are within the group. If *condition1* is met, then the DO group is executed. This means that the statements within the DO group are sequentially executed (unless of course, a transfer to a statement outside the DO group takes place). The DO group provides a means for executing more than one statement upon satisfaction of the condition (of the IF clause). The DO group must be terminated with the END; statement.
4. The IF statement with the ELSE clause,

IF condition1 THEN statement1b;
ELSE statement1a;

 causes execution of *statement1b* when *condition1* is met, and execution of *statement1a* when *condition1* fails.
5. In the program segment

IF condition1 THEN DO;
statement1b;
statement2b;
. . . .
statementm;
END;
ELSE DO;
statement1a;
statement2a;
. . . .
statementna;
END;

the first DO group is executed if *condition1* is true, and the second DO group is executed if *condition1* is false.

6. The THEN clause can be an IF statement, resulting in the nested IF statements, that is,

> If *condition1* THEN IF *condition2* THEN *statement1a;*

IF *condition1* and *condition2* are true, *statement1a* is executed. Otherwise *statement1a* is ignored. A further generalization of this nesting gives the form

> IF *condition1* THEN IF *condition2* · · · THEN IF *conditionm* THEN *statement1k;*

and again, *statement1k* is executed only if all the conditions are satisfied.

7. Nested IF statements can have ELSE clauses as in

> IF *condition1* THEN IF *condition2* THEN IF *condition3* THEN *statement1d;*
> ELSE *statement1c;*
> ELSE *statement1b;*
> ELSE *statement1a;*

where each ELSE clause is matched with the last unmatched THEN clause. Thus, if *condition1* and *condition2* are true but *condition3* is false, *statement1c* is executed. If *condition1* is met but *condition2* is failed, *statement1b* is executed. And finally, if *condition1* is false, *statement1a* is executed.

8. For proper match of ELSE clauses it is sometimes necessary to use the null ELSE written as

> ELSE;

which causes no statement execution.

9. It is sometimes convenient to employ the null THEN clause written as

> IF *condition1* THEN;

Here, if *condition1* is met, no statement execution takes place.

10. The ELSE clause can contain nested IF statements, as in

> ELSE IF *condition1* THEN IF *condition2* THEN *statement1a;*

11. The logical operators

> & meaning *and* | meaning *or*

are used to simplify certain IF statements. In

> IF *condition1* & *condition2* THEN *statement1;*

statement1 is executed if both *condition1* and *condition2* are satisfied. In

> IF *condition1* | *condition2* THEN *statement1;*

statement1 is executed if either *condition1* or *condition2* is satisfied (*statement1* is also executed if both conditions are satisfied).

The logical operators are also known as bit-string operators.

12. Labels can be used in the THEN and ELSE clauses of the IF statement as in

IF *condition1* THEN L1: *statement1a;*
ELSE L2: *statement1b;*

where L1 and L2 are statement labels.

PROBLEMS

6.1 Write a program implementing the flowcharts shown in Fig. P6.1.

6.2 Write a program coding the flowcharts in Fig. P6.2.

6.3 Code the flowchart shown in Fig. P6.3.

6.4 The program segment

$$IF (A=0 \& B>C) \mid D>A \text{ THEN } S = S+K;$$
$$A = B+S;$$

is to be rewritten without the & and | symbols.

6.5
```
PROB_5: PROCEDURE OPTIONS(MAIN);
        SUM = 0;
A:      GET LIST(B,C,D);
        IF B=C|B>C+D THEN SUM=SUM+D;
        IF B>5 THEN GO TO A;
        IF C<D THEN SUM=SUM+D;
        IF B>SUM/100 THEN SUM=SUM+2*C;
        IF B>SUM THEN GO TO A;
        PUT LIST(SUM);
        END PROB_5;
```

The data are

5.1, 8.2, −7.2, 0.2, 2.1, 0.7, 2.3, 6.5, 10, 12, 17.2, 14.2

What is the output of this program?

6.6 Correct the errors in the following programs:

(*a*)
```
PROB-6A; PROC.OPTIONS MAIN
         GET LIST A;
         IF A=0, THEN B=3;
         FOR A=1 GO TO END;
         SUM 1 = 2*A AND SUM 2 = 3*A;
         IF SUM 1=17 AND IF SUM 2=18 THEN B=4;
         PUT LIST(SUM 1, SUM 2, B);
    FINISHED:END;
```

(*b*)
```
NO-NAME PROCEDURE OPTIONS MAIN
        GET LIST 1A;
        1A = 1A + 5;
        JOE = 1A + 5 + 3 + 1;
        MOE = (JOE):1A;
        IF JOE>10 GO TO GET LIST;
                  ELSE DO NOTHING;
        PUT LIST JOE AND MOE;
        END PROCEDURE;
```

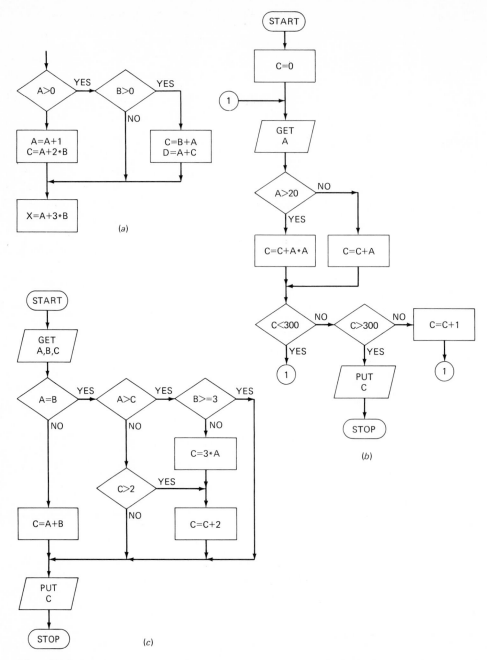

Figure P6.1

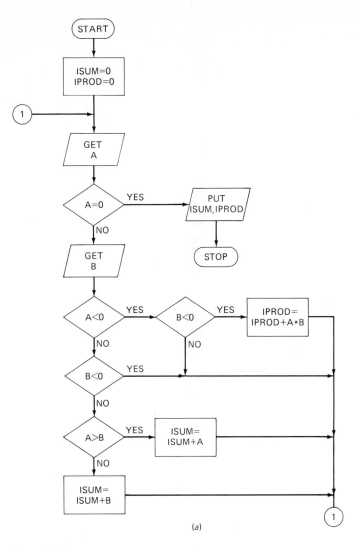

(a)

Figure P6.2

(c) **Q 2: PROC. OPTION MAIN:**
      GET FROM LIST(N&M);
      IF N¬0 THEN PRINT(N);
      IF N>0 & IF M<0 PUT(N+M)
      END 2ND QUIZ.

6.7 The data card contains one number.

    (a) Write a program to do the following:

If this number is zero, do nothing.

If this number exceeds 5, print YES.

If this number is 5 or smaller (but not zero), print NO.

    (b) Write also a program to print

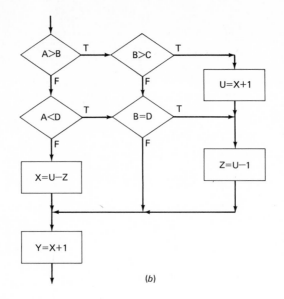

(b)

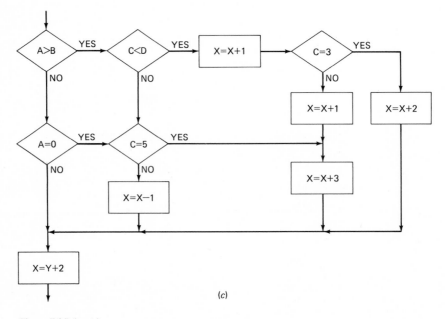

(c)

Figure P6.2 (cont.)

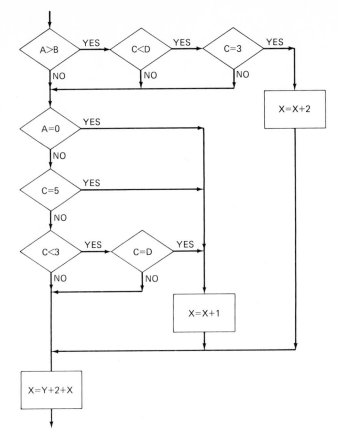

Figure P6.3

1   if the number is negative
2   if the number is larger than 1 but less than 2
3   if the number is larger than 10
4   in all other cases

6.8   The data cards contain positive integers and −1 as the last number (to be used for the termination of the program).

(*a*) Write a program which will print out only the integers divisible by 3.

(*b*) Write a program to print out the number of odd integers on data cards.

6.9   Write a program to determine whether or not four positive numbers on the data cards could be the sides of a rectangle. If so, print out YES; if not, print out NO.

6.10   Four integers are given on the data cards. Write a program that will print out either of the following, depending upon the applicable case:

(1)   ALL ARE EQUAL
(2)   THREE ARE EQUAL
(3)   TWO PAIRS OF EQUAL NUMBERS
(4)   TWO ARE EQUAL
(5)   NONE ARE EQUAL

6.11 The three nonzero numbers on data cards are A, B, C, where

$$Ax^2 + Bx + C = 0$$

Write a program to print out

TWO   if there are two positive roots
ONE   if there is 1 positive root
NONE   if there are no positive roots

6.12 The data cards contain many numbers. Each tenth number (that is, 10th, 20th, etc.) is to be printed out as is. Also the square of each 13th number is to be printed out. The other numbers are to be ignored.

The last number in the data is 1000 and is to be used only for stopping program execution. There are two other 1000s in the data (that is, the last number is the third 1000 in the data). Write a program to obtain the desired output.

6.13 Each pair of numbers on data cards gives the x, y coordinates of a point. Print each pair and

(*a*) The location in the system (for example, print FIRST if in the first quadrant, ORIGIN if in the origin, X-AXIS if on the x axis, etc.)

(*b*) The distance from the origin

(*c*) SMALL, if the distance in (*b*) is less than 10; MEDIUM, if the distance in (*b*) is 10 or more but less than 20; LARGE, if the distance in (*b*) is 20 or more

For no point is the distance from the origin in excess of 100. Consequently, a single value of 1000 is to be used to terminate the program.

Include sufficient comments to explain your program. Provide a suitable heading for your printout. The data are

1, 0	0, −4
7, −9.35	0, 0
0.2, 82	−22.3, −16.1
−14.4, 17.5	1000

(The last number is to be used to terminate program execution.)

6.14 Write a program that will test three numbers to see whether these can be the sides of a triangle. If they cannot be sides of a triangle, print out the numbers and the message

THESE 3 NUMBERS CANNOT BE THE SIDES OF A TRIANGLE

If they can be sides of a triangle, determine whether or not

(*a*) All angles are acute (that is, less than 90°)

(*b*) One angle is 90°

(*c*) One angle exceeds 90°

and print out the numbers and the appropriate message. (Show the flowchart on your printout sheet.) The numbers are

1, −1, 1.5	7.2, 7.4, 6.8
1, 1, 1.5	2.8, 3.2, 7.0
2, 3, 4	5, 6, 7
6, 4, 3	6, 8, 10

6.15 In the game of bridge, players bid or pass depending upon the "point count" of their cards and the length of the suits. It is desired to write a program that will determine the players' action using the following criteria:

Point-count evaluation:
Each Ace counts 4 points
Each King counts 3 points

Each Queen counts 2 points
Each Jack counts 1 point

Each player has 13 cards which are named a "hand."

Bidding criteria:
With a 7-card suit and less than 8 points, make a 3-level bid.
With a 8-card suit and less than 8 points, make a 4-level bid.
With a 9- or more card suit and less than 8 points, make a 5-level bid.
With no 7- or more card suit and less than 13 points, pass.
With 13 or more points, make either a 1-level or a 2-level bid.

The hand is coded as follows:
    1. Cards with pips from 2 to 10 are coded by the numbers 2 through 10.
    2. Jack is coded as 11, Queen as 12, King as 13, and Ace as 14.
    3. The cards are coded in the order spades, hearts, diamonds, and clubs.
    4. The last card of each suit is followed by a zero. For example, the hand

        ♠ J, 9, 7   ♥ K, 10, 6, 2   ♦ A, K, J, 9   ♣ 4, 2

will be coded as 11, 9, 7, 0, 13, 10, 6, 2, 0, 14, 13, 11, 9, 0, 4, 2, 0 (a hand with a void has either two consecutive zeros or starts with a zero).

Write a program which will print out the players' action. The input is

    14, 2, 0, 8, 7, 3, 0, 12, 10, 9, 8, 7, 6, 5, 3, 0, 0
    12, 11, 9, 0, 10, 6, 4, 3, 0, 3, 2, 0, 14, 10, 5, 2, 0
    6, 0, 13, 12, 11, 9, 0, 14, 13, 12, 8, 0, 14, 13, 12, 11, 0
    13, 11, 3, 0, 14, 12, 10, 8, 0, 11, 9, 7, 5, 2, 0, 14, 0

6.16 Four bridge players JOE, MOE, SUE, and MABEL play rubber bridge. The partnerships rotate after each rubber, and in the first three rubbers the pairings are
    1. JOE & MOE   SUE & MABEL
    2. JOE & SUE   MOE & MABEL
    3. JOE & MABEL   MOE & SUE
After the three rubbers the players repeat the above rotation.
    The result of each rubber is entered in data cards. For the first rubber the data read

        +1020   −1020

meaning that JOE and MOE each won 1020 points, and SUE and MABEL each lost 1020 points. Similarly, the second pair of numbers

        −570   +570

means that both JOE and SUE lost 570 points and MOE and MABEL gained 570 points.
    The last data card is used for termination and has +1, +1 on it.
    Write a program which will print out the final score of each player. The given data are

        +1020   −1020
        −570   +570
        +3280   −3280
        −810   +810
        −1520   +1520
        +60   −60
        +380   −380
        +1   +1

6.17 The tickets to theaters for performances on weekday evenings cost as follows:

Seats	Musical		Nonmusical	
	On Broadway	Off Broadway	On Broadway	Off Broadway
Top	$20.00	$14.00	$16.00	$12.00
Good	18.00	12.00	13.00	10.00
Average	15.00	9.00	11.00	8.00
Poor	12.00		8.00	
Standing	3.00	2.00	3.00	2.00

Matinee tickets cost 20 percent less rounded off to the nearest 50 cents. Weekend evening tickets cost 10 percent more rounded off to the nearest dollar.

Write a program that will print the price of a ticket. The request is coded by four numbers, where

1. The first number describes the seat, with 1 describing the top seat and 5 describing standing-room tickets.

2. In the second number, 1 describes a musical and 0 a nonmusical.

3. In the third number, a Broadway show is described by 1 and an off Broadway show by 0.

4. In the fourth number, matinee is described by -1, weekday evening by 0, weekend evening by 1.

As an example, the input

$$2, 1, 0, 1$$

is a request for the price of a good seat to a musical in an off Broadway theater on a weekend evening.

The input is

$$2, 1, 0, 1$$
$$1, 0, 0, -1$$
$$5, 1, 1, 0$$
$$3, 0, 1, 1$$
$$4, 1, 1, -1$$

6.18 It is desired to calculate the telephone charges for calls listed on the data cards. The calls were made to Boston, Chicago, Los Angeles, and Philadelphia with the following charge schedule:

	Boston	Chicago	Los Angeles	Philadelphia
Station-to-station direct dialing, initial 1 min	0.44	0.50	0.56	0.40
Station-to-station operator-assisted, initial 3 min	1.50	1.80	1.95	1.25
Person-to-person, initial 3 min	2.10	2.80	3.55	1.70
Each additional minute in all three cases	0.29	0.35	0.40	0.25

The charges for the station-to-station direct-dialed calls and the charges for additional time are subject to the following discounts using the 24-hour clock (that is, 1 A.M. = 1:00, 1 P.M. = 13:00).

Sun.–Fri.	17:00–22:59	}35% discount
Every night	23:00–7:59	
All hours on		60% discount
Sat.		
Sun.	0:00–16.59	

Fractions of a cent are ignored. Each call on a card is coded as five numbers signifying
1. Area: 1 for Boston, 2 for Chicago, 3 for Los Angeles, and 4 for Philadelphia
2. Type: 1 for direct-dialed, 2 for operator-assisted station-to-station, 3 for person-to-person
3. Day: 1 for Sunday, 2 for Monday, etc., with 7 for Saturday
4. Time: in three or four digits (for example, 1700 for 17:00)
5. Length of the call in minutes. For example,

$$2, 3, 5, 1315, 17$$

describes a call to Chicago, person-to-person, made on Thursday, at 13:15 and 17 min long.

Your output should be in the form

THE CHARGE FOR CALL #1 IS_____.

The data cards contain

$$2, 3, 4, 1315, 17$$
$$2, 1, 7, 2010, 4$$
$$1, 2, 2, 715, 5$$
$$4, 2, 5, 1020, 12$$
$$4, 1, 3, 1805, 9$$

Include ample explanations in your program.

6.19 The numbers on the data card represent amounts of money. For each amount show the bills and coins needed to pay the amount. The pay is to be made in the largest possible bills and coins (that is, in the smallest number of items). For example, for the amount $67.43, your output should be

TO PAY 67.43 WE NEED
1 FIFTY
0 TWENTY
1 TEN
1 FIVE
2 ONE
1 QUARTER
1 DIME
1 NICKEL
3 PENNY

Assume that we have no $2 bills or dollar or half-dollar coins. There should be at least one line between the outputs for different amounts. Each amount is less than $100. The last number on the data card is zero. Write a program that will give the desired output. The data are

$$67.43$$
$$98.84$$
$$12.17$$

9.52

18.62

0

6.20 The Big Wheel Bicycle Company sells a bicycle with options. Options 1, 2, and 3 cost $6 each. Option 4 costs $8, and option 5 costs $10. Furthermore, the following discounts apply. If

$$\$8\ \ < \text{cost of options} \leq \$12 \qquad 10\% \text{ discount}$$
$$\$12 < \text{cost of options} \leq \$20 \qquad 15\% \text{ discount}$$
$$\$20 < \text{cost of options} \leq \$30 \qquad 20\% \text{ discount}$$

If all five options are bought, only $28 is charged. The bicycle itself, without the options, costs $50. The discount is given only on the options.

Write a program which will calculate the cost of a bicycle. The input consists of five numbers, which are either 0 or 1. For example, the input 0, 1, 1, 0, 1 means that only options 2, 3, and 5 are desired (zeros in the first and fourth positions signify that options 1 and 4 are not wanted).

After the processing of the first input, the computer should calculate the cost for the second input, and so on, until there are no more inputs. The total input is

0, 1, 1, 0, 1   0, 1, 0, 1, 0,   1, 1, 0, 1, 1   1, 0, 1, 1, 1   1, 1, 1, 1, 1

A REVISIT TO SOME STATEMENTS

There is more to be said about several of the statements which were described in previous chapters; we did not say everything that we knew earlier, because earlier we wanted to keep these statements simple. Now we are ready to tie up the loose ends.

7.1 KEYWORDS

There are certain words in the PL/I language that have a specific meaning to the compiler. These words are named *keywords*. Examples of such keywords are

IF
ELSE
PUT
DECLARE
GO TO
LIST
BINARY

The above words do not have to be reserved for exclusive use as keywords and can be used for identifiers,[1] if so desired. The compiler recognizes whether a word is a keyword or an identifier by the context. For example, the statement

DECLARE = END + 3*DECIMAL − DO;

is a legal one. Here DECLARE, END, DECIMAL, and DO are names of variables, and the context of the statement reveals them as such. Similarly, in the statement

DECLARE END DECIMAL;

DECLARE and DECIMAL are keywords, and END an identifier, as indicated by the context.

---

[1]Recall that an identifier is the name given to a variable or a label.

We have seen earlier that certain keywords can be abbreviated. For example, DCL was the abbreviation for DECLARE, DEC the abbreviation for DECIMAL. Two other allowable abbreviations are

PROC   for   PROCEDURE
GOTO   for   GO TO

We will introduce other keywords and their abbreviations later on.

7.2 THE PROCEDURE STATEMENT

The PROCEDURE statement was said to have the form

Label: PROCEDURE OPTIONS (MAIN);

where in fact several departures are possible.

1. As just stated above, PROCEDURE can be abbreviated to PROC, resulting in the statement

    Label: PROC OPTIONS(MAIN);

2. On some compilers it is permissible to omit OPTIONS (MAIN). Thus on such compilers it is legal to use the statement

    Label: PROCEDURE;

    or abbreviated to

    Label: PROC;

3. It is permissible to use several labels for naming a procedure. Thus

    Label1: Label2: Label3: PROC OPTIONS (MAIN);

    is a valid statement.
4. We have said that the PROCEDURE statement is the first program statement. This is true, but it may be preceded by a comment (which is not a statement). Thus the program segment

    /*CALCULATION OF PAYROLL*/
    PAYROLL: PROC OPTIONS (MAIN);

    is a valid one.
5. We mentioned in Sec. 3.1 that certain identifiers may not contain more than seven characters. This limitation applies to names which are *external* (that is, which are used outside the program itself), for example, names used by the operating system[1] (we will discuss the use of external names in Sec. 22.6). The label attached to the PROCEDURE OPTIONS (MAIN); statement is external (that is, the label is used by the operating system), and hence it is limited to the maximum of seven characters.

[1]An operating system is the program which directs the processing of jobs on the computer.

7.3 THE END STATEMENT

The introduced form

END Label;

is valid and preferable.

1. If the PROCEDURE statement reads

    Label1: Label2: · · · Labeln: PROC OPTIONS (MAIN);

    we can terminate the program with

    END Labelk;

    where *Labelk* is any one of the labels preceding the PROC statement.

2. It is permissible to terminate the program with the statement.

    END;

    that is, the label following END can be omitted.

3. If there is a label preceding the DO statement, then the END terminating the DO group can be followed by a label. For example, both program segments below are legal:

    ```
    IF A>B THEN L: DO;            IF A>B THEN L: DO;
                B=B+1;                        B=B+1;
                A=A+2;                        A=A+2;
            END;                          END L;
    ```

4. The statement

    END label;

    provides a closing for all unclosed groups between the label and the end statement. For example, the program

    ```
    A:   PROC OPTIONS (MAIN);
         . . . . . . . . . . . . . . . . . . . . . .
         IF B>C THEN DO;
         . . . . . . . . . . . . . . . .
                     END;
         END A;
    ```

    in which END; closes the DO group and END A; terminates the program, can be rewritten as

    ```
    A:   PROC OPTIONS (MAIN);
         . . . . . . . . . . . . . . . . . . . . . .
         IF B>C THEN DO;
         . . . . . . . . . . . . . . . .
         END A;
    ```

Here the END A; statement also terminates the DO group. A similar situation occurs in the example

```
IF A>B THEN L1: DO;
                    A=A+1;
                    IF C>A THEN DO;
                                    C=D+3;
                                    A=C+2;
                    END;
        END;
```

We can close both DO groups with a single END L1; statement as in

```
IF A>B THEN L1: DO;
                    A=A+1
                    IF C>A THEN DO;
                                    C=D+3;
                                    A=C+2;
        END L1;
```

This technique is known as *multiple closure*. Observe that it only applies to adjacent END statements.

5. Any statement, not just a PROCEDURE statement, may have several labels. Then any one of these labels can follow the END, as in

```
IF A>B THEN L1: A2: JAK: DO;
                    . . . .
                    . . . .
                    END A2;
```

Also statements which do not require a closure may have several labels. Thus the form

Label1: Label2: · · · Labeln: Statement1;

is legal.

7.4 OTHER STATEMENTS

1. The null statement

```
;
```

consists of just the semicolon and signifies no execution. It is used whenever a statement is needed but no execution is desired, as in the null ELSE and the null THEN.

2. The assignment statement

```
A,B,C=D+3;
```

is known as *multiple assignment* and is the same as the statements

$$A = D+3;$$
$$B = D+3;$$
$$C = D+3;$$

Thus the value on the right side is assigned to each variable on the left side. Note the commas separating the variables.

3. The STOP statement

STOP;

terminates the program execution. It is used for abrupt termination as an alternative to jumping to the program-ending statement. As an illustration of its use, go back to the program shown in Sec. 3.3. Statement 8,

GO TO FINISHED;

can be replaced by

STOP;

To see the distinction between the END and the STOP statements, observe the following:

1. When the program is compiled (that is, translated into the machine language), the END statement (which closes the procedure) tells the compiler that the end of the program has been reached and that the compiler should stop compiling.
2. When the program is run, the END statement tells the computer to stop the program execution.
3. The STOP statement is an alternative for the second (that is, program run) termination. The END statement is still needed for the first (that is, program compilation) termination.

7.5 SUMMARY

In this chapter we added some bits of information on previously introduced statements. We saw that keywords can be used for identifiers and that a statement may have several labels. We discussed programming shortcuts such as (1) abbreviations for the PROCEDURE statement, (2) multiple closure, and (3) multiple assignment. We also introduced the STOP; statement for the termination of program execution.

We have also seen that PL/I is a very permissive language which allows the use of keywords for identifiers and the cluttering of statements with unneeded labels. Both such practices are confusing and result in badly written programs. This confusion does not bother the PL/I compiler but bothers the unfortunate reader of the program.

PROBLEMS

7.1 In the program

```
B: PROC OPTIONS (MAIN);
   GET LIST(A);
   PUT LIST(A,A*A);
   STOP;
   END B;
```

is the statement END B; necessary? Give reasons for your answer.

7.2 There are several integers on data cards. Write a program that will
(*a*) Count all numbers.
(*b*) Count all numbers larger than 1 and smaller than 10.
(*c*) Count all numbers between 5 and 15.

The program is to stop when −100 is encountered.

DEBUGGING OF PROGRAMS

We will now describe the various aids available to make a program work. We will also describe how to interpret the helpful messages produced by the compiler and how to eliminate the errors in a program.

8.1 AN INTRODUCTORY EXAMPLE

In the preceding pages we saw a number of programs. All those programs were "correct," that is, they produced the desired answers. However, most of those programs did not work in their initial versions because of various errors. What you saw in the text were second, third, and even later versions, with the last program being (we hope) error-free.

The process of finding errors (called debugging) is frustrating, time-consuming (on the average three to four times as long as program writing), but very necessary. Without it, we have an incorrect program which is just a pile of useless garbage.[1] Fortunately, the compiler provides a number of aids for finding errors. To describe these aids, we will start with a program having several errors. Consider the following problem:

Given

A set of numbers with only the last one being −10. Each number is smaller than 100, and there are at most three digits to the right of the decimal point.

Find
1. The count of all positive numbers
2. The count of all numbers larger than −5 and smaller than 5
3. The count of all even integers between 40 and 50 inclusive

The input on the data card is

---

[1]The term GIGO, meaning "garbage in–garbage out," is commonly used among programmers.

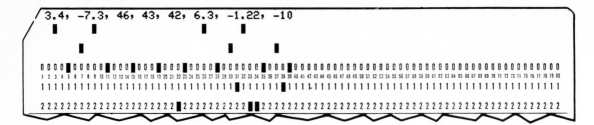

Let us assume that in our first effort we produce the program shown in Fig. 8.1 and named EX_1. This program has several errors that we should have detected with cursory inspection, but, as we said, we assume this to be our first effort, to be transformed into a working program.

Incidentally the program shown in Fig. 8.1 is named a *source program*. It shows the content of program cards (that is, source deck), with one card displayed per line. Observe that this program is on page 2. Page 1 usually (that is, if no special requests are made) lists the options used during the compilation of the program and need not concern us here. The printed program has the following features:

1. Each statement has been numbered as shown in the first column.
2. The compound statement (that is, the IF statement) counts as two statements or more. The fifth statement is followed by the seventh statement because the IF statement counts as two statements. The ninth statement is followed by the twelfth statement because the nested IF statement counts as three statements. In general, each IF clause counts as one statement, and each THEN (or ELSE) clause counts as one statement.
3. The *level number* in the second column gives information about internal procedures (to be described in a later chapter). The single main procedure in effect here is of level 1; hence the level number is 1 throughout the program. If we had an internal procedure, then its statements would have 2 as the level number.

```
        EX_1:    PROC OPTIONS(MAIN);                                                    PAGE    2

STMT LEVEL NEST
  1                 EX_1:    PROC OPTIONS(MAIN);
  2     1                    I,J,K=0              /*I COUNTS POS NUMBERS, J NUMBERS    */
  3     1          A:        GET LIST(A);         /*BETWEEN -5 AND 5, K EVEN INTEGERS  */
  5     1                    IF A>0 THEN I=I+1;    /*BETWEEN 40 AND 50 INCLUSIVE        */
  7     1                    IF -5<A<5 THEN J=J+1;
  9     1                    IF 40=>A=>50 THEN IF A/2=0 THEN K=K+1;
 12     1                    IF A=-10 THEN DO;
 14     1      1                      PUT LIST(I,J,K);
 15     1      1                      STOP;
 16     1      1                  END;
 17     1                    GO TO A;
 18     1                    END PROC;
```

Figure 8.1 First program for the example.

```
      EX_1:    PROC OPTIONS(MAIN);                                         PAGE     3,

                                         ATTRIBUTE AND CROSS-REFERENCE TABLE

 DCL NO.           IDENTIFIER            ATTRIBUTES AND REFERENCES

                   A                     AUTOMATIC,ALIGNED,DECIMAL,FLOAT(SINGLE)
                                         3,4,5,7,9,10,12

 1                 EX_1                  ENTRY,DECIMAL,FLOAT(SINGLE)

       ********** I                      AUTOMATIC,ALIGNED,BINARY,FIXED(15,0)
                                         2,6,6

       ********** J                      AUTOMATIC,ALIGNED,BINARY,FIXED(15,0)
                                         2,8,8,14

       ********** K                      AUTOMATIC,ALIGNED,BINARY,FIXED(15,0)
                                         2,11,11,14

                   SYSIN                 FILE,EXTERNAL
                                         4

                   SYSPRINT              FILE,EXTERNAL
                                         14
```

Figure 8.2 Attribute and cross-reference table for the program EX _1.

4. The *nest number* in the third column gives information about the DO groups. Statements 14 through 16 are within the DO group. Should there be a second DO group "nested" in a DO group, then this second DO group has 2 for the nest number.

Figure 8.2 shows page 3 of the output and is named *attribute and cross-reference table*. Figure 8.3 shows pages 5 and 6 of the output and displays compiler diagnostics (page 4 lists storage requirements and is of no interest here). The compiler-diagnostics printout is a major tool in debugging as we will see presently, but the attribute and cross-reference table also provides debugging help.

The compiler diagnostics lists SEVERE ERRORS, ERRORS, and WARN-INGS. *Severe errors* cannot be corrected by the compiler. With such errors, work on the program is ended after all these printouts have been produced, and no execution is made.

When *errors* occur the compiler attempts to correct them. Usually, though, these errors also cause termination as do severe errors.

Warnings draw attention to the possibility of errors but do not stop program execution.

We shall now study the compiler diagnostics of Fig. 8.3 to locate the errors in the program. Apparently, A used in statement 17 is not a label. An inspection of the attribute and cross-reference table of Fig. 8.2 reveals that A is a float, decimal, variable (and used as such in statements 3, 4, 5, 7, 9, 10, 12). Consequently, we must change A in statement 17 to a differently named label, say, AGAIN.

The second message, that statement 17 has been deleted, is of no further debugging value.

COMPILER DIAGNOSTICS:

SEVERE ERRORS.

IEM0685I   17   A IS NOT A STATEMENT LABEL ON AN EXECUTABLE STATEMENT. DUMMY REFERENCE INSERTED AFTER GO TO

                    IN STATEMENT NUMBER 17

IEM0725I   17   STATEMENT NUMBER 17 HAS BEEN DELETED DUE TO A SEVERE ERROR NOTED ELSEWHERE.

IEM0031I   3   OPERAND MISSING IN OR FOLLOWING STATEMENT NUMBER 3 .   DUMMY OPERAND INSERTED.

IEM0002I   9   INVALID PREFIX OPERATOR IN STATEMENT NUMBER 9 .   REPLACED BY PLUS.

IEM0002I   9   INVALID PREFIX OPERATOR IN STATEMENT NUMBER 9 .   REPLACED BY PLUS.

IEM0028I   18   LABEL REFERENCED ON END STATEMENT NUMBER 18 CANNOT BE FOUND. END TREATED AS HAVING NO OPERAND.

IEM0002I   14   INVALID PREFIX OPERATOR IN STATEMENT NUMBER 14 .   REPLACED BY PLUS.

IEM0031I   14   OPERAND MISSING IN OR FOLLOWING STATEMENT NUMBER 14 .   DUMMY OPERAND INSERTED.

ERRORS.

IEM0096I   2   SEMI-COLON NOT FOUND WHEN EXPECTED IN STATEMENT NUMBER 2 .   ONE HAS BEEN INSERTED.

IEM0080I   3   EQUAL SYMBOL HAS BEEN INSERTED IN ASSIGNMENT STATEMENT NUMBER 3

WARNINGS.

IEM0227I   NO FILE/STRING OPTION SPECIFIED IN ONE OR MORE GET/PUT STATEMENTS. SYSIN/SYSPRINT HAS BEEN

                    ASSUMED IN EACH CASE.

EX_1:   PROC OPTIONS(MAIN);   PAGE

IEM0764I   ONE OR MORE FIXED BINARY ITEMS OF PRECISION 15 OR LESS HAVE BEEN GIVEN HALFWORD STORAGE. THEY

                    ARE FLAGGED '**********' IN THE XREF/ATR LIST.

END OF DIAGNOSTICS.

AUXILIARY STORAGE WILL NOT BE USED FOR DICTIONARY WHEN SIZE =   66K

COMPILE TIME   .04 MINS
ELAPSED TIME   .30 MINS

Figure 8.3 Compiler diagnostics for the program EX__1.

Statement 3 misses an operand. Inspecting this statement we note that we placed the semicolon rather than colon after the label A. Thus besides correcting A to AGAIN, it must be followed by a colon instead of a semicolon.

Statement 9 has an invalid operator, which the compiler replaced by plus. The invalid operator is evidently =>, which should have been written as >=. This error occurs in two places, and the next error message tells us so.

Statement 18 has a label which cannot be found. Evidently it should be END EX_1; instead of END PROC;

An invalid operator precedes variables in statement 14. The next message tells that the compiler inserted a dummy operand in this statement. An inspection of this statement shows that | has been punched instead of I, which must be corrected.

The ERRORS message tells us that a semicolon is needed in statement 2. We inspect statement 2 and see that this is so.

The message that an equal sign has been inserted in statement 3 can be ignored. We are going to correct this statement by replacing A with AGAIN and the semicolon with the colon.

The WARNINGS are of no further interest. Thus we must make the following corrections:

Statement	Correction
17	Change A to AGAIN
3	Change A; to AGAIN:
9	Change => to >= in two places
18	Change PROC to EX__1
14	Change | to I

8.2 CORRECTIONS OF THE PROGRAM FOR THE EXAMPLE

We made the corrections and the "cosmetic" change of aligning the fifth statement. The result is the program named EX_2 shown in Fig. 8.4. The compiler diagnostics are shown in Fig. 8.5. Evidently, there are no errors in compilation. This means that

```
STMT LEVEL NEST
  1                     EX_2:      PROC OPTIONS(MAIN);
  2      1                         I,J,K=0;                /*I COUNTS POS NUMBERS, J NUMBERS     */
  3      1                AGAIN:   GET.LIST(A);            /*BETWEEN -5 AND 5, K EVEN INTEGERS   */
  4      1                         IF A>0 THEN I=I+1;  /*BETWEEN 40 AND 50 INCLUSIVE   */
  6      1                         IF -5<A<5 THEN J=J+1;
  8      1                         IF 40>=A>=50 THEN IF A/2=0 THEN K=K+1;
 11      1                         IF A=-10 THEN DO;
 13      1     1                              PUT LIST(I,J,K);
 14      1     1                              STOP;
 15      1     1                         END;
 16      1                         GO TO AGAIN;
 17      1                         END EX_2;
```

Figure 8.4 Second program for the example.

```
   EX_2:    PROC OPTIONS(MAIN);                                          PAGE      5

COMPILER DIAGNOSTICS.


WARNINGS.

   IEM0227I       NO FILE/STRING OPTION SPECIFIED IN ONE OR MORE GET/PUT STATEMENTS. SYSIN/SYSPRINT HAS BEEN

                  ASSUMED IN EACH CASE.

   IEM0764I       ONE OR MORE FIXED BINARY ITEMS OF PRECISION 15 OR LESS HAVE BEEN GIVEN HALFWORD STORAGE. THEY

                  ARE FLAGGED '*********' IN THE XREF/ATR LIST.



END OF DIAGNOSTICS.

AUXILIARY STORAGE WILL NOT BE USED FOR DICTIONARY WHEN SIZE =  66K

COMPILE TIME         .03 MINS
ELAPSED TIME         .30 MINS
```

Figure 8.5 Compiler diagnostics for the program EX__2.

we violated no PL/I rules in writing the program. Is our algorithm correct? Let us inspect the obtained output, shown in Fig. 8.6.

I is the count of positive numbers and 5 checks the given data. J counts numbers larger than -5 and smaller than 5. From the data, we see J should be 2 instead of 8 as given. Also K is evidently incorrect and should be 2 instead of 0 as given in the output.

We may now ask: Of what value is the program if we have to obtain the correct answers for I, J, and K from the data as we just did? To answer this question we must observe that we found I, J, and K for the small data set given here. Once we debugged the program, we expected the computer to deliver values of I, J, and K for *any* data set. Incidentally, in many programming problems we construct a simplified data set to test our program. To test most programs it is essential to know something about the results, so as to be able to accept or reject the computer-delivered answers.

To correct the errors in calculations of J and K we will perform "hand simulation," that is, simulate the computer by hand. Evidently the count of J counted all numbers. Using the data value of 46 in statement 6, we obtain

$$-5 < 46 < 5 \text{ THEN } J = J + 1;$$

```
5                 8                 0
```

Figure 8.6 Output of program EX__2.

Such an inequality, involving three numbers, was not defined. In fact, the computer first evaluates

$$-5 < 46$$

Since this is true, the result of comparison is the bit string '1'B. The next comparison entails

$$'1'B < 5$$

which is also true; thus J is increased by 1. This explains why J is so large. We evidently wrote the condition for J incorrectly. What we must write is

$$\text{IF } -5 < A \ \& \ A < 5 \text{ THEN } J=J+1;$$

instead. Similarly the condition for K suffers from the same error and must be written as

$$\text{IF } A >= 40 \ \& \ A <= 50 \text{ THEN IF } A/2=0 \text{ THEN } K= K+1;$$

Making these corrections we obtain the program EX_3 of Fig. 8.7, which has the output shown in Fig. 8.8. The compiler diagnostics are of no interest (there are no errors detectable by the compiler) and are thus not shown. J has the correct value now, but K does not. To check K, let us again use the data value of 46, which K should count. With this value, statement 8 reads

$$\text{IF } 46 >= 40 \ \& \ 46 <= 50 \text{ THEN IF } 46/2=0 \text{ THEN } K=K+1;$$

and reveals the error. Obviously $46/2 \neq 0$; hence K is not increased. This last condition is wrong. We wish to determine whether A is an even integer and not whether $A/2 = 0$. We can do so with

$$N=A/2;$$
$$\text{IF } A=2*N \text{ THEN } K=K+1;$$

Here if A is an odd integer or a noninteger, A would not be equal to $2*N$. Moreover, it is a bad practice to compare A in its FLOAT BIN representation with decimal numbers. To avoid such a comparison we should declare A as FIXED(5,3). Hence the needed changes are

```
      EX_3:    PROC OPTIONS(MAIN);                                          PAGE    2

STMT LEVEL NEST
  1               EX_3:    PROC OPTIONS(MAIN);
  2    1                   I,J,K=0;                /*I COUNTS POS NUMBERS, J NUMBERS    */
  3    1         AGAIN:    GET LIST(A);            /*BETWEEN -5 AND 5, K EVEN INTEGERS  */
  4    1                   IF A>0 THEN I=I+1;      /*BETWEEN 40 AND 50 INCLUSIVE        */
  6    1                   IF -5<A & A<5 THEN J=J+1;
  8    1                   IF A>=40 & A<=50 THEN IF A/2=0 THEN K=K+1;
 11    1                   IF A=-10 THEN DO;
 13    1    1                       PUT LIST(I,J,K);
 14    1    1                       STOP;
 15    1    1                  END;
 16    1                   GO TO AGAIN;
 17    1                   END EX_3;
```

Figure 8.7 Third program for the example.

```
5                              2                        0
```

Figure 8.8 Output of program EX_3.

1. A declaration for A
2. Replacement of the eighth statement by

    IF A >= 40 & A <= 50 THEN DO;
                                    N=A/2;
                                    IF A=2*N THEN K=K+1;
                        END;

With these changes, and movement of the test for A=−10 to the top of the tests (this way we will stop with A=−10 immediately and will not need to perform the other three tests), we obtain the program EX_4, shown in Fig. 8.9. Its output is shown in Fig. 8.10. Since the output agrees with the expected answers, we accept the program as a correct one.

8.3 ADDITIONAL DEBUGGING AIDS

In the preceding example we found the algorithmic errors through hand simulation. Sometimes the calculations are too involved to be done by hand. In such instances we use several output statements spaced throughout the program to calculate the desired variable values. After the completion of debugging these statements are removed from the program.

A convenient way of obtaining variable values at different program points is provided with the CHECK condition and will be discussed in Chap. 26.

Observe that the compiler diagnostics showed errors generated during the compilation. These are known as "compile time" or syntax errors. We also

```
    EX_4:     PROC OPTIONS(MAIN);                                                      PAGE    2

STMT LEVEL NEST
  1                   EX_4:     PROC OPTIONS(MAIN);
  2     1                       DCL A FIXED(5,3);
  3     1                       I,J,K=0;              /* I COUNTS POS NUMBERS, J NUMBERS   */
  4     1             AGAIN:    GET LIST(A);          /* BETWEEN -5 AND 5, K EVEN INTEGERS */
                                                      /* BETWEEN 40 AND 50 INCLUSIVE       */
  5     1                       IF A=-10 THEN DO;
  7     1    1                            PUT LIST(I,J,K);
  8     1    1                            STOP;
  9     1    1                       END;
 10     1                       IF A>0 THEN I=I+1;
 12     1                       IF A>-5 & A<5 THEN J=J+1;
 14     1                       IF A>=40 & A<=50 THEN DO;
 16     1    1                            N=A/2;
 17     1    1                            IF A=2*N THEN K=K+1;
 19     1    1                       END;
 20     1                       GO TO AGAIN;
 21     1                       END EX_4;
```

Figure 8.9 Fourth program for the example.

5   2   2

Figure 8.10 Output of program EX__4.

generated "execution time" errors, which required changes in the algorithms. There are several aids to execution errors, in that the compiler detects several exceptional occurrences, such as division by zero. Again, Chap. 26 will describe the treatment of such occurrences.

There are several common keypunching errors which should be avoided. Often a similar character is used for another. Examples of similar characters are

1. The characters 1, I, |, /, ' (we used | for I in our first program)
2. ∅ (letter) and 0 (zero)
3. − and ___

Another error is the improper use of equality or inequality as, for example,

A=B=C;	instead of	A,B=C;
A>5|>B	instead of	A>5|A>B
−5<A<5	instead of	−5<A & A<5 (as in our program)

Often an error is caused by the fact that the programmer finds a better way of writing the program after a part of the program has been written. The attempt to salvage what has been written results in a program partly written for one idea and partly for another. The only recipe for avoiding this dilemma is to think out the entire program before writing a single statement and to resist the desire to write a program quickly. After keypunching, inspect the cards to make sure that there are no silly keypunching errors, and then be careful in assembling them in their correct sequence.

Good programmers avoid errors through their program-writing "style." A good programming style in current popularity is one in which the problem to be solved is outlined first in broader and then in finer and finer detail, with the last detail being at the actual statement-writing level. This style is referred to as "structured" or "top-down" and will be described in a separate chapter. Also the use of GO TOs is avoided, because this statement causes one to shuttle between different parts of the program and results in a more difficult debugging process than does a "top to bottom" program.

8.4 SUMMARY

In this chapter we described how a program is debugged. We saw that the compiler helps in finding the errors in the incorrect use of the language, that is, syntax errors. We illustrated the hand simulation for finding algorithmic errors and described the use of output statements for the display of variables of interest.

PROBLEM

8.1 To observe the diagnostics of the compiler, deliberately make the following errors in your well-working programs:

1. Remove an END.
2. Add an extra END.
3. Add a single parenthesis to an expression.
4. Have a GO TO to a nonexistent label.
5. Keypunch your program beyond column 72.
6. Place a letter instead of a number in data.
7. Replace an expression such as $3*A$ by $3A$.
8. Misspell a keyword or a variable.
9. Divide by zero.
10. Assign to a variable a number larger than 10^{75} (see p. 43).
11. Assign to a variable a number smaller than 10^{-78} (see p. 43).
12. Declare a variable as FIXED DEC (2), and then assign to it a four-digit integer.

THE DO STATEMENT

Recall that we introduced the DO statement in Chap. 6, where it was used for grouping statements with the THEN or ELSE clauses.

The DO statement has still another use. It is a convenient and powerful tool for problems with repetitive tasks. In such problems the DO statement replaces several statements, thus simplifying and streamlining the program.

We will first review the use of the DO statement for grouping statements and then describe its application to repetitive tasks.

9.1 THE DO STATEMENT FOR GROUPING STATEMENTS

We introduced the DO statement in Sec. 6.2. We used it for grouping statements to be executed with the THEN and ELSE clauses, as in

```
IF condition1 THEN DO;
                    statement1b;
                    statement2b;
                    . . . . . . . . . . .
                    statementmb;
                END;
        ELSE DO;
                    statement1a;
                    statement2a;
                    . . . . . . . . . . .
                    statementna;
                END;
        statement2;
```

This grouping with the DO statement allows the execution of several statements with the THEN and ELSE clauses. The end of the grouping is signaled (to the compiler) by the END; statement. Thus the DO; and END; enclose the DO group.

The DO statement can also be used by itself without the THEN or ELSE clauses. For example, the program for the printout of numbers and their squares,

```
EXAMPLE: PROC OPTIONS(MAIN);
REPEAT:  GET LIST(A);
                    DO;
                        ASQUARE = A*A;
                        PUT LIST(A,ASQUARE);
                    END;
            GO TO REPEAT;
            END EXAMPLE;
```

uses the DO to group calculations. This DO is not necessary here, and the program will work just as well without the DO; and END; statements. But the grouping isolates the computational tasks, which improves readability. In long programs such grouping is recommended, with an accompanying comment describing the actions of the DO group. Such groupings and comments are of great assistance in debugging.

Recall from Sec. 6.5 that we can place a label or labels in front of the DO. Thus

$$\text{IF } C > D+1 \text{ THEN L1: DO;}$$

where L1 is a label, is a legal statement. We can also place several labels in front of the DO as discussed in Sec. 7.3. We gave there the example

$$\text{IF } A > B \text{ THEN L1: A: JAK: DO;}$$

with the DO having three labels.

9.2 THE DO STATEMENT WITH A WHILE CLAUSE

The DO group with a WHILE clause has the form

$$
\begin{aligned}
&\text{DO WHILE } (\textit{condition}); \\
&\quad \textit{statement1}; \\
&\quad \textit{statement2}; \\
&\quad \cdots\cdots\cdots \\
&\quad \textit{statementm}; \\
&\text{END}; \\
&\textit{statementn};
\end{aligned}
$$

This is a repetitive or an iterative DO group. Here, upon reaching the END; statement, the program control returns to the DO statement. If the condition is true, the group is executed. If the condition is false, we leave the group and execute *statementn*. Thus the above program segment is equivalent to

$$
\begin{aligned}
&\text{AGAIN: IF } \textit{condition} \text{ THEN DO;} \\
&\qquad\qquad \textit{statement1}; \\
&\qquad\qquad \textit{statement2};
\end{aligned}
$$

```
          . . . . . . . . . . .
        statementm;
        GO TO AGAIN;
     END;
  statementn;
```

and is portrayed by the flowchart of Fig. 9.1. As can be seen the WHILE clause provides an alternative way to program repetitive instructions. It eliminates the need for the GO TO AGAIN; statement, and it streamlines the program (no label needed with the WHILE clause).

As an example of the WHILE clause, let us list the squares and cubes of all integers from 1 to 20. We wrote such a program in the solution to Example 3.4.1, with a flowchart shown in Fig. 3.4. We will now write another program using the WHILE clause.

```
TABLE2:   PROC OPTIONS(MAIN);
          /* TABLE OF SQUARES AND CUBES FROM 1 TO 20 */
          N = 1;
          DO WHILE(N<=20);
              NSQUARE = N*N;
              NCUBE = N*NSQUARE;
              PUT LIST(N,NSQUARE,NCUBE);
              N = N + 1;
          END;
          END TABLE2;
```

This program is easier to understand than the one in the Example 3.4.1 solution. The parentheses enclosing the condition next to WHILE must always be present.

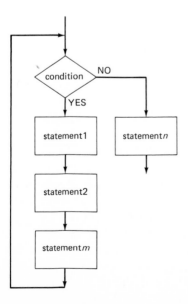

Figure 9.1 Flowchart for the DO group with the WHILE clause.

Note that the END; statement is not necessary, because the statement END TABLE2; closes the DO group also (see Sec. 7.3).

Observe that an error in the condition may give rise to an "infinite loop," for example, in the above program the statement

DO WHILE (N >0);

will cause the computer to grind out numbers indefinitely,[1] thus yielding a large bill for the computer time due to our error.

Because of the repetitive nature of the DO group, there is a "looping" from the END; statement to the DO statement. Hence this DO group is also known as a *DO loop*.

9.3 THE DO STATEMENT WITH A CONTROL VARIABLE

The DO group with a control variable has the basic form

DO   *control variable = initial value* TO *final value* BY *increment;*
       statement1;
       statement2;
       . . . .
       statementm;
END;
statementn;

This also is a repetitive DO group and thus a *DO loop*. To explain the action of this DO loop consider the following program segment:

DO   I=1 TO 10 BY 4;
       N=3+2*I;
       M=2+I;
       PUT LIST (I,N,M);
END;
X=1;

Here I is the control variable, 1 the initial value, 10 the final value, and 4 the increment. We start with the assignment of 1 to I. 1 is compared to 10, and because it does not exceed 10, the DO loop is executed. Upon reaching the END; statement, the control variable (that is, I) is increased by the increment (that is, 4); thus I is now 5. A return to the DO statement takes place, and I is again compared with 10. Since 5 is less than 10, the DO loop is executed. At the END; statement, I is increased to 9, and program control returns to the DO statement. Here I is compared with 10, and because I still does not exceed 10, the execution of the DO loop is repeated. After return to the DO statement I is 13. Now I exceeds 10, so we leave the DO loop, with a jump to the statement following the DO group (that is, X=1;).

[1] In practice, there is a time limit imposed on each program by the programmer (with control cards), which limits the charges that can be incurred.

As an example of this DO loop, let us construct again a list of the squares and cubes of all integers from 1 to 20. Such a program now reads

```
TABLE3:  PROC OPTIONS(MAIN);
         /* TABLE OF SQUARES AND CUBES FROM 1 TO 20 */
         DO N = 1 TO 20 BY 1;
             NSQUARE = N*N;
             NCUBE = N*NSQUARE;
             PUT LIST(N,NSQUARE,NCUBE);
         END;
         END TABLE3;
```

which is simpler still than the previous versions.

The increment can also be negative as in

$$DO\ N=5\ TO\ 2\ BY\ -2;$$

For a positive increment the control variable cannot exceed the final value. For a negative increment, the control variable cannot be smaller than the final value. Thus the DO loop headed by the above statement is executed first for N=5. When the DO statement is reached for the second time, N is 3, and thus the DO loop is executed again. When the DO statement is reached for the third time, N is 1, which is smaller than the final value of 2. Thus a jump out of the DO loop takes place.

We shall now give some additional examples of the DO statement.

1. DO I=−5 TO 0 BY 2;
   Here the DO loop is executed as I assumes the values of −5, −3, and −1. For the next increment I=1, which exceeds the final value of 0.
2. DO A=12 TO −2 BY −1.5;
   Now the increment is a negative noninteger. The DO loop is executed as A is assigned the values of 12.0, 10.5, 9.0, 7.5, 6.0, 4.5, 3.0, 1.5, 0.0, and −1.5. This assumes, of course, that A is declared as a FIXED DEC(2, 1) variable. With no declaration we obtain the above values for A but in floating-point form.
3. DO ACE=1.3E1 TO 1.35E1 BY 1E-1;
   This illustrates that floating-point numbers are allowable.
4. DO I=5 TO 7 BY −2;
   For a negative increment the control variable cannot be smaller than the final value. If it is, as here, the test for execution of the DO loop fails. Thus the DO loop is not executed, and a jump out of the loop takes place.
5. DO I = 5 TO 4 BY 1;
   Here the control variable exceeds the final value. Since the increment is positive, we do not satisfy the condition for execution of the DO loop, and a jump out of the loop takes place.

We will now describe further details on the DO statement with a control variable.

A The DO Statement with Expressions

The DO statement can have the more general form

DO *control variable*=*expression1* TO *expression2* BY *expression3;*

Here the expressions are first evaluated. The evaluation of *expression1* gives the initial value, while the evaluations of *expression2* and *expression3* give the final value and the increment. For example, the statement

DO JACK=7*I+N*N TO (I**3−2)/3 BY I+J;

is a legal one.

B The TO and the BY Clauses Can Be Interchanged

It is permissible to interchange the TO and BY clauses, as in

DO I=3 BY 2 TO 7;
DO I=2*N BY −(2+J) TO N;

which are equivalent to

DO I=3 TO 7 BY 2;
DO I=2*N TO N BY −(2*J);

C The BY Clause Can Be Omitted

The statement

DO *control variable* = *expression1* TO *expression2:*

with the BY clause omitted, has the same meaning as

DO *control variable* = *expression1* TO *expression2* BY 1;

Thus, with the BY clause omitted, the compiler chooses an increment of +1 by default. For example,

DO K=1 TO 100;

has the same effect as

DO K=1 TO 100 BY 1;

D The TO Clause Can be Omitted

The statement

DO *control variable* = *expression1* BY *expression3;*

is a legal one. This DO loop is executed repeatedly and can be left only through a statement in the DO group. As an example of this situation, consider the program segment

```
DO I=1 BY 2;
    PUT LIST (I,I*I);
    IF I*I>5000 THEN GO TO OUT;
END;
```

Here, an exit out of the DO loop ensues through the IF statement and not through the final value.

E The DO Statement with a WHILE Clause

The DO statement with the control variable can be further generalized to

DO *control variable* = *expression1* TO *expression2* by *expression3* WHILE(*condition*);

An example of this statement is given by

DO L=1 TO J+3/M BY 3 WHILE (M<N);

In the DO loop headed by this statement, an exit out of the loop takes place whenever either $L > J + 3/M$ or $M \geqslant N$. For example, the last program segment (illustrating the DO loop without the TO clause) can be written with the WHILE clause as

```
DO I=1 BY 2 WHILE (I*I<= 5000);
    PUT LIST (I,I*I);
END;
GO TO OUT;
```

Clearly, if the statement labeled OUT is immediately following the END; statement, the GO TO statement is not necessary.

The WHILE clause must always appear at the end of the specification. Thus

DO I=1 WHILE (I*I<= 5000) BY 2;

is an illegal statement.

F Both BY and TO Clauses Can Be Omitted

Both BY and TO clauses can be omitted as in

DO I=3;

Here, just a single execution of the DO loop takes place, with I being 3. After reaching the END; statement we leave the group. In this special case, we no longer have a repetitive DO loop.

G The DO Statement with Multiple Specifications

A still further generalization of the DO statement to the format

DO *control variable*=*expression1a* TO *expression2a* BY *expression3a*
                        WHILE(*condition1a*),

$$expression1b \text{ TO } expression2b \text{ BY } expression3b$$
$$\text{WHILE}(condition1b),$$

$$\cdots\cdots\cdots\cdots\cdots\cdots\cdots\cdots\cdots\cdots\cdots$$

$$expression1m \text{ TO } expression2m \text{ BY } expression3m$$
$$\text{WHILE}(condition1m);$$

is allowed. The specifications are separated by a comma. An example of this DO statement is given by

DO I=3, 6 TO 12, 2 BY −2 WHILE (N<I+3), 24;

Here the DO loop is executed once for the first specification, that is, for I=3. Upon completion, the DO loop is executed seven times for the second specification, that is, for I=6, 7, 8, 9, 10, 11, 12. Next, the loop is executed for the third specification, that is, for I=2, 0, −2, −4, and so on, as long as N < I+3. The fourth specification causes a single execution, for I=24. As a further example of the multiple specification, consider the program

```
EXAMPLE: PROC OPTIONS(MAIN);
         N = 1;
         DO I = 1 BY 1 WHILE(I+N<5), 13,
            3 WHILE(N+I=10), 6 BY −1 TO 4;
            PUT LIST(I,N);
            N = N + I;
         END;
         END EXAMPLE;
```

which gives the output

1	1	2	2	13
4	6	17	5	23
4	28			

We will explain this output. For I=1 the first specification satisfies the WHILE condition, because I+N = 1+1 = 2<5; thus we execute the DO loop. We print out I and N as 1 and 1 and set N=N+I=1+1=2. For I=2, the WHILE condition is I+N=2+2=4 < 5, and we execute the DO group again by printing 2 and 2. Now, N=N+I=2+2=4. For I=3, I+N=3+4=7, and the WHILE condition fails. This ends the first specification, and we execute the second specification with I=13. We print 13 and 4, and N becomes N+I=4+13=17. Since this completes the specification, we start the third specification with I=3. But N+I=17+3=20, which is not equal to 10. Thus the WHILE condition fails, and we go to the fourth specification and print 6 and 17. Now N=N+I=6+17=23; thus the second run through the DO loop results in the printout of 5 and 23. N becomes N+I= 23+5=28. Hence, the third run through the loop gives the printout 4 and 28. Upon reaching the END; statement, I becomes 3 which is lower than the final value and hence causes an exit out of the DO loop, ending the program.

H Calculation of Expressions

The calculation of expressions for the initial value, final value, and the increment is performed only once, at the start of the loop. For example, in

```
J=1;
DO  I=J TO 10*J BY 2+J;
    J=I+J;
    PUT LIST (I,J);
END;
```

the initial calculations establish the DO statement as

```
DO I=1 TO 10 BY 3;
```

and the changes in values in J do not affect it.

   If there are several specifications in the DO statements, each new specification is treated as the start of a DO loop, and the expresssions for the initial value, final value, and increment are recomputed. For example,

```
J=1;
DO  I=J TO 10*J BY 2+J, J TO 2*J;
    J=I+J;
    PUT LIST (I,J);
END;
```

establishes the first specification as

```
DO I=1 TO 10 BY 3;
```

for I=1,   J=1+1=2
    I=4,   J=4+2=6
    I=7,   J=7+6=13
    I=10, J=10+13=23

Hence J=23 at the start of the second specification, which establishes the second specification as

```
23 TO 46
```

The expression in the WHILE condition is calculated before each passage through the loop. For example,

```
J=1;
DO  I=1 TO 10 WHILE (J<10);
    J=I+J;
    PUT LIST (I,J);
END;
```

for I = 1, J=1 <10, DO loop is executed, and J=1+1=2
I = 2, J=2 <10, DO loop is executed, and J=2+2=4
I = 3, J=4 <10, DO loop is executed, and J=3+4=7

I = 4, J=7 <10, DO loop is executed, and J=7+4=11

I = 5, J=11≮10, and we leave the DO loop

Thus the printout is

1	2	2	4	3
7	4	11		

I Nested DO Loops

One can write a program with a DO loop contained within another DO loop. As an example of such a program, consider our old friend the list of squares and cubes of integers from 1 to 20. But now we want to print five asterisks after each five printouts of N,NSQUARE, NCUBE. We can obtain asterisks with the statement

PUT LIST ('*****');

executed after each five printouts. With one DO loop, the desired program reads

```
TABLE4:   PROC OPTIONS(MAIN);
          /* TABLE OF SQUARES AND CUBES FROM 1 TO 20 */
          N = 1;
REPEAT:   DO N = N TO N+4;
              NSQUARE = N*N;
              NCUBE = N*NSQUARE;
              PUT LIST(N,NSQUARE,NCUBE);
          END;
          PUT LIST('*****');
          IF N<20 THEN GO TO REPEAT;
          END TABLE4;
```

Note that initially N=1; hence the DO statement reads DO N=1 TO 5;. When we leave the DO loop, N=6 and we reenter the DO loop for the second time with N having this value. When we leave the DO loop for the second time, N=11. When we leave the DO loop for the fourth time, N=21 and we end the program execution.

With two DO loops, the program becomes

```
TABLE5:   PROC OPTIONS(MAIN);
          /* TABLE OF SQUARES AND CUBES FROM 1 TO 20 */
          DO I = 1 TO 16 BY 5;
              DO N = I TO  I+4;
                  NSQUARE = N*N;
                  NCUBE = N*NSQUARE;
              PUT LIST(N,NSQUARE,NCUBE);
              END;
              PUT LIST('*****');
          END;
          END TABLE5;
```

Here the inner DO loop (that is, the one headed by the DO N=I TO I+4; statement) is executed five times. After we leave the inner DO loop, we execute the PUT LIST ('*****'); statement and return to the outer loop. Observe that the END; statement

```
┌DO . . .
│  . . . . . . . .
│      ┌DO . . .
│      │  . . . . . . . .
│      └END;
│  . . . . . . . .
└END;
```
Figure 9.2 An illustration of nested DO loops.

preceding the END TABLE5; (which closes the outer loop) can be omitted, because the last statement closes all "open" DO loops. Also note that here the GO TO statement (with its accompanying label) has been eliminated.

In the above example, the inner loop is "nested" within the outer loop; hence such DO loops are known as *nested* DO loops. A graphical picture of such a situation is shown in Fig. 9.2. Of course, other types of nestings are possible—two examples are portrayed in Fig. 9.3. Observe that the overlapping DO loops illustrated in Fig. 9.4a cannot be achieved. The END; statement terminates the last unclosed loop, thus the inner DO loop here. Hence the compiler will interpret this program as the one of Fig. 9.4b.

J Multiple Closure

Figure 9.5 portrays the situation, discussed in Sec. 7.3, where *multiple closure* can be applied, that is, where we can close several DO loops with a single statement. As shown in the figure, the END A; statement closes all open DO loops contained within the statement labeled A and the END A; statement.

K The Control Variable

It is permissible to use the same name for the control variable in subsequent DO loops. For example, the program segment

Figure 9.3 Further illustrations of nested DO loops.

Figure 9.4 (*a*) Overlapping DO loops; (*b*) interpretation given to overlapping DO loops.

DO I =1 TO 10;

. . . .

END;

. . . .

DO I=2 BY −1 TO −5;

. . . .

END;

is a valid one. Here the same name (that is, I) is used for the control variable in subsequent DO loops.

   If the control variable is changed in the loop, then such a change will affect the number of passages through the loop. To illustrate this, consider the program segment

DO I=1 TO 20 BY 3;

. . . .

   I=I+2;

. . . .

END;

   The loop is executed for I=1. In the loop, I is changed to 3. Upon reaching the END; statement, I is increased by the increment to 6. Hence, on the second pass through the loop, I=6. Thus the DO loop is executed for I=1, 6, 11, 16. The next value of I is 21, which exceeds the final value; consequently, we leave the DO loop.

   Observe that after leaving the DO loop, the control variable has a value different from the final value. For example,

DO I=2 TO 7;

. . . .

END;

PUT LIST (I);

will cause the printout

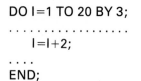

Figure 9.5 Illustration of multiple closure.

8

which is the value of I after leaving the DO loop.

Whenever the END; statement is reached, the control variable is increased by the increment. For example, in

```
DO I=7 TO 0 BY −1;
      . . . . . . . . . . . . . . . . . .
            IF X>5 THEN GO TO A;
      . . . . . . . . . . . . . . . . . .
      A: END;
```

I will increase by −1 (that is, decrease by 1) no matter whether the END; statement is reached sequentially or through a jump.

Whenever the DO statement is reached sequentially or through a jump, the control variable starts with its initial value. For example, in the program segment

```
A: DO I=7 TO 0 BY −1;
      . . . . . . . .
            IF X>5 THEN GO TO A;
      . . . . . . . . . . . .
      END;
```

for X >5, we jump to the DO statement and I starts again with its initial value of 7.

If the control variable satisfies the condition for leaving the DO loop at the beginning, the DO loop is not executed at all. For example, in

```
DO I=10 TO 1;
      . . . . . . . . .
      END;
```

I must exceed the final value of 1 for exit out of the DO loop. It does so at the start; hence, the DO loop is not executed.

L Transfers into a DO Group and Transfers out of a DO Group

We can transfer into a nonrepetitive DO group. We cannot transfer into a repetitive DO loop. For example,

```
GO TO A;
IF X>5 THEN DO;
            Y=Y+3
      A: Z= Y+X;
      END;
```

is a legal program segment. But

```
GO TO A;
DO I=1 TO 10;
      . . . . . . . . . .
```

```
              A: Z=Y+X;
              . . . . . . . . . .
              END;
```

is an illegal program segment, because no transfer into a repetitive DO is allowed. A repetitive DO can only be entered at the top, that is, at the DO statement.

We can transfer out of any DO group before reaching the END; statement. For example,

```
              DO I=1 TO 10;
              . . . . . . . . . . .
                  IF X>Y THEN GO TO A;
              . . . . . . . . . . . . . . . . . . . . . . . . .
              END;
              . . . . .
              A: PUT LIST (X);
              . . . . . . . .
```

is a legal program segment. Such transfer can occur before I exceeds the final value of 10.

It is also legal to jump within a DO loop. For example,

```
              DO I= 1 TO 10;
              A:  X=I+3;
                  Y=I+K;
                  IF X > Y THEN GO TO A;
                  PUT LIST (X,Y);
              END;
```

is a legal program segment.

M Infinite Loops

In writing programs involving DO loops extra care is needed to avoid so-called "infinite loops," that is, loops without an exit. An example of such an infinite loop was given in Sec. 9.2 with the statement

$$DO\ WHILE\ (N>0);$$

Unless an exit is provided in the DO loop, this is an infinite loop with N being always positive. Another example of a potentially infinite loop is given by

$$DO\ I=1\ BY\ 2;$$

which again requires an exit statement in the body of the DO group.

Another example of an infinite loop occurs in a program which transfers from the DO loop into the DO statement, as in

```
              A: DO  I=1 TO 10;
                     PUT LIST (I,I*I);
                     IF I*I>50 THEN GO TO A;
              END;
```

This program is performed for I=1, 2, 3, 4, 5, 6, 7, 8. For I=8, I*I=64 >50, and we jump to the DO statement, where we repeat the DO loop, starting with I=1. Hence, the output consists of pages repeatedly listing I and its square for the first eight integers. Fortunately, there is an end to this madness. There is a time limit on each computer user's program and also a limit on the number of pages. Thus a program comes to a stop eventually, but still such a programming error can be quite costly for the computer time wasted.

9.4 EXAMPLES

Example 9.4.1 It is desired to find an approximation x_0 to the real root of the polynomial equation

$$P(x) = x^3 - 4.123x^2 - 3.123x - 10.246 = 0$$

to within $\frac{1}{2}(10^{-2})$ of the true root. This means that

$$| x_0 - \text{true root} | \leq \frac{1}{2} (10^{-2})$$

Solution Because $P(0) < 0$ and $P(10) > 0$, we know that the root lies between 0 and 10. We propose the following procedure for finding the root:

1. We will calculate $P(x)$ for $x = 0$ to 10 in steps of 1 until $P(x) > 0$. Let us assume that for $x = x_k$, $P(x_k-1) < 0$ and $P(x_k) > 0$. Thus the root lies between x_k-1 and x_k.
2. We will calculate $P(x)$ for $x = x_k-1$ to x_k in steps of 0.1 until $P(x) > 0$. Let us assume that for $x = x_l$, $P(x_l -0.1) < 0$ and $P(x_l) > 0$. Thus the root lies between $x_l -0.1$ and x_l.
3. We will calculate $P(x)$ for $x = x_l -0.1$ to x_l in steps of 0.01 until $P(x) > 0$. Let us assume that for $x = x_m$, $P(x_m-0.01) < 0$ and $P(x_m) > 0$. Thus, the root lies between $x_m-0.01$ and x_m.
4. The desired approximation is

$$x_0 = \frac{1}{2} (x_m - 0.01 + x_m) = x_m - 0.005$$

We are now ready for the program:

```
ROOT:    PROC OPTIONS(MAIN);
         DO X = OEO BY 1EO
              WHILE(-10.246E0 + X*(-3.123E0 + X*(-4.123E0 + X)) < 0),
              X-1EO BY 1E-1
              WHILE(-10.246E0 + X*(-3.123E0 + X*(-4.123E0 + X)) < 0),
              X-1E-1 BY 1E-2
              WHILE(-10.246E0 + X*(-3.123E0 + X*(-4.123E0 + X)) < 0);
         END;
         X_0 = X - 5E-3;
         PUT LIST(X_0);
         END ROOT;
```

which gives the output

`5.12499E+00`

This result looks more accurate than it is because we only guarantee an error of no more than 0.005. Note further that we expressed P as

$$P = -10.246E0 + X*(-3.123E0 + X*(-4.123E0 + X)); \quad (1)$$

rather than as

$$P = -10.246 - 3.123*X - 4.123*X**2 + X**3; \quad (2)$$

We have done so because

1. The calculation is in floating-point numbers. Hence use of floating-point coefficients saves conversions.
2. For small powers, multiplication is faster than exponentiation. Hence, we avoided the use of exponentiation operators.
3. Even if we rewrite the assignment statement (2) as

$$P = -10.246E0 - 3.123E0*X - 4.123E0*X*X + X*X*X;$$

it will still require three additions (or subtractions) and five multiplications because

3.123E0*X	requires one multiplication
4.123E0*X*X	requires two multiplications (4.123E0*X is obtained first, and the result is multiplied by X)
X*X*X	requires two multiplications (X*X is obtained first, and the result is multiplicated by X)

and there are still three additions or subtractions (a subtraction requires approximately the same time as an addition) to be performed.

The assignment statement (1) requires

One addition for $-4.123E0 + X$
One addition and one multiplication for $X*(-4.123E0 + X)$
Two additions and one multiplication for $-3.123E0 + X*(-4.123E0 + X)$
Two additions and two multiplications for $X*(-3.123E0 + X*(-4.123E0 + X))$
Three additions and two multiplications for
$\quad -10.246E0 + X*(-3.123E0 + X*(-4.123E0 + X))$

hence a saving of three multiplications over the expression in (2). Since these calculations are performed repeatedly in the DO loop, there is a substantial saving in expressing P in the form of (1) rather than in the form of (2). Thus the writing of a polynomial

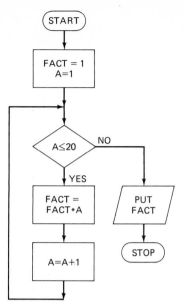

Figure 9.6 Flowchart for Example 9.4.2.

$$a_0 + a_1x + a_2x^2 + \cdots + a_nx^n$$

in the so-called "nested form"

$$a_0 + x(a_1 + x(a_2 + x(a_3 + \cdots + x(a_{n-1} + a_nx)))) \cdots)$$

constitutes good programming practice.

Example 9.4.2 Evaluate 20!

Solution The flowchart for this example appears in Fig. 9.6. Since 20! is a rather large number, we need more than the default precision. To estimate the number of digits in 20!, consider 10 as the average number, and there are 20 multiplications. Hence 20! is approximately of the order of 10^{20}. We will declare it as FLOAT DEC(16), which is the maximum available for a floating-point decimal number, and obtain the result with 16 significant digits. Hence the program is

```
FACTOR:    PROC OPTIONS(MAIN);
           DCL FACT FLOAT DEC(16);
           FACT = 1E0;
           DO A = 1E0 TO 2E1;
               FACT = FACT*A;
           END;
           PUT LIST(FACT);
           END FACTOR;
```

which gives the output

```
2.432902008176640E+18
```

Note that the DO statement implements the A=1 assignment, the A ≤ 20 test, and the A=A+1 assignment. After the completion of the DO loop, FACT has the required value.

Example 9.4.3 Tabulate the function

$$z = 2.3x^2 + 3.4y^2 + 4.5xy + 7.2x + 3.9y + 11.8$$

for

$$0 \le x \le 10$$
$$0 \le y \le 10$$
$$x^2 + y^2 \le 80$$

and choose the points of tabulation as follows.

For	x in steps of	y in steps of
$0 \le x \le 2,\ \ 0 \le y \le 1$	0.1	0.1
$0 \le x \le 2.\ \ 1 < y \le 2$	0.2	0.1
$0 \le x \le 2,\ \ 2 < y \le 10$	0.2	0.2
$2 < x \le 10,\ 0 \le y \le 5$	2	0.5
$2 < x \le 10,\ 5 < y \le 10$	2	1

Solution The program for this tabulation is

```
TAB:      PROC OPTIONS(MAIN);
L1:       DO X=0E0 TO 2E0 BY 1E-1;
             DO Y=0E0 TO 1E0 BY 1E-1;
                Z = X*(2.3E0*X + 4.5E0*Y + 7.2E0) +
                    Y*(3.4E0*Y + 3.9E0)  +11.8E0,
                PUT LIST(X,Y,Z);
          END L1;
L2:       DO X=0E0 TO 2 BY 2E-1;
             DO Y=1.1E0 TO 2E0 BY 1E-1,
                   2.2E0 TO 1E1 BY 2E-1 WHILE(X*X+Y*Y<=80);
                Z = X*(2.3E0*X + 4.5E0*Y + 7.2E0) +
                    Y*(3.4E0*Y + 3.9E0)  +11.8E0;
                PUT LIST(X,Y,Z);
          END L2;
          DO X=4E0 TO 1E1 BY 2E0;
             DO Y=0E0 TO 5E0 BY 5E-1 WHILE(X*X+Y*Y<=80),
                   6E0 TO 1E1 BY 1E0 WHILE(X*X+Y*Y<=80);
                Z = X*(2.3E0*X + 4.5E0*Y + 7.2E0) +
                    Y*(3.4E0*Y + 3.9E0)  +11.8E0;
                PUT LIST(X,Y,Z);
          END TAB;
```

Note that no WHILE clause is needed for $x \le 2$, $y \le 1$, and for $x \le 2$, $y \le 2$.

9.5 FLOWCHART SYMBOL FOR THE DO LOOP

There is no special standard symbol for a DO loop. Because of this fact, a DO loop is represented by either a nonstandard special symbol or several standard symbols. For example, the program segment

```
DO   I=3 TO 20 BY 2;
          statement1;
END;
          statement2;
```

can be portrayed by the flowchart of Fig. 9.7 An experienced programmer will implement this flowchart with a DO loop as above rather than with other statements.

Note that the representation of a DO loop requires three standard symbols picturing

1. The assignment of an initial value to the control variable
2. The test to ascertain whether or not the control variable has exceeded the final value
3. The increasing of the control variable by the increment

It is possible to portray the above three functions (requiring three standard symbols) by a single symbol, with the attendant simplification in the flowchart. One such symbol is shown in Fig. 9.8, where the initial, final, and increment values for the control variable are as before. Using this symbol, the preceding segment results in the flowchart of Fig. 9.9.

Other special symbols for the DO loop are in use. Just like the symbol of Fig. 9.8, the other symbols usually divide a rectangle or some other geometric figure into three parts, showing the initial, final, and increment values for the control variable.

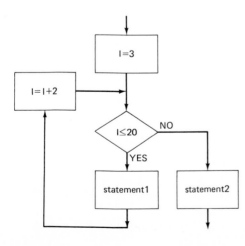

Figure 9.7 Flowchart portraying the DO loop with standard symbols.

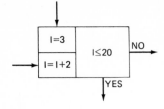

Figure 9.8 A nonstandard symbol for the DO loop.

Because of their limited acceptance neither the special symbol of Fig. 9.8 nor the other such special symbols are used in the remainder of this book.

9.6 SUMMARY

We described here the three different types of the DO statement. In the first type, the DO statement is used for grouping statements. This grouping is useful for executing several statements with the THEN or ELSE clauses.

The second and the third types of the DO statement give rise to repetitive executions of the DO group. In the second type, there is a WHILE clause. The DO group is executed repeatedly as long as the condition in the WHILE clause is true. Only if the condition is false does an exit out of the DO group take place. Because of its repetitive nature, this DO group is known as a DO loop.

The third type of DO statement also results in repetitive executions of the DO group. Thus the DO group is also named a DO loop. Here the control variable is set to an initial value, and each passage through the loop results in an addition of a specified increment to the control variable. When the control variable exceeds a specified final value, an exit out of the DO loop takes place. The initial value, the increment, and the final values can be expressions, and the DO statement can be generalized to one containing multiple specifications for the control variable, with or without WHILE clauses.

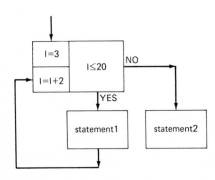

Figure 9.9 Flowchart portraying the DO loop with a nonstandard special symbol.

PROBLEMS

9.1 What is the printout for each of the following segments?

(*a*) DO I=1 TO 10;
      I=3+I;
      PUT LIST(I);
   END;

(*b*) DO J=1 TO 10;
   END;
   PUT LIST(J);

(*c*) N=3;
   DO WHILE(N<50);
      N=N*N;
      PUT LIST(N);
   END;

(*d*) DO M=10 TO 1;
      PUT LIST(M);
   END;

9.2 What is the printout for each of the following segments?

(*a*) N=1;
   DO I=N TO 3*N, 2*N TO 1 BY −3;
      N=N+1;
      PUT LIST (I,N);
   END;

(*b*) N=2;
   DO I=N TO 3*N WHILE (N>=5);
      N=N+2;
      PUT LIST (I,N);
   END;

(*c*) DO A=1E0 BY 1E0 WHILE (A*A<5);
      PUT LIST (2*A);
   END;

9.3 Given that

$$z = 1.3xy + 1.2x - 1.2y$$

calculate z in the ranges

$$\begin{matrix} 5 \le x \le 15 \\ 2 \le y \le 6 \end{matrix} \quad \text{and} \quad \begin{matrix} 5 \le x \le 10 \\ 10 \le y \le 15 \end{matrix}$$

Chose x and y in steps of 1 for both ranges.

9.4 The equation

$$x^3 - 6.2x^2 - 4.55x + 24.5 = 0$$

has three real roots between -10 and 10. Write a program for finding all three roots (see Example 9.4.1).

9.5 Find the maximum and the minimum values of

$$z = \sqrt{x} + 3.5\sqrt{y} + 1.73\,x^2 y$$

in the triangularly bounded region shown in Fig. P9.5*a* by using the following method:

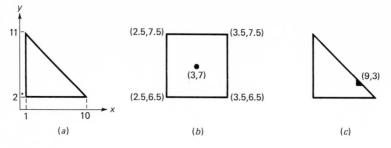

Figure P9.5

1. Find the maximum and minimum values of z at the grid points, that is, for integer values of x and y on or within the boundary.

2. If the maximum occurs in the interior of the region, search further for the maximum in the 1×1 square enclosing the initial maximum by letting x and y vary in steps of 0.1. For example, if the initial maximum occurs at $x = 3$ and $y = 7$, investigate the square bounded by (2.5, 6.5), (3.5, 6.5), (2.5, 7.5), and (3.5, 7.5), as shown in Fig. P9.5b.

If the maximum occurs on the boundary, investigate only the part of the 1×1 square inside the region. For example, if the initial maximum occurs at (9, 3), investigate only the black area, as shown in Fig. P9.5c.

3. Use the method just described to find the minimum value.

4. Print out the maximum and minimum values and their coordinates. Identify your results clearly and include ample explanation of your program in your program listing.

9.6 There are 20 pairs of positive integers on data cards. For each pair, say, I, J, print out

$$\text{I,J,N} \qquad \text{if } I^N = J$$
$$\text{J,I,N} \qquad \text{if } J^N = I$$

(no printout if neither of these conditions applies).

9.7
```
PR_7:    PROC OPTIONS(MAIN);
         I = 1;
         ISUM = 0;
AGAIN:   GET LIST(N);
         IF N=0 THEN GO TO PRINT;
         ISUM = ISUM + N;
         IF I=10 THEN GO TO PRINT;
         I = I + 1;
         GO TO AGAIN;
PRINT:   PUT LIST(ISUM);
         END PR_7;
```
Replace this program with one that
(*a*) Accomplishes the same objectives as the above program
(*b*) Has no GO TO statements (that is, eliminates the three GO TOs in the given program)

9.8 A definite integral can be approximately evaluated by the formula (known as the trapezoidal rule)

$$\int_a^b f(x)\, dx \approx h\{\tfrac{1}{2}f(a) + f(a + h) + f(a + 2h) + \cdots + f[a + (n - 1)h] + \tfrac{1}{2}f(b)\}$$

where n = number of equal subdivisions of $b - a$

$$h = \frac{b - a}{n}$$

Using this formula and 50 subdivisions, evaluate and print out

(a)

$$\int_1^{10} \frac{x^2 + \sqrt{x}}{3x + 1} \, dx$$

(b)

$$\int_2^3 \frac{1.7\sqrt[3]{x}}{1 + \sqrt{x}} \, dx$$

10

PROGRAMMING WITHOUT THE GO TO STATEMENT

We mentioned earlier (Secs. 3.3 and 8.3) that skilled programmers avoid the use of the GO TO statement. We will now expand on this topic and show how to write programs without this statement.

10.1 WHY NO GO TOs?

Computer programming is a very recent human activity and, as such, has practically no theoretical foundation. Many questions remain unanswered regarding the methods for writing bug-free and easily understood programs.

Edsger W. Dijkstra, one of the leading computer scientists, warned in a famous paper[1] that GO TO statements lead to programs which are difficult to understand and debug. Today there are many disciples of Dijkstra's thinking. Some maintain that just the avoidance of GO TOs leads to a thinking pattern which yields a "cleaner," more direct program style, resulting in fewer bugs. Up to now we wanted to present just the PL/I language with examples without worrying about the style of our programs. But now we know enough of the language so that we can start addressing ourselves to the way in which our programs are written.

Can programs be written without the GO TO statements? The answer is yes. As we will describe in Sec. 10.3, any program with a single entry and a single exit can be written with just three control structures, these being simple sequence, selection (that is, IF-THEN-ELSE), and loop control mechanism (for example, DO WHILE). Is the avoidance of GO TOs always beneficial? The answer is no. There are problems where the use of a GO TO statement is more natural than the use of other statements. However, such problems are infrequent. In fact, all the programs introduced so far can be written without the GO TO statements, as we will demonstrate in the following section.

---

[1]E. W. Dijkstra, Go To Statement Considered Harmful, *Commun. ACM,* vol. 11, no. 3, pp. 147–148, March 1968.

We may conclude that GO TO statements should be used with great frugality. If we use such statements we should do so only after constructing an alternative program without the GO TOs, and then select the program with GO TOs for some specific reason. Thus we should not accept a program with GO TOs just because it was the first implementation that came to our mind, but only as a result of careful and well-thought-out decision.

10.2 EXAMPLES OF GO TO–LESS PROGRAMS

In the previous pages we constructed a number of programs. We will redo several of these programs and show that they can be rewritten without the GO TO statement. The main replacement for the GO TO statement is the repetitive looping implemented by the DO with the WHILE clause.

Let us start with the programs in Chap. 3. In the solution to Example 3.4.2 we constructed a program for obtaining (1) the count of positive numbers, (2) the count of negative numbers, and (3) the sum of all positive numbers. The program is to stop either for zero input or when the sum of positive numbers exceeds 1000.

If we rewrite the program without the GO TO statements, we obtain

```
COUNTS: PROC OPTIONS(MAIN);
        K,L,TOTAL = 0;        /* K COUNTS POS NUMBERS,L NEG NUMBERS   */
        GET LIST(A);
        DO WHILE(TOTAL<=1000 & A¬=0);
          IF A>0 THEN DO;
                        TOTAL = TOTAL + A;
                        K = K+1;
                      END;
                 ELSE L = L+1;
          GET LIST(A);
        END;
        PUT LIST(K,L,TOTAL);
        END COUNTS;
```

Compare the above program with the one in Example 3.4.2. Observe here the following features:

1. The statement

$$\text{DO WHILE (TOTAL} <= 1000 \text{ \& A } \neg = 0);$$

eliminates the two GO TO statements

$$\text{IF A=0 THEN GO TO PRINT;}$$

and

$$\text{IF TOTAL} <= 1000 \text{ THEN GO TO REPEAT;}$$

used in the program in Example 3.4.2.

2. With

IF A>0 THEN DO;

we update TOTAL and K. In the program in Example 3.4.2 we needed a GO TO statement to jump to the statement labeled UPDATE. Hence the present construction eliminates this GO TO statement.

3. The use of the DO WHILE loop eliminates the GO TO statement

GO TO REPEAT;

used in the Example 3.4.2 program.

4. Note that the present program is more direct and readable than that in Example 3.4.2, where the four GO TO statements detracted from its clarity.

5. Observe that we use a GET LIST statement before the DO WHILE loop (to start the loop) and a GET LIST statement in the loop. This is often necessary when the condition depends on the input data, as is the case here.

A second example is the program in the solution to Example 3.4.5, which is now rewritten by including a DO loop with a control variable. The resulting program is

```
POL: PROC OPTIONS(MAIN);
    DO X = -5 TO 20 BY 0.5;
        Y = X**5 + 1.7*X - 3.4;
        PUT LIST(X,Y);
    END;
    END POL;
```

and eliminates the two GO TO statements. The advantages in brevity and clarity of this program over the one in the Example 3.4.5 solution are obvious.

The program following Example 6.2.1 has two GO TO statements. The version here

```
EXAMPLE: PROC OPTIONS(MAIN);
        TOTAL = 0;
        GET LIST(A);
        DO WHILE(A¬=0);
            IF A>0 THEN TOTAL = TOTAL+A;
            GET LIST(A);
        END;
        PUT LIST(TOTAL);
        END EXAMPLE;
```

eliminates these statements. The condition in the WHILE clause eliminates the need for

IF A=0 THEN GO TO FINISHED;

and the use of the repetitive DO WHILE loop obviates the need for

```
        GO TO REPEAT;
```

Note again that we use here the GET LIST statement to obtain the first value of A before the start of the DO WHILE loop.

The program following Example 6.2.2 can be rewritten as

```
EXAMPLE: PROC OPTIONS(MAIN);
        TOTAL,SUM_SQUARE = 0;
        GET LIST(A);
        DO WHILE(A¬=0);
            IF A>0 THEN DO;
                            TOTAL = TOTAL+A;
                            SUM_SQUARE = SUM_SQUARE+A*A;
                        END;
            GET LIST(A);
        END;
        PUT LIST(TOTAL,SUM_SQUARE);
        END EXAMPLE;
```

and the program following Example 6.3.1 becomes

```
EXAMPLE: PROC OPTIONS(MAIN);
        SUM_POS,SUM_NEG = 0;
        GET LIST(A);
        DO WHILE(A¬=0);
            IF A>0 THEN SUM_POS = SUM_POS+A;
                   ELSE SUM_NEG = SUM_NEG+A;
            GET LIST(A);
        END;
        PUT LIST(SUM_POS,SUM_NEG);
        END EXAMPLE;
```

These two programs require no further explanation.

The program in the solution to Example 6.6.2 can be more directly constructed by using the DO loop with a control variable. Such a construction is

```
VALUES: PROC OPTIONS(MAIN);
        DCL T FIXED(2,1),Y_SQUARE FIXED(3,2);
        DO T=0 TO 1 BY 0.2;
            Y_SQUARE = T*T;
            PUT LIST(T,Y_SQUARE);
        END;
        DO T=1.2 TO 2 BY 0.2;
            PUT LIST(T,Y_SQUARE);
        END;
        DO T=2.2 TO 3 BY 0.2, 3.5 TO 4.5 BY 0.5;
            Y_SQUARE = (5-T)*(5-T);
            PUT LIST(T,Y_SQUARE);
        END;
        END VALUES;
```

and eliminates the need for the two GO TO statements required in the Example 6.6.2 program.

The program in the solution to Example 6.6.3 has only a single GO TO statement, this being

$$\text{GO TO DONE;}$$

Replacing it with

$$\text{STOP;}$$

makes the program GO TO–less and eliminates the need for the label on the last statement.

The program shown in Fig. 8.9 has the GO TO statement

$$\text{GO TO AGAIN;}$$

which can be eliminated with

$$\text{DO WHILE (A}\neg = -10);$$

and the PUT LIST statement outside the loop as in

```
EX_4: PROC OPTIONS(MAIN);
      DCL A FIXED(5,3);
      I,J,K=0;                /* I COUNTS POS NUMBERS, J NUMBERS    */
      GET LIST(A);           /* BETWEEN -5 AND 5, K EVEN INTEGERS */
                             /* BETWEEN 40 AND 50 INCLUSIVE        */
      DO WHILE(A¬=-10);
         IF A>0 THEN I=I+1;
         IF A>-5 & A<5 THEN J=J+1;
         IF A>=40 & A<=50 THEN DO;
                              N=A/2;
                              IF A=2*N THEN K=K+1;
                           END;
         GET LIST(A);
      END;
      PUT LIST(I,J,K);
      END EX_4;
```

As the previous examples demonstrate, armed with our present programming experience, we can easily construct GO TO–less programs. Observe how much more readable and direct these programs are. As an extra all-important bonus, these programs require less debugging time.

The above examples are not meant to suggest that one should construct a program in any sloppy way and then replace the GO TO statements. It is a much better practice to try to formulate the solution to avoid the GO TO statements in the initial program version.

10.3 PROGRAMMING WITH SIMPLE CONTROL STRUCTURES

In the previous section we described how to write programs without the GO TO statement. We saw that programs without the GO TO statements are clearer and

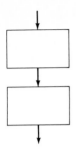

Figure 10.1 Simple sequence.

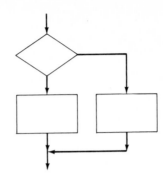

Figure 10.2 Selection.

more readable and have no thought-distracting jumps to different parts of the program.

In a later chapter we will describe how to develop a program in a so-called "structured" form. In developing such a program a division is made into separate program parts. Each of these parts is then implemented by using just a combination of three control structures, resulting in a single-entry–single-exit program[1] (that is, without any jumps in the middle). These three control structures are

1. Simple sequence, shown in Fig. 10.1
2. Selection, shown in Fig. 10.2
3. Loop control mechanism (that is, repetition), shown in Fig. 10.3

As an example, consider the flowchart of Fig. 3.6. The program implementing this flowchart appears in the solution to Example 3.4.2, and the rewritten GO TO–less version in the beginning of Sec. 10.2. The flowchart for the GO TO–less program is shown in Fig. 10.4. Replacing the part within the broken lines by the box labeled X results in the flowchart of Fig. 10.5. As we can see this flowchart can be easily decomposed into the three basic control structures. In fact, the GO TO–less implementation mirrors a flowchart constructed with just such control structures.

[1]This is always possible as shown by C. Bohm and G. Jacopini in Flow Diagrams, Turing Machines and Languages with Only Two Formation Rules, *Commun. ACM,* vol. 9, pp. 366–371, May 1966.

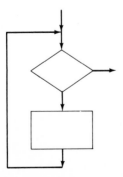

Figure 10.3 Repetition.

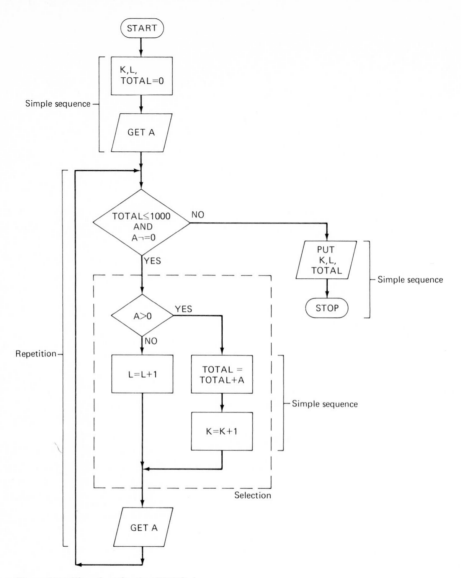

Figure 10.4 Flowchart for the GO TO–less program.

10.4 SUMMARY

We described how to write programs without the GO TO statement. We should strive to write such programs because they are usually clearer and more direct than their counterparts with the GO TO statements. Also such programs generally require a better understanding of the problem being solved, with the attendant saving in the debugging time and effort.

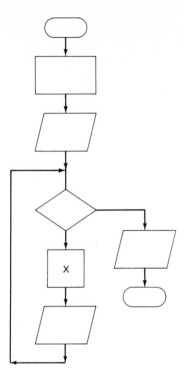

Figure 10.5 The flowchart of Fig. 10.4 with the part within the broken lines replaced by a single box.

If the construction with GO TO statements yields a more intelligible or more efficient program, use the GO TOs (see Problems 10.3 and 10.4). However, even in such cases use GO TOs sparingly.

PROBLEMS

10.1 Rewrite the following program segments into the ones with no labels (and accomplishing the same function).

    (a)   IF A > B THEN N = N+1;
                IF A > B THEN N1 = N1+2;
                IF A > B THEN GO TO SKIP;
                N2 = N2+1;
       SKIP: PUT LIST (N,N1,N2);
    (b)   IF A > C THEN X = X+2;
                IF A < C THEN GO TO L2;
                GO TO L1;
       L2: Y = X+3;
                Z = U+Y;
       L1: PUT LIST(X,Y,Z);

10.2 Write a program segment implementing the flowchart shown in Fig. P10.2 with and without labels.

10.3 Code the flowchart in Fig. P10.3 without any labels.

10.4 Code the flowchart of Fig. P10.3 with labels and GO TO statements. Did you obtain a reduction in total statements? What conclusions can be reached from this example?

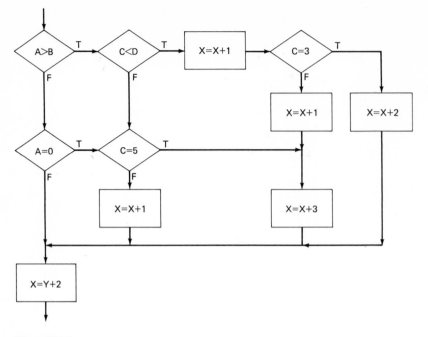

Figure P10.2

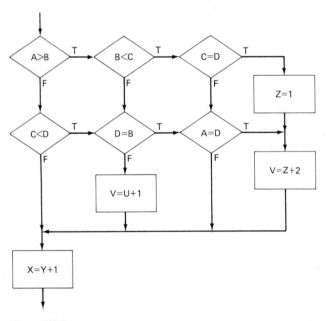

Figure P10.3

10.5 Rewrite the following program without any labels and GO TO statements.

```
P5:    PROC OPTICNS(MAIN);
       Z = 0;
       KOUNT = 1;
LOOP:  GET LIST(X);
       IF X<20 THEN GO TO OUT;
                ELSE PUT LIST(X);
       Y = X + 3;
       PUT LIST(Y);
       KOUNT = KOUNT + 2;
       IF KOUNT<100 THEN GO TO LOOP;
                ELSE Y=2*X;
       Z = X + Y;
OUT:   PUT LIST(X,Y,Z);
       END P5;
```

10.6
```
P6:        PROC OPTIONS(MAIN);
  L2:      GET LIST(M);
  L1:      GET LIST(N);
           IF N=0&M=0 THEN GO TO FINISH;
           IF N=0 THEN DO;
                       PUT LIST(M,M*M);
                       GO TO L1;
                    END;
           IF M=0 THEN DO;
                       PUT LIST(N,N*N);
                       GO TO L2;
                    END;
           PUT LIST(M,N);
           GO TO L2;
  FINISH: END P6;
```

Replace this program with one that (1) accomplishes the same objectives as the above program and (2) has no GO TO statements.

10.7 Write a program without GO TOs which will print out
  1. The count of nonzero numbers
  2. The count of negative numbers
  3. The count of nonnegative numbers (that is, positive and zero numbers)
  4. The count of zeros

No number in the data exceeds 1000, and a trailer number of 2000 (not part of the data) is placed at the end of the data to signal the end of the data deck.

10.8 Construct without GO TO statements
  (*a*) A program for Prob. 6.2*a*.
  (*b*) A program for Prob. 6.8.
  (*c*) A program for Prob. 6.13.

11 PROGRAMMING STYLE

We now know how to write programs in the PL/I language. But programs in PL/I are like compositions in English. If we ask two authors to write a composition on the same topic, we may find one composition to be decisively better than the other. The better composition is clear, well organized, and structured so that each part treats a single subtopic cohesively. The better composition displays a good writing style.

Similar consideration applies to programs. A well-constructed program is clear, well organized, and structured so that each part of the program treats a single task completely. Such a program displays a good programming style.

11.1 WHAT IS THE IMPORTANCE OF STYLE?

Programs are written to solve problems, and hence our primary interest is in the output which displays the solution. Because of this fact, we may ask: What does it matter how the program is written, as long as the printed out results are correct?

Before we answer this question, let us again use the analogy between a program and an English text. An analogous question referring to an English text may read: What does it matter how the text is written as long as the contents are valid?

The answer to the last question is obvious. It may not matter how the text is written if the text is a grocery or laundry list. However, if the text is to be read by others, or even by ourselves at a later date, it must be intelligible.

The same answer applies to the original question concerning programs. It may not matter how a simple program of a few lines, written for a one-shot use, is constructed. However, if the program is either (1) long, or (2) complicated, or (3) to be used at a later time, or (4) to be used by others, or (5) to be modified eventually, then the style of the program matters very much.

The debugging of a long, complicated, and badly constructed program is a nightmare. If a program is to be used at a later time, say, a year later, it is difficult to remember the purpose of each statement or part of the program. An unintelligible program will be of little use to someone else. To modify a poor program, which we only debugged by sheer luck, is a masochistic exercise. For all these reasons style is important, and the extra initial investment of time in the program actually produces a large saving of time. This saving is immediate in debugging time. We also save time when we use or modify the program at a later date and can easily read and understand the program.

11.2 THE ELEMENTS OF STYLE

From the preceding discussion the purpose of style is evident. We must strive to make the program as clear as possible. This is achieved by the following three elements:

1. Simplicity of statements
2. Grouping of statements into logical parts
3. Explanatory descriptions

The simplicity of statements means that the choice of the algorithm and its implementation should be direct, straightforward, and simple. Ambiguity should be avoided, and no tricks should be used that exploit some obscure peculiarities of the PL/I language.

The second element of program style is the organization of the program. By grouping the statements into logical parts connected with a simple control structure, the readability is greatly enhanced. Such a program is said to be *well structured*. As an example, consider a program of 100 statements divided into five parts, with the function of each part clearly described. We can understand the purpose and the mechanism of the entire program at a glance. As we read the program, we do not read a single program of 100 statements, but five smaller programs. It is evident that careful structuring of large programs is essential, because only with such a division and a simple control mechanism can we handle the complexity of large programs.

The last element is the documentation. A well-written program is nearly self-documented in that the program statements describe what takes place. Each logical group of statements should also be preceded by a heading, and explanatory comments should precede or accompany the statements.

In the following sections we will illustrate the use of these three elements of style in constructing an intelligible program.

11.3 SIMPLICITY OF STATEMENTS

We are adding now another aspect of programming. Not only must the program statements solve the program, but they must be easily understandable by others as well. This is principally achieved by composing the statements so as to make their purpose evident. As we write the statements we must constantly ask: Is this the simplest construction of the program segment?

Let us start with an example. Consider again the program SIDES in Sec. 3.3. The object was to determine whether three positive numbers A, B, C were equal (that is, whether they could be the sides of an equilateral triangle). An even clumsier construction than the one of Sec. 3.3 may read

```
SIDES:      PROCEDURE CPTIONS(MAIN);
            GET LIST(A,B,C);
            IF A=B THEN GO TO MAYBE;
            GO TO NO;
MAYBE:      IF A=C THEN GO TO YES;
NO:         PUT LIST
      ('THESE 3 NUMBERS CANNOT BE THE SIDES OF AN EQUILATERAL TRIANGLE');
            GO TO FINISHED;
YES:        PUT LIST
      ('THESE 3 NUMBERS CAN BE THE SIDES OF AN EQUILATERAL TRIANGLE');
FINISHED: END SIDES;
```

We have made the point before, but it is worth repeating: The jungle of GO TOs reduces the clarity of the program. We can also note that we would not solve the problem by hand in the way we programmed it. We would simply do: If A=B and A=C, then all three numbers are equal, otherwise they are not equal. And it is this approach that we implemented in the program named SIDES_2, shown in Sec. 6.6 and repeated here (with an additional explanatory heading).

```
SIDES_3: PROCEDURE OPTIONS(MAIN);
         /* THIS PROGRAM DETERMINES WHETHER OR NOT 3 POSITIVE NUMBERS
            A, B, AND C CAN BE THE SIDES OF AN EQUILATERAL TRIANGLE  */
         GET LIST(A,B,C);
         IF (A=B) & (A=C) THEN PUT LIST
      ('THESE 3 NUMBERS CAN BE THE SIDES OF AN EQUILATERAL TRIANGLE');
                       ELSE PUT LIST
      ('THESE 3 NUMBERS CANNOT BE THE SIDES OF AN EQUILATERAL TRIANGLE');
         END SIDES_3;
```

The above two programs lead to the conclusions

1. Avoid a jungle of GO TOs.
2. Program the solution that you would use in solving the problem by hand.

As the next example consider the program segment

$$X=2*Y;$$
$$Z=5+X;$$
$$U=Z+1;$$
$$V=U+3;$$

which is apparently a sequence of calculations. A direct substitution shows that this is equivalent to

$$V=(Z+1)+3=Z+4=(5+X)+4=X+9=2*Y+9$$

Therefore the segment is equivalent to

$$V=2*Y+9;$$

which shows the nature of the calculations directly, in a simple, easy-to-understand way, without cluttering up the program with four extra variables. This leads to the conclusion

3. Do not introduce unnecessary variables.

Consider next the program segment

```
        IF X<Y THEN GO TO PART1;
        X=Y+1;
PART1: PUT LIST(X);
```

which has a GO TO and a confusing skip over the $X=Y+1$; statement. It is clear that just an inversion of the condition will provide the desired cure, that is,

```
IF X >= Y THEN X = Y+1;
PUT LIST(X);
```

which is clearer than a null THEN as in

```
IF X < Y  THEN;
            ELSE X=Y+1;
PUT LIST (X);
```

This leads to the conclusion

4. If the condition in the IF statement requires a GO TO, try inverting the condition.

Consider now the program segment

```
DO I=1 TO 20;
    DO J=1 TO 20;
        PUT LIST (I*(I>J));
    END;
END;
```

Can you tell what it does?

You probably remember that $I > J$ has the value of 1 if the inequality is true and the value of 0 if the inequality is false. Hence the value of I is printed out for $I > J$, and 0 is printed out for $I \leq J$. But did you see this immediately? And someone else may not see it at all. It is therefore better to write this segment as

```
DO   I=1 TO 20;
       DO J=1 TO 20;
           IF I>J THEN PUT LIST (I);
                   ELSE PUT LIST (0)
       END;
   END;
```

which is clearer, even though it is a statement longer. This example leads to the conclusion

5. Avoid clever tricks.

We just reached five conclusions regarding individual statements from inspections of unreadable programs. Next we will consider the program organization.

11.4 PROGRAM ORGANIZATION

In the preceding section we described the need for writing clear and simple statements. These statements must be connected in a logical sequence. What we wish to achieve is a division of the program into units or modules, each performing a distinct task. With such a division the program is separated into smaller parts, which enhances the program readability. To further improve the clarity of the program we will allow only the three control structures introduced in Sec. 10.3. These are

1. Simple sequence
2. Selection
3. Repetition

As we have described in Sec. 10.3, these three control structures suffice for the construction of any single-entry–single-exit program. Note that the IF-THEN-ELSE statement realizes the selection, and the DO WHILE statement the repetition. Incidentally, the iterative DO with the control variable, which is a special case of the DO WHILE, is also allowed. This limitation on the control mechanism leads to so-called *structured programs,* to be described in more detail in Chap. 12.

To illustrate the importance of organization on readability, consider the following program:

```
EX_1:      PROC OPTIONS(MAIN);
AGAIN:     GET LIST(A);
           IF A=0 THEN STOP;
           GET LIST(B,C,D);
           IF A<B THEN IF C<D THEN PUT LIST('CASE 1');
                               ELSE IF C>D THEN PUT LIST('CASE 2');
                                           ELSE PUT LIST('CASE 4');
                     ELSE IF A>B THEN IF C>D THEN PUT LIST('CASE 1');
                                           ELSE IF C<D THEN PUT LIST
                                                     ('CASE 2');
                                           ELSE PUT LIST
                                                     ('CASE 4');
                               ELSE IF A<D THEN PUT LIST('CASE 2');
                                           ELSE IF A>D THEN PUT LIST
                                                     ('CASE 3');
                                           ELSE PUT LIST
                                                     ('CASE 1');

           GO TO AGAIN;
           END EX_1;
```

What does this program do?

To answer this question let us analyze the program. Evidently the following relationships exist between the conditions on the variables and the output:

Conditions	Output
$A < B$ and $C < D$	Case 1
$A < B$ and $C > D$	Case 2
$A < B$ and $C = D$	Case 4
$A > B$ and $C > D$	Case 1
$A > B$ and $C < D$	Case 2
$A > B$ and $C = D$	Case 4
$A = B$ and $A < D$	Case 2
$A = B$ and $A > D$	Case 3
$A = B$ and $A = D$	Case 1

This analysis would not be necessary, and the program would reveal itself at a glance, if a better organization were followed. Instead of jumping from case to case, the conditions pertaining to a single case should be consolidated. Here

Case 1 occurs when either	$A < B$	and	$C < D$
or	$A > B$	and	$C > D$
or	$A = B$	and	$A = D$
Case 2 occurs when either	$A < B$	and	$C > D$
or	$A > B$	and	$C < D$
or	$A = B$	and	$A < D$
Case 3 occurs when	$A = B$	and	$A > D$

Case 4 occurs for the remaining conditions.

Thus the program can be more simply written if we implement the above organization, leading to

```
EX_2:     PROC OPTIONS(MAIN);
          GET LIST(A);
          DO WHILE(A¬=0);
             GET LIST(B,C,D);
             IF (A<B & C<D) | (A>B & C>D) | (A=B & A=D)
                THEN PUT LIST('CASE 1');
                ELSE IF (A<B & C>D) | (A>B & C<D) | (A=B & A<D)
                        THEN PUT LIST('CASE 2');
                        ELSE IF A=B & A>D THEN PUT LIST('CASE 3');
                                          ELSE PUT LIST('CASE 4');
             GET LIST(A);
          END;
          END EX_2;
```

which is shorter and more readable.

As a second example consider the program EX_3 shown below. Again we ask: What does this program do? And again, to supply an answer analysis is necessary. To do so, we will list the conditions on the variables and the resulting output.

```
EX_3:     PROC OPTIONS(MAIN);
AGAIN:    GET LIST(A,B,C,D);
          E = A - C;
          F = B - D;
          IF E>0 THEN GO TO R1;
          IF E<0 THEN GO TO R2;
          IF F=0 THEN PUT LIST('SINGLE POINT, NO SLOPE');
                 ELSE PUT LIST('INFINITE SLOPE');
          GO TO AGAIN;
R1:       IF F>0 THEN DO;
                         PUT LIST('POSITIVE SLOPE');
                         GO TO AGAIN;
                      END;
          IF F<0 THEN DO;
                         PUT LIST('NEGATIVE SLOPE');
                         GO TO AGAIN;
                      END;
          PUT LIST('ZERO SLOPE');
          GO TO AGAIN;
R2:       IF F>0 THEN DO;
                         PUT LIST('NEGATIVE SLOPE');
                         GO TO AGAIN;
                      END;
          IF F<0 THEN DO;
                         PUT LIST('POSITIVE SLOPE');
                         GO TO AGAIN;
                      END;
          PUT LIST('ZERO SLOPE');
          GO TO AGAIN;
          END EX_3;
```

Conditions	Output
$E > 0$ and $F > 0$	Positive slope
$E > 0$ and $F < 0$	Negative slope
$E > 0$ and $F = 0$	Zero slope
$E < 0$ and $F > 0$	Negative slope
$E < 0$ and $F < 0$	Positive slope
$E < 0$ and $F = 0$	Zero slope
$E = 0$ and $F = 0$	Single point, no slope
$E = 0$ and $F \neq 0$	Infinite slope

The reference to slope yields the clue on the workings of the program. A, B and C, D are coordinates of two points, and the slope refers to the connecting line segment. Figure 11.1 illustrates this interpretation for three sets of conditions on E and F.

It is clear from the cursory inspection that the program is repetitious and badly organized. A consolidation of conditions leading to the same output would add to clarity. Also, the choice of variables X1, Y1, X2, Y2 rather than A, B, C, D is more suggestive of coordinates. There is no need for the intermediate variables E and F. With these changes, the program modifies to

```
EX_4:    PROC OPTIONS(MAIN);
         DO WHILE(1);
            GET LIST(X1,Y1,X2,Y2);
            IF (X1>X2 & Y1>Y2) | (X1<X2 & Y1<Y2)
               THEN PUT LIST('POSITIVE SLOPE');
               ELSE IF (X1>X2 & Y1<Y2) | (X1<X2 & Y1>Y2)
                       THEN PUT LIST('NEGATIVE SLOPE');
                       ELSE IF X1=X2 & Y1=Y2
                               THEN PUT LIST('SINGLE POINT, NO SLOPE');
                               ELSE IF X1=X2
                                       THEN PUT LIST('INFINITE SLOPE');
                                       ELSE PUT LIST('ZERO SLOPE');
         END;
         END EX_4;
```

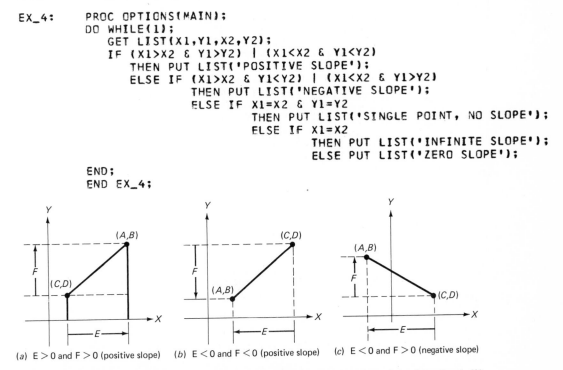

(a) $E > 0$ and $F > 0$ (positive slope)   (b) $E < 0$ and $F < 0$ (positive slope)   (c) $E < 0$ and $F > 0$ (negative slope)

Figure 11.1 Graphical interpretation of conditions on E and F: (a) $E > 0$ and $F > 0$ (positive slope); (b) $E < 0$ and $F < 0$ (positive slope); (c) $E < 0$ and $F > 0$ (negative slope).

The 1 in the WHILE condition results in an "infinite" loop which terminates when there is no more data for the GET LIST statement. Note also that the conditions on the fourth and the sixth lines can be reduced to

$$(X1-X2)*(Y1-Y2) > 0 \text{ and } (X1-X2)*(Y1-Y2) < 0$$

respectively. Such reduction does not add to the clarity of the program, which is the main issue here.

Observe that in both the examples presented in this section a simpler program ensued from just a consolidation and better grouping of the conditions. In both cases we made no changes in the algorithm. Often a better algorithm simplifies the program further, but this aspect of program writing is a large topic in itself.

11.5 DOCUMENTATION

Documentation, through meaningful explanations, further enhances readability. Appending explanations to the last program, we obtain the program EX_5 shown below, which is still easier to understand than the program EX_4.

```
EX_5:    PROC OPTIONS(MAIN);
         /* THIS PROGRAM DETERMINES THE SLOPE OF A LINE SEGMENT      */
         DO WHILE(1);
             GET LIST(X1,Y1,X2,Y2);          /*(X1,Y1) ARE THE COORDINATES
                                                 OF THE FIRST POINT, (X2,Y2)
                                                 ARE THE COORDINATES OF THE
                                                 SECOND POINT. THE LINE
                                                 SEGMENT OF INTEREST CONNECTS
                                                 THESE TWO POINTS.          */
             IF (X1>X2 & Y1>Y2) | (X1<X2 & Y1<Y2)
                THEN PUT LIST('POSITIVE SLOPE');
                ELSE IF (X1>X2 & Y1<Y2) | (X1<X2 & Y1>Y2)
                        THEN PUT LIST('NEGATIVE SLOPE');
                        ELSE IF X1=X2 & Y1=Y2
                                THEN PUT LIST('SINGLE POINT, NO SLOPE');
                                ELSE IF X1=X2
                                        THEN PUT LIST('INFINITE SLOPE');
                                             /* HERE X1=X2, Y1¬=Y2    */
                                        ELSE PUT LIST('ZERO SLOPE');
                                             /* HERE X1¬=X2, Y1=Y2    */
         END;
         END EX_5;
```

It is a good programming practice to document a program written for one's own use. Such a program can become incomprehensible even to the writer in just a couple of months. Comments should generally do the following:

1. Give a descriptive title of the program, as for example,

   /* A TABLE OF BASE 7 LOGARITHMS FOR THE FIRST 100 INTEGERS*/

2. Describe the method, for example,

```
/* STEP 3:   EVALUATION OF THE INTEGRAL
            BY TRAPEZOIDAL FORMULA      */
```

or

```
/* FIND THE MAXIMUM BY SEARCHING THROUGH THE TABLE.*/
```

3. Identify variables, for example,

```
/* VARIABLES:
   K_I           = IMPEDANCE SCALING FACTOR
   K_OMEGA       = FREQUENCY SCALING FACTOR
   OMEGA_C       = CUTOFF FREQUENCY          */
```

4. Provide chronological detail, for example,

```
/* REVISION 3.2 FEBRUARY 3, 1978 */
```

5. Describe temporary modifications, for example,

```
/* THIS COMMENT AND THE NEXT SIX STATEMENTS
   ARE TO BE REMOVED AFTER TESTING            */
```

Comments should always reveal information and not merely duplicate the program statement. The reading of a comment such as

```
A=0;    /* A IS SET TO ZERO. */
```

is a waste of time.

11.6 TECHNIQUES FOR IMPROVING READABILITY

The readability of the program can be further improved by the use of several techniques. We will enumerate four such techniques here.

A Paragraphing

We have used indentation (that is, paragraphing) extensively in DO groups, DO loops, procedures, and IF-THEN-ELSE statements, and no further illustration is needed.

B Blank Lines

A blank line may emphasize the separation between different parts of a program. A blank line is achieved by placing a blank card between the statements to be separated.

C Choice of Names

The names of variables, labels, and procedures should be chosen to suggest the quantities or processes which they represent. Thus

$$VEL = DIS/TIME;$$

is better than

$$A = B/C;$$

if A represents velocity, B distance, and C time.

D Parentheses

Parentheses, even when not necessary, may enhance readability. In the program EX_5, for example, the parentheses around X1>X2 & Y1>Y2 are not necessary (because & is of higher priority than |), but were placed there to improve clarity.

11.7 SUMMARY

We described here the elements of programming style. We saw that readable programs require simple statements, careful organization, and explanation of non-obvious program parts. We also described techniques for enhancing the clarity of programs.

11.8 FURTHER READING

For further reading on the topic of style we list the following nine references.

Brown, P. J.: Programming and Documenting Software Projects, *Comput. Surv.*, vol. 6, no. 4, pp. 213–220, December 1974.

Grabowsky, N.: What Kind of Programmer Are You?, *Datamation,* vol. 23, no. 3, p. 134, March 1977.

Halstead, M. H.: "Elements of Software Science," Chap. 7, Elsevier North-Holland, New York, 1977.

Kernighan, B. W., and P. J. Plauger: Programming Style: Examples and Counterexamples, *Comput. Surv.*, vol. 6, no. 4, pp. 303–319, December 1974.

———— and ————: "The Elements of Programming Style," 2nd ed., McGraw-Hill, New York, 1978.

Kreizberg, C. B., and Ben Shneiderman: "The Elements of FORTRAN Style: Techniques for Effective Programming," Harcourt Brace Jovanovich, New York, 1972.

Van Tassel, D.: "Program Style, Design, Efficiency, Debugging and Testing." 2nd ed., Prentice-Hall, Englewood Cliffs, NJ, 1978.

Weinberg, G. M.: "PL/I Programming: A Manual of Style," McGraw-Hill, New York, 1970.

Yourdan, E.: "Techniques of Program Structure and Design," Prentice-Hall, Englewood Cliffs, NJ, 1975.

PROBLEMS

11.1 A variable named I has the values of either 1 or 2. If I has the value of 1, change it to 2, and vice versa. Write at least six different program segments to do so, and comment on their merits (see the paper by N. Grabowsky listed in Sec. 11.8).

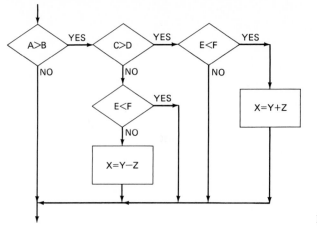

Figure P11.3

11.2 Consider again Prob. 6.9. Write two programs, one with nested IF statements and the other using ANDs and ORs. Observe how much simpler the second program is. Document both programs, and again observe the advantages of the second version.

11.3 Write two program segments for the flowchart of Fig.P11.3. One segment should use the nested IFs and the other ANDs and ORs. What conclusion can be drawn with regard to coding flowcharts with null ELSEs and THENs?

11.4 Simplify the program segment

```
DO I = 1 TO 10;
    GET LIST (A,B);
    IF A<10 THEN;
    IF A>= 10 & A< 20 THEN B = B+1;
    IF A>= 20 & A< 30 THEN B = B+2;
    IF A>= 30 & A< 40 THEN B = B+3;
    IF A>= 40 & A< 50 THEN B = B+4;
    IF A>= 50 THEN:
    PUT LIST(B);
END;
```

(*Hint:* Use a better algorithm.)

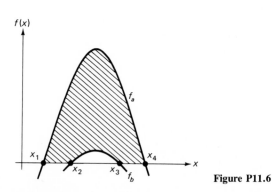

Figure P11.6

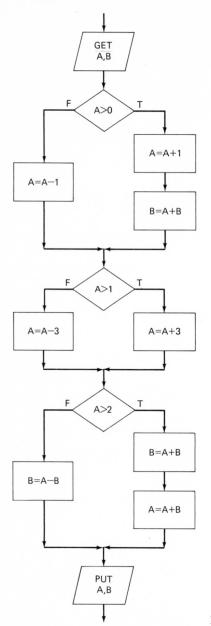

Figure P11.8

11.5 Determine the function of the program segment

$$X = X + Y + Z;$$
$$Y = X + Y - Z;$$
$$Z = 2*X - Y - 2*Z;$$
$$Y = (2*X - Y - Z)/2;$$
$$X = X - Z - Y;$$

and replace it by a simpler one, with explanatory documentation.

11.6 Write two programs to calculate the shaded area shown in Fig.P11.6, where

$$f_a = -x^2 + 6x - 5 \quad \text{and} \quad f_b = -x^2 + 5x - 6$$

using the following two approaches:

    1. Calculate x_1, x_2, x_3, x_4 and then the area as

$$\text{Area} = \int_{x_1}^{x_2} f_a \, dx + \int_{x_2}^{x_3} (f_a - f_b)dx + \int_{x_3}^{x_4} f_a \, dx$$

    2. (*a*) Calculate x_1, x_4
       (*b*) Calculate

$$\text{Area 1} = \int_{x_1}^{x_4} f_a \, dx$$

       (*c*) Calculate x_2, x_3
       (*d*) Calculate

$$\text{Area 2} = \int_{x_2}^{x_3} f_b \, dx$$

       (*e*) Area = Area 1 − Area 2

Provide documentation and comment on both approaches. To evaluate the integrals use the trapezoidal rule described in Prob. 9.8.

11.7 The program segment

$$A = B+C+D-C;$$
$$C = D+E;$$
$$C = C*C;$$
$$F = (A+B*C)*(A+B*C);$$
$$G = (A+B);$$
$$H = G**3;$$
$$P = A*A+B*B+2*A*B;$$

contains five examples of bad programming practice. Identify these five examples and replace them (see the book by M. H. Halstead listed in Sec. 11.8 and describing six classes of program inpurities).

11.8 Code the flowchart of Fig.P11.8 in the simplest possible equivalent way.

12 STRUCTURED PROGRAMMING

In Sec. 10.3 we introduced the term "structured program" We also wrote about "well-structured programs" in Sec. 11.2. We are ready now to expand on this topic.

12.1 STRUCTURED AND UNSTRUCTURED PROGRAMS

We will start with a definition of a structured program.

Definition A program is said to be *structured* if its flowchart can be constructed with only a specific set of structures.[1]

For our purposes the set of structures consists of

1. Simple sequence
2. Selection (implemented by the IF-THEN-ELSE)
3. Repetition (implemented by the DO WHILE)

these being the structures portrayed in Figs. 10.1 to 10.3.

Similarly, an *unstructured* program has a flowchart which cannot be constructed with just a combination of the above three elements.

As an illustration of a structured program consider the program named STRUC, shown below, which has the flowchart portrayed in Fig. 12.1. The inspection of the flowchart reveals that the program is structured.

```
STRUC:    PROC OPTIONS(MAIN);
          GET LIST(A,B,C);
          IF A>2*B THEN;
                ELSE IF A>B THEN C=C+A;
                            ELSE C=C+B+2*A;
          PUT LIST(C);
          END STRUC;
```

[1]This is a simplified definition which restricts only the flow of control. A broader definition also restricts the ways in which a program can be partitioned and the communication among such parts.

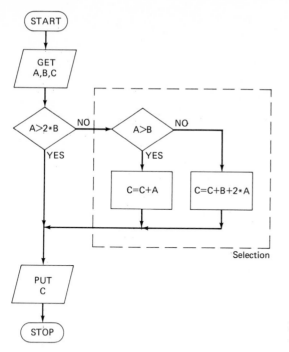

Figure 12.1 Flowchart for the program STRUC.

The program named UNSTRUC, shown below, has the flowchart displayed in Fig. 12.2. The flowchart cannot be constructed with just a combination of three basic elements (try it), and thus the program is unstructured.

```
UNSTRUC: PROC OPTIONS(MAIN);
         GET LIST(A,B,C);
         IF A>B THEN IF A>2*B THEN;
                             ELSE NO: C = C + A;
               ELSE DO;
                     C = A + B + C;
                    GO TO NO;
                 END;
         PUT LIST(C);
         END UNSTRUC;
```

As can be seen, structured programming requires an organizational discipline in the design of a program. Programmers can no longer write their programs in an arbitrary manner but must conform to specific rules.

12.2 WHY STRUCTURED PROGRAMMING?

Structured programming evidently makes the program writing more difficult, because certain statements such as GO TOs are no longer allowed. We also must

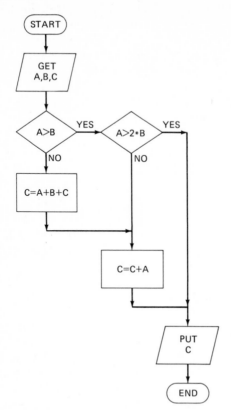

Figure 12.2 Flowchart for the program UNSTRUC.

plan our programs more carefully, and this planning requires extra time. What do we gain for surrendering the GO TOs and for the extra time spent on planning our programs more carefully?

What we gain is a saving in debugging time. Experience[1] has shown that in a typical program the finding of the algorithms for the solution of the problem and the resulting program design take approximately one-third the total time. The actual coding, that is, program writing, requires approximately one-sixth the total time. The remainder of the time, which amounts to one-half the total time, is spent on debugging. Hence, the major part of programming effort is in the debugging phase, and careful planning in the program design phase is justified because such planning reduces the debugging time. There is evidence that structured programming indeed reduces the debugging time.

It may be of interest to quote some typical numbers on the productivity of programmers. An average programmer produces approximately 10 statements each working day. Since all of us can write 10 statements in about 5 minutes, we may ask on what other activities do programmers spend the balance of the working day? We

[1]Barry W. Boehm, The High Cost of Software, in E. Horowitz (ed.), "Practical Strategies for Developing Large Software Systems," p. 7, Addison-Wesley, Reading, MA, 1975.

speak here about a large program, involving several programmers. Therefore, our average programmers attend various meetings and spend considerable time discussing how to merge (or "integrate") programs written by different programmers. They debug programs, perform the necessary rewriting and corrections, write test programs, and provide documentation for their programs. They perform many clerical duties such as bringing the programs to and picking up the programs from the computer center, determining, keypunching, and storing all the job control cards needed for various computer printouts, and maintaining a library of their programs with a description of debugging history. They also support the overhead (that is, the salaries of secretaries and administrators, the rent for the office space and computer, etc.). The result is that typically just 10 statements cost the money paid for a professional programmer's working day.

Can the programmer's productivity be increased? There is evidence that it can—with structured programming! One evidence consists of results achieved in a large programming job performed by IBM for the *New York Times*. On this project, which called for retrieval of information (and led to a program of over 80,000 statements), each programmer produced 35 statements during each working day. It is true that this large increase in productivity cannot be credited entirely to structured programming but also to two other factors. First, the IBM team was staffed by excellent personnel not found in average programming shops. Second, a novel approach, named *Chief Programmer Team* (described in Sec. 23.3), was applied to the organization and the management of the project. It is agreed, however, that the major contribution to the productivity improvement resulted from the use of structured programming. Structured programming statements had relatively few errors, thus reducing greatly the time-consuming debugging, with the attendant increase in productivity.

One advantage of structured programming is that even though it takes longer to write an initial version of a structured program, it takes less time and effort to debug it. A second advantage is that the structured program will generally be written in a better style than an unstructured program. The structured program will be more readable and better organized, allowing a modification with much less effort than an unstructured program will require.

12.3 METHODS FOR CONSTRUCTING STRUCTURED PROGRAMS

We will now introduce three methods for constructing structured programs and apply them to illustrative examples.

A Structured Flowcharts

In this method we construct a flowchart which contains only nestings of the three basic elements, that is, only simple sequence, selection, and repetition. To illustrate this method consider the following example.

Example 12.3.1 Print out the first 50 prime numbers.

Solution We can use the following method for finding the primes:

1. We print out the first three primes: 1, 2, and 3.
2. We will test the odd integers starting with 5. We name the integer tested IT and count the primes as we locate them. We use the variable KOUNT to count the primes.
3. The test consists of dividing IT by odd integers. If the remainder is zero, then IT is not a prime. By how many odd integers must IT be divided before we certify it as a prime? Evidently, it is not necessary to divide IT by integers exceeding the square root of IT, because if IT is not prime, then IT can be expressed as the product of two factors M and N, that is,

$$IT = M*N$$

Clearly, if one factor exceeds $\sqrt{IT}$ then the other factor must be less than $\sqrt{IT}$. Thus, if there are no factors less than $\sqrt{IT}$, there cannot be any factors larger than $\sqrt{IT}$.

4. One way to implement the test for primeness is through a loop which is left either if IT fails the prime number test of if the test is completed satisfactorily. We use the variable named KEY to designate the condition causing exit from the loop. We start with KEY = 0 and reset it to 1 if the test for primeness fails.

The flowchart implementing this method of solution is portrayed in Fig. 12.3. As can be seen the flowchart is structured, because it consists of nestings of just the three basic elements. The resulting structured program is named PRIMES and appears below with its output. Note that 0.1 is added to IT**0.5, because exponentiation by a fraction is approximate and a roundoff error may occur.

```
PRIMES:  PROC OPTIONS(MAIN);
         /* PRINT OUT THE FIRST 50 PRIMES                        */
         /* PRINT THE FIRST 3 PRIMES: 1, 2, AND 3                */
         DO KOUNT=1 TO 3;                /* KOUNT COUNTS PRIMES   */
             PUT LIST(KOUNT);
         END;
         /* TEST FOR PRIMENESS                                   */
         DO IT=5 BY 2 WHILE(KOUNT<=50);  /* IT IS THE INTEGER TESTED */
             J = IT**0.5 + 0.1;          /* FOR PRIME CHARACTER   */
             KEY = 0;
             DO I=3 TO J BY 2 WHILE(KEY=0);
                 N = IT/I;               /* IF IT DIVIDES BY I,   */
                 IF I*N=IT THEN KEY=1;   /* THEN N=I*N            */
             END;
             IF KEY=0 THEN DO;           /* IF KEY=0, IT IS PRIME */
                         PUT LIST(IT);
                         KOUNT = KOUNT + 1;
                     END;
         END;
         END PRIMES;
```

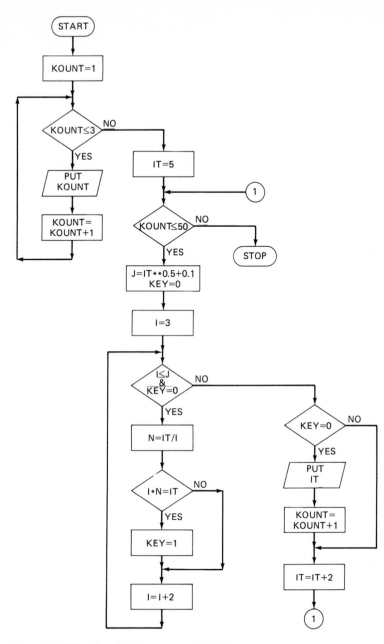

Figure 12.3 Flowchart for the program PRIMES.

1	2	3	5	7
11	13	17	19	23
29	31	37	41	43
47	53	59	61	67
71	73	79	83	89
97	101	103	107	109
113	127	131	137	139
149	151	157	163	167
173	179	181	191	193
197	199	211	223	227

Observe that in the program PRIMES we used for convenience the DO with a control variable, which is a special case of the DO WHILE.

The preceding example illustrates the method of the structured flowchart. It is the same approach as followed in the previous chapters, except that in the construction of the flowchart extra care is exercised in limiting the flowchart exclusively to the three basic elements, that is, sequence, selection, and repetition.

B N-S Charts

A chart which leads directly to a structured program has been suggested by I. Nassi and B. Schneiderman.[1] (A similar chart has been introduced by N. Chapin.[2]) Such a chart is known as an N-S chart. The chart has just three symbols, for the portrayal of simple IF-THEN-ELSE and DO WHILE statements

Figure 12.4 shows the symbols of the N-S chart. The symbols for the simple sequence are just boxes placed below one another, without any arrows. Similarly, the symbol for the IF-THEN-ELSE is a boxed triangle, where the IF-part triangle separates the THEN clause from the ELSE clause. The symbol for the DO delineates the body of the DO. The N-S chart is a succession of these symbols. We will illustrate the correspondence between the N-S chart and program segments by examples.

Example 12.3.2 Construct the N-S chart for the program segment

[1]I. Nassi and B. Shneiderman, Flowchart Techniques for Structured Programming, *SIGPLAN Notices,* vol. 8, no. 8, pp. 12–26, August 1973.

[2]N. Chapin, New Format for Flowcharts, ''Software-Practice and Experience,'' vol. 4, pp. 341–357, Wiley, New York, 1974.

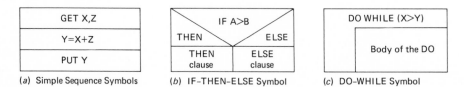

(*a*) Simple Sequence Symbols   (*b*) IF–THEN–ELSE Symbol   (*c*) DO–WHILE Symbol

Figure 12.4 Symbols for the N-S chart: (*a*) simple sequence symbols; (*b*) IF-THEN-ELSE symbol; (*c*) DO-WHILE symbol.

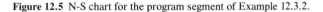

GET A,B		
IF A<B		
THEN		ELSE
C=A+B		
D=2*C+A		C=A−B
PUT D,C		
X=C−A		

Figure 12.5 N-S chart for the program segment of Example 12.3.2.

```
GET LIST (A,B);
IF A < B THEN DO;
              C=A+B;
              D=2*C+A;
         •    PUT LIST (D,C);
          END;
      ELSE C=A−B;
  X=C−A;
```

Solution The desired N-S chart is shown in Fig. 12.5. Observe again that the IF divides the chart into two parts corresponding to the THEN and the ELSE clauses. Note further that the box with X=C−A; occupies the entire width of the chart, indicating that this statement is executed after the completion of either the THEN path or the ELSE path.

Example 12.3.3 Construct the N-S chart for the program segment

```
X=  A+B;
DO  WHILE(X>0);
     Y=X+1;
     IF Y=2*B THEN Z=Y−2;
     X=X−1;
  END;
  V=U−2;
```

Solution The desired chart is shown in Fig. 12.6. Note that the ELSE path has no statements; that is, it is a null ELSE. Such a path is portrayed on the chart as the NULL statement as shown. Observe also how the statements inside the DO WHILE are bordered by the DO WHILE symbol, whereas the statement outside the DO WHILE (that is, V=U−2) occupies the entire width of the chart.

Example 12.3.4 Construct the N-S chart for the program PRIMES of Example 12.3.1.

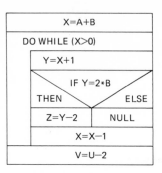

Figure 12.6 N-S chart for the program segment of Example 12.3.3.

Solution The desired chart is portrayed in Fig. 12.7. Observe the compactness of the chart. Note also that the chart results in a structured program, because only the three basic symbols are used for the chart construction. Note that the DO with the control variable (that is, DO KOUNT = 1 TO 3), which is a special case of the DO WHILE, is representable with the same symbol as the DO WHILE.

Example 12.3.5 Write a structured program for the printout of the first 30 Fibonacci numbers.

Remark: Fibonacci numbers are the integers

$$1, 1, 2, 3, 5, 8, 13, \ldots$$

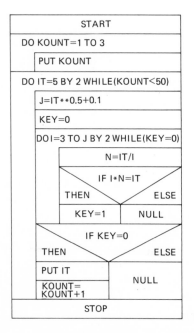

Figure 12.7 N-S chart for the program PRIMES.

START		
FIRST,SECOND=1		
KOUNT=2		
PUT FIRST,SECOND		
DO KOUNT=3 TO 30		
	LAST=FIRST+SECOND	
	PUT LAST	
	FIRST=SECOND	
	SECOND=LAST	
STOP		

Figure 12.8 N-S chart for the problem of Example 12.3.5.

Thus the first and the second numbers are both 1, and each succeeding number equals the sum of the two preceding numbers.

Solution Evidently, we must do the following:

1. Print out 1 as the first number and 1 as the second number.
2. Introduce the variables KOUNT (for counting the Fibonacci numbers) and FIRST, SECOND, and LAST (for calculating the Fibonacci numbers).

With these choices the N-S chart for the program is as shown in Fig. 12.8. The structured program following from this chart is named FIB and is shown with the resulting output:

```
FIB:  PROC OPTIONS(MAIN);
      DCL (FIRST, SECOND, LAST) FIXED BIN(31);
      FIRST, SECOND = 1;
      KOUNT = 2;
      PUT LIST(FIRST,SECOND);
      DO KOUNT=3 TO 30;
         LAST = FIRST + SECOND;
         PUT LIST(LAST);
         FIRST = SECOND;
         SECOND = LAST;
      END;
      END FIB;
```

1	1	2	3	5
8	13	21	34	55
89	144	233	377	610
987	1597	2584	4181	6765
10946	17711	28657	46368	75025
121393	196418	317811	514229	832040

The symbol of Fig. 12.4a may also stand for a process (just like the box in the conventional flowchart), requiring a separate N-S chart. Thus a complicated program may be represented by a summarizing N-S chart, with each symbol representing another N-S chart. This is analogous to the conventional flowchart where a box representing process is separately portrayed by its own flowchart.

C Pseudocode

The third method for constructing a structured program uses pseudocode. The pseudocode is a program written in a mixture of English and PL/I. Refinements of the code eliminate the English part and substitute PL/I. As before, only the three basic types of statements are allowed for either the initial PL/I statements or the substitution of the English statements. We will illustrate the method by an example.

Example 12.3.6 Write a pseudocode for the printout of the first 30 Fibonacci numbers.

Solution The pseudocode reflects our solution to the problem. Thus the pseudocode for the Fibonacci numbers may be

```
Initialize for the first two numbers, FIRST and SECOND;
Print 1, FIRST, 2, SECOND;
DO KOUNT = 3 TO 30;
    Calculate LAST;
    Print KOUNT, LAST;
    Update FIRST, SECOND;
END;
```

Further refinements lead directly to the program FIB.

In the next chapter will will discuss more extensively the method of the pseudocode as a major tool in program design.

12.4 SUMMARY

We described the reasons for the interest in structured programming. We illustrated how to construct structured programs with either structured flowcharts, N-S charts, or pseudocode.

12.5 FURTHER READING

Structured programming is still a developing field, and we list several additional references for further reading.

Aron, J. D.: "The Program Development Process," part 1, Addison-Wesley, Reading, MA, 1975.

Dahl, O. J., E. W. Dijkstra, and C. A. R. Hoare: "Structured Programming," Academic London, 1972.

Donaldson, J. R.: Structured Programming, *Datamation,* vol. 19, no. 12, pp. 52–54, December 1973.

Hughes, J. K., and J. I. Michtom: "A Structured Approach to Programming," Prentice-Hall, Englewood Cliffs, NJ, 1977.

Knuth, D. E.: Structured Programming with GO TO Statements, *Comput. Surv.,* vol. 6, no. 4, pp. 261–301, December 1975.

Marcotty, M.: "Structured Programming with PL/I," Prentice-Hall, Englewood Cliffs, NJ, 1977.

McClure, C. L.: Top-Down, Bottom-Up and Structured Programming, *Proc. First Natl. Conf. Software Eng.,* pp. 89–94, September 1975.

McCracken, D. D.: Revolution in Programming: An Overview, *Datamation,* vol. 19, no. 12, pp. 50–52, December 1973.

McGowen, C. L., and J. R. Kelly: "Top-Down Structured Programming," Petrocelli/Charter, New York, 1975.

Miller, E. F., and G. E. Lindamood: Structured Programming: Top-Down Approach, *Datamation,* vol. 19, no. 12, pp. 55–57, December 1973.

Mills, H. D.: Mathematical Foundations for Structured Programming, *IBM Rep.* FSC 72-6012, February 1972.

Mills, H.: Top-Down Programming in Large Systems, in R. Rustin (ed.), "Debugging Techniques in Large Systems," pp. 41–55. Prentice-Hall, Englewood Cliffs, NJ, 1971.

Shortt, J., and T. C. Wilson: "Problem Solving and the Computer: A Structured Concept with PL/I (PL/C)," Addison-Wesley, Reading, MA., 1976.

Weinberg, G., N. Yasukawa, and R. Marcus: "Structured Programming in PL/C," Wiley, New York, 1973.

Witt, J.: The Columbus Approach, *Proc. First Natl. Conf. Software Eng.,* pp. 14–20, September 1975.

Yohe, J. M.: An Overview of Programming Practices, *Comput. Surv.,* vol. 6, no. 4, pp. 221–245, December 1975.

Yourdan, E.: "Techniques of Program Structure and Design," Prentice-Hall, Englewood Cliffs, NJ, 1975.

PROBLEMS

12.1 Construct N-S charts for (*a*) Prob. 6.10, (*b*) Prob. 6.11, (*c*) Prob. 6.12.

12.2 Construct N-S charts for (*a*) Prob. 6.14, (*b*) Prob. 6.15, (*c*) Prob. 6.16.

12.3 Construct N-S charts for (*a*) Prob. 6.18, (*b*) Prob. 6.19.

12.4 Construct N-S charts and write structured programs for (*a*) Prob. 9.4, (*b*) Prob. 9.5.

12.5 Construct an N-S chart for a program segment performing the same function as the flowchart of Fig. P10.2

12.6 Convert the flowchart of Fig. 12.2 to a structured one.

12.7 Given four pairs of numbers. Each pair represents the *x, y* coordinates of a point. We wish to determine if the points form a square. Write a structured program to do so. Your output should be one of two messages: SQUARE or NO SQUARE. Construct test data to test your program.

13

DESIGN OF STRUCTURED PROGRAMS

In Chap. 2 we described the four steps of problem solving. We will address ourselves again to the topic of problem solving, but now we want our solution to be in the form of a structured program. We will describe here a technique for obtaining such a solution and illustrate this technique with three examples.

13.1 THE PHASES OF PROGRAM DESIGN

In Chap. 2 we described the four steps of problem solving as

1. Understanding the problem
2. Devising a plan of solution
3. Carrying out the plan
4. Examining the solution

Our present approach to problem solving is still the same. We will focus here on the second step, with the added requirement that the solution be in the form of a structured program.

We will divide the second step into three phases:

2 *a*. Devise a gross plan of solution.
   b. State the solution in pseudocode, that is, part English, part PL/I.
   c. Refine the plan until the English part is completely eliminated. Use only program constructions allowable in structured programming.

As can be seen the initial plan is a gross plan, allowing ambiguities. This plan is equally good for solving a whole family or a set of related problems. To solve our specific problem, we must refine it by adding more details. These details remove ambiguities and thus shrink the size of the set. In the plan these details are evidenced in two ways: (1) in the expansion of the pseudocode and (2) in the substitution of PL/I for English. Eventually, through successive refinements, the size of the set reduces to a single member, this being the particular solution to our specific problem. When this happens, the English part of the pseudocode vanishes, being completely replaced by structured PL/I code.

As an illustration consider the pseudocode

> obtain input;
> process input into output;
> print output;

which is a gross solution to nearly every possible problem. Nothing is said here about either input, the process, or the output. To solve a specific problem, details must be supplied on the form of the input, on the required processing, and on the desired display of the output. As we fill in the details, we refine the problem and obtain a new version of the solution. The final version is the solution in the desired form of a structured program.

The systematic application of stepwise refinements is known as *top-down structured programming*. The only way to describe it is by examples. We will do so with three such examples.

13.2 ILLUSTRATIVE EXAMPLE: FINDING THE SUM OF THE FIRST FIFTY POSITIVE NUMBERS

Up to now when we gave an example we just presented the program as a solution. We did not describe the train of thought that culminated in the completed program. We will do so here with a relatively simple example.

Example 13.2.1 Find the sum of the first 50 positive numbers on data cards.

Solution Evidently, the first possible version of solution is the problem statement itself, that is,

VERSION 1

> Start fifty;
> Obtain the sum of the first 50 positive numbers;
> END FIFTY;

Observe that we use lowercase letters for English and capital letters for PL/I.

We have solved a sufficient number of such problems to know that we must have a variable to store the sum. We also need a variable to hold the number obtained from data cards. Naming these variables TOTAL and NUMBER, respectively, we obtain the second version.

VERSION 2

```
Start fifty;
/*OBTAIN THE SUM OF THE FIRST 50 POSITIVE NUMBERS*/
DO for the first 50 positive numbers;
    GET LIST (NUMBER);
    IF NUMBER > 0 THEN add it to TOTAL;
    /*TOTAL STORES THE SUM*/
END;
PUT LIST (TOTAL);
END FIFTY;
```

indicates our train of thought in the solution of this problem. Observe that we keep the first version in a form of comment. This is the recommended procedure because it leads to a natural documentation which reflects our actual thinking in the solution process.

An examination of the psuedocode of version 2 reveals that we still must do the following:

1. Initialize TOTAL to zero.
2. Introduce the variable COUNT which counts the positive numbers.

We must also initialize COUNT to zero. These two changes result in the third version:

VERSION 3

```
Start fifty;
/*OBTAIN THE SUM OF THE FIRST 50 POSITIVE NUMBERS*/
Initialize TOTAL and COUNT;
/*TOTAL STORES THE SUM,
  COUNT COUNTS THE POSITIVE NUMBERS*/
DO WHILE (COUNT < 50);
    GET LIST (NUMBER);
    IF NUMBER > 0 THEN DO;
                            TOTAL = TOTAL + NUMBER;
                            COUNT = COUNT + 1;
                        END;
END;
PUT LIST (TOTAL);
END FIFTY;
```

Now the program is nearly complete. We must just initialize TOTAL and COUNT to zero. We also want NUMBER to be float and COUNT to be fixed. With these changes we obtain

VERSION 4

```
FIFTY:   PROC OPTIONS(MAIN);
         /* OBTAIN THE SUM OF THE FIRST 50 POSITIVE NUMBERS */
         DCL NUMBER FLOAT, COUNT FIXED, TOTAL;
         /* TOTAL STORES THE SUM, COUNT COUNTS THE POSITIVE NUMBERS */
         /* INITIALIZE TOTAL AND COUNT */
         TOTAL,COUNT = 0;
         DO WHILE (COUNT<50);
            GET LIST(NUMBER);
            IF NUMBER>0 THEN DO;
                               TOTAL = TOTAL + NUMBER;
                               COUNT = COUNT + 1;
                            END;
         END;
         PUT LIST(TOTAL);
         END FIFTY;
```

Observe that we introduced all variables in the declaration, which constitutes good practice.

The program works, but it of course assumes that there are 50 positive numbers. What happens if there are no 50 positive numbers? The program will never execute the PUT LIST statement and stop when there either is no more data or the allotted time is exceeded.

We illustrated the thought process that leads to the desired structured program. Observe that the program evolved through four versions, with each later version being a refinement of the previous one. Note also that as a by-product the documentation evolved in a natural manner.

In this problem the form of input was specified. If we could select the form of input—as is usual in most problems—would we simplify the program? Apparently not. Is the output in a good form? We could list all the numbers processed and title our output. But such cosmetic refinement is really not necessary here. So we conclude that the program is satisfactory.

13.3 ILLUSTRATIVE EXAMPLE: FINDING THE FIRST FIFTY PRIME NUMBERS

We will now trace the steps in the design of the program in Example 12.3.1. In that Example we explained the solution; here we will follow the thoughts that led to this solution.

Example 13.3.1 Print out the first 50 prime numbers.

Solution Again, as in the preceding example, the first version is the problem statement itself, that is,

VERSION 1

```
Start primes;
Print out the first 50 primes;
END PRIMES;
```

Let us now trace the thoughts leading to the next version. We want to expand

```
Print out the first 50 primes;
```

into a more detailed description. Obviously, before we can print the primes, we must first find them. There is a pool of candidates for primes, and those that meet a test for primeness are printed out. What are the primes? The integers 1, 2, and all the other candidates which satisfy the test. We do not test 1 and 2; hence these two numbers receive the special treatment of just being printed out. We will then test all the candidates starting with the first candidate. It is now clear how to expand ''Print out the first 50 primes.'' This expansion is

```
Provide special treatment for the first 2 primes, 1 and 2;
Select a pool of candidates for primes;
Select first candidate for test;
DO till the 50th prime is printed out;
      If the candidate is prime, then print it;
      Obtain next candidate;
END;
```

which results in the second version.

VERSION 2

```
Start primes;
/*PRINT OUT THE FIRST 50 PRIMES*/
Provide special treatment for the first 2 primes, 1 and 2;
Select a pool of candidates for primes;
Select first candidate for test;
DO till the 50th prime is printed out;
      If the candidate is prime, then print it;
      Obtain next candidate;
END;
END PRIMES;
```

Version 2 is considerably more detailed than version 1—and it reflects our thinking at this point. Observe that we are still telling *what to do,* rather than *how to do,* and using English for our description. The final version will be in pure PL/I, and will tell how to do. Thus, the versions can be viewed as gradual transformations from *what* to *how.*

The next version must incorporate several refinements. First, we must tell what the special treatment for the first two primes is: It is simply

Print the first 2 primes: 1 and 2;

Next we must select a pool of candidates for primes. These are the odd numbers from 3 on. By selecting the first candidate for test and giving the rule for obtaining the next candidate (in the DO loop), we are in fact selecting the pool. The first candidate is 3 and the rule is: Obtain the next odd integer. Now comes the test. We know than an integer N is prime if it is not divisible by 2, 3, 4,..., $N - 1$. For an odd integer N we can say that N is prime if it is not divisible by 3,5,7,..., $N - 2$. But this last statement is valid only for odd integers exceeding 3, so again we shall print out 3 separately and test odd integers starting with 5. With these refinements, the third version becomes

VERSION 3

```
Start primes;
/*PRINT OUT THE FIRST 50 PRIMES*/
Print the first 3 primes: 1,2, and 3;
Candidate for test = 5;
DO till the 50th prime is printed out;
    IF the candidate does not divide by 3,5, . . . , candidate−2 without
        remainder, then print out the candidate;
    Candidate = next odd integer;
END;
END PRIMES;
```

Observe that in this version we started describing *how* to do it. We tell *how* to select the first candidate, *how* to test for primeness, and *how* to select the next candidate. Now we just need to select variable names and to describe the various operations in PL/I rather than in English.

Selection of the First Candidate

Let us name the odd integer tested for primeness (that is, the candidate for test) as IT. Then clearly

Candidate for test = 5;

translates into the PL/I statement

IT = 5;

Test for Primeness

We will put down our thinking in development of the test. This test must reveal whether or not IT divides by 3,5,..., IT−2 without a remainder. Evidently if IT divides by I without a remainder then N defined by

$$N = IT/I;$$

loses no fractional part through truncation to an integer. We need another variable to tell us whether or not IT is divided without a remainder for any of the values of I. Let us name this variable KEY. Then in

```
KEY = 0;
DO I = 3 TO IT−2 BY 2;
    N = IT/I;
    IF N*I = IT THEN KEY = 1;
END;
```

the value of KEY tells us about the primeness of IT. If KEY = 0, none of the values of I are divided by IT and IT is prime.

Let us reconsider the just-developed test before we substitute it for the English text in the third version. We can see one flaw—the test continues even after we determined that IT is not prime, that is, even after we changed KEY to 1. This deficiency is easily corrected by adding a WHILE clause to the DO statement as in

```
KEY = 0;
DO I = 3 TO IT−2 BY 2 WHILE (KEY = 0);
    N = IT/I;
    IF N*I = IT THEN KEY = 1;
END;
```

where we stop testing and leave the loop once we discover that IT is not prime.

Let us again study the test. We may ask if IT must in fact be tested by all the values of I from 3 to IT − 2. Let us consider a numerical example, such as 39. The number 39 has factors 3 and 13. But we do not need to test to see if 13 is a factor. It suffices to test for factors up to $\sqrt{IT}$. If one factor exceeds $\sqrt{IT}$, then the second factor is smaller than $\sqrt{IT}$. Hence, the test can be restated as

```
J = IT**0.5;
KEY = 0;
DO I = 3 TO J BY 2 WHILE (KEY = 0);
    N = IT/I;
    IF N*I = IT THEN KEY = 1;
END;
```

As we again reread the test, we see no further faults. So we proceed to the next item.

Selection of the Next Candidate

We will replace

$$\text{candidate} = \text{next odd integer};$$

by its PL/I equivalent, which is

$$IT = IT+2;$$

With these three refinements, and the PL/I procedure statement, the next version becomes

VERSION 4

```
PRIMES: PROC OPTIONS(MAIN);
        /*PRINT OUT THE FIRST 50 PRIMES*/
        Print out the first 3 primes: 1,2, and 3;
        IT = 5; /*CANDIDATE FOR TEST      */
        DO till the 50th prime is printed out;
            /*TEST FOR PRIMENESS          */
            J = IT**0.5;
            KEY = 0;
            DO I = 3 TO J BY 2 WHILE (KEY = 0);
                N = IT/I;
                IF N*I = IT THEN KEY = 1;
            END;
        IF KEY = 0 THEN print out IT;
        IT = IT + 2; /*NEXT ODD INTEGER*/
        END;
        END PRIMES;
```

This version is mostly in PL/I, but still additional refinements are needed. To stop after printing the fiftieth prime, we must count the primes as we print them. Let us name the variable for such count as KOUNT, then after printing the first three primes, we need the initializing statement

KOUNT = 3;

The statement

DO till the 50th prime is printed out;

becomes

DO WHILE (KOUNT <= 50);

and after printing IT we must increment KOUNT by 1, with

KOUNT = KOUNT + 1;

Incorporation of the above three PL/I statements results in the next version.

VERSION 5

```
PRIMES: PROC OPTIONS (MAIN);
        /*PRINT OUT THE FIRST 50 PRIMES           */
        Print the first 3 primes: 1,2, and 3;
        KOUNT = 3; /*KOUNT COUNTS THE PRIMES*/
        IT = 5;       /*CANDIDATE FOR TEST         */
        DO WHILE (KOUNT <= 50);
            /*TEST FOR PRIMENESS                   */
```

```
J = IT** 0.5;
KEY = 0;
DO I = 3 TO J BY 2 WHILE (KEY = 0);
    N = IT/I;
    IF N*I = IT THEN KEY = 1;
END;
IF KEY = 0 THEN DO;/*IF KEY = 0, IT IS PRIME*/
                    Print out IT;
                    KOUNT = KOUNT + 1;
                  END;
IT = IT+2;              /*NEXT ODD INTEGER   */
END;
END PRIMES;
```

The fifth version has very little English left. We need only an output statement. With this addition the program becomes

VERSION 6

```
PRIMES:    PROC OPTIONS(MAIN);
           /* PRINT OUT THE FIRST 50 PRIMES                      */
           /* PRINT THE FIRST 3 PRIMES: 1, 2, AND 3              */
           DO KOUNT=1 TO 3;                /* KOUNT COUNTS PRIMES    */
               PUT LIST(KOUNT);
           END;
           IT = 5;                         /* CANDIDATE FOR TEST     */
           DO WHILE(KOUNT<=50);
           /* TEST FOR PRIMENESS                                 */
               J = IT**0.5 + 0.1;
               KEY = 0;
               DO I=3 TO J BY 2 WHILE(KEY=0);
                   N = IT/I;                /* IF IT DIVIDES BY I,    */
                   IF I*N=IT THEN KEY=1;    /* THEN N=I*N             */
               END;
               IF KEY=0 THEN DO;           /* IF KEY=0, IT IS PRIME  */
                           PUT LIST(IT);
                           KOUNT = KOUNT + 1;
                         END;
               IT = IT + 2;                /* NEXT ODD INTEGER       */
           END;
           END PRIMES;
```

and gives the output

1	2	3	5	7
11	13	17	19	23
29	31	37	41	43
47	53	59	61	67
71	73	79	83	89
97	101	103	107	109
113	127	131	137	139
149	151	157	163	167
173	179	181	191	193
197	199	211	223	227

As explained in Sec. 12.3, we add 0.1 to IT**0.5 because exponentiation by a fraction is approximate and a roundoff error may occur.

We have now a structured program. We may still ask whether the program can be simplified. We are initializing IT with IT = 5; and incrementing IT with IT = IT + 2; we can do these tasks by replacing the DO WHILE statement with

DO IT = 5 BY 2 WHILE (KOUNT <= 50);

These changes result in the final (that is, seventh) version of the program PRIMES, obtained in Sec. 12.3.

Let us reconsider how we arrived at the desired program so as to focus on the illustrated technique of program development.

Version 1	We just stated the problem, that is, said what to do.
Version 2	A more detailed statement of the problem. The first version was kept as a comment.
Version 3	Here we had the solution in English prose. The solution required some backtracking in that the special treatment accorded to the first two primes (that is, for 1 and 2) in the first version was found to be needed also for the third prime (that is, for 3).
Version 4	Here we translated the solution from English into PL/I but used the English prose as comments. We still left the output requests in English.
Version 5	We translated nearly all English into PL/I but made no choice as yet on the form of output.
Version 6	We decided how the output was to be displayed and translated the remaining English into PL/I.
Version 7	We reconsidered the program of version 6 for a possible simplification. With the simplification our task was completed and we obtained the desired structured program.

Observe again the natural manner in which the documentation was achieved. The documentation follows effortlessly from version to version rather than as an afterthought tacked on a completed program.

13.4 ILLUSTRATIVE EXAMPLE: PROCESSING OF NUMBERS

We will now illustrate the design of a program to process numbers on data cards as follows:

1. Each number in the odd position is to be rounded off to an integer and printed.
2. Each number in the even position is to be truncated to an integer and printed.
3. The last number is zero and is to be used to stop the program. There are three other zeros in the data. These four zeros are not to be included in the printout.

We start the design with the first version, this being the problem statement itself, that is,

VERSION 1

    Start processing;
    GET input;
    Round off a nonzero number in the odd position to an integer;
    Truncate a nonzero number in the even position to an integer;
    Print integer;
    Continue until fourth zero is obtained;
    END PROCESS;

We must now invent a method of solution. How would we do it without a computer? First we will establish a record of zeros. Let KOUNTZ be the name of the variable for counting zeros. How would we round off? We would inspect the number and see whether the fractional part is 0.5 or higher. How would we truncate? We will ignore the fractional part. Hence, the second version may read

VERSION 2

    Start processing;
    Initialize KOUNTZ to zero;
    DO WHILE (KOUNTZ < 4);
        GET input;
        If input = 0, increase KOUNTZ by one;
        /* ROUND OFF A NONZERO NUMBER IN THE ODD POSITION
            TO AN INTEGER*/
        If input is in the odd position and fractional part is 0.5 or larger,
            replace the input by the next higher integer. Otherwise re-
            place the input by the smaller integer;
        /* TRUNCATE A NONZERO NUMBER IN THE EVEN POSITION
            TO AN INTEGER*/
        If the input is in the even position, delete the fractional part;
        Print the integer if the input is nonzero;
    END;
    END PROCESS;

This version is still somewhat ambiguous, but it reflects our thoughts at this point. We must add further details. First let us choose some more variable names. Let

$$A = \text{input number}$$
$$N = \text{integer obtained from } A$$
$$POS = \text{position}$$

Then a possible roundoff statement is

$$N = A + 0.5;$$

but such a roundoff is only valid for positive A. For a negative A, as for -7.63, for example, the roundoff must be to -8 which is achieved by subtracting -0.5. Note that in version 2 we suggested an incorrect roundoff for a negative input. Errors in early versions can be tolerated, but the later versions must critically reexamine the suggested algorithms. Here, for example, we must replace the roundoff by

```
IF A > 0 THEN N = A + 0.5;
     ELSE  N = A − 0.5;
```

The truncation is simply

```
N = A;
```

which leads to the third version as

VERSION 3

```
PROCESS: PROC OPTIONS (MAIN);
          KOUNTZ = 0; /*INITIALIZATION                              */
          DO WHILE (KOUNTZ < 4);
              GET LIST (A);
              IF A = 0, THEN KOUNTZ = KOUNTZ + 1;
                      /*ROUND OFF A NONZERO NUMBER IN
                        THE ODD POSITION TO AN INTEGER  */
                    ELSE IF POS = odd THEN DO;
                        IF A > 0 THEN N = A + 0.5;
                            ELSE N = A − 0.5;
                                    END;
                      /*TRUNCATE A NONZERO NUMBER IN
                        THE EVEN POSITION TO AN INTEGER*/
                            ELSE N = A;
              IF A ¬ = 0 THEN PUT LIST (N);
          END;
          END PROCESS;
```

It remains only to determine the position. We really do not care to know the actual position, but only whether it is even or odd. We will be satisfied if POS had just two values, 1 for odd and 2 for even. Each time we process a number we change POS from 1 to 2, and vice versa. To do so we change the DO WHILE loop to

```
DO WHILE (KOUNTZ < 4);
    GET LIST (A);
    IF A = 0 THEN DO;
                    KOUNT = KOUNTZ + 1;
                    IF POS =1 THEN POS = 2;
                            ELSE POS = 1;
              END;
              /* ROUND OFF A NONZERO NUMBER IN
                THE ODD POSITION TO AN INTEGER*/
```

```
                        ELSE IF POS = 1 THEN DO;
                            IF A > 0 THEN N = A + 0.5;
                                    ELSE N = A − 0.5;
                        POS = 2:
                                END;
                    /* TRUNCATE A NONZERO NUMBER IN THE EVEN
                    POSITION TO AN INTEGER*/
                                ELSE DO;
                                        N = A;
                                        POS = 1;
                                    END;
                    IF A ¬ = 0  THEN PUT LIST (N);
                END;
```

This leads to the fourth version as

VERSION 4

```
PROCESS: PROC OPTIONS(MAIN);
        KOUNTZ = 0;                                    /* INITIALIZATION   */
        POS = 1;                                       /* INITIALIZATION   */
        DO WHILE(KOUNTZ<4);
            GET LIST(A);
            IF A=0 THEN DO;
                        KOUNTZ = KOUNTZ + 1;
                        IF POS=1 THEN POS = 2;
                                ELSE POS = 1;
                    END;
            /* ROUND OFF A NONZERO NUMBER IN THE ODD POSITION TO
                                                AN INTEGER */
            ELSE IF POS=1 THEN DO;
                            IF A>0 THEN N = A + 0.5;
                                    ELSE N = A − 0.5;
                            POS = 2;
                        END;
            /* TRUNCATE A NONZERO NUMBER IN THE EVEN POSITION TO
                                                AN INTEGER */
                        ELSE DO;
                                N = A;
                                POS = 1;
                            END;
            IF A¬=0 THEN PUT LIST(N);
        END;
        END PROCESS;
```

Let us inspect this program with respect to two questions:

1. Is it clear?
2. Can the program be improved?

The answer to both questions is yes. The program is clear, but it can be improved. For one, the changing of position can be performed once, at the end. And by inverting the test for zero, the program can be streamlined. With these changes the fifth and final version becomes

VERSION 5

```
PROCESS: PROC OPTIONS(MAIN);
        KOUNTZ = 0;                              /* INITIALIZATION  */
        POS = 1;                                 /* INITIALIZATION  */
        DO WHILE(KOUNTZ<4);
           GET LIST(A);
           IF A¬=0 THEN DO;
                        /* ROUND OFF A NONZERO NUMBER IN THE ODD */
                        /* POSITION TO AN INTEGER                */
                        IF POS=1 THEN IF A>0 THEN N = A + 0.5;
                                          ELSE N = A - 0.5;
                        /* TRUNCATE A NONZERO NUMBER IN THE EVEN */
                        /* POSITION TO AN INTEGER                */
                                    ELSE N = A;
                        PUT LIST(N);
                     END;
                 ELSE KOUNTZ = KOUNTZ + 1;
        IF POS=1 THEN POS = 2;
              ELSE POS = 1;
        END;
        END PROCESS;
```

As an illustration, the last two programs with the input

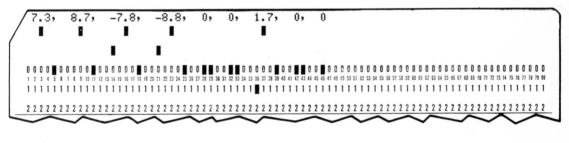

gave the output

7   8   -8   -8   2

Again observe the documentation which evolved as we went from version to version.

13.5 SUMMARY

We described here how to go about obtaining a structured program which solves a given problem. The method consists of a description of the evolution in our thinking as we add improvements to our initial solution. In this evolution we translate from English prose into PL/I, with the final version being the desired structured program.

13.6. FURTHER READING

Eleven references are listed below for further reading on the topic of top-down structured program design.

Cheng, L. L.: "Some Case Studies in Structured Programming," *MITRE Tech. Rep.* MTR-2647 VI, June 1973, the MITRE Corp., Bedford, MA.

Conway, R., and D. Gries: "An Introduction to Programming," 2d ed., pt. III, Winthrop Publishers, Cambridge, MA., 1975.

——— and ———: "Primer on Structured Programming," pts. II and III, Winthrop Publishers, Cambrindge, MA., 1976.

Dijkstra, E. W.: "A Discipline of Programming," Prentice-Hall, Englewood Cliffs, NJ, 1976.

Henderson, P., and R. Snowdon: An Experiment in Structured Programming, BIT 12, pp. 38–53, 1972.

Hughes, J. K., and J. I. Michtom: "A Structured Approach to Programming," Prentice-Hall, Englewood Cliffs, NJ, 1977.

Kieburtz, R. B.: "Structured Programming and Problem Solving with PL/I," Prentice-Hall, Englewood Cliffs, NJ, 1977.

McGowan, C. L., and J. R. Kelly: "Top-Down Structured Programming," Petrocelli/Charter, New York, 1975.

Wirth, N.: "On the Composition of Well Structured Programs," *Comput. Surv.,* vol. 6, no. 4, pp. 247–259, December 1974.

———: "Systematic Programming: An Introduction," Prentice-Hall, Englewood Cliffs, NJ, 1973.

Yourdan, E.: "Techniques of Program Structure and Design," Prentice-Hall, Englewood Cliffs, NJ, 1975.

PROBLEMS

13.1 Using stepwise refinements, construct programs for (*a*) Prob. 6.10, (*b*) Prob. 6.11, (*c*) Prob. 6.12.

13.2 Using stepwise refinements, construct programs for (*a*) Prob. 6.13, (*b*) Prob. 6.15, (*c*) Prob. 6.16.

13.3. Using stepwise refinements, construct programs for (*a*) Prob. 6.20, (*b*) Prob. 9.5.

13.4 There are several positive integers on data cards. No number exceeds 100. Print out each number and all its divisors. If the number is prime, print out the number with the description PRIME NUMBER. Use stepwise refinements to obtain the program.

The data are

$$64, 81, 17, 23, 29, 82, 12, 36, 70$$

13.5 Fixed-composition resistors used in electric circuits can be purchased only in standard values. For resistors having 20 percent tolerance, these values (measured in ohms) are

$$10, 15, 22, 33, 47, 68, 100$$

or with a decimal multiplier (divider) for larger (smaller) values.

The data cards contain numbers between 10 and 1000 inclusive. Obtain and print each number and the nearest standard resistor value. Provide two columns for your output and title each column appropriately. The program execution should stop upon finding a zero in the data. (The zero should not be processed.)

The data are

$$17.5, 184, 35, 22.2, 68, 283, 492, 712, 0$$

Obtain your program through stepwise refinements.

13.6 Given three pairs of numbers. Each pair represents the x, y coordinates of a point. We wish to determine if the points form a triangle and if so, which one. Obtain your program through stepwise refinements. Your output should be one of the following messages:

NO TRIANGLE
EQUILATERAL TRIANGLE
ISOSCELES TRIANGLE
PYTHAGOREAN TRIANGLE   (that is, with a 90° angle)
ACUTE TRIANGLE   (that is, each angle is less than 90°)
OBTUSE TRIANGLE   (that is, one angle exceeds 90°)

Construct the test data to test your program.

13.7 Given four pairs of numbers. Each pair represents the x, y coordinates of a point. We wish to determine if a connected sequence of the points (with the last point connected to the first point) forms a quadrilateral, and if so, which one. Obtain your program through stepwise refinements. Your output should be one of the following messages:

NO QUADRILATERAL
PARALLELOGRAM   (includes rhombus)
RECTANGLE   (includes square)
TRAPEZOID
QUADRILATERAL

Construct the test data to test your program.

14 PROCESSING OF ARITHMETIC DATA

We will now describe the workings of the PL/I compiler in processing numbers. In particular, we will describe the order in handling arithmetic expressions, the processing of input data, and the operations on numbers with mixed attributes.

We can give two reasons for reading the contents of this chapter. First, by knowing how arithmetic expressions are evaluated, we can eliminate redundant parentheses and thus simplify the writing of such expressions. Second, by knowing how numbers with different attributes are handled, we will know how to specify numbers so as to prevent inaccuracies and unnecessary (and costly) computer operations.

14.1 ORDER OF EVALUATION OF EXPRESSIONS

To motivate this section consider the following question. What value is assigned by the statement

$$I = 5+3*6/2*5;$$

to the variable I?

To answer this question, we must know the order in which the numbers are calculated and the priorities of the arithmetic operations. The arithmetic and logical priorities are

1. **   prefix +   prefix −
2. *   /
3. infix +   infix −
4. <   ¬<   <=   =   ¬=   >=   >   ¬>
5. &
6. |

The first category denotes operation of the highest priority, the sixth category, the lowest one. A prefix operator is the sign in front of a number, as in

$$-3.1 \quad \text{or} \quad +4.7$$

An infix operator is the operator in between numbers. Thus, infix $+$ is addition, infix $-$ is subtraction. In $3 + 5$, for example, the $+$ sign is an infix operator.

The order in which an expression is evaluated is subject to the following three rules:

1. An operation of higher priority is performed before the operation of lower priority. For example, in calculating

$$1+4*2**3$$

2**3 is calculated first, since exponentiation is of highest priority. At this point, the expression is

$$1 + 4*8$$

and the multiplication 4*8 is calculated next, giving

$$1 + 32$$

from which the result of 33 follows.

2. Operations of the same priority are evaluated from right to left for the highest priority (that is, for **, prefix $+$, prefix $-$) and from left to right for all other priorities. For example, in calculating the value for I in

$$I = 5+3*6/2*5;$$

the expression on the right side is evaluated left to right as shown:

$$5+\underbrace{3*6}_{1}/2*5$$

where numbered braces indicate the order of operations, these being

1. $3*6 = 18$
2. $18/2 = 9$
3. $9*5 = 45$
4. $5 + 45 = 50$

Thus the number 50 is assigned to I. As a second example, consider the expression

$$3**2**3$$

This expression is perhaps ambiguous to us but not to the computer. The computer will evaluate it in the order

$$3**\underbrace{2**3}_{1}$$

2**3 is obtained first because the order of exponentiation operations (highest priority) is from right to left. Thus the result is

$$3**2**3 = 3**8 = 6561$$

with the brace indicating the first operation to be performed.

3. The terms enclosed in a parenthesis are evaluated as a separate expression following the above priority rules. For example, in

$$2*(3+4)$$

3+4 is evaluated first, giving 7, and then 2*7 is evaluated, giving 14. Observe that

$$2*3+4 \quad \text{means} \quad (2*3) + 4 = 10$$

while

$$2*(3+4) = 14$$

4. Redundant parentheses are permitted. For example, the four statements

$$I = 3+4*3+7;$$
$$I = 3+(4*3)+7;$$
$$I = (3+4*3)+7;$$
$$I = 3+((4*3)+7);$$

are equivalent. Observe that knowledge of priority rules allows us to dispense with unnecessary parentheses, if computer evaluation of an expression coincides with the desired one. Sometimes, however, unnecessary parentheses are written for better readability of expressions.

Incidentally, there are no easy rules on the order of evaluation of several parenthetical expressions. For example, in the expression

$$(5+3) * (7+8)$$

there are no simple rules to tell whether $(5+3)$ is evaluated first or last. But then, it is really of no practical import. What is important is that the additions in parentheses take place prior to multiplication.

Several examples of PL/I expressions without redundant parentheses are shown in the table on page 181.

The list of priorities of operations also includes inequalities and logical expressions. These are used in conditions. Thus, for example,

$$A<= (B+1)$$

can be written as

$$A<= B+1$$

because the addition is of higher priority than the inequality. Hence, the addition is performed before the comparison, and the parentheses are unnecessary. Similarly, the condition

Arithmetic expression	PL/I expression	PL/I expression without redundant parentheses
$A + \dfrac{BC}{D+E}\,F$	$A + ((B{*}C)/(D + E)){*}\,F$	$A + B{*}C/(D + E){*}\,F$
$(A + B)(C + D)$	$(A + B){*}(C + D)$	$(A + B){*}(C + D)^{a}$
$(A^{B})^{C}$	$(A{*}{*}B){*}{*}C$	$(A{*}{*}B){*}{*}C^{a}$
$A^{(B^{C})}$	$A{*}{*}(B{*}{*}C)$	$A{*}{*}B{*}{*}C$
$-(A^{B+C})$	$-(A{*}{*}(B + C))$	$-A{*}{*}(B + C)$
$(-A)^{B+C}$	$(-A){*}{*}(B + C)$	$(-A){*}{*}(B + C)^{a}$
$\dfrac{A}{B} + \dfrac{C}{D}$	$(A/B) + (C/D)$	$A/B + C/D$

[a] Note that these examples contain no redundant parentheses.

$$(((A{+}B) \neg {>} C{*}D)\ \&\ (E \neg {=} F))\ |\ (G{>}H)$$

can be written as

$$A{+}B \neg {>} C{*}D\ \&\ E \neg {=} F\ |\ G{>}H$$

because this expression is evaluated in the order

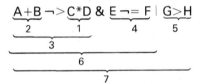

which is the same as in the expression using the parentheses.

14.2 PROCESSING OF INPUT DATA

We will now address ourselves to the following two questions:

1. How do we enter our data on cards or in the program? We know how to do so for decimal real numbers but not for binary or complex numbers.
2. In what form do numbers appear in the output printout?

Let us consider the first question on the form of input.

A Form of Input

We will now describe how numbers must be written (in the program, or on data cards) for computer operations.

1. A fixed-point decimal number, say, 12.34 is written the usual way as 12.34.
2. A floating-point decimal number, say, 1.234×10^{1} is written as 1.234E1. This number can also be written in its equivalent forms as 12.34E0, 0.1234E2, 0.01234E3, or 12340E−3, and so on.

3. A fixed-point binary number, say, 11.01 is written 11.01B. Here the letter B tells the compiler that 11.01 is a binary number. Incidentally, this number has the decimal value of $1 \times 2^1 + 1 \times 2^0 + 0 \times 2^{-1} + 1 \times 2^{-2} = 3.25$.

4. A floating-point binary number, say, 1.101×2^3 is written as 1.101E3B. This number can also be written as 11.01E2B, 110.1E1B, 1101E0B, 110100E−2B, and its other equivalent forms. Observe that the mantissa is a binary number, while the exponent is a decimal number. Again note that the letter B is appended to the number.

5. Complex numbers are written in the usual notation, with the letter I at the end. Examples of complex numbers are

$$3.5 + 6.3E-1I$$
$$7.5 + 3.92I$$
$$.75E3 + .392E-1I$$
$$1.011B + 0.11BI$$
$$1.01E2B - 11.1E-7BI$$

The following additional rules apply:

1. A sign may precede a number, as, for example,

$$+12.34$$
$$+1.234E-1$$
$$-12.34$$

2. The mantissa of a floating-point number is written just like a fixed-point number. The exponent is an integer of at most two digits for a decimal floating-point number or of at most three digits for a binary floating-point number. A sign (prefix) may precede either the mantissa or the exponent. The following are valid representations:

$$+12.34E+03 \qquad \text{a one-digit exponent may be preceded by a zero}$$
$$12.34E3$$
$$12.34E03$$

3. All characters used to describe numbers, such as ., prefix +, E, B, and I, must be adjacent to the number—no space separation is allowed.[1] Thus the following numbers are not well represented:

+ƀ12.34	space between + and 1*
12.ƀ34	space between . and 3
12.3ƀE3	space between 3 and E
12.3Eƀ3	space between E and 3
1.01ƀB	space between 1 and B
1.011B + 0.11BƀI	space between B and I

---

[1]Space is allowed between the two numbers comprising a complex number; thus 5 + 3I is a legal representation.

*The symbol ƀ denotes a space.

4. For System/360 and System/370 implementations the maximum allowable number of digits is

Fixed-point decimal number, 15 digits
Fixed-point binary number, 31 digits
Floating-point decimal number:
    Mantissa, 16 digits
    Exponent, 2 digits
    (the exponent may range from -78 to 75)
Floating-point binary number:
    Mantissa, 53 binary digits
    Exponent, 3 decimal digits
    (the exponent may range from -260 to 252)

The presence or absence of characters ., $+$, $-$, E, B, I in the number does not affect the maximum permitted number of digits.

5. In general, one should try to express the numbers in the simplest form. However, PL/I will accept human frailties and interpret correctly numbers such as

0034	unnecessary zeros preceding a number
01.230E1	unnecessary zero preceding and following a number
1.	unnecessary decimal point not followed by digits
1.E3	unnecessary decimal point in front of E
0.32	unnecessary zero in front of decimal point

Let us now consider the second question, regarding the form of the output.

B Form of Output

We just described how numbers are presented to the computer. As we have seen, there is considerable flexibility on the form of the input numbers. The output, however, is standardized, and a number appears on the printout in a unique form.

1. A fixed-point decimal number will be printed with its declared precision. For example, the program segment

```
DCL JOE FIXED (6,3);
JOE = 52.3;
PUT LIST (JOE);
```

will cause the following:

  a. 52.3 in the declared form, that is, 052.300 is assigned to JOE. Hence 052.300 in the computer's internal representation is stored in the location reserved for JOE.

  b. In the printout the front zeros are suppressed. Thus the output will appear as

52.300

In the above example, the precision attribute extended the given number. It can also cause truncation as in the program segment

```
DCL JACK FIXED (3,2);
JACK = 3.7512;
PUT LIST (JACK);
```

which will cause the following:

c. 3.7512 in the declared form, that is, 3.75 is assigned to JACK. Hence, 3.75 in the computer's internal representation is stored in the location reserved for JACK.

d. The printout will give

3.75

2. Floating point decimal numbers, if undeclared, are of precision (6), and will appear in the form:

x.xxxxxE+yy	for positive mantissa and positive exponent
x.xxxxxE−yy	for positive mantissa and negative exponent
−x.xxxxxE+yy	for negative mantissa and positive exponent
−x.xxxxxE−yy	for negative mantissa and negative exponent

which leads to the conclusions:

The mantissa is a decimal fraction with one nonzero digit preceding the decimal point and five digits to the right of the decimal point.

Only the minus sign is shown in front of the mantissa.

The exponent is always a two-digit number (a one-digit exponent is preceded by a zero).

The sign of the exponent is always shown.

Some examples of floating-point numbers in the output are

$$-1.23456E+02$$
$$-7.83472E-07$$
$$8.32142E+13$$
$$6.14729E-21$$

If a floating-point number has a declared precision p, then p rather than 6 is the number of digits in the mantissa. The mantissa still has only one digit in front of the decimal point and p-1 digits to the right of the decimal points. The remaining rules remain unchanged. Thus, for example, the program segment

```
DCL A FLOAT(3), B FLOAT(7), C FLOAT(4);
A = 12.34;
B = 0.04321;
C = -148;
PUT LIST (A, B, C);
```

will produce the outputs

```
1.23E+01          loss of a digit caused by truncation of mantissa
4.321000E-02
- 1.480E+02
```

Incidentally, there are only two precisions available internally in System/360 and System/370, namely, (6) and (16). Thus all internal computations are performed in either one of these two precisions,[1] with the output number truncated to conform with its declaration. The precision (6) is named *single precision* and is used whenever we specify a precision of 6 or less. Similarly, precision (16) is named *double precision* and is used for precisions of 7 or greater.

3. Fixed-point binary number representation exists only within the computer. A declared fixed-point binary number appears. in the output as a fixed-point decimal number. Again, only two precisions exist within the computer, one of 15 binary digits (named single precision) and the other of 31 binary digits (that is, double precision). Thus 15 digits are used for any number declared with a precision of 15 or fewer digits. Similarly 31 digits are used for all numbers declared to have 16 or more digits.

4. Floating-point binary number exists also only within the computer. In the output such a number is shown as a decimal floating-point number. Again, there are only two precisions, one of 21 binary digits (for the mantissa only) and the other of 53 binary digits. Twenty-one digits (that is, single precision) are used for all numbers with declared precision of 21 or less digits; 53 digits (that is, double precision) are used for all numbers with declared precision of 22 or more digits.

5. Complex numbers in the output are always displayed in the same scale; that is, the real and imaginary parts are either both floating-point numbers or both fixed-point numbers. Observe that it is not possible to declare a complex number to have two different scales—which is no practical drawback.

*14.3 EVALUATION OF EXPRESSIONS WITH MIXED ATTRIBUTES

We will now consider further what happens when numbers with different attributes are combined in the same expression. As an example, in the addition of a binary number to a decimal number, a conversion to a common base must take place first,

---

[1]Actually, neither System/360 nor System/370 contains FLOAT DECIMAL numbers. In fact, all calculations requiring FLOAT DECIMAL numbers are performed in FLOAT BINARY numbers, with FLOAT BINARY (21) being used for FLOAT DECIMAL(6), and FLOAT BINARY (53) being used for FLOAT DECIMAL(16). Evidently, the planners of PL/I believed that PL/I would be implemented on computers with circuitry capable of performing arithmetic operations on floating-point decimal numbers. We are still waiting for such computers.

*If time does not permit the coverage of the entire chapter, the starred sections can be omitted without any loss of continuity.

prior to the addition. Is the binary number converted to the decimal? It is true that often we do not care (or care to know) which conversion takes place. Thus, the material of this section, especially the material treating operations on numbers with different precisions, is of the reference type, to be used only when needed.

The conversions are performed automatically and for the operations of addition, subtraction, multiplication, and division are given by the following rules:

1. If the two numbers have different bases, the decimal number is converted to a binary one, and the result is binary.
2. If the two numbers have different modes, the real number is converted to a complex one (by adding an imaginary zero part of the same attributes as the real part), and the result is complex.
3. If the two numbers have different scales, the fixed-point number is converted to a floating-point number, and the result is in floating-point.

Recall that by the priority rules on the order of evaluation of expressions, we operate on only two numbers at a time. If an expression involves several numbers, the above rules still suffice. To see that, consider as an example the program segment

```
DCL A FLOAT DEC, B FLOAT BIN, C FIXED DEC,
    D FIXED BIN, E FIXED DEC CPLX;
E = B * 14.3 * (A+D) + C/3E1;
```

By the priority rules, the first operation is the one inside the parentheses, involving A+D. This and the remaining operations are

1. A is FLOAT DEC REAL and D is FIXED BIN REAL. By the above rules A is converted to FLOAT BIN REAL and D to FLOAT BIN REAL. The sum A+D is obtained as a FLOAT BIN REAL number.
2. The next operation is B*14.3. B is FLOAT BIN REAL, and 14.3 is evidently a FIXED DEC REAL number. Hence, 14.3 is converted to FLOAT BIN REAL, and the multiplication gives the product B*14.3 in FLOAT BIN REAL.
3. The product just obtained is multiplied by numbers representing A+D. Since both numbers have the same attributes no conversion is needed.
4. The FIXED DEC REAL number C is to be divided now by 3E1, which is a FLOAT DEC REAL number. Thus C is first converted to FLOAT DEC REAL, and then the division is performed.
5. We must now add the number representing B*14.3*(A+D) to the number obtained for C/3E1. The first number is in FLOAT BIN REAL form and the second in FLOAT DEC REAL form. Thus the second number is to be converted to FLOAT BIN REAL form. In fact, the second number requires no conversion (see the footnote on page 185). The result of the addition is again a FLOAT BIN REAL number.
6. The result just obtained is assigned to E, which is a FIXED DEC CPLX number. Thus a conversion to the specified attributes of E must now take place. This is done by converting the result to FIXED DEC REAL form and then

adding a zero imaginary part. The zero imaginary part is expressed also as a FIXED DEC number and has the same precision as the real part.

Observe that the above example requires five arithmetic operations and five conversions. Thus a substantial amount of computer time can be saved by specifying numbers with the same attributes to avoid time-consuming conversions.

For exponentiation automatic conversion also takes place. If A or B or both are complex, A**B is complex. A**B is usually FLOAT BINARY, but there are the following four exceptions:

1. If A is DEC FIXED or FLOAT and B is DEC FIXED or FLOAT, the result is FLOAT DEC.
2. If A is FLOAT DEC and B is a FIXED BIN nonzero integer, the result is FLOAT DEC.
3. If A is FIXED DEC and B is an unsigned (that is, no + or − sign precedes the number) nonzero integer (BIN or DEC) and the precision of A**B (we will discuss rules on precision shortly) does not exceed 15 (maximum allowed for FIXED DEC), the result is FIXED DEC.
4. If A is FIXED BIN and B is an unsigned nonzero integer (BIN or DEC) and the precision of A**B does not exceed 31 (maximum allowed for FIXED BIN), the result is FIXED BIN.

We have not said anything so far about the conversion of the precision. For example if a FLOAT DEC REAL (4) number is converted to the FIXED DEC REAL form, what is the precision? That is, how many digits are obtained for the fixed number? This and similar questions are answered by Table 14.1. This information is principally for reference, to be consulted whenever precision questions arise.

Incidentally, the number 3.32 which occurs in Table 14.1 is the value of $\log_2 10$. It signifies that it requires 3.32 binary digits to represent the number 10, and thus if decimal representation requires D digits, binary generally requires 3.32*D.

As an example consider the program segment

```
DCL A FLOAT BIN (3), B FIXED BIN (6,4);
A,B = 1.11E−2B;
PUT LIST (A,B);
```

The decimal value of 1.11 E−2B is

$$1.11E-2B = (1 \times 2^0 + 1 \times 2^{-1} + 1 \times 2^{-2})2^{-2} = (1.75) \, \tfrac{1}{4} = 0.4375$$

In the printout, A will appear as FLOAT DEC. Thus a conversion from FLOAT BIN to FLOAT DEC takes place. The precision (3) converts to (1) (*p* converts to *p*/3.32, as in Table 14.1), hence in the printout A is FLOAT DEC (1), giving

$$4E-01$$

as the printout for A.

Table 14.1

Number to be converted has the attributes	If the result of conversion has the attributes	Then the precision of the result is
FIXED DEC (p, q)	FLOAT DEC	(p)
	FIXED BIN	$(1 + 3.32*p, 3.32*q)^{a,b}$
	FLOAT BIN	$(3.32*p)^c$
FIXED BIN (p, q)	FLOAT BIN	(p)
	FIXED DEC	$(1 + p/3.32, q/3.32)^{d,e}$
	FLOAT DEC	$(p/3.32)^d$
FLOAT DEC (p)	FIXED DEC	See note f
	FLOAT BIN	$(3.32*p)^c$
	FIXED BIN	See note f
FLOAT BIN (p)	FIXED BIN	See note f
	FLOAT DEC	$(p/3.32)^d$
	FIXED DEC	See note f

[a] If $1 + 3.32*p$ exceeds 31(which is the maximum allowable number of digits for FIXED BIN), replace $1 + 3.32*p$ by 31. If $1 + 3.32*p$ is not an integer, round it to the smallest integer exceeding $1 + 3.32*p$.

[b] If $3.32*q$ is not an integer, round it to the smallest integer exceeding $3.32*q$ for $q>0$. For $q<0$, round it to the largest integer not exceeding $3.32*q$. Thus $q = 1$ gives 4, and $q = -1$ gives -4 (-4 is the largest integer not exeeding -3.32).

[c] If $3.32*p$ exceeds 53 (which is the maximum allowable number of digits for FLOAT BIN), replace $3.32*p$ by 53. If $3.32*p$ is not an integer, round it to the smallest integer exceeding $3.32*p$.

[d] If $p/3.32$ is not an integer, replace it by the smallest integer exceeding $p/3.32$.

[e] If $q/3.32$ is not an integer, round it to the smallest integer exceeding $q/3.32$ for $q>0$. For $q<0$, round it to the largest integer not exceeding $3.32/q$.

[f] All the conversions from FLOAT to FIXED can occur only through an assignment statement. But in this case the precision of the result of conversion is specified, either through a declaration or by default.

Similarly, in the printout B becomes FIXED DEC. The precision of B from Table 14.1 is

$$(1 + p/3.32, q/3.32) = (1 + 6/3.32, 4/3.32) = (3, 2)$$

Thus in the output B is FIXED DEC (3, 2), giving

$$0.43$$

as the printout for B.

Another question involving precision is: If we operate on two numbers of different precision, to what precision is the result calculated? Again, this information is of reference type only. Usually our calculations have sufficient default precision, and it is rare that we worry about the precision of the result. The precision rules are "common sense," and can be derived just from considerations of numbers. For example, if we add two fixed-point numbers:

The number	xx.xx	which has precision (4, 2)
And the number	x.xxxx	which has precision (5, 4)
Result can have the form	xxx.xxxx	which has precision (7, 4)

and that is the precision provided for this addition. In fact, formulas are tabulated for the precision of the result of an operation, if the precisions of the two operands are known. For such formulas, the reader is referred to the IBM literature.[1]

14.4 SUMMARY

We discussed here the processing of arithmetic data. We considered first arithmetic expressions and stated the order in which the terms of an expression are evaluated. Next, we described the forms of input and output. We saw that the numbers are introduced into the computer in the familiar form and that there is flexibility in the form of input. The output format, that is, the printout of numbers, follows a unique format.

The last section treats the evaluation of expressions with different attributes. We gave the conversion rules, which are followed by the computer automatically (that is, do not have to be programmed) prior to arithmetic operations on numbers with different attributes.

PROBLEMS

14.1 In the program

```
P1:  PROC OPTIONS(MAIN);
     I = 7 + 3**2*2 + 3*3/2;
     PUT LIST(I);
     END P1;
```

what number is printed out for I?

14.2 N is given by the assignment statement

$$N = 3*2/4+2*7/2**3-2+(1+7)/3;$$

and there is no DCL statement associated with N. What value is stored for N?

14.3 What is the printout of the following programs?

(a)
```
P3A:  PROC OPTIONS(MAIN);
      I = 7*2**3>5+7/3 = 2;
      PUT LIST(I);
      END P3A;
```

(b)
```
P3B:  PROC OPTIONS(MAIN);
      B = 8*(-1+7*5/2)/2**2/3+1;
      PUT LIST(B);
      END P3B;
```

(c)
```
P3C:  PROC OPTIONS(MAIN);
      N = 2*3**2/2 + 3*7**2/2**3;
      PUT LIST(N);
      END P3C;
```

[1]See, for example, "IBM System/360 Operating System PL/I(F) Language Reference Manual," IBM Systems Reference Library, order no. GC28-8201, pp. 278–280.

14.4 What is the output of the following program?

```
P4: PROC OPTIONS(MAIN);
    J = 7.2;
    A = J/3;
    N = 5 + 9/2**2 - 2*3 + 2;
    PUT LIST(A,J,N);
    END P4;
```

14.5 What is the output resulting from the following program segment?

```
DCL A FIXED BIN(5),
    B FIXED DEC(4,1),
    C FIXED DEC(5,2);
A = 25;
B = 172.88;
C = A*B;
PUT LIST(A,B,C,A*C,B*C);
```

LIST- AND DATA-DIRECTED INPUT

15

We have introduced the GET LIST statement in Chap. 3 already, and we have used this statement repeatedly. With this statement numbers and characters are "put into" the computer—thus the GET LIST statement is named *list-directed input statement*. We will describe one other way of giving input to the computer—with the *data-directed input statement*. (There are still other ways, to be described in Chaps. 24 and 25.) We will also describe some details on the use of these statements, as well as three available options.

15.1 LIST-DIRECTED INPUT

We shall first describe how the computer handles input operations. Let us assume that the program and data are on cards and are read in through the card reader. Here the following takes place:

1. The program and data are stored on a secondary memory device, such as a disk.
2. At some later instant, the program is compiled and executed.
3. During the execution phase the program requests data. The data is then taken from the secondary memory and stored in the main memory. This transfer is usually accompanied by a conversion of data, as will be described below.

Consider the statement

GET LIST (*name1, name2, . . . , namek*);

where *name1, name2, ..., namek* are names of variables, and their listing in parentheses is called *data list* or *simple list*. This statement requests the computer to read the input (that is, the data) and to store the data in the computer's main memory in the locations assigned to the variables on the list.

The data on the data card is viewed as a continuous stream of characters. The individual items of the data are separated by blanks or commas. This stream is placed first in the secondary storage as described above. As an item is picked out from the secondary storage, it is converted to the form of its computer representation and stored in its assigned main memory location. For example, consider a program with the statement

GET LIST (A,M);

and the associated data card with the data

8   17,   6   21

Here the following takes place:

1. The GET LIST statement requests data located now on the secondary storage. The program receives the first number in the stream, this being 8.
2. Eight is now converted to the computer representation of 8 and assigned to the variable A. If there is no declaration on A, it is by default FLOAT DEC (6). Thus 8 is converted to the floating-point form, that is, to the computer representation of 8.00000E0. This number is then stored in the location allocated to the variable A.
3. The program requests the next data item, this being 17. As before, 17 is converted to its computer representation and assigned to the variable M. Since M is by default FIXED BIN (15), 17 is converted to the fixed-point binary form. This number is then stored in the location reserved for M.
4. Since M is the last variable on the list, there is no more data reading to be done and the GET LIST statement has been executed.
5. Observe that the remaining numbers in the stream are ignored, because the list specified the assignment of data to just A and M. The next input request (that is, the next GET LIST statement) will be directed at the next number, that is, 6.

Recall that data on a data card can be written in all 80 columns. Since the stream of data is continuous, column 80 of the first card is followed by column 1 of the second card. Thus, if we have the numbers

123   in columns 78 to 80 of a card

and

45   in columns 1 and 2 of the following card

the computer reads this as a single number, 12345.

Again recall the rules on writing numbers:

1. Two numbers are separated from one another by a space or a comma.
2. Whenever one space is allowed, several spaces are allowed also.
3. A + sign may be written in front of a number.
4. Since a space signals the end of the number no space is allowed within the number. Thus there can be no space between a prefix sign and the number. Similarly, if letters such as E, B, or I are used to describe the number, the number must be written without any intervening spaces.

Consider the following problem:

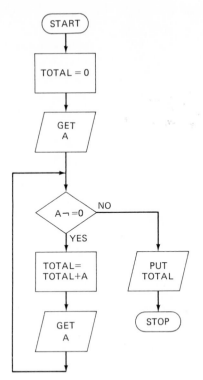

Figure 15.1 Flowchart for the summing program.

Given

A set of numbers, with the last number being the only zero in the set.

Find

The sum of these numbers.

> **Solution** The flowchart appears in Fig. 15.1. In fact, a simple program like this one can be written without the flowchart and is

```
SUMMING: PROC OPTIONS(MAIN);
         TOTAL = 0;
         GET LIST(A);
         DO WHILE(A¬=0);
             TOTAL = TOTAL+A;
             GET LIST(A);
         END;
         PUT LIST(TOTAL);
         END SUMMING;
```

The program is simple enough. Let us now consider the accompanying data card as being

$$112E0, \ 112E0, \ 7.2E-1, \ 7.2E-1, \ 7.2E-1, \ 3.2 \ 0$$

As can be seen, there is a repetition of input numbers. In fact, A remains the same through the first and second cycles, acquires a new value in the third cycle, and remains unchanged in the fourth and fifth cycles. Is a shorthand notation available to simplify the writing of such repetitive numbers?

The answer is yes. If we wish the variable to remain unchanged, we write no value between two consecutive commas. Thus the data card can be written as

$$112E0, , 7.2E-1, , , 3.2\ 0$$

where consecutive commas signify that the variable on the list (that is, A) is to remain at its previous value. Incidentally, in computer jargon the presence of two consecutive commas is named a *null field*. Similarly, the statement

$$\text{GET LIST (A,B,C);}$$

if accompanied by the data card

$$2, , 2.1E0$$

means

$$A = 2;$$
$$B = \text{previous value};$$
$$C = 2.1E0$$

Consider now, the same program, but now the data card is

$$112E0, , 7.2E-1, , , 3.2$$

Thus the last zero is missing. What happens now?

Evidently, after acquiring 3.2, the program repeats its cycle, and in this process attempts to execute the GET LIST (A); statement. But there is no value for A. Since the computer cannot do what it is asked to do, it interprets the lack of value as an error. This type of error is named the ENDFILE condition. The computer then prints out that the ENDFILE condition has occurred, the number of the statement where this occurred (all statements are numbered consecutively, thus the GET LIST statement will be the third statement), and terminates the program.[1]

In our program, there would be no output, and thus the program would not work. However, often the fact that the computer stops the program execution where there are no data for a GET LIST statement is used intentionally for terminating a program. For example, if the program is rewritten as

```
SUMMING: PROC OPTIONS(MAIN);
        TOTAL = 0;
        DO WHILE(1);
           GET LIST(A);
           TOTAL = TOTAL+A;
           PUT LIST(TOTAL);
        END;
        END SUMMING;
```

[1]The ENDFILE condition is described in more detail in Sec. 26.1.

and the data card is again

$$112E0, , 7.2E-1, , , 3.2$$

we print the consecutive values of TOTAL. When the program execution stops due to the lack of data, the last printout is the desired value for TOTAL. Hence, in the above program we intentionally used the computer's reaction to the ENDFILE condition to stop the program.

Note also that the program is similar to the first program in Sec. 3.2, where we used the ENDFILE condition for stopping the program just as here.

15.2 DATA-DIRECTED INPUT

There are two data-directed statements. The first one is

GET DATA (*name1, name2, . . . , namek);*

and requires the associated data card to have the form

name1 = value, name2 = value, ..., namek = value;

As an example,

GET DATA (M1,JACK,BILL);

with the associated data card

M1=353,JACK=13 BILL=2.1E1;

shows a valid use. The GET DATA statement is subject to the following rules:

1. When the GET DATA statement is used, the data card must show values in the form of an assignment statement. Observe the difference from the GET LIST statement, where just the values are shown.
2. A space or a comma serves to separate the individual data items on the data card. As usual a + sign may precede the number, and whenever one space is allowed, several spaces are allowed too, and there can be a space between any separations such as the value and the comma as in

M1 = 352 ,JACK=+13 BILL=2.1E1 ;

3. The associated data include all items up to the semicolon. Hence the last item on the data card is terminated with a semicolon.
4. As before, the list of variables in the parentheses is named *data list* or simply *list*. All variables on the data card must be included in the list. Thus the statement

GET DATA (A,B,C);

with the associated data card

A=3 C=4 D=7;

will result in an error, because D is not present on the list.

5. Not all variables on the list must appear on the data card. A variable for which there is no value on the card remains at its old value. As an example consider the program

```
EXAMPLE: PROC OPTIONS(MAIN);
         DO WHILE(1);
           GET DATA(I,J,K);
           PUT LIST(I,J,K);
         END;
         END EXAMPLE;
```

and the data card

$$I=3, J=4, K=6; I=6; ; J=11, K=13; J=1;$$

What numbers are printed out?

In the first cycle: 3, 4, and 6.

In the second cycle, only I changes to 6, J and K remain unchanged; thus we print 6, 4, and 6.

In the third cycle, there is no change at all; thus we print 6, 4, and 6.

In the fourth cycle: 6, 11, and 13.

In the fifth cycle: 6, 1, and 13.

In the sixth cycle, there are no more data; thus the computer stops and notifies us that the ENDFILE condition has occurred.

6. The variables on the list and the variables on the data card do not have to occur in the same order. Hence the statement

$$\text{GET DATA (A,B,C);}$$

can have a data card reading

$$B=3.7E0, C=17 \ A=2.1;$$

7. As before, the data cards constitute a continuous stream. Thus all 80 columns of a card are immediately followed by column 1 of the next card. Hence, for example, the card with

$$\text{JACK} = 12;$$

can be replaced by two cards with

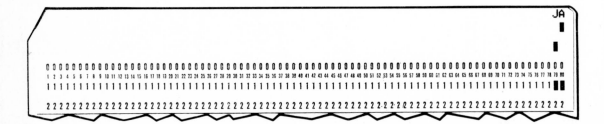

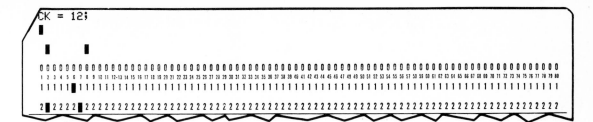

because to the card reader the characters JA are immediately followed by the characters CK, as before.

The second data-directed statement is simply

GET DATA;

Thus there is no list here. The associated data cards are as before, that is,

$$name1 = value, name2 = value,...,namek = value;$$

and the input reader obtains all data up to the semicolon.

15.3 INPUT OPTIONS

We can do more than merely obtain data, In computer jargon, we have several *options* available. These are the COPY, FILE, and SKIP options.

A The COPY Option

This option causes the copying of the input data, exactly as given, with one data item per line. This option can appear either after GET or at the end of the input statement as in

```
GET LIST (A,B,C) COPY;
GET COPY LIST (A,B,C);
GET DATA (A,B,C) COPY;
GET DATA COPY;
```

For example, the program

```
EXAMPLE: PROC OPTIONS(MAIN);
         DCL C,K;
         GET LIST(A,I)COPY;
         GET COPY DATA(J,B);
         GET DATA COPY;
         END EXAMPLE;
```

with the input

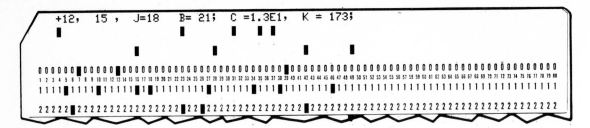

gives the output

```
+12,
15
J=18
B=21;
C=1.3E1,
K=173;
```

(The comma after 15 is not printed because of the intervening space.)

B The FILE Option

PL/I has facilities for several sources of input. In computer jargon these sources are named *files*. The files have names; thus we can obtain data from different files. There is one standard file, which is usually the card reader. This file is named SYSIN (for system input). If we use the standard file, we do not have to specify it because by default the compiler selects the SYSIN file. Thus the statements

GET FILE (SYSIN) LIST (A,B);

and

GET LIST (A,B);

accomplish the same thing. However, if we use a nonstandard file, which we named BULK, we must write

GET FILE (BULK) LIST (A,B,C);

Considerably more can be said about files. They have to be declared and other statements are needed for their use. However, we only intend to tell here of the existence of files, and their discussion is reserved to Chap. 25. More information on files can be found in the programming literature.[1]

---

[1]"IBM System/360 Operating System PL/I(F) Language Reference Manual," IBM Systems Reference Library, order no. GC28-8201-3, pp. 91–98; F. Bates and M. L. Douglas, "Programming Language/One," 3d ed., pp. 202–225, Prentice-Hall, Englewood Cliffs, NJ, 1975; Joan K. Hughes, "PL/I Programming," pp. 455–565, Wiley, New York, 1973.

C The SKIP Option

This option tells that input is to be obtained from the next card. The statements

GET LIST (A);
GET LIST (B) SKIP (2);

together with data cards

First card	2, 3, 4
Second card	5, 6, 7
Third card	8, 9, 61

cause the following:

1. A acquires the value of 2.
2. Before obtaining B, we skip twice to the data of the third card. Thus B acquires the value of 8.

Note that the skip occurs before reading of the input. The keyword SKIP can also be placed after GET as in

GET SKIP (3) DATA (A,B);

Further rules on this option are:

1. Just SKIP can be written for SKIP(1). Thus

GET LIST(A,B)SKIP;

is the same as

GET LIST(A,B)SKIP(1);

2. There can be an expression in the parentheses instead of a number. Thus

GET LIST(A,B)SKIP(3*I/6);

is a legal statement. Here the expression 3*I/6 is evaluated first, and then SKIP takes place.
3. If the number in parentheses following SKIP is less than 1, it is interpreted as 1. Thus

GET LIST(A,B)SKIP(−3.7);

is the same as

GET LIST(A,B)SKIP;

4. If the number in parentheses is larger than 1 but not an integer, it is interpreted as the integer obtained by truncation of the decimal fraction; thus

$$GET \ DATA(A,B)SKIP(3.72);$$

is the same as

$$GET \ DATA(A,B)SKIP(3);$$

5. The SKIP command can be a separate statement as in

$$GET \ SKIP(8);$$

which is just a directive for the input reader.
6. The keyword SKIP asks the input reader to obtain the data contained on a new card. If the input is to be on a new card anyway, the SKIP is redundant.

Observe that all the above three options can be used simultaneously in a single statement, as in

$$GET \ FILE(SYSIN)DATA(A,B)SKIP(3)COPY;$$

15.4 SUMMARY

We discussed the viewing of data as a continuous stream of characters, with the individual items separated by blanks or commas. We discussed the list- and data-directed inputs and the difference in data cards for these two types of inputs. We also discussed three options available, these being, the COPY, FILE, and SKIP options.

PROBLEMS

15.1 We wish to place a string of 100 characters on data cards. Assume that the first character is punched in column 5. Where are the remaining characters punched?

15.2 Which of the following statements are invalid?
(a) GET DATA (M1, 3*M);
(b) GET LIST (M1, 3*M);
(c) GET LIST (A, A);
(d) GET DATA (A, A);
(e) GET LIST (A, , , C);
(f) GET LIST (1, '1', 'JOE');

15.3 The data card contains

$$A = 1, B = 2, C = 3;$$

Which of the following are valid statements?
(a) GET DATA (C, A, B);
(b) GET DATA (C);
(c) GET DATA (B, A);
(d) GET DATA (A, B, D);
(e) GET DATA (A, B, C, D);

15.4 The program

```
P4: PROC OPTIONS(MAIN);
    GET LIST(A,B);
    GET LIST(C,D);
    GET DATA;
    G = A + B + C + D + E + F;
    PUT LIST(G);
    END P4;
```

requires data. It is known that A,B,C, and E are 1 and that D and F are 2. Show the needed data card.

16 LIST-AND DATA-DIRECTED OUTPUT

The features described in the last chapter pertaining to the input are mirrored in similar features pertaining to the output. We are already familiar with the PUT LIST statement, which is named the *list-directed output statement*. We will introduce here the *data-directed output statement,* and some details on the use of both these output statements. We will also describe several available options.

16.1 LIST-DIRECTED OUTPUT

The basic form of the PUT LIST statement is

PUT LIST *(name1, name2, . . ., namek);*

where *name1, name2, . . ., namek* are names of variables. As before, the list in parentheses is named *data list,* or simply *list.* This statement requests the computer to print out the data stored in the computer memory, in the locations assigned to the variables on the list.

A generalization is possible in that the items on the list can be expressions. For example, the statement

PUT LIST (I,I*K+3, (L-M)/3);

is a legal one. Hence we can write

PUT LIST *(expression1, expression2, . . ., expressionk);*

as a generalization of the basic statement.

In fact, the list in parentheses can be even more general and can contain expressions, variables, and constants.[1] Thus it can have the form

PUT LIST *(expression1, expression2, . . ., expressionk, constant1, constant2, . . ., constantl);*

[1] Constant is a specific quantity (for example, the number 12.3).

202

where, as before, *expression1, expression2, . . ., expressionk* are either expressions showing operations on variables or constants, or names of variables, and *constant1, constant2, . . ., constantl* are constants. These constants can be either numbers or characters. A constant composed of characters is named a *character-string* constant. Thus we have *numerical constants* and *character-string constants*. Let us next describe the details involved in the display of these constants.

16.2 NUMERICAL CONSTANTS

The decimal constants appearing on the list are printed essentially as they are written, except that

1. A decimal fraction such as

$$.xxx$$

will be printed as

$$0.xxx$$

Thus a zero will precede the decimal point.
2. A floating-point number such as

$$xx.xxEy$$

will be printed in its standard form, this being

$$x.xxxE+zz$$

Thus, in the mantissa, there is just one digit in front of the decimal point, and the exponent part consists of two digits preceded by a sign. One of these two digits can be zero, and the sign is either + or −.
3. Leading zeros are suppressed; hence

$$0xx.xx$$

will be printed as

$$xx.xx$$

4. The real and imaginary parts of a complex constant are displayed in the output with the same scale and the same precision. If the complex number on the list has parts of different precisions, the printed output portrays the higher precision for both parts. If the complex number on the list has different scales, the printed output has both parts in floating-point form.

We are ready now for some examples. First consider

PUT LIST (13E−1, 012, .073);

which results in the output

$$1.3E+00 \qquad 12 \qquad 0.073$$

Incidentally, the statement

PUT LIST (1E1);

gives the output

$$1E+01$$

rather than 1.0E+01. There is a reason for it, of course, which has to do with the precision. The compiler assigns a precision attribute to each number, and in case of a constant, the precision is the *apparent precision,* that is, the precision with which the number is written. Recall that the precision of a floating-point number is the number of digits in the mantissa; hence 1E1 has precision (1), and the output can display only one digit. The precision of 1.0E1 is (2), and thus

PUT LIST (1.0E1);

prints out

$$1.0E+01$$

To illustrate the printout of complex numbers, consider

PUT LIST (1.1 + 1.234I);

which results in the output

$$1.100+1.234I$$

with the precision of the real part increased to match the one of the imaginary part through the addition of extra zeros. Similarly, the statement with a complex number in floating-point scale

PUT LIST (2.13E0 + 1E0I);

yields the printout

$$2.13E+00+1.00E+00I$$

where again the precision was adjusted as asserted. Finally, consider the case where both parts are in different scales, as in

PUT LIST (1.27 + 2.6E0I);

which gives the output

$$1.27E+00+2.60E+00I$$

showing adjustments in both scale (to floating point) and precision.

Binary constants can also be included in the list of the PUT LIST statement. Since the computer assumes that there is little interest in these numbers in the output, they are converted to decimal form. Specifically, fixed-point binary numbers are converted to fixed-point decimal numbers, and floating-point binary numbers to floating-point decimal numbers. For example, the statement

PUT LIST (1101B, 1.1B, 11.01E2B);

where the binary numbers correspond to the decimal numbers 13, 1.5, and $3.25*2^2$ $= 13 = 1.3E1$, results in the printout

13   1.5   1.3E+01

The listing of binary numbers in the list is probably of little interest, but, while we are at it, we may note that there may be a loss of digits in the output. For example,

PUT LIST (0.11B);

will print out

0.7

rather than the correct value of 0.75. Again, the reason lies in precision. The precision of 0.11B is (3,2), which converts by Table 14.1 to a fixed-point decimal number with precision (1+3/3.32, 2/3.32), or (2, 1). Hence there is only room for two digits, the first of which is zero. Thus only 0.7 can be displayed. Similarly,

PUT LIST (1101.1E3B)

is a floating-point binary number of precision (5). Now,

$$1101.1E3B = 13.5 \times 2^3 = 108 = 1.08E2$$

but by Table 14.1, the precision of the floating-point decimal number resulting from conversion is 5/3.32, or (2). Hence a mantissa of only two digits can appear in the output, and, sure enough, the printout is

1.0E+02

16.3 CHARACTER-STRING CONSTANTS

Recall that if we want to print a text, we enclose the text in single quotation marks. Hence

PUT LIST ('ANYTHING');

will print out

ANYTHING

without the quotes. Similarly,

PUT LIST ('JOE DOE');

will print out

JOE DOE

In these cases, the item on the list consists of characters rather than a variable. Since this item does not change, it is called a *character-string constant*. It can be a number as well, as in

$$\text{PUT LIST ('1.35');}$$

or any mixture of the characters on the keyboard.

Sometimes we wish to use a quotation mark as a character. To allow the compiler to distinguish between the quotes enclosing a character-string constant and a quote as a character, we use a pair of quotes for the character. Thus

$$\text{PUT LIST ('IT''S MINE');}$$

will print out

$$\text{IT'S MINE}$$

Similarly, if we wish to print out

$$\text{''IT'S MINE,'' SAID JOE}$$

we write it as

$$\text{PUT LIST ('''''IT''S MINE,'''' SAID JOE');}$$

with four quotes used for the double quotes of the printout.

In the above illustration we used just the single quotes. The keyboard also contains a double quote as a single character. If we use the double quotes, we write

$$\text{PUT LIST ('"IT''S MINE," SAID JOE');}$$

to obtain

$$\text{"IT'S MINE," SAID JOE}$$

as printout.

A measure associated with a character string is its *length*. This is simply the number of characters in the string. Thus

$$\text{'JOE DOE'}$$

is a string of seven characters, because the blank (or space) is also a character and is counted as such. If we put three spaces to separate JOE from DOE, as in

$$\text{'JOEƀƀƀDOE',}$$

where we used the symbol ƀ for space, we have a string of nine characters. We only count characters in the output. Thus the string

$$\text{'''''ITS''S MINE,'''' SAID JOE'}$$

which will be printed as

$$\text{''IT'S MINE,'' SAID JOE}$$

has 23 characters in the latter form (two quotes count as two characters), and this is its length. In fact, we can have a string of no characters, this being one of zero length, and described by two adjacent single quotes, as in

$$\text{''}$$

and named the *null string*.

A shortcut for writing character strings is provided by the repetition factor. For example,

'YES∲YES∲YES∲'

can be written as

(3)'YES∲'

where (3) preceding the string signifies that the string is to be written three times. Therefore

PUT LIST ((3)'*', (10)'X', (3)'*');

will print out

***   XXXXXXXXXX   ***

The repetition factor in parentheses must be a nonnegative integer (it cannot be an expression). Incidentally,

(0)'ANYTHING'

is the null string, because any string written zero times is the null string.

16.4 FORMAT OF THE OUTPUT

We will now describe the format of the output printout. The printout takes place on a large sheet of paper named a *page*. In standard use with the IBM System/360 or System/370 there are 60 lines to the page and 120 columns on each line. Thus up to 120 characters can be displayed on each line. The PUT LIST statement results in the printout of five items on each line. For example, the statement

PUT LIST (A1,A2,A3,A4,A5,A6,A7);

will print the values of A1,A2,A3,A4, and A5 on one line and the values of A6 and A7 on the following line.

The 120 columns divide into five fields for printout of data. Because there are 120 columns on each line, each field has $^{120}/_5 = 24$ columns. As a consequence, the first data field occupies columns 1–24, the second columns 25–48, the third columns 49–72, the fourth columns 73–96, and the fifth columns 97–120. Thus the page has the appearance as shown in Fig. 16-1.

To illustrate the display of the data items on the page, consider the program

```
PRINT:  PROC OPTIONS(MAIN);
        I = 1;
        J = 12;
        K = 123;
        A = I;
        PUT LIST(I,J,K,A);
        END PRINT;
```

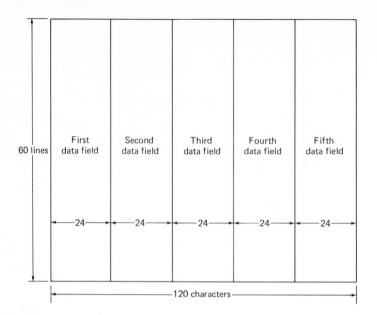

Figure 16.1 Format of the output page.

The resulting output is

ƀƀƀƀƀƀƀƀ1   ƀƀƀƀƀƀƀ12   ƀƀƀƀƀƀ123   ƀ1.00000E+00
↑   ↑   ↑   ↑
col. 1 (start of   col. 25 (start of col. 49 (start of col. 73 (start of fourth
first field)   second field)   third field)   field)

The first three numbers are integers, the last one a floating-point number. Observe the presence of blanks preceding the numbers. Note that there are eight blanks in front of 1. We shall explain their presence. Recall that I has by default the attributes FIXED BIN (15,0). Before printout, the value of I (which is 1) is converted by Table 14.1 to FIXED DEC of precision (1 + 15/3.32, 0/3.32), or (6,0). At this point we have 1 in the computer representation as FIXED DEC (6,0), that is, as 000001. Now, for printout, the computer further converts this number to a character string[1] (because the printer prints out characters) of length $p + 3$ (where p is the precision, being 6 here), that is, one with $p + 3$, or nine characters.[2] The extra three characters and the five leading zeros are replaced by blanks, and this is the reason for the eight blanks.

The conversions for the variable J are the same, and J is converted to a character string of length 9. Since the number 12 occupies two columns, it is

[1]For details see IBM System/360 Operating System PL/I(F) "Language Reference Manual," pp. 272–274, and fig. F-8 on p. 277, IBM Systems Reference Library, order no. GC 28-8201.

[2]The reason for the extra three characters is discussed in Sec. 17.8.

preceded by seven blanks, and 12 appears in columns 32 and 33. Similarly, K results in a character string of nine characters, and since 123 requires three columns there is room for six leading blanks. Therefore 123 appears in columns 55, 56, and 57.

The floating-point number is preceded by only one blank which is the space for the sign (as usual, the plus sign is not shown). The variable A is by default FLOAT DEC (6). The rules for the floating-point to character-string conversion give a character string of length $p + 6$, thus $6 + 6$ or 12 here.[1] Because the number

$$1.00000E+00$$

requires 11 characters for its representation, there is room for one leading blank only (that is, the space left for a possible minus sign).

As the next example, consider the statement

PUT LIST ('12345678901234567890l2345', 'A');

which results in the output

```
12345678901234567890l2345     A
↑                             ↑
col. 1                        col. 49
```

Observe that A is printed in the third field. This is because the 25-digit character string occupies one character of the second field. Hence A is printed on a new field, this being the third field.[2]

Note that the statement

PUT LIST ('A', 'b̸', 'B');

results in the output

```
A                             B
↑                             ↑
col. 1                        col. 49
```

Thus we skipped the second field. The printer "printed" a blank in column 25, and this item took up the second field. This technique can be used to separate output. As an example,

PUT LIST ('A', 'b̸', 'b̸', 'b̸', 'b̸', 'B');

will skip a line after printing A, giving

```
A
B
↑
col. 1
```

---

[1]The reason for the extra six characters is discussed in Sec. 17.8.

[2]In fact, even a string of 24 characters will cause the printout of A on the third field. The compiler automatically adds a blank (for separation) to the string, thus making it in effect a string of 25 characters, and as such requiring two fields.

because the fields 2, 3, 4, and 5 are skipped. Fortunately, this technique does not have to be employed to skip a line after printing, because there is an easier way to handle it. This is done with an option (the SKIP option) to be discussed in Sec. 16.6.

16.5 DATA-DIRECTED OUTPUT

Recall that there were two data-directed input statements. These were GET DATA *(list of variables);* and GET DATA;. Similarly, there are two data-directed output statements. The first one is

PUT DATA (name1,name2, . . .,namek);

and results in the printout

$$name1 = value \; name2 = value. \ldots . name5 = value$$
$$\ldots\ldots\ldots\ldots\ldots\ldots\ldots\ldots\ldots\ldots\ldots\ldots$$
$$\ldots\ldots\ldots\ldots namek = value;$$

Observe the following:

1. Each variable is identified in the output, as shown above.
2. The last item in the output is terminated by a semicolon.
3. The format of the output page is as before. Thus five items are printed on each line as in the PUT LIST format. As an example, recall the PRINT program of the previous section. We will repeat the program here, but with the data-directed output statement, obtaining

```
PRINT:   PROC OPTIONS(MAIN);
         I = 1;
         J = 12;
         K = 123;
         A = I;
         PUT DATA(I,J,K,A);
         END PRINT;
```

The resulting output is

```
I=ƀƀƀƀƀƀƀƀ1        J=ƀƀƀƀƀƀƀ12         K=ƀƀƀƀƀƀ123        A=ƀ1.00000E+00;
↑                  ↑                   ↑                  ↑
col. 1 (start of first field)   col. 25 (start of second field)   col. 49 (start of third field)   col. 73 (start of fourth field)
```

Thus the blanks are present as before, but now we have the name of the identifier and the equal sign in front of the number. We also have a semicolon after the last number.

4. The first character of the variable name is always printed in the first column of a field. Thus, if an item on the list requires more than one field, the next item is printed at the start of the subsequent field. For example, the program

```
EXAMPLE: PROC OPTIONS(MAIN);
         JOE__LONG__NAME,I = 1;
         PUT DATA(JOE__LONG__NAME,I);
         END EXAMPLE;
```

gives the output

```
JOE__LONG__NAME=        1                    I=           1;
↑                       ↑                    ↑
col. 1                  col. 25              col. 49
```

and illustrates the case where the first item occupies more than the first field. As a consequence, the second item (that is, I) is printed in the third field. In fact, even if the first item were only 24 characters long, the next item is still printed in the third field, because the compiler automatically adds a blank for separation, and this blank occupies the second field. For example, the program segment

```
MIKE_LONG_NAME,I = 1;
PUT DATA(MIKE_LONG_NAME,I);
```

results in the output

```
MIKE_LONG_NAME=         1                    I=           1;
↑                       ↑                    ↑
col. 1                  col. 24              col. 49
```

as asserted.

5. There can be no constants or expressions on the list of the PUT DATA statement, because on the output each value is accompanied by the name of the variable, but a constant or expression has no associated name. Thus, for example, the statements

$$\text{PUT DATA (1.2);}$$
$$\text{PUT DATA (3*A);}$$
$$\text{PUT DATA (N+K);}$$
$$\text{PUT DATA ('YES');}$$

are all illegal.

The second data-directed output statement is

$$\text{PUT DATA;}$$

that is, without a list of identifiers. This results in the printing out of all variables known to the program at the time of execution of the PUT DATA; statement. The output format is the same as the one with a list of identifiers, that is, with five items on each line, each item being of the form *name=value*.

16.6 OUTPUT OPTIONS

We have some control over the output format. In computer jargon, we have several options available. We will describe the more important ones.

A The FILE Option

Recall that we introduced this option in Sec. 15.3 for the input. We said there that we have facilities for several sources of input named files. Similarly, there may be several output devices such as printer, magnetic tape, or punched cards. We can choose the form of output that we desire (provided, of course, that our computer system has this form of output) and call the output device file. We give a name to each file. There is always one standard output file, which is usually the printer. This file is named SYSPRINT (system printer). If we use the standard file, we do not have to specify it, because by default the compiler selects the SYSPRINT file. Thus the statements

PUT FILE (SYSPRINT) LIST (A,B);

and

PUT LIST (A,B);

accomplish the same thing. However, if we use a nonstandard file, say, JUNK, we must write

PUT FILE (JUNK) LIST (A,B);

Considerably more can be said about files. They have to be declared, and other statements are needed for their use as we will see in Chapter 25. Here, we intended to tell only about their existence, but not about their use. For references on this topic see footnote on page 198.

B The SKIP Option

The statement with this option reads

PUT LIST (A,B) SKIP (*n*);

where *n* is a number. It requests the printer to skip *n* lines from its present position and then to print A and B. For example, the program for obtaining the integers from 1 to 20 and their squares

```
EXAMPLE: PROC OPTIONS(MAIN);
         DO I=1 TO 20;
            PUT LIST(I,I*I)SKIP(1);
         END EXAMPLE;
```

will print as follows:

1. It will skip the first line and print 1 in the first field of the second line and 1 $(=1^2)$ in the second field of the second line.
2. When executing the PUT LIST instruction again, it will skip to the third line and print 2 in the first field and 4 in the second field.
3. It will continue printing the integer and its square on new lines, giving the output

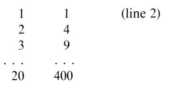

1	1	(line 2)
2	4	
3	9	
. . .	. . .	
20	400	

Observe that without the SKIP option, the output will be

1	1	2	4	3	(line 1)
9	4	16	5	25	
. . .	. . .	. . .	. . .	. . .	
324	19	361	20	400	

which is certainly harder to read

This option can also be used with the PUT DATA statement, as in

PUT DATA (A,B) SKIP(4);

Further rules on this option are

1. Just SKIP can be written for SKIP(1). Hence

PUT LIST (A,B)SKIP;

is the same as

PUT LIST (A,B) SKIP (1);

2. There can be an expression in the parentheses following SKIP instead of the number. Thus

PUT DATA (A,B) SKIP(3*I/5);

is a legal statement. The expression 3*I/5 is evaluated first, then the carriage (of the printer) skips, and finally the printer prints the output.
3. If the number in parentheses following SKIP is zero, the carriage is requested to return to column 1 of same line. This allows underlining or overprinting. For example, the statements

PUT LIST ('HEADING');
PUT LIST ((7)'__')SKIP(0);

will first cause the printer to print out HEADING. Then the carriage of the printer returns to the first column of the same line and underlines HEADING, yielding

HEADING

Similarly, the statements

PUT LIST ((5)'V');
PUT LIST ((5)'I')SKIP(0);

create

VVVVV

by overprinting the output.

4. The keyword SKIP can also be placed after PUT, as in

PUT SKIP (7) DATA (A,B);

which is the same as

PUT DATA (A,B) SKIP (7);

with the SKIP taking place first and then the printout.

5. The statement

PUT SKIP (n);

is a valid one. It requests the carriage to skip n times, but nothing else is executed.

6. It may be instructive to consider PL/I action due to an ambiguous or erroneous SKIP instruction. Consider these cases

a. The number in parentheses following SKIP is not an integer. PL/I action: the number is truncated to an integer. For example,

PUT DATA (A,B) SKIP (2.7);

is interpreted as

PUT DATA (A,B) SKIP (2);

b. The number in parentheses following SKIP is negative. PL/I action: the number is made zero. For example,

PUT LIST (A,B) SKIP (−3);

causes the same printout as

PUT LIST (A,B) SKIP (0);

7. If the SKIP option lands us on the next page, the printer prints on the first line of the new page. As an example, assume that we just printed an output on line 50 (that is, the printer is now on line 50). Then either of the three statements

PUT LIST (A) SKIP (15);
PUT LIST (A) SKIP (20);
PUT LIST (A) SKIP (75);

accomplishes the same thing—causes the printout of A on the first line of the next page. Observe that in the last example the number 75 exceeds the number of lines on the page (that is, 60).

8. If the printer were to skip on its own to a new line, the SKIP option has no effect on the printout. For example, in

PUT LIST (1,2,3,4,5);
PUT LIST (6);

the printer will skip to a new line for the printout of 6. The program segment

PUT LIST (1,2,3,4,5);
PUT SKIP LIST (6);

results in an identical output. Thus the SKIP option here has no effect on the printout, as asserted.

C The LINE Option

The statement with this option reads

PUT LIST (A,B) LINE (*n*);

where *n* is a number. It causes the printer to advance to line *n* and then to print A and B (on line *n*). Note that we have now an alternative for the SKIP option, a further example of the richness of the PL/I language. The line option can also be used with the PUT DATA statement, as in

PUT DATA (A,B) LINE(*n*);

The following details apply to this option;

1. There can be an expression in the parentheses following LINE instead of the number. Thus

PUT DATA (A,B) LINE (3*I+I*J/7);

is a legal statement. The expression 3*I+I*J/7 is evaluated first, then the carriage moves to the correct line, and then finally the printing takes place.

2. The keyword LINE can also be placed after PUT, as in

PUT LINE (*n*) DATA (A,B);

which is the same as

PUT DATA (A,B) LINE (*n*);

3. The statement

PUT LINE (*n*);

is a valid one. Here the carriage advances to line *n*, but nothing else is executed.

4. The carriage of the printer cannot go backward; it can only return to the beginning of the line or advance forward. We can overprint by repeating the line number, as in

PUT LIST (1) LINE (10);
PUT LIST (2) LINE (10);

which gives the output

2

that is, 2 overprints 1. We can use this technique for underlining.

5. Whenever we advance to a new page, we will print on the first line of the new page. As an example, assume that the printer is on line 10. Then either of the two statements

PUT DATA (A) LINE (70);

or

PUT DATA (A) LINE (8);

will cause the same thing—the printout of A on the first line of the next page. Note that in the first example the line number 70 exceeds the number of lines on the page (which is 60). The printer advances toward line 70, and after line 60 it reaches line 1 of the new page, at which time it prints A. Similarly, in the second example, the printer advances toward line 8 (which is on the next page) but must print A upon reaching line 1 of the new page.

6. Again, the following interpretation is made by PL/1:

a. If the number in parentheses following LINE is not an integer, the number is truncated to an integer. For example,

PUT LIST (A,B) LINE (3.9);

is interpreted as

PUT LIST (A,B) LINE (3);

b. If the number in parentheses following LINE is less than 1, it is interpreted as 1. For example,

PUT DATA (A,B) LINE (−9.3);

is interpreted as

PUT DATA (A,B) LINE (1);

D The PAGE Option

A statement with this option has the form

PUT LIST (A,B) PAGE;

and causes the printout of A and B on line 1 of the next page.

This option can also be used with the PUT DATA statement, as in

> PUT DATA (A,B) PAGE;

The keyword PAGE can also appear after PUT, as in

> PUT PAGE DATA (A,B);

with the same meaning as before. We can also have just

> PUT PAGE;

which is a legal statement, causing positioning of the carriage on a new page.

The LINE and PAGE options can appear together as in

> PUT LINE (*n*) PAGE;

or

> PUT PAGE LINE (*n*);

or

> PUT LIST (A,B) PAGE LINE (*n*);

or

> PUT PAGE DATA (A,B) LINE (*n*);

In all cases the PAGE option is exercised first, positioning the carriage on the first line of the new page, then the LINE option positions the carriage on the *n*th line, and finally the printout of the output is made. Also, the FILE, LINE, PAGE, and LIST (or DATA) can appear together, as in

> PUT FILE(SYSPRINT)PAGE DATA (A,B) LINE(*n*);

Again, the PAGE option is executed first.

The LINE and SKIP options and the SKIP and PAGE options cannot appear together in the same statement; hence

> PUT LINE (3) LIST (A,B) SKIP (2);

or

> PUT PAGE SKIP (3) DATA (A);

are illegal statements.

E The LINESIZE Option

Recall that each line accommodates 120 characters. This number can be decreased or increased with the statement

> OPEN FILE (SYSPRINT) LINESIZE(*n*);

For example,

OPEN FILE (SYSPRINT) LINESIZE(90);

will only allow 90 characters on each line. Here we have four fields of data, these being as before columns 1–24, 25–48, 49–72, and 73–90. After printing in column 90, the printer prints in column 1 of the next line, since with the above statement we have chosen a line of 90 characters only. In fact, there is room for 132 characters on the line; thus the statement

OPEN FILE (SYSPRINT) LINESIZE(132);

will allow 132 characters on each line. Here we have six fields of data, the previous five occupying columns 1–120 as before, and the sixth one in columns 121–132.

At times we wish two different line output formats in the same program. To do so, we use the OPEN FILE statement for the first output format. After the PUT statement (that is, the printout), we must first ''close'' the file with the statement

CLOSE FILE (SYSPRINT);

and then open a new file with a new line format. As an example, consider the program

```
EXAMPLE: PROC OPTIONS(MAIN);
         OPEN FILE(SYSPRINT) LINESIZE(72);
         PUT LIST(1,2,3,4,5,6);
         CLOSE FILE(SYSPRINT);
         OPEN FILE(SYSPRINT) LINESIZE(48);
         PUT LIST(7,8,9);
         END EXAMPLE;
```

which gives the output

1	2	3	}on the first page
4	5	6	
7	8		}on the second page
9			

Note that the first PUT LIST statement causes the printout of three items on each line. The reopening of the SYSPRINT fill results in the start of a new page. The second output statement has only a 48-column, two-field line, and thus only two numbers (7 and 8) can be printed on the line. Hence the third number (9) has to be placed on a new line.

Observe that without the LINESIZE option the default condition of 120 columns per line prevails. Similarly, after the CLOSE FILE statement the default condition of 120 columns reestablishes itself. If there is a new LINESIZE option, as in the program of the example, it overrides the default condition.

F The PAGESIZE Option

Recall that each page accommodates 60 lines. This number can be decreased or increased with

OPEN FILE (SYSPRINT) PAGESIZE(m);

For example

OPEN FILE (SYSPRINT) PAGESIZE(50);

will only allow 50 lines on each page. There is in fact room for 66 lines on each page. Hence the statement

OPEN FILE (SYSPRINT) PAGESIZE(64);

will produce pages of 64 lines. In fact, we can "make" pages of more than 66 lines. For example, the statement

OPEN FILE (SYSPRINT) PAGESIZE(100);

will produce "pages" of 100 lines. It will do so by printing 100 lines consecutively. Thus the first physical page will have 66 lines (the maximum) and the second page the remaining 34 lines. The computer treats these two pages as a single page of 100 lines, and after printing the 100 lines, it will move the printer to the new page, this being the first line of the third page.

As before, to remove the option we use

CLOSE FILE (SYSPRINT);

The LINESIZE and PAGESIZE options can be used together, as in

OPEN FILE (SYSPRINT) LINESIZE(100) PAGESIZE(40);

The CLOSE FILE statement removes both options and reestablishes default conditions.

In closing, note that the CLOSE FILE statement can be used optionally (that is, it can either appear in the program or be deleted) when our output is printed with a single format.

16.7 SUMMARY

We described the list- and data-directed outputs and the way numerical and character-string constants are portrayed in the printed output. We also described the layout of the output and the appearance of data on the printed page. We then discussed the output options, such as FILE, SKIP, LINE, PAGE, LINESIZE, and PAGESIZE. Note that PL/I provides considerable control over the layout of the output. A further form of output, with even more control over the printout, will be described in Chap. 24.

PROBLEMS

16.1 Write a program to printout

JOE'S BOOK

in the fourth column of the third field on the fifth line from the top.

16.2 What is the output of the following programs?

(a)
```
P2A: PROC OPTIONS(MAIN);
     N = 2;
     DO I=1 BY 1;
         A = 2*N +(N+1)/3;
         IF A<0 THEN STOP;
         PUT LIST(A);
         N = N - 1;
     END;
     END P2A;
```

(Incidentally, can you improve on this program style?)

(b)
```
P2B: PROC OPTIONS(MAIN);
     K = 3;
     N = 4*(K+2)/3 + (K-1)/(K+1);
     A = N/(K+1);
     PUT LIST(A,N/K,N);
     END P2B;
```

16.3 The program

```
P3: PROC OPTIONS(MAIN);
    A,B,N = 3;
    DO WHILE(A¬=0);
        GET LIST(A,B,N);
        PUT LIST(A*B,N/A);
    END;
    END P3;
```

has the data

$$2, 1, , 3, , 4$$

What is the output?

16.4 Show the exact printout of the following program (columns need not be given):

```
P4: PROC OPTIONS(MAIN);
    N = 3;
    DO WHILE(N¬<0);
        M,A = N + N*N/2E0;
        PUT LIST(N,10*A);
        PUT LIST(M,A) SKIP(N);
        N = N - 1;
    END;
    END P4;
```

16.5
```
P5: PROC OPTIONS(MAIN);
    SUM = 0;
A:  GET LIST(B,C,D);
    IF B=C|B>C+D THEN SUM = SUM + D;
    IF B>5 THEN GO TO A;
    IF C<D THEN SUM = SUM + D;
```

```
    IF B>SUM/100 THEN SUM = SUM + 2*C;
    PUT LIST(SUM);
    IF B>SUM THEN GO TO A;
    END P5;
```

The data are

$$5.1, 8.2, -7.2, 2.1, 0.7, 2.3, 6.5, 10, 12, 17.2, 14.2$$

(*a*) What is the output of this program?

(*b*) Rewrite this program without the GO TOs.

16.6 Show the output of the following programs.

(*a*)
```
P6A: PROC OPTIONS(MAIN);
     DO WHILE(1);
         GET LIST(A,N);
         IF N=3 THEN A = A - N;
                 ELSE A = A + N;
         N = N + A;
         PUT LIST(A,N);
     END;
     END P6A;
```

(*b*)
```
P6B: PROC OPTIONS(MAIN);
     DO WHILE(1);
         GET LIST(A,N);
         A = A + N;
         N = N + 1;
         PUT LIST(N,A);
         IF A>N+5 THEN PUT SKIP LIST(N);
     END;
     END P6B;
```

The data are

$$1, 2.3, 7.7, 2.1, 5.7, 0.2$$

for both *a* and *b*.

16.7 Make a table listing the first 20 integers, their squares and cubes, in three columns in fields 2,3, and 4. Each column should be headed by the correct description (for example, NUMBER, SQUARE, CUBE). Each heading should be underlined, correctly centered, and one line above its column. The entire table should be centered in the middle of the page and bordered by a rectangle of asterisks, approximately even-spaced from the table.

The third line of the page should have a descriptive title of the table and list the name of the programmer, as, for example,

TABLE OF THE FIRST 20 INTEGERS, THEIR SQUARES, AND CUBES
BY
HENRY RUSTON

properly centered.

16.8 Write a program to print out a 3×3 inch square and a description of the method that you used. The output should have the following form:

Title:	METHOD OF SOLUTION	centered and underlined on line 5
	BY	centered on line 6
	HENRY RUSTON	your name centered on line 7

A description of your method should start on line 9 and be between the margins of columns 5 and 115, with each new paragraph starting in column 10.

The remainder of the page should portray a 3×3 inch square, centered both vertically and horizontally in the unprinted area. If your narrative is of great length and there is not enough space for the square, show the square on the next page.

16.9 Joe Computer discovered errors in his paycheck, dating back to 2/1/71. He received the following pay:

Period	Salary received	Total money received in period
2/1/71–11/30/71	$330.92/month	$2521.91
12/1/71–1/31/72	$160.05/2 weeks	$ 278.67
2/1/72–8/31/72	$173.59/2 weeks	$1957.03
9/1/72–10/18/72	$178.88/2 weeks	$ 465.09

According to his union contract, Joe should have been paid

2/1/71–11/30/71	$337.84/month
12/1/71–1/31/72	$349.34/month
2/1/72–8/31/72	$384.83/month
9/1/72–10/18/72	$396.09/month

Observe that Joe's company converted to biweekly payments on 12/1/71. The biweekly pay is calculated with the formula

$$\text{Biweekly pay} = \frac{(\text{monthly pay}) (12) (10)}{261}$$

Write a computer program to calculate:
1. Correct salary per pay period (which is monthly initially, and biweekly later on)
2. Adjustment due per pay period
3. Total adjustment due

Present your output under appropriate headings. Show on the computer printout the time period, correct salary, salary received, total money received in a period, the adjustment due in a period, and the sum of all the adjustments.

16.10 A consumer organization monitors prices of five foods for 4 weeks. The initial prices of these foods are

Sugar	= 16 cents/lb
Bread	= 27 cents/lb
Milk	= 39 cents/qt
Meat	= $1.39/lb
Cereal	= 63 cents/box

The prices in the following 4 weeks were as follows:

	Sugar	Bread	Milk	Meat	Cereal
First week	0.17	0.26	0.40	1.37	0.64
Second week	0.19	0.27	0.39	1.36	0.66
Third week	0.18	0.28	0.39	1.31	0.66
Fourth week	0.18	0.26	0.42	1.30	0.62

Prepare the input in data-directed form. Show only the prices that have changed from the previous week. Print out the output as follows:

CHANGES IN PRICES IN A 4-WEEK PERIOD	centered on line 1
THE INITIAL PRICES	centered on line 3
	the initial prices in data-directed
	form in the third field of lines 5 through 9
FIRST WEEK PRICES	centered on line 12
	all prices in data-directed form
	on line 14, followed by the following messages:

SUGAR COSTS *number* MORE IT HAS INCREASED BY *number* PERCENT

or   SUGAR COSTS *number* LESS, IT HAS DECREASED BY *number* PERCENT

or   SUGAR HAS NOT CHANGED IN PRICE

Write one such message for each item. Skip one line and repeat for the remaining weeks.

17 CHARACTER STRINGS

In Sec. 16.3 we described character-string constants. Now we will expand on this topic by introducing character-string variables and operations that can be performed on character strings. These operations make PL/I an exceptionally convenient language for nonnumerical tasks, such as translation, editing of written text, or decoding of messages.

17.1 CHARACTER-STRING CONSTANTS

We described the character-string constants in Sec. 16.3. For convenience, we will summarize the three main features:

1. A character-string constant must be enclosed in single quotation marks on the list of a PUT LIST statement, as, for example,

    PUT LIST ('METS WON');

2. A string of no characters is described by two adjacent quotation marks, as in

    ''

    and is named the *null string*.

3. A shortcut for writing character-string constants within the program is provided by the repetition factor. For example,

    'MMMM'

    can be written as

    (4)'M'

    with the repetition factor being 4 here. The repetition factor must be a nonnegative integer. If the repetition factor is zero, the expression is a null string.

17.2 CHARACTER-STRING VARIABLES

A Declaration

At times we wish a variable name, say, A, to represent a character string rather than a number. We must then do the following:

1. We must tell the compiler that A is a character string to prevent the usual conversions which accompany numbers. Here we wish to preserve A intact and must thus tell the compiler to leave A alone.
2. We must tell the compiler how much space is to be reserved for A. We do so by specifying the number of characters of A, that is, by giving the length of A. A can be as short as 1 character or as long as 32,767 characters (which is the maximum in System/360 and System/370).

The DECLARE statement is the vehicle for describing the variable A. If, for example, A has eight characters, we state

DECLARE A CHARACTER(8);

which tells that A is a character-string variable consisting of eight characters.

B Input

Consider now the statements

DCL A CHARACTER(8);
GET LIST (A);

The first statement declares A to be a character-string variable of eight characters. The second statement reads A from a data card. Since A is a character-string variable, the data for it must be enclosed in single quotes, as, for example,

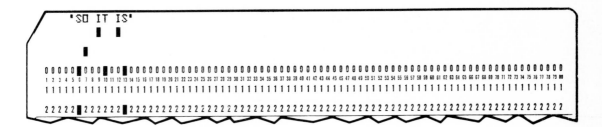

Similarly, the statement

GET DATA(A);

requires data of the form

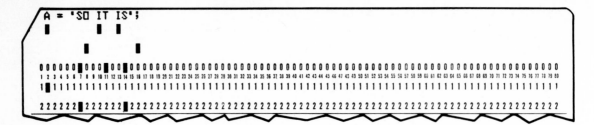

that is, quotes must enclose the character string.

C Output

The output statement

PUT LIST (A);

prints the output

SO IT IS

hence, without the quotes. Incidentally, this output is displayed in columns 1–8 of the first field.

The statement

PUT DATA (A);

prints the output

A='SO IT IS';

that is, with the quotes (and the semicolon). As in the case of numbers, A is displayed in column 1 of the first field (assuming of course that the printer is positioned on a new line), and the remaining characters occupy consecutive spaces (that is, = sign in column 2, ' in column 3, and so on).

D Assignment Statement

The statement

A = 'SO IT IS';

assigns the character string 'SO IT IS' to A. Note again the presence of quotes.

E Example

The program

```
EXAMPLE: PROC OPTIONS(MAIN);
         DCL(A,C) CHARACTER(4), B CHARACTER(3);
         GET LIST(A,C);
         B = 'AND';
         PUT LIST(A,B,C);
         END EXAMPLE;
```

with the data card

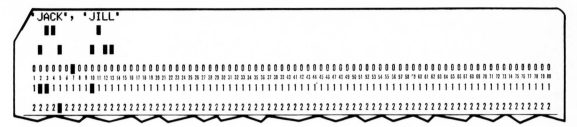

will print out

JACK   AND   JILL
↑   ↑   ↑
col. 1   col. 25   col. 49

Note the "factoring" of attributes in the above program. This factoring was described in Sec. 5.2 for numerical variables but is equally valid for character-string variables.

17.3 FURTHER DETAILS ON CHARACTER STRINGS

A Insufficient Length

Consider the program segment

```
DCL A CHARACTER(5);
A = 'PENCIL';
PUT LIST (A);
```

Obviously, the five characters reserved for A are insufficient to store the character string 'PENCIL' assigned to A. In such a case the string is truncated on the right side to the specified length, and just 'PENCI' is assigned to A. Consequently, the printout is

```
PENCI
```

B Excess Length

Consider the program segment

```
DCL A CHARACTER(10);
A = 'PENCIL';
PUT DATA (A);
```

Now 10 characters are reserved for A. Since A has only six characters, an extra four blanks are added on the right side, and the character string PENCILbbbb is assigned to A. Consequently, the printout is

```
A = 'PENCILbbbb';
```

C The VARYING Attribute

If we do not specify enough length, we lose characters. If we specify extra length, we have redundant blanks. We can avoid truncating characters and padding with extra blanks through the use of the VARYING attribute, as in

DCL A CHARACTER (10) VARYING;

which specifies that A has a length of up to 10 characters. Now we do not have to worry about specifying the actual length of A—this is done for us by the compiler. As A is acquired, an automatic assignment of space takes place, up to the given maximum length. As an example consider the program

```
EXAMPLE: PROC OPTIONS(MAIN);
         DCL A CHARACTER(10) VARYING;
         DO I=1 BY 1;
             GET LIST(A);
             PUT DATA(A);
         END;
         END EXAMPLE;
```

with the data card

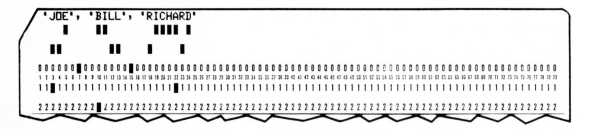

which results in the output

```
A='JOE';              A='BILL';              A='RICHARD';
↑                     ↑                      ↑
col. 1                col. 25                col. 49
```

Here automatic assignment of adequate space takes place as asserted. Observe that the program stops when the input device tries to acquire data on the fourth cycle. Since there are no more data (that is, the ENDFILE condition described in Sec. 15.1 occurs), the program execution is terminated.

D Abbreviations

Two abbreviations exist:

CHAR   for CHARACTER
VAR   for VARYING

Thus the DCL statement in the last program can be written more compactly as

DCL A CHAR (10) VAR;

E The Length Attribute

The length attribute, that is, the number following CHARACTER, can be an expression. Thus

DCL A CHAR (I*3+1);

is a legal statement (a noninteger result will be truncated).

17.4 OPERATIONS ON CHARACTER STRINGS

A Concatenation

An operation, named concatenation and denoted by the symbol

| |

unites two character strings into a single one. For example, the expression

'PROGRAMMING LANGUAGE/'| |'ONE'

is equivalent to

'PROGRAMMING LANGUAGE/ONE'

Several concatenations in a single expression are possible. For example,

PUT LIST ('THE' | |' LONE' | |' RANGER');

will print out

THE LONE RANGER

Since concatenation is an operation, it has a place on the list of priorities of operations. This list was given in Sec. 14.1. With the concatenation the list becomes

1. **   prefix +   prefix −
2. *   /
3. infix +   infix −
4. | |
5. <   ¬<   <=   =   ¬=   >=   >   ¬>
6. &
7. |

As stated in Sec. 14.1, the operations in the first priority are performed from right to left and all others from left to right. Thus, for example, in

'BI'| |'CYC'| |'LE'

the concatenation

$$'BI'||'CYC'$$

is made first, and then the concatenation

$$'BICYC'||'LE'$$

takes place.

B The SUBSTR Function

In solving various mathematical problems we often need the values of certain functions, such as the value of a sine or a logarithm. The PL/I language contains the sine, the logarithm, and several other functions as part of the language. The functions provided in PL/I are named *built-in functions* and will be described in Chap. 21. For example, the common logarithm (that is, base 10 logarithm) of a number X is denoted in PL/I as LOG10(X). Whenever the compiler sees LOG10(X), it transfers to an internal "built-in" program which calculates the base 10 logarithm of X. It then substitutes the calculated value for LOG10(X). For example, the program segment

```
X = 20;
Y = LOG10(X);
PUT LIST (X,Y);
```

will cause the printout of

$$2.00000E+01 \qquad 1.30103E+00$$

giving 20 and log 20 in floating-point form. Here LOG10 is the name of the function, and X is the argument. Note how convenient it is to have this function. Without it, we would have to write a program for its calculation. The LOG10 function has a single argument. Some functions have several arguments; hence a built-in function has the general form

function name (argument1, argument2, . . ., argumentk)

The LOG10 function is an example of a mathematical function. PL/I also provides functions for the handling of character strings. Perhaps the most useful is the SUBSTR function, which copies a part of a string (that is, a substring). This function has the form

SUBSTR *(argument1,argument2,argument3)*

where *argument1* = name of the character string from which the substring is to be copied

argument2 = the position of the starting character of the substring, counting from the left

argument3 = number of characters in the substring, that is, the length of the substring

As an example, consider the program

```
EXAMPLE: PROC OPTIONS(MAIN);
         DCL A CHAR(8), B CHAR(5)VAR;
         A = 'CALENDAR';
         B = SUBSTR(A,3,3);
         PUT LIST(B)SKIP;
         B = SUBSTR(A,1,5);
         PUT LIST(B)SKIP;
         B = SUBSTR(B,2,3);
         PUT DATA(B)SKIP;
         END EXAMPLE;
```

The output is

```
LEN
CALEN
B='ALE';
```

because the first use of the SUBSTR function copies three characters from the string 'CALENDAR', starting with the third character (that is, L). Thus 'LEN' is copied and assigned to B. Similarly, the second use of the SUBSTR function copies five characters from A, starting with the first character. Now 'CALEN' is assigned to B. And finally, three characters are copied from B (which is equal to 'CALEN'), starting with the second character. The result is 'ALE'. Thus the output is as shown. Observe the use of the VARYING attribute in the DCL statement for B, which allows B to have up to five characters.

The SUBSTR function can also be given without the third argument, that is, with just two arguments. The first argument is still the name of the character string and the second argument the place of the starting character, as before. But now, the length is assumed to be the remainder of the string beginning with the starting character. For example,

$$B = SUBSTR('CALENDAR',4);$$

gives the same result as

$$B = SUBSTR('CALENDAR',4,5);$$

and in both cases 'ENDAR' is copied from the string and assigned to B.

In the above examples, the SUBSTR function appears on the right side of the assignment statement. It is also allowable to place the SUBSTR function on the left side of the assignment statement, as if it were a variable. In this case, we name the SUBSTR function a *pseudovariable* (that is, a false or pretended variable). For example, the program segment

$$A = 'CALENDAR';$$
$$SUBSTR(A,3,5) = 'NISTE';$$
$$PUT LIST (A);$$

will cause the printout of

CANISTER

because with the second statement we have placed the string 'NISTE' in the five places of A, starting with the third character. Hence here the SUBSTR function modifies a string, where previously it merely copied a part of a string. We will illustrate in the next section applications for both uses of the SUBSTR function.

The arguments in the SUBSTR function can be expressions. For example, the first argument can be a character-string expression such as in the program segment

```
A = 'CALENDAR';
B = SUBSTR(SUBSTR(A,1,3) | |SUBSTR(A,6),2,4);
PUT LIST (B);
```

which gives the output

ALDA

because

```
SUBSTR(A,1,3) = 'CAL'
SUBSTR(A,6)   = 'DAR'
'CAL' | |'DAR'   = 'CALDAR'
```

and hence

SUBSTR('CALDAR',2,4) = 'ALDA'

Similarly, the second and the third arguments can be arithmetic expressions. If the expression results in a decimal fraction, then truncation to an integer takes place. Likewise, a floating-point number is converted to an integer. For example, any one of the assignment statements

```
B = SUBSTR(A,3.1,3.9);
B = SUBSTR(A,7/2,0.36E1)
B = SUBSTR(A,3.1E0,16/5);
```

gives the same result as

```
B = SUBSTR(A,3,3);
```

The second argument represents the starting place of the substring; hence the resulting integer must be no less than 1 and no greater than the length of the string (that is, no greater than the total number of characters in the string.) For example, the statements

```
B = SUBSTR('CALENDAR', 0,3);
B = SUBSTR('CALENDAR',9,1);
```

are both illegal.

The third argument represents the number of characters in the substring. This number cannot be less than zero and cannot exceed the available string length. For example

$$B = SUBSTR('CALENDAR',3,0);$$

is legal and gives the null string. However,

$$B = SUBSTR('CALENDAR',3,8);$$

is illegal, since there are no eight characters in 'CALENDAR' beyond the third place (but six at most).

C The INDEX Function

The INDEX function is a built-in function for locating a string in another, usually longer, string. This function has the form

$$INDEX(string1, string2)$$

where *string1* = string to be searched

string2 = string that we wish to locate

The INDEX function gives (or *returns*, in computer jargon) the position where *string2* was found. For example,

$$N = INDEX('CARNIVAL','NIV');$$

assigns 4 to N, because the string 'NIV' is located in the fourth place of the string 'CARNIVAL'. If *string2* is not found in *string1*, the INDEX function returns zero. For example,

$$N = INDEX('CARNIVAL', 'NEV');$$

assigns 0 to N, because the string 'NEV' is not found in the string 'CARNIVAL'. And finally, if *string2* exists in *string1* several times, then the first location will be given. For example, in

$$N = INDEX('CARNIVAL','A');$$

the number 2 (first location of 'A') is assigned to N.

Both *string1* and *string2* can be expressions.

17.5 EXAMPLES

We are ready now for three examples which will illustrate operations on character strings.

Example 17.5.1 Assume that there is an English text on data cards, which comprises a character string of 20,000 characters. We wish to substitute the name 'WILL' for the name 'DICK' in the string and to print out the result. It is known that the name 'DICK' does not occur at the beginning of the text nor is it followed by a punctuation mark. It is further known that each punctuation mark is followed by a space.

Solution We will use the method of structured design to construct the program. The first version is

VERSION 1

```
          Start Example 1;
          GET text;
          Replace each 'DICK' by 'WILL';
          PUT text;
          END Example 1:
```

This leads immediately to the second version as

VERSION 2

```
          Start Example 1;
          GET text;
          /*REPLACE EACH 'DICK' BY 'WILL'*/
          Locate 'DICK' in the text;
          DO WHILE ('DICK' was found in the text);
              Replace 'DICK' by 'WILL';
              Locate 'DICK' in the text;
          END;
          PUT text;
          END Example 1;
```

We observe that we should really locate the string 'ƀDICKƀ'. We should enclose DICK within the two extra spaces to avoid locating 'DICK' within another word, such as 'DICKENS'.

We shall now name the variables. Let

$$\text{TEXT} = \text{the input string}$$
$$N = \text{the position of 'ƀDICKƀ' in TEXT}$$

Then the third version is the desired program as shown below.

VERSION 3

```
EX_1: PROC OPTIONS(MAIN);
      /* THIS PROGRAM IS TO REPLACE EACH            */
      /* ' DICK ' BY ' WILL ' IN A GIVEN TEXT       */
      DCL TEXT CHAR(20000);
      GET LIST(TEXT);
      /* LOCATE ' DICK ' IN TEXT                     */
      N = INDEX(TEXT,' DICK ');         /* N = THE POSITION OF    */
                                        /* ' DICK ' IN TEXT       */
      DO WHILE(N¬=0);
          SUBSTR(TEXT,N,6) = ' WILL '; /* REPLACE ' DICK ' BY    */
                                        /* ' WILL '               */
          N = INDEX(TEXT,' DICK ');     /* NEXT POSITION OF       */
                                        /* ' DICK ' IN TEXT       */
```

```
END;
PUT LIST(TEXT);
END EX_1;
```

   Incidentally, if we remove the restrictions imposed in the example (that is, 'DICK' may occur at the beginning of the text, etc.) the program requires several modifications. The solution of this more general problem is left as an exercise (see Prob. 17.10).

Example 17.5.2 Assume that there is an English text on data cards, which comprises a character string of 10,000 characters. We wish to know how many times the article 'THE' was used. It is known that the article THE is never followed by another THE or a punctuation mark and that each punctuatic mark is followed by a space.

Solution This is a counting problem. The first version is

VERSION 1

```
                Start Example 2;
                GET text;
                Count all 'THE' in the text;
                PUT count;
                END Example 2;
```

   The second version is

VERSION 2

```
                Start Example 2;
                GET text;
                /*COUNT ALL 'THE' IN THE TEXT*/
                Locate 'THE' in the text;
                DO WHILE ('THE' was found in the text);
                     Increase count of 'THE';
                     Locate 'THE' in the text;
                END;
                PUT count;
                END Example 2;
```

There are still several details to be added. Let us consider them here:

1. To avoid locating 'THE' as part of another word, we will search for 'ƀTHEƀ'. We will place a space in front of the text to allow for the possible 'THEƀ' in the beginning of the text.
2. We must initialize the count of 'ƀTHEƀ'.

3. We must ensure that each 'ᵇTHEᵇ' is counted just once. One approach is to remove the part of the string containing the 'ᵇTHEᵇ' already counted.

With these additions the next version reads

VERSION 3

```
Start Example 2;
GET text;
Place a space in front of text;
/*COUNT ALL 'ᵇTHEᵇ' IN THE TEXT*/
Locate 'ᵇTHEᵇ' in the text;
DO WHILE ('ᵇTHEᵇ' was found in the text);
    Increase count of 'ᵇTHEᵇ';
    Eliminate the part of string containing the text
        with the 'ᵇTHEᵇ' already counted;
    Locate 'ᵇTHEᵇ' in the text;
END;
PUT count;
END Example 2;
```

If we name the input text TEXT, the location of 'ᵇTHEᵇ' N, and the count ICOUNT, we obtain the fourth version in the form of the desired program as

VERSION 4

```
EX_2:    PROC OPTIONS(MAIN);
         DCL TEXT CHAR(10001)VAR;
         GET LIST(TEXT);
         TEXT = ' '||TEXT;     /* WE PLACE A SPACE IN FRONT OF TEXT     */
         ICOUNT = 0;           /* ICOUNT COUNTS THE NUMBER OF ' THE '   */
         N = INDEX(TEXT,' THE ');
         DO WHILE(N¬=0);
             ICOUNT = ICOUNT+1;
             TEXT = SUBSTR(TEXT,N+4);   /* WE HAVE ELIMINATED THE PART OF
                                           THE TEXT WITH THE ' THE ' ALREADY
                                           COUNTED                        */
             N = INDEX(TEXT, ' THE ');
         END;
         PUT LIST(ICOUNT);
         END EX_2;
```

Example 17.5.3 Assume again that we have our English text of 10,000 characters on data cards. Now we wish to substitute the word COLOR for COLOUR (the British spelling). It is known that the word 'COLOUR' is not followed by a punctuation mark and that each punctuation mark is followed by a space.

Solution We will place a space in the front of the string to allow for a possible 'COLOUR' at the beginning of the text. We then locate the word 'ᵇCOLOURᵇ' with the INDEX function. We substitute 'ᵇCOLORᵇ' for 'ᵇCOLOURᵇ', which really results in the word $'\text{ɓCOLORɓɓ}'$, hence with a redundant space. We delete the space with concatenation of two substrings. Before printing out the result, we eliminate the space in front of the string. The program is shown below (The reader should construct as an exercise the preceding versions.)

```
EX_3:     PROC OPTIONS(MAIN);
          DCL TEXT CHAR(10001)VAR;
          GET LIST(TEXT);
          TEXT = ' '||TEXT;
          N = INDEX(TEXT,' COLOUR ');
          DO WHILE(N¬=0);
              SUBSTR(TEXT,N,7) = ' COLOR ';
              TEXT = SUBSTR(TEXT,1,N+6)||SUBSTR(TEXT,N+8);
              /* THE ABOVE CONCATENATION REMOVES THE EXTRA SPACE
                  IN THE (N+7)-TH PLACE                              */
              N = INDEX(TEXT,' COLOUR ');
          END;
          TEXT = SUBSTR(TEXT,2); /* ELIMINATES THE EXTRA FRONTAL SPACE*/
          PUT LIST(TEXT);
          END EX_3;
```

The above three examples illustrate operations on character strings which may occur in text-editing tasks. Note the versatility of PL/I in handling such nonnumerical jobs.

17.6 THE LENGTH AND REPEAT BUILT-IN FUNCTIONS

A The LENGTH Function

The LENGTH built-in function

$$\text{LENGTH}\,(string1)$$

gives the length of *string1*, that is, the number of characters in *string1*. For example, the program segment

```
DCL A CHAR(8) VAR;
A = 'EXAMPLE';
N = LENGTH(A) + LENGTH(SUBSTR(A,3));
PUT LIST(N);
```

prints

$$12$$

because

```
LENGTH(A) = LENGTH('EXAMPLE') = 7
LENGTH(SUBSTR(A,3)) = LENGTH('AMPLE') = 5
```

and their sum is 12.

Example 17.6.1 Assume that we have a string of at most 10,000 characters on data cards. We wish to obtain a "reverse" string, that is, to place the first character in the last position, the second character in the next-to-last position, and so on. With this process, for example, the string 'ABCD' will reverse into 'DCBA'.

Solution Evidently, we must determine the length of the string first and then construct the reversed string through the use of the SUBSTR function. The program is then

```
EXAMPLE: PROC OPTIONS(MAIN);
         DCL (STRING,REVSTRING)CHAR(10000)VAR;/* STRING IS THE GIVEN */
         GET LIST(STRING);                    /* STRING, REVSTRING   */
         REVSTRING = STRING;                   /* THE REVERSED STRING */
         L = LENGTH(STRING);
         DO I = 1 TO L;
            SUBSTR(REVSTRING,I,1) = SUBSTR(STRING,L+1-I,1);
         END;
         PUT LIST(REVSTRING);
         END EXAMPLE;
```

Observe that the statement REVSTRING = STRING; establishes the length of REVSTRING.

B The REPEAT Function

The REPEAT built-in function

$$REPEAT(string1,k)$$

will construct a string which consists of k repetitions of *string1*. The argument *string1* can be a character-string constant, a character-string variable, or a character-string expression. k must be an integer constant (that is, cannot be a variable or an expression) but may be signed (a negative integer is interpreted as zero). For example,

$$B = REPEAT('ABC',1);$$

assigns 'ABCABC' to B. Observe that if there is one repetition of 'ABC', then 'ABC' appears twice in the result 'ABCABC'. Therefore, in k repetitions of *string1*, *string1* will appear $k + 1$ times. Note that there are two other ways of accomplishing the repetitions for a character-string constant, either with a repetition factor or with concatenation; for example,

$$B = REPEAT('BOOM',2);$$

has the same effect as

$$B = (3)'BOOM';$$

or

$$B = 'BOOM' \mid \mid 'BOOM' \mid \mid 'BOOM';$$

Observe the differences among the repetition factor, the REPEAT function, and the concatenation:

1. The repetition factor can only be associated with a character-string constant.
2. The REPEAT function is more general and can be used with a character-string expression.
3. The concatenation is not limited to identical strings and is valid for character-string expressions.

17.7 COMPARISONS WITH CHARACTER STRINGS

We made use of comparisons with the IF statements, as in

IF *condition1* THEN *statement1;*

where *condition1* entailed a comparison. For example, in

IF X=Y THEN D = D+1;

D+1 is assigned to D if X=Y. In the past, X and Y were numbers or expressions in numerical variables, but the comparison is equally valid if X and Y are character strings. In fact, we can also use inequalities for such X and Y. For example, the program segment

```
DCL D CHAR(3) VAR;
X = 'ABC';
Y = 'ABB';
IF X > Y THEN D = 'YES';
        ELSE D = 'NO';
PUT DATA(D);
```

is a valid one and causes the printout of

D = 'YES';

which brings up the question of the rules governing the comparison of character strings.

The PL/I language contains 60 characters. Each of the 60 characters is represented in the computer by 8 bits (that is, 8 binary digits). Thus each character has internally a numerical value, and their ordering from smallest to largest is named a *collating sequence*. Many assignments of numbers to characters are possible. The assignment used in IBM System/360 and System/370 follows a code named Extended Binary-Coded-Decimal Interchange Code (abbreviated as EBCDIC). The collating sequence for the EBCDIC is

(1)	b̷	(16)	⅄	(31)	G	(46)	V
(2)	•	(17)	_	(32)	H	(47)	W
(3)	<	(18)	>	(33)	I	(48)	X
(4)	(	(19)	?	(34)	J	(49)	Y
(5)	+	(20)	:	(35)	K	(50)	Z
(6)	|	(21)	#	(36)	L	(51)	0
(7)	&	(22)	@	(37)	M	(52)	1
(8)	$	(23)	'	(38)	N	(53)	2
(9)	*	(24)	=	(39)	O	(54)	3
(10)	)	(25)	A	(40)	P	(55)	4
(11)	;	(26)	B	(41)	Q	(56)	5
(12)	¬	(27)	C	(42)	R	(57)	6
(13)	−	(28)	D	(43)	S	(58)	7
(14)	/	(29)	E	(44)	T	(59)	8
(15)	,	(30)	F	(45)	U	(60)	9

In the above sequence $'b̷'$ is represented by the smallest number and $'9'$ by the largest number. Observe that the sequence includes the question mark, which has no use in the PL/I language but can be used in a comment.[1]

In an inequality involving two strings, comparison is made character by character, starting with the leftmost characters.

Clearly, it follows from the collating sequence that

$$'C' > 'B'$$

and hence

$$'ABC' > 'ABB'$$

thus $X > Y$, causing the assignment of $'YES'$ to D, as indicated in the preceding program segment.

In any comparison involving character strings, the strings have the same length, that is, the same number of characters, on both sides of the comparison sign. This is achieved by extending the string of shorter length with extra blanks on the right. For example, in the comparison

$$'ABC' > 'AB'$$

'AB' is adjusted to 'ABb̷'; hence the expression is effectively

$$'ABC' > 'ABb̷'$$

which is *true* because $'C' > 'b̷'$.

---

[1]The keypunch contains four other characters which are not in the PL/I language. These characters are ¢, !, ", and the 0·8·2 punch. The line printer prints the double quotes but not the other three characters (they will appear on the printout sheet as blanks). Because these four characters are also represented internally by 8 bits, they can be positioned within the collating sequence (in fact, ¢ follows b̷, ! follows &, " follows =, and 0·8·2 follows R).

*17.8 CONVERSION OF DATA

We will consider now operations on mixed data, such as arithmetic data (that is, numbers) and character-string data. Because the operations require uniformity of data, a conversion must take place; that is, either the character string is converted into a number or the number into a character string. We will discuss the rules governing such conversions.

A Conversion of a Character String to a Number

PL/I is very accommodating and tries to perform all instructions that have a semblance of sense. It will reject only those that are totally meaningless. It will perform operations involving character strings and numbers. For example, the program segment

```
DCL X FIXED (3,1);
X = '12.45' + 7.2;
PUT LIST (X);
```

is a valid one. However, the result is subject to a PL/I rule. This rule states that in an infix operation (that is, an operation where the operand is in between two quantities, as in A*B) involving a character string which represents a fixed-point number, the conversion of the character string to fixed point will cause a loss of the fractional part. Thus the character string '12.45' will be converted to the number 12.45, but because of the addition performed (which is an infix operation), 12.45 is truncated to 12 and the result 19.2 assigned to X, giving the printout

19.2

In general, any character string in the form of a signed or unsigned arithmetic constant will be converted to the arithmetic constant. For example, in the program segment

```
DCL(A,B) CHAR(3), (C,D,E) FIXED(4,2);
A = '9.8';
B = '−12';
C = A+A*B;
D = A;
E = B;
PUT LIST (A,B,C,D,E);
```

all statements are legal and give the output

9.8   −12   −99.00   9.80   −12.00

---

*If time does not permit the coverage of the entire chapter, the starred sections can be omitted without any loss of continuity.

where again observe that the infix operation in the assignment statement for C causes a truncation of A to 9, so that $C = 9+9*(-12) = -99.00$ as printed out.

The arithmetic constant comprising the character string can also be in floating-point form, as in

$$A = '1.2E2';$$
$$\text{PUT DATA(A)};$$

which gives the output

$$A= ␢1.20000E+02;$$

because A is by default a floating-point number.

It is also legal to include spaces in front of or in back of the constant, as in

$$A = '␢123␢␢';$$

which is interpreted just as

$$A = '123';$$

B Conversion of a Number to a Character String

We encountered the conversion of numbers to character strings in Sec. 16.4. Recall that for printout a conversion is made from the computer representation of a number to a character string. Consider now the program segment

```
DCL A CHAR(10);
A = 13;
PUT DATA (A);
```

which requires the conversion of 13 to a character string. What is the resulting output?

1. The number 13 is FIXED DEC(2). We stated in Sec. 16.4 that such a number converts to a character string of length $p + 3$ (where p is the precision, being 2 here), or five characters. Hence the string '␢␢␢13' is assigned to A.
2. A is extended to its declared length of 10 characters by the addition of extra blanks on the right side. Thus the string '␢␢␢13␢␢␢␢␢' is stored for A.
3. The resulting printout is therefore

$$A ='␢␢␢13␢␢␢␢␢';$$

   ↑   ↑

   col. 1   col. 15

Incidentally, the reason why a FIXED DEC(p) number converts to a string of $p + 3$ characters is because such a number may require up to $p + 3$ characters for its portrayal. These three extra characters are for the

1. Sign in front of the number

2. Decimal point
3. Zero in front of the decimal point

For example, the two-digit number $-.13$ is of precision $(2,2)$. It is printed in the output in the standard form as -0.13 which requires five (that is, $p + 3$) characters, as asserted.

As a further example, the statement

PUT LIST ('THE ANSWER IS' | |13);

will cause the output

THE ANSWER ISꞵꞵꞵ13

Here the number 13 is converted to the character string 'ꞵꞵꞵ13', because only character strings can be concatenated. After the conversion, the concatenation of the two strings takes place, giving the indicated output. Consider now the statements

A = 3.7E0;
PUT LIST ('THE ANSWER IS' | |A);

which cause the output

THE ANSWER ISꞵ3.7E+00

Here the following takes place:

1. The floating-point number 3.7E0 is converted to the standard form of $3.7E+00$ and is stored in the location assigned to A.
2. To perform the concatenation, A must be converted to a character string. By the conversion rules stated in Sec. 16.4, a FLOAT DEC(p) number converts to a character string of $p + 6$ characters. Since 3.7 is of precision 2, it converts to

'ꞵ3.7E+00'

yielding the indicated output.

Note again that there is a reason for these six extra characters. They are for the

1. Sign in front of the number (only the negative sign is shown)
2. Decimal point
3. Four characters needed for the exponent part (that is, E+00 here)
   For example, the number

A = −3.7E0;

is of precision (2) and converts to the character string

'−3.7E+00'

thus requiring all eight (that is, $p + 6 = 2 + 6 = 8$) characters for its portrayal.

C Illegal Conversions

As we have seen, conversions that make sense will be made either from a character string into a number or from a number into a character string. However, one can construct statements that do not make sense. For example, in

$$D = 'CAT';$$

D is by default a FLOAT DEC(6) number. The conversion of the character string 'CAT' to a floating-point number is obviously an erroneous request, and PL/I interprets it as such. Such an error is named a CONVERSION condition and stops the execution of the program. We will say more about this condition in Chap. 26. Other illegal statements requiring illegal conversions are exemplified by

$$A = '4+2'; \quad \text{(but A = '4'+'2'; is legal)}$$
$$X = 'AB'*2;$$
$$A = 2*'*12';$$
$$\text{PUT LIST('AB' +1 | |'AB');}$$

and cause the CONVERSION condition.

17.9 SUMMARY

We reviewed the character-string constants and described the handling of character-string variables. The concatenation operation as well as the SUBSTR and the INDEX built-in functions were introduced, and examples were given on their use. We also discussed the LENGTH and REPEAT built-in functions and the comparisons with character strings. We saw that PL/I attempts to execute statements requiring conversion from characters to numbers or from numbers to characters. Only those statements that do not make sense will result in a CONVERSION error and stop the program.

PROBLEMS

17.1 Write a program to print out
   (a) 123 in columns 50 to 52 of the third line
   (b) 123 in columns 12 to 14 and 456 in columns 82 to 84 of the fiftieth line
17.2 What is the output resulting from the following program segment?

```
DCL(A,B,C) CHAR(10)VAR;
A = 'MATHEW';
B = 'ALONG';
C = 'ARRANGEMENT';
A = SUBSTR(A,3,3);
B = SUBSTR(B,2);
SUBSTR(B,4,1) = SUBSTR(A,3);
C = SUBSTR(C,3,6);
SUBSTR(C,6) = SUBSTR(C,1,1);
PUT LIST(A||' '||B||' '||C);
```

17.3 The program

```
P3: PROC OPTIONS(MAIN);
    N = 2;
    PUT LIST('THE RESULT IS',N);
    END P3;
```

gives the output

THE RESULT IS   2

↑
col. 1   19 spaces

Change the PUT LIST statement to another PUT LIST statement to give the output

THE RESULT IS 2

↑
col. 1

that is, with only a single space preceding 2.

17.4 A string of 200 characters is on data cards. Write a program which will replace each name JOE by JACK and each name JACK by JOE. It is known that both JOE and JACK are always preceded and followed by blanks. In your replacement do not create any extra spaces in the string.

17.5 The data cards contain an English text of 100 characters. It is desired to replace each name JOE by JAMES. It is known that the text does not start with the name JOE and that JOE is either followed by a blank or by a comma. Print out the new text.

17.6 A text of at most 100 characters appears on data cards. Write a GO TO–less program which removes all spaces from the text (that is, it replaces PERRY MASON by PERRYMASON) and prints the new text.

17.7 Print out an equilateral triangle, with the sides formed from dots. The base is to consist of 11 dots in columns 60 through 70 of line 30.

17.8 Write a program which reads in names (that is, character strings) punched on data cards and prints out the *longest* name and its position in the data stream.

Assume that no name is longer than 24 characters. If there are several names of equal length, print out the one which occurs first. The last name is 'END'.

17.9 Replace in a text of 200 characters each period by a comma and each comma by a period.

17.10 Modify Example 17.5.1 to include the possibility that 'DICK' can occur at any place in the text (for example, in the beginning) and is followed by either a blank or a punctuation mark.

17.11 Write a program which uses as input character strings of up to 200 characters in length, consisting of English words separated by one or more blanks, and removes all but one of the blanks between any two words in the string. The program should print out the original and final strings.

17.12 Write a program which uses as input character strings of up to 200 characters, consisting of left parentheses [(] and right parentheses [)] *only* (assume there are no blanks separating them), and determine whether the strings are "well formed."

A well-formed set of parentheses is one where

1. There is an equal number of left and right parentheses in the string.
2. For every right parenthesis, there must be a left parenthesis which appears earlier in the string.

Print the original string and a message stating whether or not the string constitutes well-formed parentheses. For example,

(( ) ( )) ( )	well formed
) ( ) (( ))	not well formed; unmatched right parentheses
((( ))	not well formed; too many left parentheses

17.13 Write a program which will take a character string composed of at most 100 characters. Each character is a letter (that is, there are no blanks or punctuation marks). Replace each letter in the string by one that follows it, so that A is replaced by B, B is replaced by C, and so on (Z is replaced by A). Print out the original string and the new string. For example,

'SILVER'

is replaced by

'TJMWFS'

17.14 Write a program that reads in a variable-length character string of at most 200 characters, determines if it is a palindrome, prints out the string and YES if it is and NO if it is not. A new string is then read in. The program stops when it reads in 'THE END'.

(*Note:* A palindrome is a string that is the same when read backwards or forward. Examples: TOOT, 525131525.)

17.15 The input consists of names having the form

'LAST__NAME,FIRST__NAME'

Each such name is to be printed out in the form

FIRST__NAMEbLAST__NAME

For example,

'DOE,JOE'

is to be printed out as

JOEbDOE

Write a program to give the desired output even if the keypunch operator inserts extra blanks in front of the last and first names. For example,

'bbLAST__NAME,bbbFIRST__NAME'

is to be printed out as before, that is,

FIRST__NAMEbLAST__NAME

The program is to stop through the ENDFILE condition. No name, inclusive of blanks, exceeds 40 characters.

17.16 The data cards contain a character string of at most 200 characters consisting of words. There are no one-letter words and no punctuation marks. Only a single space separates words. There are no spaces in the beginning or in the end of the string. Write a program to switch the first two letters of each word (that is, 'JOE AND BILL' will be replaced by 'OJE NAD IBLL') and print out the result.

17.17 Find the number of A's in a text. Do not count double or multiple A's. The text is at most 200 characters long.

17.18 Using the code

H J L T V Y R P N F D B A C E G O Q S X Z W U M K I
A B C D E F G H I J K L M N O P Q R S T U V W X Y Z

for

translate into code the message

DOING PROGRAMMING HOMEWORKS IS JOE'S IDEA OF HAVING FUN

and decode the message

NS XPHX SE?

17.19 The input cards contain several words. The last world is 'END'. There are no other such words in the input. There are at most 20 words in the input, and no word exceeds six characters. The input is

'NOW' 'IS' 'THE' 'TIME' 'FOR' 'ALL' 'GOOD' 'MEN' 'TO'
'COME' 'TO' 'THE' 'AID' 'OF' 'THE' 'PARTY' 'END'

(*a*) Show your input with the copy option.

(*b*) Form the words into a sentence but ignore the last word END. Separate the words with a single space. Place a period after the last word. Print out the sentence.

(*c*) Print out the reverse of the sentence, that is, YTRAP EHT, etc. The period should now be at the end, that is, after WON.

(*d*) Print out the words of the original sentence in reverse, that is, PARTY THE, etc., with the period at the end, that is, after NOW.

(*e*) Remove each article THE. There should still be only a single space after each word. Print out the result.

(*f*) Replace each article THE by either 'A' (before a consonant) or 'AN' (before a vowel). Print out your result.

(*g*) Your program should be general enough to work with any input described in the first paragraph.

17.20 The input consists of the first paragraph of Chap. 17. Write a program to

(*a*) Acquire and print the input.

(*b*) Reprint the input in the margins 1–100 (that is, columns 1–100). Indent the first line by five columns. Break up words to meet the margin requirements.

(*c*) Print as in (*b*) but do not break up words.

(*d*) Reprint as in (*c*) but fully "justified." This means that the last letter of the last word or punctuation mark must end in the 100th column. Add the additional blanks to the spaces between words starting in the beginning of the line by doubling each space as needed.

(*e*) Print the original input with each period replaced by the $ sign.

(*f*) Print the original input, underlining each letter S.

18 BIT STRINGS

We will now describe bit strings, which occupy the no-man's-land between character strings and numbers. We encountered them briefly at the end of Sec. 6.4 as results of a decision process. We will expand here on the use of bit strings for decisions and other applications. We shall see that the rules governing bit strings are very similar to the rules governing character strings.

18.1 RULES GOVERNING BIT STRINGS

The rules governing bit strings are very similar to the rules governing character strings.

A Form

A bit string is a string of 0s and 1s (that is, a string of binary digits or bits) enclosed in single quotes and immediately followed by the letter B, as, for example,

```
'101011'B
'0'B
'001'B
```

B Repetition Factor

We can use the repetition factor for writing bit strings. Thus

$$(3)'110'B$$

is the same as

$$'110110110'B$$

where the repetition factor must be an unsigned nonnegative integer constant (i.e., a sign in front of the integer is now allowed).

C Null Bit String

A null bit string is a string with no digits between quotes, that is,

$$' \, 'B$$

A repetition factor of zero also produces a null bit string; thus

$$(0)'1101'B$$

is a null string.

D Length

The length of a bit string is the number of digits in the string. The letter B is not counted. Hence

$$'1001'B$$

is a bit string of length 4.

E Bit-string Constants and Variables

A bit string, just like other quantities, can exist in a program in two forms:

1. As a constant, that is, in the described form for the bit string. For example,

$$'11011'B$$
$$(3)'11'B$$

   are bit-string constants.
2. As a variable. Here the name of the variable stands for the bit string, which is stored in the location assigned to the variable. In this case, the computer must be told that the variable represents a bit string of a certain length. This message to the computer is carried by the DECLARE statement.

F The DECLARE Statement

The DECLARE statement for a bit-string variable A has the form

$$\text{DCL A BIT(4);}$$

where 4 is the length of A. (For IBM System/360 and System/370 the maximum length is 32,767 bits.)

G Insufficient Length

If the declared length for a variable is insufficient, the rightmost digits are truncated. For example, in the program segment

```
DCL A BIT(3);
A = '10011'B;
PUT LIST (A);
```

the printout is

'100'B

thus '10011'B has been truncated on the right side to '100'B and then assigned to A.

H Excess Length

If the declared length for a variable exceeds the length of a string, extra zeros on the right side are added to the string. For example, in the program segment

```
DCL A BIT(3);
A = '11'B;
PUT LIST (A);
```

the printout is

'110'B

thus an extra zero was added to '11'B to satisfy the declared length of A.

I The VARYING Attribute

As for character strings, we can specify the maximum length of a bit-string variable A with the statement

DCL A BIT(10) VARYING;

which specifies that A has a length of up to 10 characters. Now, the length of A is adjusted automatically. For example, the output of the program

```
EXAMPLE: PROC OPTIONS(MAIN);
        DCL(A,B) BIT(5) VARYING;
        A = '101'B;
        B = '1011'B;
        PUT DATA(A,B);
        END EXAMPLE;
```

is

```
A='101'B                B='1011'B;
```

Thus automatic adjustments of lengths in A and B took place.

The VARYING attribute can be abbreviated to VAR, as, for example,

DCL JOE BIT (7) VAR;

J Input

Bit-string input data must appear in its defined form either on a data card or in an assignment statement. The program segment

```
DCL A BIT (4);
GET LIST (A);
```

requires a data card with a bit string for A, such as

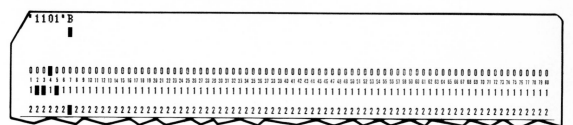

The program segment

```
DCL (A,B) BIT (3);
GET DATA (A,B);
```

requires a data-directed input card such as

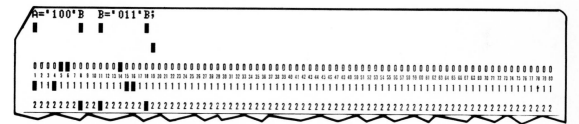

with the inevitable semicolon after the last item.

The assignment of a bit string to a bit-string variable was illustrated already, as, for example,

```
DCL A BIT(4);
A = '1001'B;
```

with A being a declared bit-string variable.

K Output

A bit-string constant can appear in the list of a PUT LIST statement, as in

```
PUT LIST ('1011'B);
```

which gives the output

```
'1011'B
```

To further illustrate the appearance of bit-string variables in the output, consider the program segment

```
DCL (A,B) BIT (3);
A, B = '101'B;
```

PUT LIST (A);
PUT DATA (B);

which gives the output

'101'B   B = '101'B;

Thus quotes always accompany the bit-string output.

18.2 OPERATION ON BIT STRINGS

The so-called *logical* operators

$\neg$ & |

can be employed on bit strings. We will describe the use of these operators.

A The NOT Operator

The NOT operator

$\neg$

changes 0s to 1s, and vice versa. For example,

$\neg$'0'B = '1'B
$\neg$'1'B = '0'B
$\neg$'01011'B = '10100'B
$\neg$'00100'B = '11011'B

In decision making we associate *true* with the bit string '1'B and *false* with the bit string '0'B. Hence

$\neg$'1'B

means *not true,* that is, *false,* and can thus be expressed as

'0'B

which follows the rules of logic and explains why $\neg$ is named a *logical* operator.

Since $\neg$ is an operation, it has a place on the list of priorities of operations. This list was given in Sec. 17.4A. In fact, $\neg$ is the last operation to be introduced, and the list of priorities is now complete.

1. **   prefix +   prefix − $\neg$
2. *   /
3. infix +   infix −
4. ||
5. < $\neg$<   <=   = $\neg$=   >=   > $\neg$>
6. &
7. |

Note that the ¬ operation is of highest priority. Recall that in an expression with several operations of the highest priority, such operations are performed from right to left.

B The AND Operator

The AND operator

$$\&$$

operates on two bit strings in accordance with the four rules

$$'0'B \& '0'B = '0'B$$
$$'0'B \& '1'B = '0'B$$
$$'1'B \& '0'B = '0'B$$
$$'1'B \& '1'B = '1'B$$

Again, associating '0'B with *false* and '1'B with *true,* the four rules state

False statement AND false statement = false statement
False statement AND true statement = false statement
True statement AND false statement = false statement
True statement AND true statement = true statement

Since these rules are logical, it explains why the AND operator is named a logical operator. The four rules are also known as the *truth table* for the AND operations. Observe that by these rules the result will be true only if both statements are true.

The & operator can be applied to bit strings containing more than 1 bit. In such cases the operation is applied to the two bit strings bit by bit. For example, in the operation

$$'011'B \& '101'B$$

the first (that is, leftmost) bit of the first bit string (which is 0) is compared to the first bit of the second bit string (which is 1). The result is 0. Similar comparison of the second bit of the first bit string (which is 1) with the second bit of the second bit string (which is 0) gives 0 as the result. Continuing with the third bit gives the overall result '001'B. Thus

$$'011'B \& '101'B = '001'B$$

Other examples of the & operation are

$$'10011'B \& '01010'B = '00010'B$$
$$'110'B \quad \& '010'B \quad = '010'B$$
$$'111'B \quad \& '001'B \quad = '001'B$$

If the strings are of different length, the shorter string is extended (with zeros on the right side) to the longer length. Thus

$$'101'B \& '10011'B = '10100'B \& '10011'B = '10000'B$$

C The OR Operator

The OR operator

operates on two bit strings in accordance with the four rules

$$'0'B \mid '0'B = '0'B$$
$$'0'B \mid '1'B = '1'B$$
$$'1'B \mid '0'B = '1'B$$
$$'1'B \mid '1'B = '1'B$$

Using the association of $'0'B$ with *false* and $'1'B$ with *true,* the interpretation of the rules is that if either the first statement is true OR the second statement (or both) is true, then the result is true. This OR is known as the inclusive OR, and the above four rules are named the truth table for the OR. Again, because of its use in logic, the OR operator is named a logical operator.

The OR operation on bit strings containing more than 1 bit is performed bit by bit, as in the AND operation. Thus, for example,

$$'101'B \quad \mid '110'B \quad = '111'B$$
$$'10110'B \mid '00100'B = '10110'B$$

and bit strings of unequal length are made equal by extending the shorter string with zeros (on the right side). For example,

$$'1'B \mid '01100'B = '10000'B \mid '01100'B = '11100'B$$

D Concatenation

Two bit strings can be concatenated, just like character strings. For example,

$$'1001'B \mid\mid '110'B = '1001110'B$$
$$'1'B \mid\mid '001'B = '1001'B$$

Thus the concatenation of two bit strings results in another bit string.

E Examples

We will now illustrate several of the operations just described.

Example 18.2.1

$$\neg '100'B \mid ('0110'B \ \& \ '01'B \mid\mid '011'B) = ?$$

Solution We first evaluate the expression inside the parentheses. By the list of priorities concatenation is performed first, yielding

$$'01' \mid\mid '011'B = '01011'B$$

The & operation is performed next, giving

$$'0110'B \ \& \ '01011'B = '01100'B \ \& \ '01011'B = '01000'B$$

We have now

$$\neg \ '100'B|'01000'B$$

Since the $\neg$ operation has higher priority than the | operation, it is performed next. Then finally,

$$'011'B|'01000'B = '01100'B|'01000'B = '01100'B$$

Example 18.2.2

$$'10'B \ \& \ ('010'B|(\neg '0'B \ \& \ '10'B)) = ?$$

Solution:

$$\neg '0'B \ \& \ '10'B = '1'B \ \& \ '10'B = '10'B \ \& \ '10'B = '10'B$$
$$'010'B \ | \ '10'B = '010'B \ | \ '100'B = '110'B$$
$$'10'B \ \& \ '110'B = '100'B \ \& \ '110'B = '100'B$$

Example 18.2.3 We will illustrate operations with null bit strings.

$\neg ''B = ''B$	NOT of a null string is still a null string.
$''B| \ |''B = ''B$	Concatenation of null strings results in a null string.
$''B| \ |'011'B = '011'B$	Concatenation of a null string with a string A results in A.
$''B|''B = ''B$	
$''B|'101'B = '000'B|'101'B$ $= '101'B$	OR operation on a null string and a string A results in A.
$''B \ \& \ ''B = ''B$	
$''B \ \& \ '110'B = '000'B \ \& \ '110'B$ $= '000'B$	AND operation on a null string and a string A results in a bit string having only zeros and the length of A.

*18.3 CONVERSIONS WITH BIT STRINGS

It is possible to use bit strings with other types of data in arithmetic expressions. In such applications, conversion to uniform data must take place. Also conversion

---

*If time does not permit the coverage of the entire chapter, the starred sections can be omitted without any loss of continuity.

may have to be performed as a result of an assignment statement. We will discuss such conversions with bit strings.

A Bit String to Character String

The bit 1 converts into character 1, the bit 0 converts into character 0, and the B disappears. This conversion occurs in concatenation of a bit string and a character string or in an assignment statement. For example,

PUT LIST ('100'B| |'ⅥACES');

will cause the printout of

100ⅥACES

because the bit string '100'B is converted to the character string '100'. Similarly, the program segment

DCL A CHAR(3);
A = '100'B;
PUT DATA (A);

will print

A = '100';

with the conversion taking place by assignment to meet the specifications of A.

B Character String to Bit String

This conversion is possible for character strings having only 0s and 1s as characters. Conversion of any other characters is illegal and causes the CONVERSION condition (that is, conversion error). For example,

DCL A BIT(3);
A = '1000';
PUT DATA (A);

will print

A = '100'B;

thus conversion and truncation of the character string (to the declared length of A) take place.

C Number to Bit String

The absolute value of the number is converted first to a binary integer. The precision of the binary integer is

3.32*$(p - q)$ if the number[1] is FIXED DEC(p, q)
3.32*p if the number[1] is FLOAT DEC(p)

[1]If 3.32*$(p - q)$ is not an integer, replace it by the smallest integer exceeding 3.32*$(p - q)$. Similarly, a noninteger 3.32*p must be replaced by the smallest integer exceeding 3.32*p.

$p - q$ if the number is FIXED BIN(p, q)

p if the number is FLOAT BIN(p)

The binary integer is converted next to the bit string. For example,

```
DCL A BIT(4);
A = 2;
PUT DATA (A);
```

gives the printout

A = '0010'B;

because 2 being FIXED DEC(1, 0) converts to FIX BIN(3.32*($p - q$)) or FIXED BIN(4). Therefore, 2 converts to 0010. A being BIT(4) accepts all four digits, giving the indicated printout.

Observe that the program segment

```
DCL A BIT(3), B BIT(5);
A, B = 2;
PUT DATA (A, B);
```

yields

A = '001'B   B= '00100'B;

because A is truncated to 3 bits and B is extended (by addition of an extra zero) to 5 bits.

Similarly, the program segment

```
DCL A BIT(2);
A = −2.5;
PUT DATA (A);
```

gives the output

A = '00'B;

where, again, 2.5 is converted to 0010, because the absolute value of the number is converted to a binary integer (that is, the negative sign and the fractional part are ignored). Since A is BIT (2), only the first 2 bits of 0010 are assigned to A, giving the indicated output.

D Bit String to Number

The bit string is interpreted as a binary integer. If the bit string has more than 56 bits (the maximum default precision), bits on the left are ignored. The result of the conversion is a positive number.

The null bit string converts to zero.

The conversions of bit strings to numbers occur either as results of arithmetic operations involving bit strings or by assignment. For example, the program segment

```
DCL A BIT(4);
A = '1011'B;
PUT LIST(2*A, 2+A);
```

will result in the output

$$22 \qquad 13$$

because '1011'B is converted to the binary number 1011, which in printout appears as the equivalent decimal number 11. Hence the printout is as shown.

Observe that conversions are risky, because truncation or padding may give wrong results. They are also time-consuming and should generally be avoided.

18.4 COMPARISON OPERATIONS

Recall that at the end of Sec. 6.4 we described briefly how PL/I handles the decision process. We said there that the condition part is evaluated, and if satisfied it receives the bit string '1'B. If the condition is not satisfied it receives the bit string '0'B. Thus, in the statement

IF X>Y THEN X = X + 2;

the comparison X>Y is evaluated. If X>Y then the result is '1'B, and after the evaluation the statement reads as

IF '1'B THEN X = X + 2;

'1'B signifies that the comparison is satisfied, that is, comparison is *true;* hence the THEN clause is executed. Similarly, if X $\not>$ Y, the result is '0'B, and the statement reads as

IF '0'B THEN X = X + 2;

'0'B signifies the comparison to be *false;* hence the THEN clause is not executed, and the control passes to the next statement. Similarly, any other comparisons

```
X ¬ > A+7
1 ¬ = JACK**JILL+7
JOE + BILL<= ELLEN*HELEN+2
```

have either the value of '1'B or '0'B.

Observe that the statement

IF '1'B THEN X = X + 2;

is always executed and is therefore equivalent to

X=X+2;

Similarly, the statements

$$\text{IF } '0'B \text{ THEN } X = X + 2;$$
$$\text{ELSE } X = X - 1;$$

are equivalent to the single statement

$$X = X - 1;$$

because the ELSE clause is always executed.

Because a comparison always yields either a bit string $'1'B$ or $'0'B$, the assignment statement

$$X = A+(B>C);$$

is a valid one. The comparison in parentheses is executed first. If $B>C$, then, in effect,

$$X=A+'1'B$$

and because of the conversion rules, the assignment statement is equivalent to

$$X = A+1;$$

If $B \not> C$, then the assignment statement reads

$$X = A+'0'B;$$

which is equivalent to

$$X = A+0;$$

or

$$X = A;$$

Another example is provided by

$$A = (B = C);$$

Here $A = 1$ if $B = C$, and zero otherwise. The first equal sign is for the assignment statement, the second for the comparison operation. Thus parentheses can be eliminated, as in

$$A = B = C;$$

and PL/I will still interpret this expression as identical to $A = (B = C)$; this is why the equal sign appears in the list of priorities as an operation.

If the data in a comparison operation is not uniform, a conversion will take place. For arithmetic data of different base, scale, precision, or mode, the conversion to uniform attributes is made in accordance with the rules of Sec. 14.3. If we compare an arithmetic expression with a character string, the character string is converted to a number (if possible to do so). For example, the comparison

$$'123' < 1.23$$

is converted to

$$123 < 1.23$$

If we compare an arithmetic expression with a bit string, the bit string is converted to a binary integer. Thus

$$123 < \, '1011'B$$

is converted to

$$123 < 1011_2 \qquad \text{(that is, 1011 is base 2)}$$

which then causes the conversion of 123 to binary base, that is, to $1111011_2 (=123)$, so that the comparison has the form

$$1111011_2 < 1011_2$$

If we compare a bit string with a character string, the bit string is converted to a character string. The two strings are made equal by the addition of blanks (on the right side) to the shorter string.

As a further example consider the meaning of the assignment statement

$$\text{JOE} = \neg \, A\&B > C+1 = 3*D;$$

By the priority rules, the expression is evaluated in the order (see list of priorities in Sec. 18.2A)

$$
\begin{array}{c}
\neg \, A\&B \; > \; C+1 \; = \; 3*D \\
\underbrace{}_{1} \quad \underbrace{}_{3} \quad \underbrace{}_{2} \\
\underbrace{}_{4} \\
\underbrace{}_{5} \\
\underbrace{}_{6}
\end{array}
$$

To see what number is assigned to JOE, let

$$A='011'B$$
$$B=2$$
$$C=3$$
$$D=4$$

Then the above expression becomes

$$\neg'011'B \, \& \, 2 > 3+1 = 3*4$$
$$'100'B \, \& \, 2 > 3+1 = 3*4$$
$$'100'B \, \& \, 2 > 3+1 = 12$$
$$'100'B \, \& \, 2 > 4 = 12$$
$$'100'B \, \& \, '0'B = 12 \qquad \text{(conversion of bit string to binary number)}$$
$$'100'B \, \& \, 0 = 12 \qquad \text{(12 is converted to binary number)}$$
$$'100'B \, \& \, 0 = 1100_2$$
$$'100'B \, \& \, '0'B \qquad \text{(bit string }'0'B\text{ is extended to }'000'B)$$
$$'100'B \, \& \, '000'B$$
$$'000'B$$

Thus, finally, the assignment is made

$$JOE = '000'B;$$

which may require a further conversion to the attributes of JOE.

The use of comparisons in an assignment statement has occasional applications. As an example, consider the following problem.

Given

An integer N followed by a set of numbers on data cards. The last number is zero. There are no other zeros in the data.

Find

A sum which includes only the numbers on data cards which are less than N.

The program for this problem is rather simple. Here it is:

```
PROB: PROC OPTIONS(MAIN);
      GET LIST(N);
      TOTAL = 0;
      GET LIST(A);
      DO WHILE(A¬=0);
          IF A<N THEN TOTAL = TOTAL + A;
          GET LIST(A);
      END;
      PUT DATA(TOTAL);
      END PROB;
```

With the comparison operation in the assignment statement the program reads

```
PROB_2: PROC OPTIONS(MAIN);
        GET LIST(N);
        TOTAL = 0;
        GET LIST(A);
        DO WHILE(A¬=0);
            TOTAL = TOTAL + (A<N)*A;
            GET LIST(A);
        END;
        PUT DATA(TOTAL);
        END PROB_2;
```

Here we have replaced the statement

$$\text{If } A < N \text{ THEN TOTAL} = \text{TOTAL} + A;$$

with the statement

$$\text{TOTAL} = \text{TOTAL} + (A < N)*A;$$

where for $A < N$ we obtain $'1'B$ for the comparison and thus

$$\text{TOTAL} = \text{TOTAL} + A;$$

while for A $\not<$ N we obtain '0'B for the comparison, resulting in

$$\text{TOTAL} = \text{TOTAL};$$

This is further evidence of the many possible ways of constructing a program. The second version may appear to be more "clever" but is harder to understand and as such should be avoided.

It is also legal to have a statement of the form

IF A THEN *statement1;*

where A is a bit string. If any bit in A is 1, then *statement1* is executed. If all bits in A are 0, the THEN clause is ignored and control passes to the next statement (or an associated ELSE clause).

For example,

IF '1010'B THEN PUT LIST ('YES');

will cause the printout of

YES

In fact, A can be any number, since a conversion to a bit string will take place. Thus the statement

IF 5 THEN PUT LIST ('YES');

will result in the printout of

YES

as before.

18.5 BUILT-IN FUNCTIONS

A The SUBSTR Function

The SUBSTR function

SUBSTR*(argument1, argument2, argument3)*

where *argument1* = name of string from which substring is to be copied
argument2 = the place of starting character of substring
argument3 = length of substring
also applies to bit strings.

For example, the program segment

```
DCL (A,B) BIT CHAR (10) VAR;
A = '10111'B;
B = SUBSTR(A,3,2);
PUT DATA (B);
```

gives the output

$$B = '11'B;$$

As before, if the third argument is not specified, the length of the substring is the entire string from the starting point. For example, the program segment

```
DCL (A,B) BIT CHAR(6)VAR;
A = '10111'B;
B = SUBSTR(A,3);
PUT LIST (B);
```

gives

$$'111'B$$

We can also use the SUBSTR function as a *pseudovariable* on the left side of the assignment statement, as in

```
DCL A BIT CHAR(5);
A = '10111'B;
SUBSTR(A,3,2) = '00'B;
PUT LIST (A);
```

which replaces the third and fourth bits by 00 and yields the output

$$'10001'B$$

B The INDEX Function

The INDEX function

$$INDEX(string1,string2)$$

where *string1* = string to be searched
     string2 = string that we wish to locate
can also be used with bit strings. For example,

```
DCL A BIT(6), (B,C) BIT(3);
A = '0101101'B;
B = '011'B;
C = '000'B;
N1 = INDEX(A,B);
N2 = INDEX(A,C);
PUT LIST (N1,N2);
```

gives the output

$$3 \hspace{4cm} 0$$

because N1 is 3 and N2 is 0 (the bit string C cannot be found in the bit string A).

C The LENGTH Function

The LENGTH function

$$\text{LENGTH}(string1)$$

gives the number of bits in the bit *string1*. For example,

```
DCL A BIT(10)VAR;
A='001101'B;
N=LENGTH(A);
PUT LIST (N);
```

prints

$$6$$

as the output.

D The REPEAT Function

The REPEAT function

$$\text{REPEAT}(string1,k)$$

will construct a string which consists of k repetitions of the bit string *string1*. For example,

```
N=REPEAT('001'B,2);
```

has the same effect as

```
N='001001001'B;
```

Note again that k is an integer constant. A sign in front of k is allowed, and a negative integer is interpreted as zero.

E The BOOL Function

The four built-in functions just discussed are usable for both character strings and bit strings. We will now describe a new built-in function, the BOOL function. But first, let us go back to the & operation.

Assume that we have three bit strings, named *string1*, *string2*, and *string3*. Then in the operation

$$string1 \ \& \ string2 \ = \ string3$$

string3 is obtained through bit-by-bit comparisons of *string1* and *string2* in accordance with the following rules:

Bit in *string1*	Bit in *string2*	Bit in *string3*
0	0	0
0	1	0
1	0	0
1	1	1

The above rules are known as the truth table for the & operation. We can imagine an operation which has the following truth table:

Bit in *string1*	Bit in *string2*	Bit in *string3*
0	0	1
0	1	0
1	0	1
1	1	0

The BOOL built-in function allows us to specify an operation such as the last one. The BOOL function has the form

$$\text{BOOL}(string1, string2, string3)$$

where *string1* and *string2* are two bit strings on which the BOOL operation is to be made, and *string3* is a 4-bit string which describes the truth table for the BOOL operation. For example, for the & operation *string3* is '0001'B; for the last truth table *string3* is '1010'B. Thus *string3* is the bit string read vertically in the last column of the truth table.

As an example, let

> *string1* = '011'B
> *string2* = '110'B
> *string3* = '1010'B   (this describes the last truth table)

Then

$$\text{BOOL('011'B, '110'B, '1010'B)}$$

gives the result

$$'001'B$$

because in accordance with the given truth table,

Comparison of bits of *string1* and *string2* in first position, that is, 0 and 1, gives 0
Comparison of bits of *string1* and *string2* in second position, that is, 1 and 1, gives 0
Comparison of bits of *string1* and *string2* in third position, that is, 1 and 0, gives 1

giving the indicated results of '001'B.

Consider as the next example

$$A = BOOL('00110'B, '1'B, '0110'B)$$

First, the shorter string (that is, *string2*) must be extended with zeros to the length of the longer string. Hence, we consider in effect

$$A = BOOL('00110'B, '10000'B, '0110'B)$$

The third bit string describes the following truth table:

0	0	0
0	1	1
1	0	1
1	1	0

Hence

$$A = '10110'B$$

is the result.

Observe that the & operation between two strings A and B

$$A \& B$$

is the same as

$$BOOL(A,B,'0001'B)$$

because '0001'B gives the truth table for the &. Similarly, the | operation

$$A \mid B$$

is the same as

$$BOOL(A,B,'0111'B)$$

because '0111'B gives the truth table for the |. Thus the BOOL function includes the & and | operations as special cases. Since 4 bits give rise to 16 different expressions, there are 14 more truth tables (16 with & and |) that can be implemented with the BOOL function.

18.6 EXAMPLE

The Quickbuck Corporation, a maker of mousetraps, has announced a contest for its salesmen. Each salesman who sells mousetraps in excess of his quota in 6 or more months throughout the year will be a winner of the contest. A salesman's performance is entered as a 12-bit string (1 bit for each month), with 1 describing sales in excess of quota and 0 describing sales at or below quota. The data on each salesman are entered on a data card as two items, the first giving the salesman's number and the second giving his performance record as a bit string. For example, if salesman number 145 exceeded his quota in January, March, and December, his data will appear as

EXAMPLE **267**

145, '101000000001'B

with 1 in the first (for January), third (for March), and twelfth (for December) position, and 0 everywhere else.

It is desired to print the number of the winners of the contest. There are no more than 600 salesmen, and their numbers are at most three digits. The printout of the winners should have the form

SALESMAN NUMBER N EXCEEDED HIS QUOTA M TIMES

where N is the number of a winning salesman and M the number of times he exceeded his quota (where of course $M \geq 6$).

The flowchart for the problem is shown in Fig. 18.1. Note the following:

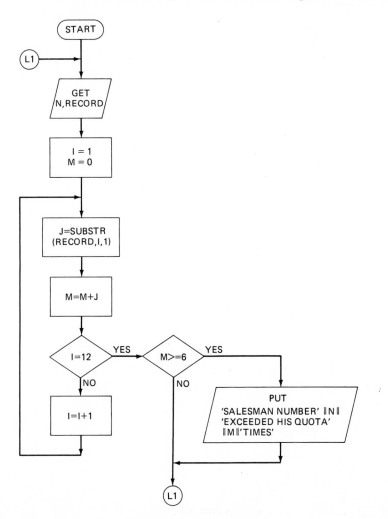

Figure 18.1 Flowchart for the CONTEST program.

1. We are naming RECORD the salesman performance record, given by the 12-bit string.
2. I will be used to access the individual bits and is initially set to 1.
3. J = SUBSTR(RECORD,I,1); thus J = first bit of the bit string. If J=1, the salesman exceeded his sales quota, and M is increased by 1.
4. If I=12, all 12 bits were investigated. Now we check if M ≥ 6. If so, the salesman is a winner and we print the output. If M < 6. we obtain a new input.
5. If I ≠ 12, then I<12. We increase I by 1 and investigate the next bit of the bit string RECORD.
6. Observe the concatenation of character strings with numerical variables N and M. Recall that for concatenation the numerical values of N and M are converted to character strings (see Sec. 17.8B).
7. There is no stop. The program will stop by itself when there is no more input data (that is, through the ENDFILE condition).

The input data was

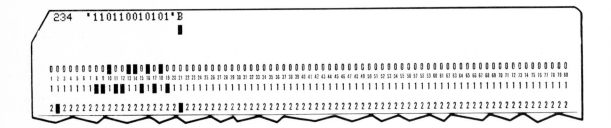

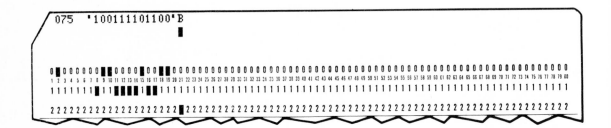

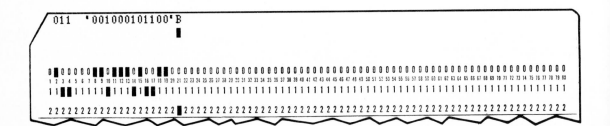

EXAMPLE **269**

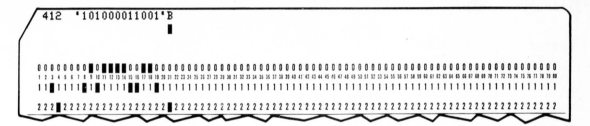

412 '101000011001'B

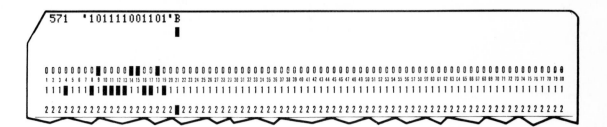

571 '101111001101'B

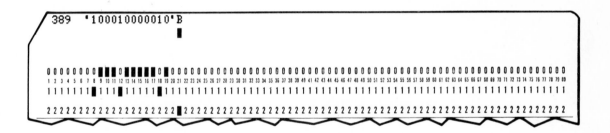

389 '100010000010'B

and gave the output

```
234
'110110010101'B
SALESMAN NUMBER      234 EXCEEDED HIS QUOTA      7 TIMES
075
'100111101100'B
SALESMAN NUMBER       75 EXCEEDED HIS QUOTA      7 TIMES
011
'001000101100'B
412
'101000011001'B
571
'101111001101'B
SALESMAN NUMBER      571 EXCEEDED HIS QUOTA      8 TIMES
389
'100010000010'B
```

The program is

```
CONTEST: PROC OPTIONS(MAIN);
         DCL RECORD BIT(12);
         DO WHILE(1);
             M = 0;
             GET LIST(N,RECORD)COPY; /* N IS THE SALESMANS'S NUMBER */
             DO I = 1 TO 12;
                 J = SUBSTR(RECORD,I,1);
                 M = M + J;
             END;
             IF M>=6 THEN PUT LIST('SALESMAN NUMBER'||N||
                 ' EXCEEDED HIS QUOTA'||M||' TIMES');
         END;
         END CONTEST;
```

Note the use of the COPY option to record the input. Also note the blanks in front of the numbers in the output. Incidentally, we can eliminate the blanks easily enough (see Prob. 17.3), but a better way to do so will be given in Chap. 24.

18.7 SUMMARY

We described bit strings, their use in logical operations and comparisons, and their applications. As we learned, bit strings are useful in program writing for describing records which can be coded numerically, such as check-off answers to questionnaires. We also learned that because comparisons generate the bit strings '0'B and '1'B, we can write assignment statements containing equalities or inequalities in the expressions on the right side of such statements.

The bit strings follow nearly the same rules as character strings. There are applications where either a bit string or a character string can be used. In such cases, bit strings are preferable because they require less storage. (Character strings require 8 bits for each character, while bit strings need only 1 bit for each bit of a bit string. Thus bit strings need only one-eighth the storage requirements of character strings.)

PROBLEMS

18.1 What bit string corresponds to
  (a) (4)'1010'B
  (b) (0)'1010'B
  (c) (2)'101'B || (3)'1100'B

18.2 What output results from the following program segment:

```
DCL A BIT(3), B BIT(6), C BIT(10) VAR;
A,B,C = '10111'B;
PUT LIST(A,B,C);
```

18.3 What bit string corresponds to

 (*a*) '1011'B & '110'B

 (*b*) '1011'B | '10001'B

 (*c*) '10011'B & '10'B | '001'B || '1001'B

18.4 Replace the following expressions by conventional program segments:

 (*a*) Y = (X > 1)*(B > 3);

 (*b*) A = B > C;

 (*c*) A = B = C = D;

18.5 Find the bit string given by

 (*a*) BOOL('110'B, '10001'B, '1010'B)

 (*b*) BOOL('100'B, '1'B, '0110'B)

 (*c*) BOOL('01011'B, '1001'B, '1100'B)

18.6 Redo Prob. 6.17. Now the request for a ticket is coded as a 7-bit bit string, where

 (*a*) The first 3 bits (that is, leftmost bits) describe the seat quality

 (*b*) The fourth bit describes a musical or a nonmusical

 (*c*) The fifth describes location

 (*d*) The sixth and seventh bits describe

 10 matinee (replaces −1)

 00 weekday evening

 01 weekend evening.

for example, the previous input of

$$2,1,0,1$$

will now be described by the bit string

$$'0101001'B$$
$$\underbrace{}_{(a)}\quad\underbrace{}_{(d)}$$

18.7 Redo Prob. 6.20. Now the five options are coded as a 5-bit bit string. For example, the previous input

$$0,1,1,0,1$$

will now be described by the bit string

$$'01101'B$$

18.8 A 10-question examination was given. The results are coded in the form

     '*name*' 20-bit bit string

with each 2 bits indicating the grade for each question as follows:

 00 means −5 percent

 01 means 0 percent

 10 means +5 percent

 11 means +10 percent

Thus the first 2 bits give the grade for the first question, the next 2 bits give the grade for the second question, and so on.

 Write a program to compute and print out each student's total grade.

 The last card has just the string 'END' on it. No name exceeds 20 characters.

 The input is

'AMAR'	'1101111100011100111'B
'DOW'	'01011011000110100111'B
'HARDY'	'11111111111110111111'B
'KRUSE'	'11111111001101011011'B
'IKAR'	'11111110101110011011'B
'JONES'	'00101010011101110001'B
'END'	

18.9 A true-false 10-question test was given in a history course. The results are coded in the form

$$'student's \ name' \qquad 10\text{-bit bit string}$$

with the 1s indicating correct answers and 0s indicating incorrect answers. Write a program which will do the following:

(*a*) Compute and print out each student's grade (each correct answer is worth 10 percent, each incorrect answer 0 percent).

(*b*) Find the frequencies (in percent) of correct answers to each question. The leftmost bit (that is, the first bit) represents the first question, the next bit the second question, and so on. For example, if 9 out of 10 students correctly answered the fifth question, then this question has 90 percent as frequency of correct answers.

The last card has just the string 'END' on it. No name exceeds 20 characters. The input is

'AMAR'	'1010111101'B
'BROCK'	'0011110101'B
'CHEVER'	'1010001000'B
'DOW'	'0111110111'B
'EDSON'	'1011100001'B
'FINLEY'	'1010110110'B
'GORDON'	'1011100000'B
'HARDY'	'0011111101'B
'IKAR'	'1111111111'B
'JONES'	'1010111111'B
'END'	

18.10 A multiple-choice 5-question test was given in an economics course. The results are coded in the form

$$'student's \ name' \qquad \text{five 5-bit bit strings}$$

with the student's answer being indicated by 1 in a bit string. For example,

OMAR	'01000'B
	'00010'B
	'10000'B
	'00000'B
	'00001'B

indicates that the student named Omar marked the second answer in the first question, the fourth answer in the second question, and so on. Note that all zeros means that this question was not answered.

Write a program to do the following:

(*a*) Calculate and print each student's grade. Each correct answer is worth 20 percent. Each incorrect answer is −6 percent. No answer (that is, a bit string with only 0s) and a multiple answer (that is, a bit string with two or more 1s) are not counted.

(*b*) Print out the frequency (in percent) of correct answers to each question.

The correct answers are

$$\begin{array}{c}
'01000'B \\
'00100'B \\
'10000'B \\
'00001'B \\
'00001'B
\end{array}$$

and the input is

'JAIN'	'01000'B
	'00100'B
	'01000'B
	'00001'B
	'00000'B
'ANDREWS'	'00100'B
	'01100'B
	'11011'B
	'00001'B
	'00101'B
'SIMS'	'01000'B
	'00100'B
	'10000'B
	'00001'B
	'10000'B
'BROOKS'	'00010'B
	'00100'B
	'00000'B
	'00001'B
	'00010'B

The last name is used for termination and is

$$'END'$$

19   ARRAYS

We often have problems involving large amounts of similar data in which each data item is identically processed. As an example, the data may consist of balances of a bank's customers. The processing may be a uniform deduction of the monthly service charge. In such an instance PL/I affords a simplified shorthand notation, which lets us deduct the service charge from all customers' balances by means of a single assignment.

In computer jargon a collection of similar data is named an *array*. In this example, all customers' balances are similar items, and we will find it convenient to represent them by an array. We will describe here the advantages of grouping data into arrays, as well as the details on the use of arrays.

19.1 AN INTRODUCTORY EXAMPLE

We will consider now the writing of a program for scoring a chess match of 100 rounds and involving four players. In each round the players form two pairs, with each pair playing a chess game. Let us name the players as PLAYER_1, PLAYER_2, PLAYER_3, and PLAYER_4. Upon the completion of each round, the scores are entered on a data card, with the first score for PLAYER_1, the second for PLAYER_2, and so on; the scores are 1 for win, 0.5 for tie, and 0 for loss or sit-out. The input consists of 100 cards, each with four numbers, denoting the scores on each round, and the output should be the total score for each player. Hence the program to do so reads

```
CHESS:    PROC OPTIONS(MAIN);
          PLAYER_1,PLAYER_2,PLAYER_3,PLAYER_4 = 0;
          DO I=1 TO 100;
             GET LIST(SCORE_1,SCORE_2,SCORE_3,SCORE_4);
             PLAYER_1 = PLAYER_1 + SCORE_1;
             PLAYER_2 = PLAYER_2 + SCORE_2;
             PLAYER_3 = PLAYER_3 + SCORE_3;
             PLAYER_4 = PLAYER_4 + SCORE_4;
          END;
          PUT DATA(PLAYER_1,PLAYER_2,PLAYER_3,PLAYER_4);
          END CHESS;
```

This program has 11 statements. Incidentally, a program for more players will require more items in the second, the GET LIST, and the PUT DATA statements, as well as an extra assignment statement for each additional player. Thus a program for 100 players will require $11 + 96 = 107$ statements, and three of these statements will be very long. We will do much better with arrays which exploit the identity in processing of each player's score, that is, in the initialization, the acquiring of the score, and in the adding of the score. In fact, with the use of arrays this program will have only nine statements. Furthermore, only nine statements will suffice for a program for more players. To repeat, where the extension of the first program to 100 players will lengthen the first program to 107 statements, a program using arrays will still be only nine statements long. Thus the saving in program writing is evident and justifies an expansion of effort for learning about arrays.

19.2 TYPES OF ARRAYS

In the example of the preceding section, we gave a different name to each player (that is, PLAYER_1, PLAYER_2, etc.) Had we used arrays, a common name would be given to all the players. If the common name is PLAYER, then PLAYER would be the name of the array. The individual players are the elements of the array and are designated as

PLAYER (1)
PLAYER (2)
PLAYER (3)
PLAYER (4)

The numbers in parentheses are named *subscripts*. Because only a single subscript suffices to identify a particular element in the array PLAYER, this array is named a *one-dimensional* array. If an array requires two subscripts for the description of an element, such an array is a *two-dimensional* array.

As an example of a two-dimensional array, assume that the price of an encyclopedia depends upon the make and the edition. Then the array ENCYCLO-PEDIA is a two-dimensional array. To make this example more specific, let the encyclopedia makes be Americana, Britannica, and Colliers, and let the editions be standard and deluxe. Let the make be the first subscript, and let us associate 1 with Americana, 2 with Britannica, and 3 with Colliers. Similarly, let us consider the edition to be the second subscript, with 1 designating the standard edition and 2 the deluxe edition. Then the array ENCYCLOPEDIA can be envisioned as a two-entry table as shown in Fig. 19.1, with the price given in the table. From the table we see, for example, that

ENCYCLOPEDIA (2,1) = 450

and

ENCYCLOPEDIA (3,2) = 500

Observe that we could have specified ENCYCLOPEDIA as a one-dimensional array of six elements. Then perhaps

MAKE \ EDITION	1	2
1	500	650
2	450	600
3	400	500

Figure 19.1 The array ENCYCLOPEDIA.

ENCYCLOPEDIA(1) describes the standard edition of Americana
ENCYCLOPEDIA(2) describes the deluxe edition of Americana
ENCYCLOPEDIA(3) describes the standard edition of Britannica
ENCYCLOPEDIA(4) describes the deluxe edition of Britannica
ENCYCLOPEDIA(5) describes the standard edition of Colliers
ENCYCLOPEDIA(6) describes the deluxe edition of Colliers

but the use of two subscripts in a two-dimensional array is more convenient. It is easier to remember that 1,2,3 in the first subscript stand for Americana, Britannica, and Colliers, respectively, and that 1 and 2 in the second subscript stand for standard and deluxe editions, respectively. Thus the choice of dimensionality of an array is a matter of convenience, and not something natural in the array.

We can similarly envision a *three-dimensional* array as being one with three subscripts. In the PL/I F-level compiler we can have an array of as many as 32 dimensions, that is, an array with up to 32 subscripts. The arrays are typified by their dimensions; thus the type of an array is the number of its dimensions.

19.3 THE DECLARE STATEMENT

Evidently, an array requires more storage than a simple variable (that is, a scalar variable). Hence we must tell the compiler that a name represents an array. We must also tell the compiler what the allowed subscripts of each dimension are. We do so with the DECLARE statement. For example, the statement

DCL ENCYCLOPEDIA (1:3, 1:2);

tells the compiler that ENCYCLOPEDIA is a two-dimensional array, with the subscripts of the first dimension being the integers 1,2, and 3. Similarly, the subscripts of the second dimension are 1 and 2. The compiler knows that the array ENCYCLOPEDIA has six elements and reserves the space accordingly.

The numbers 1 and 3 are named *bounds* of the first dimension: 1 is named the *lowbound* and 3 is named the *highbound* of the first dimension. Similarly, 1 is the lowbound and 2 the highbound of the second dimension: PL/I allows any lowbound (but not smaller than −32,768) and any highbound (not exceeding 32,767). It is only required that the subscripts be interpreted by the compiler as integers increasing by

1; hence the highbound must not be smaller than the lowbound. If we wish, for example, an array A with the subscripts from 9 to 23, we declare

$$\text{DCL A(9:23);}$$

Thus the notation $i{:}j$ specifies i as the lowbound and j as the highbound of the array. The subscripts can also be negative, as in

$$\text{DCL B(−2:3);}$$

which describes an array with the elements

$$
\begin{array}{l}
\text{B(−2)}\\
\text{B(−1)}\\
\text{B(0)}\\
\text{B(1)}\\
\text{B(2)}\\
\text{B(3)}
\end{array}
$$

It is permissible to include a plus sign in front of the subscript and to have spaces before or after the subscripts and signs. For example,

$$\text{DCL C(−1 : + 12);}$$

is legal.

A noninteger subscript will be truncated to an integer. For example, the declarations

$$\text{DCL E(2:7);}$$

and

$$\text{DCL E(2.35: 7.8);}$$

accomplish the same thing—declare E as a one-dimensional array with the subscripts running from 2 to 7. Incidentally the declarations

$$\text{DCL F(1:10);}$$

and

$$\text{DCL F(10);}$$

are the same. Thus, when the lowbound is 1 (the most common case), only the highbound needs to be shown.

Although we principally used one-dimensional arrays for simplicity's sake in the preceding examples, the same rules apply to subscripts of arrays with several dimensions. Thus

$$\text{DCL AUTO(−2:1, 0:5, 10);}$$

declares an array with the subscripts of the first dimension being $-2, -1, 0, 1$, subscripts of the second dimension being $0, 1, 2, \ldots, 5$, and the subscripts of the third dimension being $1, 2, \ldots, 10$. Incidentally, the number of subscripts in a dimension is named the *extent* of the dimension. Thus here the extents of the three dimensions are 4 for the first dimension, 6 for the second, and 10 for the third. The number of elements contained in an array is the product of the extents of the dimensions. The array AUTO, for example, has $4*6*10=240$ elements.

The attributes of an array are the attributes of the elements. Thus the array

DCL N(3, 5);

is an array of elements having the attributes of N, these being BINARY REAL FIXED (15,0). If we desire different attributes, say, FIXED DECIMAL (4,3), we accomplish it with the declaration

DCL N(3,5)FIXED DEC (4,3);

The numbers next to the name of the array name denote subscripts, and the numbers next to DEC denote precision. It is also possible to specify the initial values of an array, as in

DCL YES(10) INIT (1);

which sets the first element of the array YES to 1. If we want to initialize the entire array, we can do this with

DCL YES(10) INIT ((5)1, (2)2, (3)0);

which sets the first five elements [that is, YES(1), YES(2), . . . , YES(5)] to 1, the next two elements [that is, YES(6), YES(7)] to 2, and the last three elements [that is, YES(8), YES(9), YES(10)] to 0. Note the use of multipliers, and parentheses around them. In a two-dimensional array, the statement

DCL NO(10,5) INIT ((20)1,(15)2,(15)3);

specifies that the first 20 elements are 1. This brings up the question of how multidimensional arrays are ordered in the computer's memory; that is, which are the first 20 elements?

The ordering is always such that the subscripts of a dimension vary more rapidly than the subscripts of a dimension to the left of it. For example, the ordering of the array A(2:5,3:6) is

A(2,3)   A(2,4)   A(2,5)   A(2,6)   A(3,3)   A(3,4), . . . A(5,6)

Hence the second subscript varies more rapidly than the first subscript (which is to the left of the second dimension). As a second example, consider the array B(6,−2:1,2). Its ordering is

B(1,−2,1)   B(1,−2,2)   B(1,−1,1)   B(1,−1,2)   B(1,0,1) . . . B(6,1,2)

Coming back to our DECLARE statement, it is evident now that the values specify

NO(1,1), NO(1,2), . . . , NO(1,5),

NO(2,1), . . . , NO(2,5), . . . , NO(4,5)	as 1
NO(5,1), NO(5,2), . . . , NO(7,5)	as 2
NO(8,1), NO(8,2), . . . , NO(10,5)	as 3

In closing note that the statement

DCL A(4:2);

is illegal, because the lowbound exceeds the highbound. But

DCL B(10:10);

is legal and denotes an array B consisting of a single element. This element is denoted as B(10).

In the declaration

DCL A(3:5,10) FIXED DEC (5,1);

the specification of subscripts [that is, (3:5,10)] is known as the *dimension attribute*. This attribute, just like other attributes, can be "factored." For example,

DCL (A,B) (−2:3, 2:5);

is the same as

DCL A(−2:3, 2:5), B(−2:3, 2:5);

19.4 INPUT AND OUTPUT STATEMENTS

The program segment

DCL A(10,10);
GET LIST (A);

acquires 100 numbers for the 100 elements of A. Thus the GET LIST statement is equivalent to the 100 statements

GET LIST (A(1,1));
GET LIST (A(1,2));
. . . .
GET LIST (A(10,10));

which shows an advantage of using the arrays—one statement replaces 100. Similarly, for the same array A, the statement

PUT LIST (A);

causes the printout of 100 numbers in the usual order, that is,

A(1,1), . . . , A(1,10), A(2,1), . . . , A(10,10)

with the usual format of five numbers per line. Again, for the array A, the statement

GET DATA (A);

will acquire 100 numbers for the elements of A. But now, the input must be of the form

A(1,1) = *value*   A(1,2) = *value*   . . .   A(10,10) = *value;*

As before, the last item must be terminated in a semicolon. The input data do not have to be ordered, and not all elements must be present. For example, the statement

GET DATA(A);

with the input

A(7,3) = 1.7E1   A(2,1) = 0.3   A(9,2) = 0;

will change just A(7,3), A(2,1), and A(9,2). It will leave the other elements unchanged.

The statement

GET LIST (A(3,4));

is legal. It acquires a value and assigns it to A(3,4). But the statement

GET DATA (A(3,4));

is illegal. We must use instead

GET DATA (A):

and a data card with

A(3,4) = *value;*

On the output, both statements

PUT LIST (A(3,4));

and

PUT DATA (A(3,4));

are allowed.

As a further example, consider the program segment

DCL A(3,2), B(4);
GET LIST (A,B);
PUT DATA (A,B);

Here the six elements of the array A are acquired first and then the four elements of the array B. The printout similarly portrays all the six elements of A first and then the four elements of B.

19.5 OPERATIONS ON ARRAYS

A Assignments

The statements

DCL A(3,10);
A = 1.5E0;

assign 1.5E0 to each element of A.

The statement

$$A = A+1;$$

is equivalent to the statements

$$A(1,1) = A(1,1) +1;$$
$$A(1,2) = A(1,2) +1;$$

. . . .

$$A(3,10) = A(3,10) +1;$$

that is, 1 is added to each element of A. Similarly in the statement

$$A = 5*A;$$

each element of A is multiplied by 5. In

$$A = A/5;$$

each element of A is divided by 5.

The statement

$$A(2,5) = 5;$$

assigns 5 to the single element A(2,5) of the array A. In an assignment statement the subscripts can be expressions, as in

$$I = 3;$$
$$J = 5;$$
$$A(5*I/(J+2), 2*J/I) = A(3, (J-1)/I);$$

with the last statement being equivalent to

$$A(15/7,10/3) = A(3,4/3);$$

or

$$A(2,3) = A(3,1);$$

B Operations with Arrays

If there are arithmetic operations with two or more arrays, then all the arrays must have identical bounds (that is, identical subscripts). The result is an array with the same bounds as the original arrays. As an example, assume that the arrays A, B, C, and D are defined by

$$DCL (A,B,C,D) (2:3,2) FIXED;$$
$$A(2,1) = 1;$$
$$A(2,2) = 2;$$
$$A(3,1) = 3;$$
$$A(3,2) = 4;$$
$$B = 2*A;$$
$$C = A+B;$$
$$D = A/B;$$

the assignment statement for C is equivalent to

$$C(2,1) = A(2,1) + B(2,1);$$
$$C(2,2) = A(2,2) + B(2,2);$$
$$C(3,1) = A(3,1) + B(3,1);$$
$$C(3,2) = A(3,2) + B(3,2);$$

and the assignment statement for D is equivalent to

$$D(2,1) = A(2,1)/B(2,1);$$
$$D(2,2) = A(2,2)/B(2,2);$$
$$D(3,1) = A(3,1)/B(3,1);$$
$$D(3,2) = A(3,2)/B(3,2);$$

Similarly, in

$$E = A * B;$$

an element of E equals the product of the corresponding elements in A and B.

19.6 THE DO LOOPS

We frequently use DO loops with arrays. With a DO loop we can conveniently perform operations on all or some array elements. As an example of the use of a DO loop, consider the chess-scoring problem of Sec. 19.1. Let now PLAYER denote an array of four elements. Then the program reads

```
CHESS2:   PROC OPTIONS(MAIN);
          DCL PLAYER(4) INITIAL((4)0);
LOOP:     DO I=1 TO 100;        /* I COUNTS THE ROUNDS */
            DO J=1 TO 4;        /* J COUNTS THE PLAYERS*/
              GET LIST(SCORE);
              PLAYER(J) = PLAYER(J) + SCORE;
          END LOOP;
          PUT DATA(PLAYER);
          END CHESS2;
```

In the program, I counts the rounds and J the players. For $J = 1$, we read the input and obtain a new score for PLAYER(1). We now increment J to 2 and repeat the process for PLAYER(2). After updating the score for PLAYER(4), we increase I by 1 and update the scores for the next round. Thus the inner loop is executed four times for each cycle of the outer loop.

Observe that this program has only nine statements, as asserted in Sec. 19.1. Note that an extension of this program to 100 players will only require a new DCL statement, such as

```
DCL PLAYER(100) INITIAL ((100)0);
```

and a new DO statement such as

DO J = 1 to 100;

but no additional statements. Thus just nine statements will suffice, instead of the 107 statements as with the program of Sec. 19.1.

As a further example, let us assume that we wish the output to be displayed with just one item on each line (rather than five items per line). Then we need a DO loop on the output and replace the statement

PUT DATA (PLAYER);

by

DO I = 1 TO 100;
PUT DATA (PLAYER(I)) SKIP;

(No END; statement is needed because the END CHESS; statement provides a closure for the DO loop.)

The DO loop also provides a convenient tool for manipulating just a part of an array and for various processings of arrays. We will illustrate such manipulations and processings by examples. To do so, let us assume that we have an array A, which has been declared by the statement

DCL A(10,10);

that is, as a 10×10 array. Incidentally, such an array is known as a 10×10 matrix in the language of mathematics.

Example 19.6.1 We wish to enter data for just the third row of the array. We do this with

DO I = 1 TO 10;
GET LIST (A(3,I));
END;

Example 19.6.1 We wish to enter data for just the main diagonal elements. We do this with

DO I = 1 TO 10;
GET LIST (A(I,I));
END;

Example 19.6.3 We wish to add to the elements of the second column the corresponding elements of the seventh column. We do this with

DO I = 1 TO 10;
A(I,2) = A(I,2) + A(I,7);
END;

Example 19.6.4 We wish to add to the elements of the second column the corresponding elements of the seventh row. We do this with

```
DO I = 1 TO 10;
      A(I,2) = A(I,2) + A(7,I);
   END;
```

Example 19.6.5 We wish to print out just the inner elements of the array, that is, all elements except those on the first and tenth rows and those on the first and tenth columns. We do this with

```
DO I = 2 to 9;
   DO J = 2 TO 9;
      PUT DATA (A(I,J));
   END;
END;
```

The increment does not have to be 1, and the WHILE form of the DO loop can also be used. For example, to print out all the elements of A below the main diagonal, we write

```
DO I = 1 TO 10;
   DO J = 1 TO 10 WHILE (J<I);
      PUT DATA (A(I,J));
   END;
END;
```

Note that the printout gives the values of

$$A(2,1), A(3,1), A(3,2), A(4,1), \ldots, A(10,9)$$

that is, the elements below those on the main diagonal, as desired.

A special form of the DO loop can be used with the GET LIST, PUT LIST, and PUT DATA statement (not with GET DATA statements). For example, the statement

```
GET LIST ((A(I) DO I = 1 TO 5));
```

is legal. It acquires five values for A(1), A(2), . . . , A(5). Observe the two sets of parentheses, of which one is required for the list specification and the other to enclose the item with the DO loop. Also note that no END statement is necessary. Another example of this form of the DO loop is

```
GET LIST (((A(I,J) DO J = 1 TO 5) DO I = 1 TO 5));
```

The DO J = 1 TO 5 constitutes the inner loop, and the DO I = 1 TO 5 constitutes the outer loop. Hence this statement is equivalent to

```
DO I = 1 TO 5;
   DO J = 1 TO 5;
      GET LIST (A(I,J));
   END;
END;
```

Further examples include the following:

1. PUT LIST ((A(I), (B(I,J) DO J = 1 TO 5) DO I = 1 TO 4),C);
   Here the DO I = 1 TO 4 serves for both the A array and B array. Observe that
   C is not an array. The output is printed in the order

   A(1),B(1,1),B(1,2),B(1,3),B(1,4),B(1,5),A(2),B(2,1), . . . ,C

2. PUT DATA ((A(I) DO I = 17, 3 TO 10 BY 3 WHILE(I*I<25)));
   The DO loop has multiple specifications plus a WHILE clause.
3. GET LIST (N,(A(I) DO I = 1 TO N), B);
   The value for N is aquired first; thus N is known when the DO loop is executed.

19.7 THE ASTERISK NOTATION

Consider a two-dimensional array A. With our notation A stands for the entire
array, while A(2, 3) stands for a particular element. It is also possible to represent a
single row or column of an array. For example,

$$A(3,*)$$

represents the third row of A, while

$$A(*,7)$$

represents the seventh column of A. The asterisk notation specifies that all subscripts are to be used. For example,

DCL A(5,5);
PUT DATA (A(3,*));

is the same as

DCL A(5,5);
PUT DATA ((A(3,I) DO I = 1 TO 5));

which shows the shorthand notation provided by the asterisk.

It is also convenient to use the asterisk notation for operations on rows and
columns. For example,

DCL A(5,5)
A(3,*) = A(3,*) + 2 * A(*,2);

is equivalent to

DCL A(5,5);
DO I = 1 TO 5;
    A(3,I) = A(3,I) + 2 * A(I,2);
END;

but the asterisk notation is, of course, more compact.

Incidentally,

$$A(*,*)$$

specifies the entire array. The asterisk notation can be employed in arrays of any dimension. For a three-dimensional array A,

$$A(*,*,*)$$

represents the entire array, while

$$A(3,*,5)$$

represents a one-dimensional array, which is an intersection of two cross sections of A. Because of this feature, an array with the asterisk notation is known as a *cross section* of an array.

19.8 ARRAYS OF CHARACTER STRINGS AND BIT STRINGS

The elements of an array can be character strings rather than numbers. For example,

DCL A(3:5,10) CHAR (10);

defines A as a two-dimensional array, with each element being a string of 10 characters. The VARYING attribute can be used. Thus

DCL A(5,5) CHAR (10) VAR;

defines A as a two-dimensional array, with each element being a string of no more than 10 characters.

We can similarly have an array of bit strings. For example,

DCL A(4,3) BIT (3);

declares A to be an array whose each element is a 3-bit string.

Again note that the dimension attribute must immediately follow the name of the variable. Thus in

DCL NAME (10) CHAR (20) VAR;
DCL NAME CHAR (20) VAR (20);

the first declaration is legal and the second illegal. If there is, however, a factoring of attibutes, the dimension attribute must be shown immediately after the right parenthesis, as in

DCL (N FLOAT, A FIXED (5,3), B CHAR (4) VAR) (3:6);

19.9 THE DEFINED ATTRIBUTE

Arrays may have many elements and thus occupy large storage. There are applications in which the computer storage is critical and must be used wisely. There are also many applications involving arrays in which one array contains other arrays.

There are problems where such large number of locations needed for all the arrays cannot be spared. Fortunately, PL/I provides a mean for coping with this problem. It allows two or more arrays to share storage. It does so through the DEFINED attribute. For example, the statement

DCL A(5,6), B(5,6) DEFINED A;

says that the array B will occupy the same storage as A. In computer nomenclature, A is said to be the *base* or *defining variable*, and B is said to be the *defined variable*.

There are two restrictions on the use of the DEFINED attribute:

1. The defined array cannot have the INITIAL attribute.
2. The base array cannot have the DEFINED attribute itself.

In the above declaration the element B(I,J) is the same as the element A(I,J). This is also so when the defined array has different bounds than the base array. For example, in

DCL A(5,6), B(2,3) DEFINED A;

we have the relations

$$B(1,1) = A(1,1)$$
$$B(1,2) = A(1,2)$$
$$B(1,3) = A(1,3)$$
$$B(2,1) = A(2,1)$$
$$B(2,2) = A(2,2)$$
$$B(2,3) = A(2,3)$$

Similarly, in

DCL A(5,6), B(2:3,3:5) DEFINED A;

we have the associations

$$B(2,3) = A(2,3)$$
$$B(2,4) = A(2,4)$$
$$\dots\dots\dots\dots$$
$$B(3,5) = A(3,5)$$

thus in general

$$B(I,J) = A(I,J)$$

as asserted.

Note that the statement

DCL A(5,6), B(3:7,2) DEFINED A;

is invalid, because there is no A(7,1) or A(7,2) to associate with B(7,1) and B(7,2). Similarly,

$$\text{DCL A(5,6), B(20) DEFINED A;}$$

is invalid for the same reason.

The base and defined arrays can have a more general correspondence than the $B(I,J) = A(I,J)$ one. This is done by giving subscripts to the base array following the DEFINED attribute. The subscripts are written as iSUB, where i is an integer indicating the dimension. Thus 1SUB represents the subscripts of the first dimension of the defined array, 2SUB represents the subscripts of the second dimension of the defined array, and so on. For example,

$$\text{DCL A(5,6), B(2,2) DEFINED A(2*2SUB, 1SUB);}$$

provides the association

$$B(I,J) = A(2*J,I)$$

or

$$
\begin{aligned}
B(1,1) &= A(2,1) \\
B(1,2) &= A(4,1) \\
B(2,1) &= A(2,2) \\
B(2,2) &= A(4,2)
\end{aligned}
$$

Similarly,

$$\text{DCL A(5,6), B(3:7,7:10) DEFINED A(1SUB-2, 2SUB-5);}$$

provides the association

$$B(I,J) = A(I-2,J-5)$$

If there are no subscripts following the base array, the base and the defined arrays must have the same dimensions. If there are subscripts, the base and defined arrays may have different dimensions. For example,

$$\text{DCL A(5,6), B(4) DEFINED A(1SUB, 1SUB+1);}$$

specifies the correspondence

$$B(I) = A(I,I+1);$$

Similarly,

$$\text{DCL A(10), B(5,5) DEFINED A(1SUB+2SUB);}$$

results in the association

$$B(I,J) = A(I+J)$$

The DEFINED attribute can be abbreviated to DEF. Thus the last statement can be written as

$$\text{DCL A(10), B(5,5) DEF A(1SUB+2SUB);}$$

The DEFINED attribute can also be used for nonarray variables, as in

$$\text{DCL A FIXED DEC(3,1), B FIXED DEC (3,1) DEF A;}$$

Observe that the defined variable B above has the same attributes as the base variable A. This is required. For example, the statement

DCL A(10) FIXED (3,2), B(10) DEF A;

is illegal, because the attributes of B [being by default FLOAT DEC (6)] are not identical with the attributes of A.

The DEFINED attribute can be specified to several variables in a single DCL statement, as in

```
DCL  A(20),
     B(10,10),
     C(10) DEF A,
     D(2,3) DEF B,
     E(5,5) DEF B(2SUB+1, 1SUB+2);
```

19.10 DYNAMIC STORAGE ALLOCATION

Before the execution of a program, the compiler scans the program and assigns storage to the variables. It is possible to control the assignment of the storage and to release the storage when it is no longer needed. Such control over the storage is known as *dynamic storage allocation*. It begins with the statement

DCL A CONTROLLED;

which tells the compiler that no storage is to be reserved for A before the execution of the program. When we wish to assign storage to A, we do so with the statement

ALLOCATE A;

When we wish to release the storage reserved for A, we do so with the statement

FREE A;

Even though the dynamic storage allocation can be applied to any variable, the need to conserve storage arises mostly in problems involving arrays.

As an illustration of the use of the dynamic storage allocation, consider the following examples:

Example 19.10.1 Given two arrays, the 600×500 array A and the 400×500 array B, find

1. The 300×300 array A1 comprising the elements of A in the first 300 rows and the first 300 columns
2. The 300×300 array B1 comprising the elements of B in the first 300 rows and the first 300 columns
3. The array A1 + B1

Solution A typical program for this problem is

```
EX_1: PROC OPTIONS(MAIN);
      DCL A(600,500),
          B(400,500),
          (A1,B1,C)(300,300);
      GET LIST(A,B);
      DO I=1 TO 300;
          DO J=1 TO 300;
              A1(I,J) = A(I,J);
              B1(I,J) = B(I,J);
          END;
      END;
      C = A1 + B1;
      PUT DATA(A1,B1,C);
      END EX_1;
```

The above program may not work. It requires $300,000 + 200,000 + 3 \times 90,000$ = 770,000 memory locations just for the arrays A, B, A1, B1, and C. The memory capacity is specified in units called bytes. Each byte is 8 bits. A binary integer of 15 binary digits requires 16 bits (1 bit for sign) and hence 2 bytes. A floating-point decimal number requires 4 bytes. However, a large computer such as the IBM System/360 or System/370 typically has a memory capacity of 2×10^6 bytes.[1] Such a computer actually stores less than 500,000 floating-point numbers because the program (and the compiler) is stored; thus the program also requires some storage space. Therefore the above program is infeasible, since it demands storage for 770,000 floating-point numbers. We can write a valid program with 390,000 memory locations if we release the storage which is no longer required. We can do so with the program

```
EX_2: PROC OPTIONS(MAIN);
      DCL A(600,500) CONTROLLED,
          B(400,500) CONTROLLED,
          (A1,B1,C)(300,300) CONTROLLED;
      ALLOCATE A, A1;
      GET LIST(A);
      DO I=1 TO 300;
          DO J=1 TO 300;
              A1(I,J) = A(I,J);
          END;
      END;
      FREE A;
      PUT DATA(A1);
      ALLOCATE B, B1;
      GET LIST(B);
```

[1]Some computers have a "virtual memory," which is a technique for allowing the use of larger memory capacity than actually available. A computer with an actual memory of 2×10^6 bytes (called "real" memory) may have a virtual memory of 16×10^6 bytes.

```
DO I=1 TO 300;
   DO J=1 TO 300;
      B1(I,J) = B(I,J);
   END;
END;
FREE B;
PUT DATA(B1);
ALLOCATE C;
C = A1 + B1;
PUT DATA(C);
END EX_2;
```

The abbreviation CTL can be used for CONTROLLED, as, for example,

$$DCL (A,B,C, RESULT) (400,500) CTL;$$

A variable cannot have both the DEFINED and CONTROLLED attributes. For example, the statement

$$DCL A(2), B(2) CTL DEF A;$$

is illegal.

Since no allocation of storage takes place for a controlled variable at the declaration, it is allowable to replace dimensions by asterisks and to specify the actual dimensions with the ALLOCATE statement. For example, the program segment

```
DCL A(*,*) CTL;
GET LIST (N1,N2,N3,N4);
ALLOCATE A(N1:N2,N3:N4);
GET LIST (A);
PUT LIST (A);
FREE A;
```

is a legal one.

19.11 EXAMPLES

Example 19.11.1 Given four 4×4 arrays A, B, C, and D, find a program for the construction of an array E such that:

1. The first row of E is the sum of the first column of A and the second row of B.
2. The second row of E is the product of the third column of B and the second row of C.
3. The third row of E is the fourth column of A less 7 times the third row of D.
4. The fourth row of E is the first row of C divided by the third column of A.

Solution By the division of a row by a column we mean, of course, the division of the corresponding elements. Using the asterisk notation, the program for formation of E is

```
EX_1:      PROC OPTIONS(MAIN);
           DCL(A,B,C,D,E)(4,4);
           GET LIST(A,B,C,D);
           E(1,*) = A(*,1) + B(2,*);
           E(2,*) = B(*,3) * C(2,*);
           E(3,*) = A(*,4) - 7*D(3,*);
           E(4,*) = C(1,*) / A(*,3);
           PUT DATA(E);
           END EX_1;
```

Example 19.11.2 Given two 4×4 matrices A and B, find the matrix product C=AB.

Solution The formula for the element c_{ij} of the product matrix C is

$$c_{ij} = \sum_{k=1}^{4} a_{ik} b_{kj}$$

Hence the program is

```
EX_2:      PROC OPTIONS(MAIN);
           DCL(A,B,C)(4,4);
           GET LIST(A,B);
L1:        DO I=1 TO 4;
              DO J=1 TO 4;
                 C(I,J)=0;
                 DO K=1 TO 4;
                    C(I,J) = C(I,J) + A(I,K)*B(K,J);
           END L1;
           PUT DATA(C);
           END EX_2;
```

Example 19.11.3 Given 100 names on data cards. No name exceeds 20 characters. Sort them out in alphabetical order, and print out the sorted names.

Solution There are several methods for sorting. We will illustrate one of the simplest (but not very efficient) sorting methods for the names

EULER

ZOLA

BYRON

GAUSS

1. We compare the first two names, EULER and ZOLA. Because these are in their proper order, we proceed to the next comparison.

2. We compare the second and the third names, ZOLA and BYRON. Their order is wrong, so we interchange them and return to the beginning.
3. Now we start again with the list

EULER
BYRON
ZOLA
GAUSS

The first comparison forces the interchange of EULER and BYRON. We again return to the beginning.
4. Now we start with

BYRON
EULER
ZOLA
GAUSS

and we interchange ZOLA with GAUSS and return to the beginning.
5. The list has now the names

BYRON
EULER
GAUSS
ZOLA

Since no interchange is needed in a pass through the list, the sorting is completed.

Recall that by Sec. 17.7 we can sort character strings just like numbers. Hence the flowchart for this problem is as shown in Fig. 19.2. Note that we use STORE to store the value of A(I) needed for the interchange. The program is then

```
EX_3:    PROC OPTIONS(MAIN);
         DCL (A(100),STORE) CHAR(20)VAR;
         GET LIST(A);
         DO I=1 TO 99;
            IF A(I)>A(I+1) THEN DO;
                                    STORE = A(I);
                                    A(I)  = A(I+1);
                                    A(I+1)= STORE;
                                    I = 0;
                                 END;
         END;
         PUT LIST(A);
         END EX_3;
```

Observe that when there is an interchange I is set to 0. When the END; statement of the DO loop is reached, I is increased to 1, and thus the DO loop is restarted with I = 1.

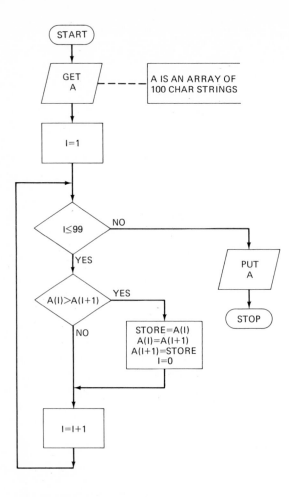

Figure 19.2 Flowchart for Example 19.11.3.

19.12 SUMMARY

We discussed arrays as a convenient tool for performing operations on a collection of similar data. We saw that the use of arrays can greatly reduce the number of program statements, as in the chess-scoring example. We discussed the types of arrays, the specification of subscripts, and the operations on arrays. We illustrated the use of DO loops for various types of array problems. We learned that we can form arrays of character strings and of bit strings. We also described techniques for handling problems encountered with arrays requiring a storage capacity in excess of the available one.

PROBLEMS

19.1 Consider the following declarations and array values:

DCL A(4,4) FIXED, V(4) FIXED;

$$A = \begin{bmatrix} 4 & -2 & 3 & 6 \\ -1 & 0 & 7 & 1 \\ 2 & 6 & 3 & 4 \\ 7 & 1 & 2 & -8 \end{bmatrix} \quad V = \begin{bmatrix} 1 \\ 2 \\ 3 \\ 4 \end{bmatrix}$$

(a) What are the values of the expressions

$$A(3,4) + V$$

and

$$A(*,2)*A(3,*)$$

(b) Show the values of V given by

$$V = V + A(1,*) + V(3);$$

(c) Show the values which are displayed as a result of executing the following PUT statement, assuming initial values of A and V.

    PUT LIST(((A(J,I) + V(I) DO J=2 TO 3) DO I = 4 TO 3 BY −1));

19.2 There are 100 numbers on data cards. Write a program to print out
   (a) The average of these 100 numbers
   (b) These numbers in the reverse order (that is, the last number is printed first, etc.)

19.3 The array A is defined by

    DCL A(10,10);

Write a program segment to print out (see Fig. P19.3)
   (a) The first five columns of A in the column order, that is,

       A(1,1),A(2,1), . . . A(10,1), A(1,2), . . . A(10,5)

   (b) The remaining elements in the row order, that is,

       A(1,6), A(1,7), . . . A(1,10),A(2,6) . . . A(10,10)

19.4 The elements of a 100 × 100 array are on data cards.
   (a) Add 1 to the elements on the right-to-left diagonal, as shown in Fig. P19.4a. Print out the new array.
   (b) Print out one element per line in the order

                 A(51,51)
                 A(51,52)
                 . . . .
                 A(100,100)
                 A(51,1)
                 A(51,2)
                 . . . .
                 A(100,50)
                 A(1,1)
                 . . . .
                 A(50,100)

That is, in the quarters portrayed in Fig. P19.4b.
   (c) Double each element just above and just below the main diagonal. Print out the new array.

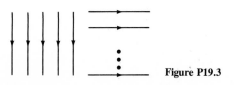

Figure P19.3

Add 1 to these elements

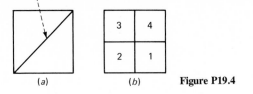

(a)   (b)   **Figure P19.4**

19.5 The elements of an 101×101 array are on data cards. Obtain this array and print out just the elements indicated in Fig. P19.5a (starting with the center element) and b. In c print out the entire array in the usual row order after adding 1 to the shaded elements in the 2nd, 50th, 52nd, and 100th rows and columns. No element is to be printed more than once. Start each part with the original array.

19.6 The input consists of several data cards. The last data card contains just the character string 'END'. The other data cards contain either the character 'A' and six numbers or the character 'B' and six numbers.

Write a program to do the following:

(a) Acquire the data from each card.

(b) If the character is 'A', the numerical data is to be printed in the form

$$
\begin{array}{l}
x \\
x\ x \\
x\ x\ x
\end{array}
$$

(c) If the character is 'B', 1 is to be added to each number, and the numbers are to be printed out in the form

$$
\begin{array}{l}
x\ x\ x \\
x\ x \\
x
\end{array}
$$

(d) There are to be two lines of space between each set of data (that is, between each set of six numbers).

(e) The program is to stop when the last card is encountered.

19.7 The following 21-statement program reads in an array A, performs some calculations, and prints out the result. Simplify the program so that the same results are obtained using 12 or fewer statements and no GO TOs. Assume that $1 \leqslant N \leqslant 100$.

```
PROB_7: PROC OPTIONS(MAIN);
        DCL A(100);
        GET LIST(N);
        I = 1;
LOOP_A: IF I>N THEN GO TO COMP;
        GET LIST(A(I));
        I = I + 1;
        GO TO LOOP_A;
COMP:   S = 0;
        I = 1;
LOOP_B: IF I>(N-1) THEN GO TO NEXT;
        IF A(I)=0 THEN GO TO NEXT;
        S = A(I) + S;
        I = I + 1;
        GO TO LOOP_B;
NEXT:   S = S + A(N);
        PUT SKIP;
```

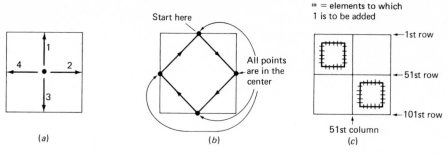

Figure P19.5

```
PUT SKIP;
PUT DATA(S);
STOP;
END PROB_7;
```

19.8 The first 10 numbers on the data cards are in ascending order. These are followed by 15 more numbers, also listed in ascending order. Write a program to print a single list with all 25 numbers ordered in ascending order (that is, we want to merge these two sets of numbers).

19.9 There are 30 numbers on data cards. Print them out, but identical numbers are to be printed out only once.

19.10 The input consists of a 5 × 5 array A with the elements

$$
\begin{array}{ccccc}
1 & 2 & 4 & 9 & 15 \\
15 & 9 & 4 & 2 & 1 \\
3 & 7 & 7 & 7 & 3 \\
1 & 4 & 2 & 8 & 7 \\
5 & 4 & 9 & 3 & 8
\end{array}
$$

(a) Write a program to acquire A.

(b) Print out A.

(c) Form and print out an array B consisting of

The first column of B = fourth row of A.
The second column of B = third column of A + 2* first row of A.
The third column of B = fourth column of A + second column of B.
The fourth and fifth columns of B are the same as those of A.

(d) Form an array C consisting of the inner 3 × 3 elements of A. Print out C with three elements on each line.

(e) Print out the arrays D=C*C and E=A+B. Identify all arrays with appropriate headings.

19.11 There are 1000 numbers on data cards. Write a program to

(a) Acquire the numbers.

(b) Print out the numbers, with one number on each line, and a space between each 10 numbers (that is, a line is skipped between each set of 10 numbers).

(c) Call the above order of numbers to be from 1 to 1000, that is, $a_1, a_2, \ldots, a_{1000}$. Print out the numbers now in the reverse order, that is, from a_{1000} to a_1, with two numbers on each line.

(d) Print out the numbers in the order

$$a_{500} \text{ to } a_1$$
$$a_{501} \text{ to } a_{750}$$

$$a_{1000} \text{ to } a_{751}$$

with four numbers on each line.

Do all these parts in a single program.

19.12 Write a program that reads in a square array A of 10 rows and 10 columns and determines if the array is in upper-diagonal form. Upper-diagonal form means that

$$A(I,J) = 0 \text{ for } J < I$$

and

$$A(I,I) \neq 0$$

19.13 A survey is being conducted by the Grocers Association. They have selected 100 buyers and asked each of them to purchase 10 grocery items. The Association wants to find

    (*a*) The average purchase

    (*b*) The largest purchase

    (*c*) The smallest purchase

Write a computer program to do so. The input consists of 100 data cards. Each card lists in the same order the cost of each of the 10 items purchased by the buyer.

19.14 The elements of a 100 × 100 array A are on data cards.

    (*a*) Obtain the array A.

    (*b*) Find the transpose of A. [If A′ is the transpose of A. then A′(I,J) = A(J,I).]

    (*c*) Find the array B defined by

$$B = A + 2*A'$$

    (*d*) Print out B,A′,A. Do not use more memory than needed for two 100 × 100 arrays.

19.15 The Eagle-eye Bird Watching Society has 10 members. The Pigeon-eye Bird Feeding Society has 8 members. The membership lists are as follows:

Eagle-eyes	Pigeon-eyes
1. Apeman	1. Alligator E.
2. Wolf	2. Pigeon
3. Fox	3. Butcher
4. Alligator J.	4. Kong
5. Alligator E.	5. Rat
6. King	6. Mouse
7. Kong	7. Mustang
8. Rabbit	8. Horse
9. Rat	
10. Mouse	

Write a program which will give a output the printout of

    (*a*) A list of those who are members of both societies.

    (*b*) A list of those who are either members of Eagle-eye, Pigeon-eye, or of both societies

These lists should contain no duplicates.

19.16 Write a program to print out 50! as an integer, showing all its digits in the usual groups of three (with a space between each three digits).

19.17 The data cards contain the elements of a 4 × 4 array. Write a program which will

    (*a*) Multiply the second column by 1.5 and print the resulting array.

    (*b*) Add to the first row the corresponding elements of the third column and print out the array.

    (*c*) Manipulate the elements to obtain the "upper triangular" form (that is, all elements below the main diagonal are to be zero), by adding or subtracting suitable fractions of rows.

(*d*) Manipulate the array elements to obtain the "diagonal" form (that is, all elements below and above the main diagonal are zero).

(*e*) Use the methods of (*c*) and (*d*) to evaluate the determinant of the 4 × 4 array.

The output for parts (*a*) to (*d*) is to be displayed with four elements on each line, suitably identified and titled. Your program should have ample comments. In all parts the input is the original array, given by the data

```
1.   1     4    -1     5      2.  1     3     1    -1
     2    10     1    18          2     0     1     1
    -2   -10    -2   -16          0    -1     4     1
     0     2     5     7          0     1     1    -5

3.   2     1    -3     5      4.  1     2     3     4
     2    -2     3     9          5     6     7     8
     4     5   -13     8          9    10    11    12
     0    -3     8     0         13    14    15    16
```

Upper triangular form:

$$\text{Determinant} = a_{11}\,a_{22}\,a_{33}\,a_{44} = \begin{vmatrix} a_{11} & a_{12} & a_{13} & a_{14} \\ 0 & a_{22} & a_{23} & a_{24} \\ 0 & 0 & a_{33} & a_{34} \\ 0 & 0 & 0 & a_{44} \end{vmatrix}$$

Diagonal form:

$$\text{Determinant} = b_{11}\,b_{22}\,b_{33}\,b_{44} = \begin{vmatrix} b_{11} & 0 & 0 & 0 \\ 0 & b_{22} & 0 & 0 \\ 0 & 0 & b_{33} & 0 \\ 0 & 0 & 0 & b_{44} \end{vmatrix}$$

If a_{11}, a_{22}, or a_{33} is zero during any stage of the computation of the upper-triangular form, you cannot proceed any further, and neither form exists. Print out what you have and go to the next array.

If a_{11}, a_{22}, and a_{33} are nonzero but $a_{44} = 0$, then you have a complete upper-triangular form, but the diagonal form does not exist and you cannot proceed. Print out what you have and go to the next array.

Compute the determinant from both forms. The results must, of course, be the same.

19.18 It is required to prepare a program for a computer dating service. Each male client of the service is to obtain the name of a female client. The input data on the clients is of the form

$$\text{'\b BETTY\b\b MARTINI\b\b\b/12301300'}$$
$$\text{'JOE\b\b\b CHAMPAGNE\b/13022211'}$$

that is, first name, last name, and eight digits denoting scores in eight questions of a questionnaire. A slash separates the name from the scores, and blanks are freely inserted before, in between, and after the names.

The dating match is achieved by calculating a disparity number between clients. To do so, we first calculate differences between the respective digits of the questionnaire. The disparity number is the sum of these differences. For example, the disparity number between BETTY MARTINI and JOE CHAMPAGNE is

```
1  2  3  0  1  3  0  0    BETTY's score
1  3  0  2  2  2  1  1    JOE's score
0  1  3  2  1  1  1  1    Differences in scores
```
$$\text{Disparity number} = 0 + 1 + 3 + 2 + 1 + 1 + 1 + 1 = 10$$

A good match requires a low disparity number.

The data for the male clients is

```
'JOEƀƀƀCHAMPAGNEƀ/13022211'
'BENƀBEERƀƀƀ/22131201'
'BERTƀƀƀBURGUNDY/12123100'
'ƀƀƀSTEVEƀƀSECTƀƀ/11132212'
'ƀCHARLIEƀCOGNACƀ/21120321'
```

The data for the female clients is

```
'ƀBETTYƀƀMARTINIƀƀƀ/12301300'
'ƀMARYƀMANHATTAN/01112130'
'ƀƀƀJULIAƀƀPINKLADY/21323012'
'WILMAƀƀWHISKYSOURƀƀ/32312021'
'BRENDAƀƀBRANDYALEXANDERƀƀ/21200122'
'GINGERƀƀGINGERALEƀ/20021233'
'BELAƀBACARDIƀƀƀƀ/02212331'
'CELLIAƀƀCUBALIBREƀ/22112111'
```

Each male client is to be matched with the most compatible female client. It is allowable to match several male clients with the same female client.

(*a*) Write a computer program to do the match. The program should be general enough so that only minor changes are required to provide the match for a large number of clients.

(*b*) Print out your match results in the form

LAST_NAME_OF_FEMALE_CLIENT,ƀFIRST_NAME_OF_FEMALE_CLIENTƀ-
ƀLAST_NAME_OF_MALE_CLIENT,ƀFIRST_NAME_OF_MALE_CLIENTƀ
(DISPARITY_NUMBER)

There should be one-line spacing between the matching results.

19.19 After learning bridge through Probs. 6.15 and 6.16, Joe Poly went to a bridge tournament in which 10 pairs of players participated. Each pair was numbered from 1 to 10 and played one board (that is, one deal) against five of the other pairs. The actual scores on each board are shown in the following table:

Board	Pairs									
	1	2	3	4	5	6	7	8	9	10
1	+120	−110	+150	−100	+600	−120	+110	−150	+100	−600
2	+90	−80	+50	+110	+100	+80	−50	−110	−100	−90
3	−680	−630	−650	−620	+100	+650	+620	−100	+680	+630
4	+110	+130	+110	+110	−50	−110	+50	−110	−130	−110
5	+400	+150	+140	+200	+150	−150	−400	−150	−140	−200

Construct a program which will print out the total score of each pair by using the following rules:

1. The total score of each pair is the sum of the relative scores obtained on each board.

2. To obtain the relative scores of each pair on a board, we compare separately the actual scores of pairs 1 through 5 and the actual scores of pairs 6 through 10.

3. A pair receives 1 point for "beating" each pair and ½ point for tying each pair. For example, on board 5, the actual scores for the first five pairs are

```
Pair 1    +400
Pair 2    +150
Pair 3    +140
Pair 4    +200
Pair 5    +150
```

Hence,

Pair 1 beat 4 pairs and obtains	4
Pair 2 beat 1 pair, tied 1 pair, and obtains	1.5
Pair 3 beat 0 pairs and obtains	0
Pair 4 beat 3 pairs and obtains	3
Pair 5 beat 1 pair, tied 1 pair, and obtains	1.5

19.20 A popular contest in tournament bridge is the team event in which two opposing teams play with identical cards at two different tables. Each team fields two pairs of players. One pair takes the North-South positions at one table, while their teammates take the East-West seats at the second table.

Each match consists of seven deals (that is, boards). The scores for each board are compared, and the net difference is calculated. The net difference is then converted to so-called IMPs (International Match Points). The conversion table is as follows:

Difference in points	IMP	Difference in points	IMP	Difference in points	IMP
20–40	1	370–420	9	1500–1740	17
50–80	2	430–490	10	1750–1990	18
90–120	3	500–590	11	2000–2240	19
130–160	4	600–740	12	2250–2490	20
170–210	5	750–890	13	2500–2990	21
220–260	6	900–1090	14	3000–3490	22
270–310	7	1100–1290	15	3500–3990	23
320–360	8	1300–1490	16	4000 and up	24

As an example, assume that team 3 is playing against team 5 and has the scores of +420 and −170 on a board. Thus, team 3 has gained the net of +250 points and hence +6 IMPs on this board. Similarly, team 5 obtains −6 IMPs on the same board.

The IMPs for the seven boards are then totaled. The net sum is in turn converted to so-called victory points in accordance with the following table:

Team A wins by IMPS	Team A victory points	Team B victory points
0	10	10
1–2	11	9
3–4	12	8
5–7	13	7
8–10	14	6
11–13	15	5
14–16	16	4
17–19	17	3
20–23	18	2
24–27	19	1
28–31	20	0
32–39	20	−1
40–47	20	−2
48–up	20	−3

As an example, assume that team 3 beat team 5 by 15 IMPs on the seven boards of the match. Thus team 3 gained 16 victory points, while team 5 gained only 4 victory points on this match.

The data for scoring the match is prepared as follows. First, the pairing information is given in the form of a character string. For example, '3vs5' means that team 3 played team 5. There are no blanks in the string. Next there are seven pairs of scores, giving the results of the seven-board match. The scores are for the first team in the string. For example, the pair of scores

$$+170 \qquad -140$$

means that team 3 had the score $+170$ at one table and the score -140 at the other table. Evidently, team 5 had the negative scores -170 and $+140$ on the same board.

Write a program to calculate (and print) the victory points of each team after the seven-board match, listing the teams in ascending order. The input is given in the following table:

'3vs5'		'1vs6'		'2vs4'	
+170	−140	+120	−150	+800	+110
−420	−50	−620	+650	−650	−100
+650	+100	+420	−450	−140	+140
+980	−480	+140	−730	+100	−100
−500	+420	+920	−990	+430	−400
+90	−80	+120	−180	−110	+140
+110	−140	+50	−100	+170	−620

STRUCTURES

In the preceding chapter we described an array as a collection of similar data. All elements of an array have the same attributes, and no mixture of elements of different types, such as character strings and numbers, is allowed.

There are, however, problems which require a grouping of dissimilar data. In such problems we wish to identify with a single name a collection of data having different attributes (that is, character strings and numbers) but some logical tie-in. For handling such problems, PL/I provides special programming features known as *structures*.

20.1 AN INTRODUCTORY EXAMPLE

Consider the information that a bank needs to process a monthly payment on a loan. Such data contain

1. Name of the borrower
2. Address of the borrower
3. Initial amount of loan
4. Present balance of the loan (that is, before payment)
5. Yearly interest on the loan
6. Regular monthly payment due
7. Monthly payment received
8. Payment due date
9. Date on which payment was credited
10. Charge (if any) for a late payment
11. Charge for monthly interest
12. Total charges
13. Payment on principal
14. Present balance of the loan (i.e., after payment on the principal)

As one can see, even such a simple business transaction as recording a payment on a loan requires the processing of a large amount of data. Let us write a program for this transaction. Specifically, the program is to do the following:

1. Acquires items 1 through 9 in the above data on each customer.
2. Determines whether a late charge is due (item 10).
3. Calculates the monthly interest due (item 11).
4. Calculates the total charges (item 12) as the total of regular monthly payment due and late charge.
5. Calculates the payment on the principal (item 13).
6. Calculates the present balance of the loan (item 14) by subtracting the payment on the principal.

Various refinements are desired in a practical program, such as (1) a message if the underpayment exceeds some amount (that is, $50); (2) a message if the customer is consistently late in his or her payment; (3) handling the last payment on a loan, which can be smaller than the regular monthly payment. We will not incorporate these refinements into our program.

We will assume that the payment due date and the date on which payment was credited are both two-digit numbers, giving just the day of the month when payment is received. Assuming commonsense attributes for the variables, the program reads

```
LOAN:      PROC OPTIONS(MAIN);
           DCL BORROWER_NAME CHAR(30) VAR,
               BORROWER_ADDRESS CHAR(40) VAR,
               INITIAL_LOAN FIXED(6,2),
               PRESENT_LOAN FIXED(6,2),
               YEARLY_INTEREST FIXED(4,2),
               PAYMENT_REGULAR FIXED(5,2),
               PAYMENT_RECEIVED FIXED(5,2),
               DATE_DUE FIXED(2),
               DATE_CREDITED FIXED(2),
               LATE_CHARGE FIXED(3,2),
               INTEREST_DUE FIXED(5,2),
               TOTAL FIXED(5,2),
               PRINCIPAL FIXED(5,2);
           GET LIST(BORROWER_NAME,
                   BORROWER_ADDRESS,
                   INITIAL_LOAN,
                   PRESENT_LOAN,
                   YEARLY_INTEREST,
                   PAYMENT_REGULAR,
                   PAYMENT_RECEIVED,
                   DATE_DUE,
                   DATE_CREDITED,
                   LATE_CHARGE,
                   INTEREST_DUE,    /*THESE ARE INCLUDED FOR THE   */
                   TOTAL,           /*SAKE OF UNIFORMITY. THE INPUT*/
                   PRINCIPAL);      /*DATA ARE JUST ZEROS OR COMMAS*/
           /* DETERMINE LATE CHARGE                 */
```

```
IF DATE_CREDITED>DATE_DUE THEN;
                           ELSE LATE_CHARGE=0;
/* DETERMINE INTEREST DUE              */
INTEREST_DUE = YEARLY_INTEREST*PRESENT_LOAN/1200;
/* DETERMINE TOTAL PAYMENT DUE         */
TOTAL = PAYMENT_REGULAR + LATE_CHARGE;
/* DETERMINE PAYMENT ON PRINCIPAL      */
PRINCIPAL = PAYMENT_RECEIVED - INTEREST_DUE - LATE_CHARGE;
/* DETERMINE PRESENT LOAN              */
PRESENT_LOAN = PRESENT_LOAN - PRINCIPAL;
PUT LIST(BORROWER_NAME,
         BORROWER_ADDRESS,
         INITIAL_LOAN,
         PRESENT_LOAN,
         YEARLY_INTEREST,
         PAYMENT_REGULAR,
         PAYMENT_RECEIVED,
         DATE_DUE,
         DATE_CREDITED,
         LATE_CHARGE,
         INTEREST_DUE,
         TOTAL,
         PRINCIPAL);
END LOAN;
```

Observe that in this program the principal effort is in listing all the input and output variables. We did the listing three times: in the DCL, GET LIST, and PUT LIST statements. There are relatively few calculations here. This is typical in business problems. It is for such problems that *structures* are useful, because they allow a single name for all the variables of the program. With a single name, the GET LIST and the PUT LIST statements have only a single identifier in their lists (that is, within parentheses) instead of the 13 identifiers shown in the program. To achieve this economy in program writing, we must first order the data into a logical hierarchical grouping; that is, we must organize it into a *structure*. In the next section we will describe how such organization is performed.

20.2 ORGANIZATION OF DATA INTO A STRUCTURE

A collection of dissimilar but logically connected data, such as the data on the borrower in the preceding example, can be organized into a hierarchy. A possible organization is shown in Fig. 20.1. This organization is named a *structure*. Observe the following:

1. The structure has four levels. At the first (top) level is the name BORROWER. BORROWER is the name of the so-called *major structure*.
2. At the second level there are four names. NAME and ADDRESS have no further components and are named *elements* (or *elementary names*). LOAN and PAYMENT have components and are named *minor structures*.

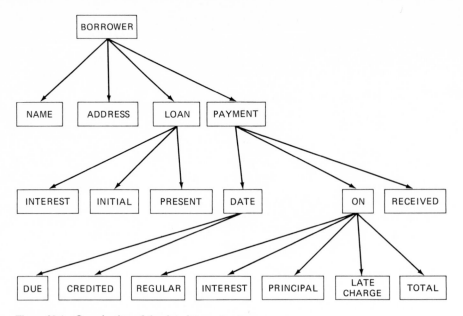

Figure 20.1 Organization of the data into a structure.

3. The minor structure LOAN has three elements, these being INTEREST, INITIAL, and PRESENT. The minor structure PAYMENT contains two minor structures DATE and ON, and the element RECEIVED.
4. The minor structure DATE has two elements DUE and CREDITED. The minor structure ON has five elements named REGULAR, INTEREST, PRINCIPAL, LATE CHARGE, and TOTAL.
5. The data are contained only in the elements.
6. The name of a minor structure provides a single name for the substructure extending downward. The minor structure PAYMENT, for example, identifies the grouping extending downward from the name PAYMENT.
7. The name of the major structure provides a single name for the entire grouping.

In general, any logically connected data can be organized into a structure. On the first level we have the name of the major structure. On the second and lower levels we have the names of minor structures and elements. Thus each minor structure and each element are associated with a level number. The level number determines the position or the rank within the structure. The compiler must be informed of this organization or "structuring" of data, and thus a structure requires a special declaration. We will describe such a declaration in the following section.

20.3 DECLARATION OF A STRUCTURE

Consider again the diagram of Fig. 20.1. Assume that we wish to describe the information of the diagram but without any figures. One possibility is to assign level numbers 1, 2, 3, and 4 to each item in the diagram. With such level numbers, the description is

```
1 BORROWER
 2 NAME
 2 ADDRESS
 2 LOAN
      3 INTEREST
      3 INITIAL
      3 PRESENT
 2 PAYMENT
      3 DATE
           4 DUE
           4 CREDITED
      3 ON
           4 REGULAR
           4 INTEREST
           4 PRINCIPAL
           4 LATE_CHARGE
           4 TOTAL
      3 RECEIVED
```

Observe that this description portrays the structuring of the data. It shows, for example, that the minor structure LOAN is on the second level of the hierarchy, and that it contains the elements INTEREST, INITIAL, and PRESENT which are on the third level of the hierarchy. In fact, the DECLARE statement for the structure uses the above form of the description. Appending the attributes to the elements, the DECLARE statement for the structure BORROWER reads

```
DCL 1 BORROWER,
      2 NAME CHAR (30) VAR,
      2 ADDRESS CHAR (40) VAR,
      2 LOAN,
           3 INTEREST FIXED (4,2),
           3 INITIAL FIXED (6,2),
           3 PRESENT FIXED (6,2),
      2 PAYMENT,
           3 DATE,
                4 DUE FIXED (2),
                4 CREDITED FIXED (2),
           3 ON,
                4 REGULAR FIXED (5,2),
                4 INTEREST FIXED (5,2),
                4 PRINCIPAL FIXED (5,2),
                4 LATE_CHARGE FIXED (3,2),
                4 TOTAL_FIXED (5,2),
           3 RECEIVED FIXED (5,2);
```

Note the following:

1. Each item of the structure has a level number, which precedes the item.
2. Only the name of the major structure (that is, BORROWER) has 1 as a level number.
3. The major structure contains minor structures and elements. The minor structures and elements have level numbers larger than 1.
4. The names of minor structures and elements do not have to be unique. It is permissible, as in the above DCL statement, to give the same names to different items. For example, we named INTEREST the element of the minor structure LOAN and the element of the minor structure ON.
5. Each structure item in the DCL statement is followed by a comma. There is a blank between the level number and the associated name.
6. Only elements contain data. Thus only elements can have arithmetic or string attributes.
7. The indentation of items in the DCL statement is just to improve readability. The compiler does not require it.

The level numbers of minor structures do not have to be consecutive integers. The hierarchy of the structure is equally well described by any other integer level numbers chosen so that a minor structure A having the level number N contains all the items which

1. Have level numbers larger than N
2. Are between A and the next item with a level number smaller than or equal to N.

As an example, the two declarations

```
DCL   1 A,
         2  B,
            3  C,
               4  D1,
               4  D2,
         2  E,
            3  F;
```

and

```
DCL   1 A,
         3  B,
            5  C,
               8  D1,
               6  D2,
         2  E,
            7  F;
```

describe the same structure.

We are almost ready to redo the introductory example using structures. But first we must tell how to identify an element of a structure. We will do so in the following section.

20.4 QUALIFIED NAMES

A major structure, a minor structure, or an element can be identified by its name. Such an identification suffices if the name is unique. However, we allow the use of the same name for different members of the structure. For such a member, we employ a so-called *qualified name* to resolve the ambiguity. The *qualification* consists of the listing of the minor structure or structures to which the member belongs. As an example, inspect the DCL statement for BORROWER in the preceding section.

1. The elements NAME and ADDRESS have unique names. Hence just their names suffice to identify these elements.
2. The minor structures LOAN, PAYMENT, DATE, and ON also have unique names. Thus just their names suffice to identify them.
3. The elements INITIAL, PRESENT, DUE, CREDITED, REGULAR, PRIN-CIPAL, LATE_CHARGE, TOTAL, and RECEIVED have unique names. Thus just their names identify them.
4. The element INTEREST has a nonunique name. To designate the element INTEREST in the minor structure LOAN, we write

BORROWER.LOAN.INTEREST

which shows the minor structure to which INTEREST belongs. This is named *qualification,* and BORROWER.LOAN.INTEREST is named a *qualified name.* Observe the period between the names in a qualified name (it is allowable to have blanks before and after the period). The names appear in the order of the structure; that is, the first name in a qualified name has a smaller level number than the second name, and so on. In computer jargon, the name

BORROWER.LOAN.INTEREST

is a *fully qualified name,* because we gave full information on the position of the element INTEREST in the structure. Often full qualification is not necessary. For example, the qualified name

LOAN.INTEREST

suffices to identify the desired element.
5. The element INTEREST in the minor structure ON is identified either by the fully qualified name

BORROWER.PAYMENT.ON.INTEREST

or by any one of the qualified names

```
BORROWER.PAYMENT.INTEREST
BORROWER.ON.INTEREST
PAYMENT.ON.INTEREST
PAYMENT.INTEREST
ON.INTEREST
```

As a further example of qualification, consider the structure defined by the declaration

```
DCL 1 A,
       2 B1,
          3 C,
          3 D,
       2 B2,
          3 C,
          3 D,
       2 B3,
          3 C,
             4 D;
```

The five elements of the structure can be identified as

```
B1.C
B1.D
B2.C
B2.D
B3.C.D or B3.D or C.D
```

The minor structure C has the qualified name

```
B3.C
```

The names of minor structures and elements must be chosen so that qualification removes ambiguity *completely*. Thus the structure

```
DCL 1 A,
       2 B,
          3 C,
       2 C;
```

has badly chosen names, because the second C is ambiguous, even with qualification.

We are ready now to redo the introductory example of Sec. 20.1 by using structures. We will do so in the following section.

20.5 THE INTRODUCTORY EXAMPLE WITH STRUCTURES

We will now use structures to write a program for the introductory example of Sec. 20.1. The DECLARE statement is as the one written in Sec. 20.3. The program then reads

```
LOAN2:     PROC OPTIONS(MAIN);
           DCL 1 BORROWER,
                2 NAME CHAR(30) VAR,
                2 ADDRESS CHAR(40) VAR,
                2 LOAN,
                   3 INTEREST FIXED(4,2),
                   3 INITIAL FIXED(6,2),
                   3 PRESENT FIXED(6,2),
                2 PAYMENT,
                   3 DATE,
                      4 DUE FIXED(2),
                      4 CREDITED FIXED(2),
                   3 ON,
                      4 REGULAR FIXED(5,2),
                      4 INTEREST FIXED(5,2),
                      4 PRINCIPAL FIXED(5,2),
                      4 LATE_CHARGE FIXED(3,2),
                      4 TOTAL FIXED(5,2),
                   3 RECEIVED FIXED(5,2);
           GET LIST(BORROWER);
           /* DETERMINE LATE CHARGES         */
           IF CREDITED>DUE THEN;
                              ELSE LATE_CHARGE = 0;
           /* DETERMINE INTEREST DUE         */
           ON.INTEREST = LOAN.INTEREST*PRESENT/1200;
           /* DETERMINE TOTAL PAYMENT DUE    */
           TOTAL = REGULAR + LATE_CHARGE;
           /* DETERMINE PAYMENT ON PRINCIPAL*/
           PRINCIPAL = RECEIVED - ON.INTEREST - LATE_CHARGE;
           /* DETERMINE PRESENT LOAN         */
           PRESENT = PRESENT - PRINCIPAL;
           PUT DATA(BORROWER);
           PUT DATA(PAYMENT)SKIP(2);
           END LOAN2;
```

Observe that this program is considerably shorter than the one of Sec. 20.1, because we did not have to repeat the entire listing of all identifiers, as done in Sec. 20.1, in the GET LIST and the PUT DATA statements.

The GET LIST statement requires data cards with a value or a null field (that is, a comma) for each element of the structure. An example of a possible input is shown in Fig. 20.2. The input values are assigned in order, that is, the first input value, this being 'JOE BADRISK', to the first element, this being NAME, and so on.

The PUT DATA (BORROWER); statement results in the printout of all the elements of the structure. The name of each element is given in the fully qualified form; hence the output is

```
BORROWER.NAME='JOE BADRISK'                    BORROWER.ADDRESS='333 SCHOOL DRIVE, PARIS, N.Y. 12345'
BORROWER.LOAN.INTEREST=  12.00                 BORROWER.LOAN.INITIAL=  2000.00
BORROWER.LOAN.PRESENT=   872.95                BORROWER.PAYMENT.DATE.DUE=    15
BORROWER.PAYMENT.DATE.CREDITED=    13          BORROWER.PAYMENT.ON.REGULAR=  120.00
BORROWER.PAYMENT.ON.INTEREST=    9.83          BORROWER.PAYMENT.ON.PRINCIPAL= 110.17
BORROWER.PAYMENT.ON.LATE_CHARGE=  0.00         BORROWER.PAYMENT.ON.TOTAL= 120.00
BORROWER.PAYMENT.RECEIVED=  120.00;
```

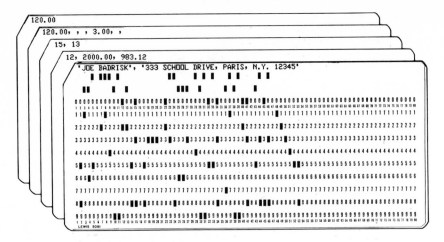

Figure 20.2   Input data cards for the example.

Incidentally, the statement

PUT DATA (PAYMENT);

will result in the printout of all elements of the minor structure PAYMENT. The output will appear as

```
BORROWER.PAYMENT.DATE.DUE=      15        BORROWER.PAYMENT.DATE.CREDITED=     13
BORROWER.PAYMENT.ON.REGULAR=   120.00     BORROWER.PAYMENT.ON.INTEREST=      9.83
BORROWER.PAYMENT.ON.PRINCIPAL=  110.17    BORROWER.PAYMENT.ON.LATE_CHARGE=   0.00
BORROWER.PAYMENT.ON.TOTAL=   120.00       BORROWER.PAYMENT.RECEIVED=  120.00;
```

thus in the fully qualified form as above.

20.6 USE OF ARRAYS

Consider the DECLARE statement for the structure

DCL 1 A,
        2 B,
            3 C1,
            3 C2,
            3 C3,
        2 D;

Evidently, the declaration of the structure will be shorter if we combine C1, C2, and C3 into an array. Then the DCL statement reads

DCL 1 A,
        2 B,

```
                    3 C(3),
                  2 D;
```

In this structure the elements of the minor structure B form an array. It is possible to have a situation in which the major structures or the minor structures can be arranged into arrays. As an example of the first case, consider the declaration

```
            DCL 1 A1,
                  2 B,
                    3 C,
                    3 D,
                  2 E,
              1 A2,
                  2 B,
                    3 C,
                    3 D,
                  2 E;
```

which describes two major structures A1 and A2. Again, using arrays simplifies the DCL statement to

```
            DCL 1 A(2),
                  2 B,
                    3 C,
                    3 D,
                  2 E;
```

with the major structure being an array.

An example of a structure where the minor structure can be organized into an array is given by the declaration

```
            DCL 1 A,
                  2 B1,
                    3 C,
                    3 D,
                  2 B2,
                    3 C,
                    3 D;
```

Combining the B's into an array, the DCL statement reads

```
            DCL 1 A,
                  2 B(2),
                    3 C,
                    3 D;
```

Note that the dimension attribute [that is, (2)] is appended to the structure name in the last two examples. In fact, the dimension attribute is the only attribute that can be associated with the name of a major or a minor structure. All the other attributes must be associated with elements of the structure.

As a further example, consider the DECLARE statement

```
DCL 1 JOE(2:3),
      2 MOE(2),
        3 SUE(2,2),
        3 LOU,
      2 JACK;
```

which describes the structure

```
1 JOE(2),
  2 MOE(1),
    3 SUE(1,1),
    3 SUE(1,2),
    3 SUE(2,1),
    3 SUE(2,2),
    3 LOU,
  2 MOE(2),
    3 SUE(1,1),
    3 SUE(1,2),
    3 SUE(2,1),
    3 SUE(2,2),
    3 LOU,
  2 JACK,
1 JOE(3),
  2 MOE(1),
    3 SUE(1,1),
    3 SUE(1,2),
    3 SUE(2,1),
    3 SUE(2,2),
    3 LOU,
  2 MOE(2),
    3 SUE(1,1),
    3 SUE(1,2),
    3 SUE(2,1),
    3 SUE(2,2),
    3 LOU,
  2 JACK;
```

Hence the use of arrays provides a simplification in the description of a structure, as asserted.

To identify a particular element, we use a qualified name and the correct subscripts. For example, to identify the element SUE(2,1) in JOE(3) and MOE(2), we write

```
JOE(3).MOE(2).SUE(2,1)
```

It is allowable to move the subscripts either to the left or to the right, as long as their order is preserved. Thus the last element can also be identified by either

JOE(3,2,2,1).MOE.SUE

or

JOE(3).MOE(2,2,1).SUE

or

JOE(3,2).MOE(2,1).SUE

or

JOE.MOE.SUE(3,2,2,1)

and other such expressions.

The shifting of subscripts allows the elimination of names. For example, the last element can be identified as

MOE.SUE(3,2,2,1)

or as

SUE(3,2,2,1)

In this connection observe that an array in a structure possesses besides its own dimensions the dimensions of the containing structures. Here SUE is a four-dimensional array, having its own two dimensions and the two dimensions of the containing structures (that is, JOE and MOE).

20.7 THE INITIAL AND LIKE ATTRIBUTES

A The INITIAL Attribute

The elements in a structure can be initialized through the use of the INITIAL attribute. As an example, consider the declaration

```
DCL 1 JOE,
      2 MOE,
        3 SUE FIXED (3,1) INIT(12.6),
        3 FRAN CHAR(3) INIT ('DOG'),
      2 JACK FLOAT INIT (3.1E0);
```

which specifies initial values for the elements SUE, FRAN, and JACK.

B The LIKE Attribute

Consider the declaration

```
DCL 1 CHESS_TOURNAMENT,
```

```
            2 DATES,
               3 LOCAL CHAR(6),
               3 REGIONAL CHAR(6),
               3 NATIONAL CHAR(6),
            2 FEES,
               3 REGULAR_EVENTS FIXED (3,2),
               3 SPECIAL_EVENTS FIXED(3,2),
         1 BRIDGE_TOURNAMENT,
            2 DATES,
               3 LOCAL CHAR(6),
               3 REGIONAL CHAR(6),
               3 NATIONAL CHAR(6),
            2 FEES,
               3 REGULAR_EVENTS FIXED (3,2),
               3 SPECIAL_EVENTS FIXED (3,2);
```

Here the BRIDGE_TOURNAMENT structure is the same as the CHESS_TOURNAMENT structure. We can tell that to the compiler without duplicating declarations, as above, by writing simply

```
      1 BRIDGE_TOURNAMENT LIKE CHESS_TOURNAMENT;
```

The complete DCL statement then reads

```
DCL 1 CHESS_TOURNAMENT,
      2 DATES,
         3 LOCAL CHAR(6),
         3 REGIONAL CHAR(6),
         3 NATIONAL CHAR(6),
      2 FEES,
         3 REGULAR_EVENTS FIXED(3,2),
         3 SPECIAL_EVENTS FIXED(3,2),
      1 BRIDGE_TOURNAMENT LIKE CHESS_TOURNAMENT;
```

The LIKE attribute can be used for any two structures, be it two major (as above), two minor, or one minor and one major. As an example, consider

```
DCL 1 A,
      2 B,
      2 C,
         3 D,
         3 E,
      2 F LIKE C,
   1 JOE LIKE C;
```

which describes the structures A and JOE as

```
1 A,
   2 B,
   2 C,
```

```
            3 D,
            3 E,
          2 F,
            3 D,
            3 E,
        1 JOE,
            3 D,
            3 E;
```

The LIKE attribute duplicates only the *structure* below the name given in the LIKE statement. The *dimensions* that are associated with the name are not copied. Hence, for example, the declaration

```
DCL 1 JOE(10),
      2 BILL(5),
      2 JACK CHAR(6),
    1 SUE LIKE JOE;
```

is equivalent to

```
DCL 1 JOE(10),
      2 BILL(5),
      2 JACK CHAR(6),
    1 SUE,
      2 BILL(5),
      2 JACK CHAR(6);
```

and the dimensions associated with the name JOE are not copied for the name SUE.

If we want the structure SUE to have the dimensions of JOE, we write

```
1 SUE(10) LIKE JOE;
```

We can also specify different dimensions, as in

```
1 SUE(3,2:5) LIKE JOE;
```

In

```
DCL 1 A,
      2 B INIT(1),
      2 C INIT(2),
    1 JOE(2,2) LIKE A;
```

JOE(1,1).B is initialized to 1 and JOE(1,1).C is initialized to 2. The remaining elements have no specified initial values.

20.8 THE BY NAME OPTION

Consider two structures described by the DECLARE statement

```
DCL 1 FIRST,
       2 JOE,
       2 MOE,
         3 SUE,
         3 FRAN,
       2 JACK,
     1 SECOND,
       2 BURT,
       2 MOE,
         3 ANNE,
         3 FRAN,
         3 DALE,
       2 JACK
       2 GEORGE;
```

Then the assignment statement

$$\text{FIRST} = \text{SECOND, BY NAME;}$$

tells the compiler that only names common to both structures are to be used in the assignment statement. Hence this statement is equivalent to

$$\text{FIRST.MOE.FRAN} = \text{SECOND.MOE.FRAN;}$$
$$\text{FIRST.JACK} = \text{SECOND.JACK;}$$

Observe that it is not necessary for both structures to have the same form (that is, the same structuring). The minor structure MOE of FIRST has two elements, while the minor structure MOE of SECOND has three elements. Also, SECOND has three elements on the second level (beside the minor structure MOE), while FIRST has only two elements there.

The BY NAME assignment can also be used with minor structures. For example, in the structure defined by the last declaration,

$$\text{FIRST.MOE} = \text{SECOND.MOE, BY NAME;}$$

is equivalent to

$$\text{FIRST.MOE.FRAN} = \text{SECOND.MOE.FRAN;}$$

We can also use the BY NAME option for more than two structures. As an example, if three structures are defined by the declaration

```
DCL 1 A1,
       2 B,
       2 C,
         3 D,
         3 E,
         3 F,
     1 A2,
       2 B,
       2 C,
```

```
              3 D,
              3 G,
              3 F,
           1 A3,
              2 C,
                 3 I,
                 3 D,
              2 J;
```

then the assignment statement

A2 = A1 + A3, BY NAME;

means, as before, that only names common to *all three structures* are to be used in the assignment statement. In this example, only the elements named D satisfy this requirement. Thus the statement is equivalent to

A2.C.D = A1.C.D + A3.C.D;

Note that in carrying out the BY NAME option, only the first name in a qualifying name is different. All the other names must be identical. Hence a statement such as

A.B.C = A1.B.C + A1.D.C;

can never arise from a BY NAME statement.

20.9 OPERATIONS WITH STRUCTURES

All operations involving structures are operations on the elements of the structures. Consider the declaration

```
          DCL 1 A,
              2 B,
                 3 C,
                 3 D,
              2 E,
                 3 F,
                 3 G,
                 3 H,
           1 JOE,
              2 JACK,
                 3 MOE,
                 3 TOM,
              2 SUE,
                 3 FRAN,
                 3 ANNE,
                 3 MARY,
          N FLOAT;
```

Then

$$A + N$$

describes the operations

$$C + N$$
$$D + N$$
$$F + N$$
$$G + N$$
$$H + N$$

and

$$A + JOE$$

means the operations

$$C + MOE$$
$$D + TOM$$
$$F + FRAN$$
$$G + ANNE$$
$$H + MARY$$

Only in the BY NAME assignment may we have expressions with structures having different structuring. In all other operations we must have identical structuring of the component structures. Identical structuring means that there is the same breakdown into minor structures and that we have the same number of elements in the corresponding positions. Also corresponding arrays must have the same bounds.

As usual, the attributes of corresponding elements do not have to be identical. As an example, for the two structures defined by

```
DCL 1 A,
      2 B FIXED(3,2),
      2 C FLOAT,
    1 AA,
      2 D FLOAT,
      2 C FIXED BIN;
```

the operation

$$AA = AA + 2*A;$$

is legal.

20.10 EXAMPLES

Example 20.10.1 A stockroom fills orders for different departments of a company. There are 20 departments, and the supplies consist of pens, pencils, nuts, and bolts. There is less than a thousand of each type. We wish to construct a program which will update and print out the inventory in the stockroom.

Solution Let us organize the supplies into a structure such as

```
1 SUPPLIES,
 2 OFFICE,
  3 PENS,
  3 PENCILS,
 2 HARDWARE,
  3 NUTS,
  3 BOLTS;
```

Let us further assume that SUPPLIES is an array of 21 elements. The first 20 elements represent the 20 departments, and the twenty-first element represents the present stockroom inventory, that is, before filling the orders. Then the program reads

```
INVENT:   PROC OPTIONS(MAIN);
          DCL 1 SUPPLIES(21),
                 2 OFFICE,
                  3 PENS FIXED(4),
                  3 PENCILS FIXED(4),
                 2 HARDWARE,
                  3 NUTS FIXED(4),
                  3 BOLTS FIXED(4);
          /* WE MUST CLEAR THE ARRAY BEFORE GETTING NEW DATA */
          SUPPLIES = 0;
          GET DATA(SUPPLIES);
          DO I=1 TO 20;
             SUPPLIES(21) = SUPPLIES(21) - SUPPLIES(I);
          END;
          PUT DATA(SUPPLIES(21));
          END INVENT;
```

The printout of SUPPLIES(21) gives the updated inventory, as desired. This program requires data-directed input. For such input, the names must be *fully qualified* on the data cards.

Incidentally, it is permissible to factor out the attributes in the declaration of a structure. With such factoring, we could have shortened the DCL statement to

```
DCL 1 SUPPLIES(21),
     2 OFFICE,
      ( 3 PENS,
        3 PENCILS) FIXED(4),
     2 HARDWARE,
      ( 3 NUTS,
        3 BOLTS) FIXED(4);
```

Example 20.10.2 A mail-order garden supply store receives orders from its customers. If the order does not exceed the customer's credit, the order is filled. (The credit may be the money sent with the order, or the credit extended to the customer, or a sum of both.) Otherwise, the order is not filled. We want a program which will compute the cost of the order, check it against the customer's credit, and print out an instruction as to the filling or not filling of the order. Assume that the store has four products, these being

Flower seeds at \$3.25/lb
Vegetable seeds at \$3.25/lb
Flower plants at 10 cents each
Vegetable plants at 30 cents each

The input consists of customer's name, address, credit, and order. A missing item in the order (for example, no flower seeds ordered) is represented by a comma (that is, a null field).

Solution Let us organize the customer into a structure such as

```
1 CUSTOMER,
  2 NAME,
  2 ADDRESS,
  2 CREDIT,
  2 ORDER,
    3 SEEDS,
      4 FLOWERS,
      4 VEGETABLES,
    3 PLANTS LIKE SEEDS.
```

We will assume that no order exceeds 1000 lb of any seeds or 1000 of any plants and that no credit is granted in excess of \$1000. The program stops when there is no more data (that is, on the ENDFILE condition) and reads

```
GARDEN:   PROC OPTIONS(MAIN);
          DCL 1 CUSTOMER,
                2 NAME CHAR(30) VAR,
                2 ADDRESS CHAR(40) VAR,
                2 CREDIT FIXED(6,2),
                2 ORDER,
                  3 SEEDS,
                    (4 FLOWERS,
                     4 VEGETABLES) FIXED(4),
                  3 PLANTS LIKE SEEDS,
              COST FIXED(6,2);
          DO WHILE(1);
            CUSTOMER = 0;
            GET LIST(CUSTOMER);
            COST = (SEEDS.FLOWERS + SEEDS.VEGETABLES)*3.25 +
                    PLANTS.FLOWERS*0.1 + PLANTS.VEGETABLES*0.3;
```

```
   IF COST>CREDIT THEN PUT SKIP LIST('THE ORDER OF',NAME,
                                     'IS NOT TO BE FILLED');
                 ELSE PUT SKIP LIST('THE ORDER OF',NAME,
                                     'IS O.K.');
   END;
   END GARDEN;
```

20.11 SUMMARY

We described here the use of structures. With structures we can give a single name to dissimilar data which is grouped together in a ranked order.

Names in structures do not have to be unique. A nonunique name A is made unique through qualification, that is, by appending the names of minor or major structures to A.

Through the use of arrays, we can construct large structures with a limited listing in the DECLARE statement. Arrays can be formed for major structures, minor structures, and elements.

The LIKE attribute allows a saving in the writing of the declaration of a structure. The BY NAME option provides a saving in the writing of assignment statements.

The operations involving two or more structures reduce to the operations involving the corresponding elements of the structures.

PROBLEMS

20.1 A structure is described by the declaration

```
DCL 1 A,
      2 B,
      2 C,
      2 D,
        3 E,
          4 F1,
          4 F2,
      2 X,
        3 Y,
          4 P,
          4 Q;
```

(*a*) Which is the major structure?
(*b*) Which are the minor structures?
(*c*) Which are the elements of X?
(*d*) Can you simplify the declaration with the LIKE attribute?

20.2 Two structures are described by

```
DCL 1 A1,
      2 B1,
        3 C1,
        3 C2,
```

```
            2 B2,
               3 C21,
               3 C22,
         1 A2,
            2 B3,
               3 C1,
               3 C3,
            2 B4,
               3 C21,
               3 C22,
               3 C23;
```

The elements of the structure A1 have the value of 1; the elements of the structure A2 have the value of 2. What happens as the result of the following statements (in each case start with the initial values)?

(*a*) A1 = 2*A2, BY NAME;

(*b*) B1 = B2 + B3;

(*c*) A1.C1 = A2.B3.C3*A2.B4.C23;

(*d*) Write an assignment statement assigning to the variable X the sum of the two C21 (that is, X = first C21 + second C21).

20.3 Modify Example 20.10.2 to maintain inventory of the four products. Assume that initial numbers of these products are read in, and as the customer's order is filled, the quantity is decreased accordingly. Provide also for the situation when an order cannot be filled because of shortage of a product.

20.4 The Glibtalk Travel Agency markets different tours to Siberia:

1. DELUXE costs $1000 and includes five free stopovers in Siberian cities. Additional stopovers cost $30 each. Additional days on the tour cost $50 each.

2. STANDARD costs $800 and includes two free stopovers. Additional stopovers cost $20 each. Additional days on the tour cost $35 each.

3. ECONOMY costs $600. Extra stopovers cost $18 each. Additional days on the tour cost $30 each.

The tour can accommodate 50 passengers. Set up a record for each client and calculate the client's cost of the tour. Provide test data to test your program.

20.5 The Big Wheel Bicycle Company produces four types of bicycles—Racer, Standard, Banana, Child—and four options—pump, carrier, bag, water bottle.

Each of these bicycles comes with either a man's or woman's frame. With each sale a card is filled giving:

Type
Frame
Actual purchase price
Region in which sold
Listed purchase price
List of options

Write a program to print out each month

(*a*) Total number of bicycles sold

(*b*) Total dollar sales

(*c*) Most popular bicycle (type and frame)

(*d*) Most popular option

(*e*) Region with the highest sales

(*f*) Region with the lowest sales

(*g*) Regions with the highest and lowest discounts

(*h*) Region with the highest profit

Assume eight regions and provide test data to test your program. Provide the needed inputs (that is, list prices for the four types of bicycles), assuming reasonable numbers.

20.6 An insurance company needs a program to calculate the commission due to an agent on premiums paid by his or her clients. The company sells the following policies in various dollar coverages:

Life	term
Life	20 years
Auto	injury
Auto	collision
Auto	theft
Home	fire
Home	theft

The company employs 200 agents. The commission rate on the above policies is not uniform and is recorded for each agent. The commission on auto insurance distinguishes between preferred-risk drivers and other drivers. There is also an additional bonus in commission on each new policy.

Make reasonable assumptions as needed, and provide for return of commission due to cancellation of policy. Provide test data to test your program.

20.7 An honorary engineering fraternity wants a program to identify candidates for membership. Engineering senior students with a 3.0 grade average and juniors with a 3.2 grade average are to be identified. Seniors are those with 90 or more credits, juniors with 60 to 89 credits. Write a program to do so. Assume that you will enter records of 40 students and that each record will include

Student's name
Major (EE,ME,AE,CE,CHEM.E)
Address
Courses taken
Credits of each course
Grade in each course
Grade point average

Your output should print out the information on the selected students. Provide test data to test your program.

20.8 Joe Computer wants to divide his computer literature into books and articles. He wishes to divide both of these further into major topics such as architecture, languages, compilers, hardware, data structures, operating systems, and software engineering. Joe decides to classify each topic by author and list under each author the title of the publication, coauthors, date, and source of publication. He wants to be able to retrieve any publication by either the title or the author. Write a program to do so. Provide the data to test your program.

21 BUILT-IN FUNCTIONS

PL/I provides several programs, called built-in functions, stored in the computer's memory, with each program identified by its name. We encountered these functions in Sec. 17.4, where we gave the example of the LOG10 built-in function and described the SUBSTR and the INDEX built-in functions. We will describe here several more such built-in functions.

21.1 GENERAL FORM

A built-in function has the form

$$function\_name \ (arg1, arg2, \ldots, argn)$$

The arguments *arg1, arg2, . . . , argn* are the data that have to be supplied for calculating the value of the function. The arguments are always enclosed in parentheses and separated by commas. In computer jargon, the parentheses enclose an *argument list*. There are built-in functions with no arguments (which will not be discussed here), as well as built-in functions with one or more arguments.

A generalization is possible in that we may have expressions instead of arguments. In such a case the built-in function has the form

$$function\_name \ (expression1, expression2, \ldots, expressionn)$$

The built-in function can appear on the right side of an assignment statement, as, for example,

$$A = function\_name \ (X1,X2,X3);$$

or in an operation, as in

$$A = B * function\_name \ (X1,X2);$$

In both cases, the computer calculates the value of the function from the given arguments. In computer jargon, the computer *returns* the value of the function corresponding to the given arguments. If each argument is a *scalar,* then so is the return.

21.2 MATHEMATICAL BUILT-IN FUNCTIONS

A The Logarithmic Built-in Functions

In Sec. 17.4, we described the LOG10(X) built-in function as

LOG10(X)   meaning log X, that is, the common or base 10 logarithm of X

There are two more logarithmic built-in functions, namely,

LOG(X)   meaning ln X, that is, the natural or base e logarithm of X
LOG2(X)   meaning $\log_2$ X, that is, the base 2 logarithm of X

As an example, the program

```
EXAMPLE: PROC OPTIONS(MAIN);
         X = 20;
         Y = LOG(X);
         Z = LOG2(X);
         PUT DATA(Y,Z);
         END EXAMPLE;
```

will cause the printout of

Y= 2.99573E+00   Z= 4.32192E+00;

giving in floating-point form the natural and base 2 logarithms of 20.

B The SQRT Built-in Function

The function

$$SQRT(X)$$

means $\sqrt{X}$, which is an alternate[1] way of expressing the exponentiation

$$X**0.5$$

___

[1] The computer calculates SQRT(X) by using a numerical approximation (that is, the Newton-Raphson method). X**0.5 is evaluated as $e^{0.5 \ln x}$ [that is, as EXP(0.5*LOG(X))], using the built-in function EXP to be discussed in Sec. 21.2D. The calculation with SQRT(X) is faster than with X**0.5.

If X is positive, the return is positive. A nonpositive or complex X must be declared as complex, and the return is complex. For example, the program segment

```
DCL (X,Y)CPLX;
X = − 1;
Y = SQRT(X);
PUT LIST (Y);
```

will result in the output

$$0.00000E+00+1.00000E+00I$$

C The Trigonometric Built-in Functions

The trigonometric built-in functions are

SIN(X)	meaning sin X, with X given in radians
SIND(X)	meaning sin X, with X given in degrees
COS(X)	meaning cos X, with X given in radians
COSD(X)	meaning cos X, with X given in degrees
TAN(X)	meaning tan X, with X given in radians
TAND(X)	meaning tan X, with X given in degrees
ATAN(X)	meaning $\tan^{-1}$ X (that is, arctangent of X), with the result (that is, the return) expressed in radians
ATAND(X)	meaning $\tan^{-1}$ X, with the result expressed in degrees
ATAN(X,Y)	meaning $\tan^{-1}$ (X/Y), with the result expressed in radians
ATAND(X,Y)	meaning $\tan^{-1}$ (X/Y), with the result expressed in degrees

Example 21.2.1 Given the angle α in degrees and the sides B1 and C1 in the triangle ABC of Fig. 21.1, find the side A1 and the angles β and γ.

Solution By the cosine law, A1^2 is given as

$$A1^2 = B1^2 + C1^2 - 2 (B1)(C1) \cos \alpha$$

from which A1 follows. By the same law

$$\cos \beta = \frac{A1^2 + C1^2 - B1^2}{2(A1)(C1)}$$

$$\cos \gamma = \frac{A1^2 + B1^2 - C1^2}{2(A1)(B1)}$$

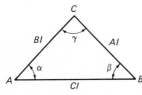

Figure 21.1 The triangle for Example 21.2.1.

Since

$$\tan x = \frac{\sqrt{1-\cos^2 x}}{\cos x}$$

hence

$$\beta = \tan^{-1} \frac{\sqrt{1-\cos^2 \beta}}{\cos \beta}$$

$$\gamma = \tan^{-1} \frac{\sqrt{1-\cos^2 \gamma}}{\cos \gamma}$$

Using the above formulas, the desired program is

```
TRIG:      PROC OPTIONS(MAIN);
           GET LIST(B1,C1,ALPHA);
           /* CALCULATION OF A1 USING THE COSINE LAW     */
           A1 = SQRT(B1*B1 + C1*C1 - 2*B1*C1*COSD(ALPHA));
           /* CALCULATION OF THE COSINES                 */
           COS_BETA = (A1*A1 + C1*C1 - B1*B1)/(2*A1*C1);
           COS_GAMMA= (A1*A1 + B1*B1 - C1*C1)/(2*A1*B1);
           /* CALCULATION OF THE ANGLES                  */
           BETA = ATAND(SQRT(1-COS_BETA**2), COS_BETA );
           GAMMA= ATAND(SQRT(1-COS_GAMMA**2),COS_GAMMA);
           PUT DATA(A1,BETA,GAMMA);
           END TRIG;
```

Note that the list of trigonometric built-in functions shows two ways of expressing the arctan (that is, $\tan^{-1}$) function. In the first way, the function

ATAND(X)

has one argument and returns an angle between -90 and $90°$, corresponding to the value of X. In the second way, the function

ATAND(X,Y)

has two arguments and returns an angle between -180 and $180°$, corresponding to the values of the numerator X and denominator Y. For example, in

PUT LIST(ATAND(1/−1), ATAND(−1/1));

both expressions are calculated as -1 and result in the printout of

−4.49999999999999E+01   −4.49999999999999E+01

this being $-45°$ in floating point with $p = 15$ as its precision.[1] However, the

---

[1]By the rules of PL/I, $1/-1$ is calculated to precision (15, 14). The precision of ATAND(X) is the same as the precision of the argument X, which is 15 here.

statement

> PUT LIST (ATAND(1.000, −1.000), ATAND(−1.000, 1.000));

gives the printout as

> 1.349E+02   −4.499E+01

because

$$\frac{1}{-1} = \tan 135° \quad \text{and} \quad \frac{-1}{1} = \tan(-45°)$$

The built-in function ATAND(X) returns an angle in the first and fourth quadrants. Observe that the arctan function is multivalued. Hence ATAND(X) selects the branch of the function between −90 and 90°, the so-called *principal value* of the function.

The built-in function ATAND(X,Y) returns an angle in the four quadrants. Note that this angle is given in the range −180 to 180° rather than in the range 0 to 360°.

The functions ATAN(X) and ATAN(X,Y) are analogous to ATAND(X) and ATAND(X,Y), but the returned angle is in radians. For example,

> PUT LIST (ATAN(1/−1), ATAN (−1/1));

gives

> −7.85398163397448E−01   −7.85398163397448E−01

while

> PUT LIST (ATAN)1.000, −1.000), ATAN(−1.000, 1.000));

gives

> 2.356E+00   −7.853E−01

D The Exponential Built-in Function

The function

$$EXP(X)$$

means e^X, where e is the base of the natural logarithms.

E The Hyperbolic Built-in Functions

These are

SINH(X)   meaning sinh $X\left(=\dfrac{e^X - e^{-X}}{2}\right)$

COSH(X)   meaning cosh $X\left(=\dfrac{e^X + e^{-X}}{2}\right)$

$$\text{TANH(X)} \qquad \text{meaning tanh X} = \frac{\text{sinh X}}{\text{cosh X}}$$

$$\text{ATANH(X)} \qquad \text{meaning tanh}^{-1} \text{ X}$$

The arguments of the mathematical built-in functions should be in floating-point scales. A non–floating-point argument is converted to floating-point form; hence the use of floating-point representations saves on conversions. The return is also in floating-point form.

The functions

LOG(X)	EXP(X)
SQRT(X)	SINH(X)
SIN(X)	COSH(X)
COS(X)	TANH(X)
TAN(X)	ATANH(X)
ATAN(X)	

can have complex arguments. The return is then also a complex number. The functions

LOG10(X)	TAND(X)
LOG2(X)	ATAND(X)
SIND(X)	ATAN(X,Y)
COSD(X)	ATAND(X,Y)

must have real arguments and return a real value. More generally, the argument can be an array (or even an array expression). The return is then also an array of the same dimension and bounds as the argument, with the built-function operating on each element of the argument array. For example, the program segment

```
DCL A(2,2);
A(1,1) = 0;
A(1,2) = 30;
A(2,1) = 60;
A(2,2) = 90;
PUT LIST (COSD(A));
```

gives the printout

    1.00000E+00   8.66025E−01   4.99999E−01   1.82864E−10

these being the floating-point values of cos 0°, cos 30°, cos 60°, and cos 90° (observe that the actual output of cos 90° is a very small number rather than zero). If a built-in function has several array arguments, then all such arrays must be of the same dimensions and bounds. For example, if the arrays A, B, and C are defined by

```
DCL (A,B,C) (2,2);
```

then

```
C = ATAND (A,B);
```

is the same as

$$C(1,1) = ATAND(A(1,1), B(1,1));$$
$$C(1,2) = ATAND(A(1,2), B(1,2));$$
$$C(2,1) = ATAND(A(2,1), B(2,1));$$
$$C(2,2) = ATAND(A(2,2), B(2,2));$$

21.3 ARITHMETIC BUILT-IN FUNCTIONS

A The MOD Built-in Function

The function

$$MOD(X1,X2)$$

gives (that is, returns) the remainder of the division X1/X2. This remainder is the smallest positive remainder. For example,

MOD(16,5)   returns 1 (that is, remainder of the division $^{16}\!/_5$).

MOD(-16,5)   returns 4. Here the division is executed to give a positive remainder, that is,

$$\frac{-16}{5} = \frac{-20+4}{5} = -4 + \frac{4}{5}$$

Hence the smallest positive remainder is 4.

MOD(16,-5)   returns 1. Here $16/-5 = -3 + 1/-5$; hence the remainder is 1.

MOD(7,10)   returns 7.

MOD(11.3,1.5)   returns 0.8.

To illustrate the use of the MOD function, consider the following example.

Example 21.3.1 Given a set of integers on the data cards. Print out only the integers which are divisible by 7.

Solution Without the use of the MOD function, the program reads

```
EX_1:    PROC OPTIONS(MAIN);
         DO WHILE(1);
            GET LIST(N);
            K = N/7;
            L = N-7*K;   /* L IS THE REMAINDER */
            IF L=0 THEN PUT LIST(N);
         END;
         END EX_1;
```

with the execution terminated by the ENDFILE condition.

With the MOD function, we can write

```
EX_2:     PROC OPTIONS(MAIN);
          DO WHILE(1);
             GET LIST(N);
             IF MOD(N,7)=0 THEN PUT LIST(N);
          END;
          END EX_2;
```

which is obviously a simpler program.

B The SIGN Built-in Function

The function

SIGN (X)   returns 1   if X > 0
            returns 0   if X = 0
            returns −1 if X < 0

C The FIXED and FLOAT Built-in Functions

The function

FIXED(X,*p,q*)   returns X in fixed-point form with precision (p,q). If X is in binary base, the return is binary too; if X is decimal, so is the return.

FIXED(X,*p*)   is the same as FIXED (X,*p*,0).

FIXED(X)   on the IBM System/360 or System/370 is the same as FIXED (X,15,0) if X is binary, and the same as FIXED (X,5,0) if X is decimal.

FLOAT(X,*p*)   returns X in floating-point form with precision p. The base of the return is the same as the base of X.

FLOAT(X)   on the IBM system/360 or System/370 is the same as FLOAT(X,21) for a binary X, and the same as FLOAT(X, 6) for a decimal X.

D The FLOOR and CEIL Built-in Functions

The function

$$FLOOR(X)$$

returns the largest integer not exceeding X. For example,

FLOOR(5.73)   returns 5
FLOOR(−5.73)   returns −6

Note that −5 exceeds −5.73, while −6 is smaller than −5.73.

The function

$$CEIL(X)$$

returns the smallest integer that is greater than or equal to X. For example,

CEIL(5.73)   returns 6
CEIL(−5.73)   returns −5

Observe that if we have a number whose integer part is N and whose fractional part is α, where $0 < \alpha < 1$, then

$$N < N + \alpha < N+1$$

Here N is FLOOR(N+α), and N+1 is the CEIL(N+α). The name CEIL suggests ceiling, that is, the next higher integer of a fraction.

E The ROUND and TRUNC Built-in Functions

The function

$$ROUND(X,n)$$

for a fixed-point X returns a number rounded at the nth digit after the decimal point. For example,

ROUND(3.8562,2)   returns 3.8600
ROUND(3.8562,0)   returns 4.0000
ROUND(385.62,−1)   returns 390.00

For a floating-point X the rules are somewhat different. This case is less important practically. The details are described in the IBM PL/I "Language Reference Manual."[1]

The function

$$TRUNC(X)$$

truncates (that is, deletes) the fractional part. For example,

TRUNC(5.73)   returns 5 [that is, FLOOR(5.73)]
TRUNC(−5.73)   returns −5 [that is, CEIL(−5.73)]

F The MIN and MAX Built-in Functions

The function

$$MIN(X1,X2, \ldots ,XN)$$

returns the value of the minimal argument on the list. For example,

$$MIN(1.23, 12.2, −3, −2.5)$$

[1] IBM Systems Reference Library, order no. GC28-8201, p. 292.

returns -3.00. The precision of the return is given by the one or two arguments having the highest number of digits to the left of the decimal point and the highest number of digits to the right of the decimal point. Here, we have xx.xx as the highest precision, or (4, 2). Since front zeros are suppressed in the printout, -3.00 is the return.

The function

$$\text{MAX(X1,X2, . . . ,XN)}$$

returns the value of the maximal argument. For example,

$$\text{MAX(1.23, 12.2, } -3, -2.5)$$

returns 12.20. The precision rule is the same as for the MIN function.

For both functions, if any number on the list is in floating-point form, the result is also in floating-point form. There must be at least two arguments on the lists of both functions.

G The ABS Built-in Function

The function

$$\text{ABS(X)}$$

means X , that is, the absolute value, or the magnitude of X. For real X, the return is the positive value of X. For complex X, the return is the magnitude of X (that is, the positive square root of the sum of squares of the real and imaginary parts). For example, the statement

$$\text{PUT LIST (ABS(-1.23), ABS($3+4$I));}$$

gives the output

$$1.23 \qquad 5$$

Observe that the precision of the return is the same as that of the argument.

H The REAL, IMAG, CONJG, and COMPLEX Built-in Functions

There are several built-in functions for operations on complex quantities. If X is complex, then

REAL(X)	returns the real part of X
IMAG(X)	returns the imaginary part of X
CONJG(X)	returns the conjugate of X

As an example, the program segment

```
DCL X CPLX;
X = 1.23 - 4.5I;
PUT LIST(X,REAL(X),IMAG(X),CONJG(X));
```

gives the output

```
1.22999E+00-4.50000E+00I            1.22999E+00        -4.50000E+00
1.22999E+00+4.50000E+00I
```

with the returns having the attributes of X.

The function

$$COMPLEX(X,Y)$$

returns a complex number having X as its real part and Y as its imaginary part. For example,

```
N = 3;
PUT LIST (COMPLEX(3*N, N−1));
```

gives the printout

$$9+2I$$

Note that the two arguments X and Y must be real.

Example 21.3.2 There are several complex numbers on data cards. These numbers are in the cartesian (that is, rectangular) form. Print out for each number its magnitude and angle.

Solution The form

$$\alpha + j\beta$$

is the cartesian form of a complex number. The magnitude M and the angle θ of $\alpha + j\beta$ are given by

$$M = |\alpha + j\beta| \qquad \theta = \tan^{-1}\frac{\beta}{\alpha}$$

Using these formulas, the desired program is

```
EXAMPLE: PROC OPTIONS(MAIN);
         DCL X CPLX;
         DO WHILE(1);
            GET LIST(X);
            PUT SKIP LIST(X,ABS(X),ATAND(IMAG(X),REAL(X)));
         END;
         END EXAMPLE;
```

The arguments of the functions

MOD(X,Y)	TRUNC(X)
SIGN(X)	MIN(X1,X2, . . . ,XN)
FLOOR(X)	MAX(X1,X2, . . . ,XN)
CEIL(X)	COMPLEX(X,Y)

must be real. The functions

$$FIXED(X,p,q), FIXED(X,p), FIXED(X)$$
$$FLOAT(X,p), FLOAT(X)$$
$$ROUND(X,n)$$
$$ABS(X)$$
$$REAL(X)$$
$$IMAG(X)$$
$$CONJG(X)$$

may have complex arguments.

As a rule the attributes of the return are the same as the attributes of the argument.[1] As for the mathematical built-in functions, the arguments in the arithmetic built-in functions may be arrays or array expressions. In such a case, the return is an array of the same dimensions and bounds as the argument, with the built-in function operating on each element of the argument array. For example, the program segment

```
DCL X(2) CPLX FIXED(2), (M,N)(2);
X(1) = 3 + 4I;
X(2) = 4 − 3I;
M(1) = 5;
M(2) = 9;
N(1) = 3;
N(2) = 5;
PUT LIST (ABS(X), MOD(M,N));
```

gives the printout

$$5 \quad 5 \quad 2 \quad 4$$

because the PUT LIST statement is equivalent to

```
PUT LIST (ABS(X(1)), ABS(X(2)), MOD(M(1), N(1)), MOD(M(2), N(2)));
```

thus yielding the indicated output.

21.4 BUILT-IN FUNCTIONS FOR ARRAY MANIPULATIONS

A The LBOUND and HBOUND Built-in Functions

The function

$$LBOUND(X,n)$$

returns the lower bound (that is, the *lowbound*) of the nth dimension of the array X.

---

[1]There are some exceptions. The precise rules are described in IBM System/360 Operating System PL/I (F) "Language Reference Manual," secs. F and G, IBM Systems Reference Library, order no. GC 28-8201.

For example, in the program segment

```
DCL A(3:17, −2:3, 5:13);
GET LIST (A);
N = LBOUND (A,3);
PUT LIST (N);
```

the output is 5, this being the lowbound of the third dimension of A.
  The function

$$HBOUND(X,n)$$

returns the upper bound (that is, the *highbound*) of the nth dimension of the array X. For example, in the program segment

```
DCL A(3:17, −2:3, 5:13);
GET LIST (A);
M = HBOUND (A, 1);
PUT LIST (M);
```

the output is 17, this being the highbound of the first dimension.

B The DIM Built-in Function

The function

$$DIM(X,n)$$

returns the *extent* of the nth dimension of the array X. Recall that extent is the number of elements (that is, the number of subscripts) in a dimension. For example, in the program segment

```
DCL A(3:17, −2:3, 5:13);
GET LIST (A)
L = DIM(A,2);
PUT LIST (L);
```

the output is 6, this being the extent of the second dimension.

C The SUM and PROD Built-in Functions

The function

$$SUM(X)$$

returns the sum of all elements of the array X. For example, in the program segment

```
DCL A(2,2);
A=3;
B=SUM(A);
PUT LIST (B);
```

the output is

$$1.20000E+01$$

this being the sum of all elements of A (12 in floating-point form).

The function

$$PROD(X)$$

returns the product of all the elements of the array X. For example, in the program segment

```
DCL A(2,2);
A=3;
B=PROD(A);
PUT LIST (B);
```

the output is

$$8.10000E+01$$

this being the product of all elements of A (81 in floating-point form).

D The POLY Built-in Function

Let A and X be one-dimensional arrays defined by the DECLARE statement

$$DCL\ A(M:N),\ X(P:Q);$$

then

$$POLY\ (A,X)$$

calculates

$$A(M) + A(M+1) * X(P)$$
$$+ A(M+2) * X(P) * X(P+1)$$
$$+ A(M+3) * X(P) * X(P+1) * X(P+2)$$
$$\dots\dots\dots\dots\dots\dots\dots\dots\dots\dots$$
$$+ A(M+N-M) * X(P) * X(P+1) * \dots * X(P+N-M-1)$$

if $P+N-M-1 < Q$ (Q is the highest subscript of X, and calculates

$$A(M) + A(M+1)*X(P)$$
$$+ A(M+2)*X(P)*X(P+1)$$
$$\dots\dots\dots\dots\dots\dots\dots\dots$$
$$+ A(M+N-M) * X(P) * X(P+1)* \dots *X(Q)$$

if $P+N-M-1> = Q$, since X may contain no subscript higher than Q (all subscripts of X exceeding Q are replaced by Q). In the special case where A is still the same array as above and X is a single-valued variable, (that is, a scalar variable), then

$$POLY\ (A,X)$$

calculates

$$\begin{aligned}
&A(M) + A(M+1)*X \\
&\quad + A(M+2)*X*X \\
&\quad \cdots\cdots\cdots\cdots \\
&\quad + A(M+N-M)\ \underbrace{*X*X*\ldots*X}_{N-M\ \text{factors}}
\end{aligned}$$

Hence, in this case,

$$POLY\ (A,X)$$

calculates

$$\sum_{I=0}^{N-M} A(M+I)*X^I$$

that is, the value of a polynomial. This is why the function has its name. Incidentally, a compact formula for the POLY function is

$$POLY(A,X) = A(M) + \sum_{I=1}^{N-M}\left[A(M+I)*\prod_{J=0}^{I-1} X(P+J)\right]$$

where again, if J is such that $P+J >=Q$, then $X(P+J)$ is placed by $X(Q)$. Note that if $M=N$, then the return is just $A(M)$.

Example 21.4.1 The program segment

```
DCL A(2:4), X(4);
A = 2;
X = 3;
Y = POLY (A,X);
PUT DATA (Y);
```

calculates Y as

$$\begin{aligned}
&A(2) + A(3)\ *X(1) \\
&\quad + A(4)\ *X(1)*X(2) = 2 + 2*3 + 2*3*3 = 26
\end{aligned}$$

Hence the printout is

$$Y = 2.60000E+01;$$

Example 21.4.2 The program segment

```
DCL A(4), X(2:3);
A = 2;
X = 3;
Z = POLY (A,X);
PUT DATA (Z);
```

calculates Z as

A(1) + A(2)*X(2)
    + A(3)*X(2)*X(3)
    + A(4)*X(2)*X(3)*X(3) = 2 + 2*3 + 2*3*3 + 2*3*3*3 = 80

The resulting printout is

$$Z = 8.00000E+01;$$

Example 21.4.3 The program segment

```
DCL A(0:3);
X=2;
DO I= 1 TO 4;
    A(I−1) = I;
END;
PUT LIST (POLY(A,X));
```

calculates the built-in function as

$$A(0) + A(1)*X + A(2)*X**2 + A(3)*X**3$$

$$= 1 + 2*2 + 3*2^2 + 4*2^3 = 49$$

The printout is

$$4.90000E+01$$

21.5 BUILT-IN FUNCTIONS FOR STRING HANDLING

We described the built-in functions for handling strings earlier: the SUBSTR and the INDEX functions in Sec. 17.4, the LENGTH and the REPEAT functions in Sec. 17.6, and the BOOL function in Sec. 18.5. It is only to be added that the arguments in the SUBSTR, INDEX, LENGTH, and BOOL functions can be arrays (or array expressions). In the REPEAT function, the first argument can be an array, but the second argument must be an integer constant. In such a case, the REPEAT function operates on each array element.

21.6 SUMMARY

We described here several built-in functions. These are programs stored in the computer's memory and available when identified by their names. We introduced mathematical built-in functions, arithmetic built-in functions, built-in functions for array manipulations, as well as built-in functions for handling strings.

For the sake of brevity, we omitted a detailed discussion of attributes of the arguments and of the returns of the built-in functions. We also omitted the description of several additional functions.[1]

[1] For such material, see IBM System/360 Operating System PL/I (F) "Language Reference Manual," secs. F and G, IBM Systems Reference Library, order no. GC28-8201.

PROBLEMS

21.1 There are 20 numbers on data cards. Write a concise program to print out only those numbers which exceed the average.

21.2 There are 100 positive integers on data cards. No number exceeds 100. Print out only those numbers which are not prime numbers.

21.3 There are 100 positive integers on data cards. Write a program to print out only the integers divisible by either 5 or by 7 (but not the integers divisible by both 5 and 7).

21.4 Given the sides AB, BC, and the angle β (in degrees) shown in Fig. P21.4. Write a program to print out the area of the triangle.

21.5 The data cards contain the values for the side AB and the angles α and β (in degrees) of the triangle ABC shown in Fig. P21.5. Write a program for printing the area of the triangle.

Hint: By the sine law $\dfrac{a}{b} = \dfrac{\sin \alpha}{\sin \beta}$

21.6 What output occurs for each of the following programs?

```
A: PROC OPTIONS(MAIN);
   I = ABS(7/(-3*2));
   PUT LIST(I);
   END A;


B: PROC OPTIONS(MAIN);
   I = SQRT(2);
   PUT LIST(I);
   END B;


C: PROC OPTIONS(MAIN);
   I = MOD(5,3) + SIGN(-12.3);
   PUT LIST(I);
   END C;


D: PROC OPTIONS(MAIN);
   I = FLOAT(FIXED(12.31)) + 0.5;
   PUT LIST(I);
   END D;


E: PROC OPTIONS(MAIN);
   DCL A(2:5,3:5);
   I = LBOUND(A,2)*DIM(A,1);
   PUT LIST(I);
   END E;
```

Figure P21.4

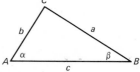

Figure P21.5

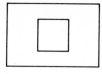

Figure P21.7

21.7 The data cards contain the elements of a 20 × 30 array (Fig. P21.7). Print out the elements of the inner 10 × 10 square with the following modifications.

(*a*) If the element is an integer, print it out in the integer form (that is, not in the float form).

(*b*) If the element is a noninteger, print its absolute value (in float form).

21.8 There are 20 numbers on data cards. Round each number to the nearest integer. Write a program to print all such integers and the count of all even positive integers (after roundoff) which are divisible by 7.

21.9 There are several hundred positive integers on data cards. We wish to acquire the first 50 numbers and to divide them into the following three classes:

ACCEPTABLE   a number which is a perfect square, or a multiple of a perfect square, and is less than 30^2

DESIRABLE   a number which is both acceptable and also less than 100

NOT ACCEPTABLE   a number which does not meet the above criteria

The output should be each number and its status on one line.

21.10 Forty numbers forming the elements of two 5×4 arrays A and B are on data cards. Write a program which will print out a third 5×4 array of *integer* numbers formed in the following fashion:

1. Each element in the two outside columns is the rounded-off value of the corresponding element in A or B, whichever is larger. "Rounded-off" means rounding up when the fractional part is 0.5 or larger, and rounding down when the fractional part is less than 0.5.

2. The elements in the two inner columns are either 0 or 1. An element is 0 if the corresponding element in A is smaller than the element in B; otherwise it is 1.

Print out the integer array in data-directed format, one row per line.

21.11 Write a program to determine the minimum element and its location in a two-dimensional array A. The array A has integer elements and dimensionality (5, 5). The program should print the element value and its location. You may assume that there is a single smallest value.

21.12 Write a program to process 20 positive values of the variable x. The program should print out either

$$e^x \qquad \text{or} \qquad \sin x \qquad \text{or} \qquad \ln x$$

depending on which of the quantities

$$|e^x - x| \qquad |\sin x - x| \qquad |\ln x - x|$$

is smaller. Thus the program should print out the value of e^x, $\sin x$ or $\ln x$, depending on which is closer to x.

21.13 Given that

$$y = a_5x^5 + a_4x^4 + a_3x^3 + a_2x^2 + a_1x + a_0$$

calculate y for

(*a*) all a's of 1 $x = 1.5$

(*b*) $a_k = k + 2$ $x = 1.3$

(*c*) $a_5 = 1.8$

$a_4 = 1.6$ $a_1 = 0.83$

$a_3 = -0.3$ $a_0 = -0.8$

$a_2 = 1.42$ $x = 1.45$

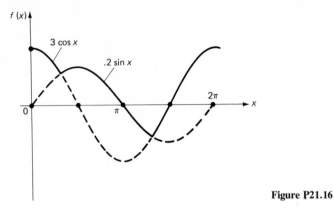

Figure P21.16

21.14 The function

$$Z(s) = \frac{s^2 + 3s + 1}{s^3 + 2s^2 + 2s + 1}$$

is to be evaluated for several given complex values of s. The resulting complex number for $Z(s)$ is to be printed in both cartesian and polar forms with identifying headings. Write a program to do so. The given values are

$$1 - j$$
$$1 + j$$
$$0.5 - j0.73$$
$$4.2 + j6.2$$

21.15 There are 100 integers on 100 consecutive data cards. Write a program to print out
    (*a*) All the 100 integers
    (*b*) All the even integers in the set preceded by an appropriate title
    (*c*) All the odd integers in the set preceded by an appropriate title

21.16 $f(x)$, shown by the solid-line curve of Fig. P21.16, is either 3 cos x or 2 sin x, whichever is larger. Write a program to calculate the area under $f(x)$ on the interval between $x = 0$ and $x = 6$, using 10 strips (that is, 11 points) and trapezoidal integration.

21.17 Given the five-sided figure (Fig. P21.17), where

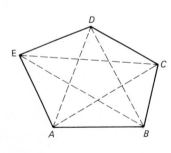

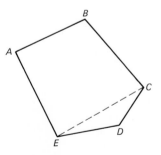

Figure P21.17

Figure P21.18

$$AB = 1.92 \text{ m} \qquad \sphericalangle \, EAB = 112.7°$$
$$BC = 1.35 \text{ m} \qquad \sphericalangle \, DEC = 36.8°$$
$$CE = 2.84 \text{ m} \qquad \sphericalangle \, ECD = 29.7°$$
$$EA = 1.63 \text{ m}$$

find

(*a*) Sides CD, DE, BE, BD, CA, DA

(*b*) Angles ABC, BCD, DEA, DAC, EBD, ACE, BDA

(*c*) The area of the pentagon

21.18 Given the five-sided figure (Fig. P21.18), with

Sides AB, BC, EA
Diagonal CE
Angles ABC, CED, ECD

List

(*a*) All five sides AB, BC, CD, ED, EA

(*b*) All five angles ABC, BCD, CDE, DEA, EAB

(*c*) Sum of five angles (for check, it should be 540°)

The data are

$$AB = 3.5 \text{ inches} \qquad \sphericalangle \, ABC = 97°$$
$$BC = 4.2 \text{ inches} \qquad \sphericalangle \, CED = 18.6°$$
$$EA = 3.7 \text{ inches} \qquad \sphericalangle \, ECD = 31.4°$$
$$CE = 5.6 \text{ inches}$$

21.19 In the six-sided figure ABCDEF shown in Fig. P21.19, the sides EF and FA are to be calculated.

The following are given:
Sides AB, BC, CD, DE
Diagonal EA
Angles ABC, CDA, DEF, FAB

The following data are given for five figures. For each figure print the desired two sides properly identified. If there is no possible answer, print NO ANSWER.

AB	BC	CD	DE	EA	$\sphericalangle$ABC	$\sphericalangle$CDA	$\sphericalangle$DEF	$\sphericalangle$FAB
4	5	3	45	7	120°	20°	120°	130°
7	12	6	3	16	140°	25°	62°	45°
5	4	2	3	4.5	85°	12°	152°	148°
8	9	8	7.5	6.2	72°	18°	135°	135°
6	6	6	6	6	82.7°	41.3°	150°	165°

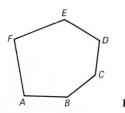

Figure P21.19

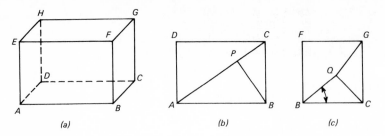

Figure P21.20

21.20 The following information is given on a parallelepiped (that is, rectangular block) shown in Fig. P21.20*a*:

    1. The segments AB, BP, PA, on the rectangular base ABCD (P lies on the diagonal AC, see Fig. P21.20*b*)

    2. The segment BQ, the angle QBC, and the segment QG on the rectangular face BCGF. Q is an interior point, not generally on the diagonal (see Fig. P21.20*c*).

Write a program to find the volume of five parallelepipeds. (In general, AB, BC, and CG are not equal.) If the data are such that there is no solution, print a message to this effect.

    The data are

AB	BP	PA	BQ	⊀QBC	QG
3	2.6	2.8	2	40°	4
18	12	15	14	45°	13
10	6.8	20	7	62°	13
10	6.8	7.3	7	39°	7
10	4.2	7.3	7	14.2°	6

PROCEDURES

22

We will introduce here the two types of procedures: function procedures and subroutine procedures.

The function procedures can be viewed as extending the capabilities of the built-in functions described in Chap. 21. With function procedures, we have the facility to use any function that we desire and are no longer limited to just the built-in ones. However, now we must write our own programs for the functions that we wish to define. In Sec. 22.1 we will show how to do so.

A function procedure *returns a single result* to the point in the program where the name of the function appears. The subroutine procedure takes over the control of the program and upon the completion of its task *returns this control*. We will describe in detail the uses of both these procedure types.

There are several good reasons why procedures are used. Three of the reasons are:

1. Procedures allow the division of a program into separate smaller units, each of which can be written and tested independently. It is much easier to test and "debug" (that is, correct) several small programs than a single, long program.
2. Procedures make the writing of a large program by several programmers possible. In such an instance, each programmer writes separate procedures, and then a single programmer ties them together into a unified program.
3. We can use existing, well-working programs as parts of a new program.

22.1 FUNCTION PROCEDURES

Consider the following problem:

Given

The sides AB, BC, CD, DE, EA, AD, and BD in the pentagon of Fig. 22.1.

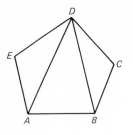

Figure 22.1 The pentagon for the illustration of a function procedure.

Find

The area of the pentagon.

The area of the pentagon is the sum of areas of the triangles ADE, ABD, and BCD. Recall that if we have three sides of a triangle, and these sides are *a*, *b*, and *c*, then the area of the triangle is given by

$$\text{Area} = \sqrt{s(s-a)(s-b)(s-c)}$$

where $s = \frac{1}{2}(a + b + c)$.

Using the above formulas, the program for the calculation of the area can be written as

```
PENTA:    PROC OPTIONS(MAIN);
          GET LIST(AB,BC,CD,DE,EA,AD,BD);
          S = (AD+DE+EA)/2;
          AREA_1 = SQRT(S*(S-AD)*(S-DE)*(S-EA));
          S = (AB+BD+AD)/2;
          AREA_2 = SQRT(S*(S-AB)*(S-BD)*(S-AD));
          S = (BC+CD+BD)/2;
          AREA_3 = SQRT(S*(S-BC)*(S-CD)*(S-BD));
          AREA = AREA_1 + AREA_2 + AREA_3;
          PUT LIST(AREA);
          END PENTA;
```

Let us assume now that there exists a built-in function

TR_AREA(X,Y,Z)

where the *arguments* X, Y, and Z are the sides of a triangle, and that this function *returns* the area of the triangle. As described in Chap. 21, whenever the compiler sees TR_AREA(X,Y,Z), it substitutes for it the area of the triangle (having X, Y, and Z as its sides). With such a function, the program reads

```
PENTA2:   PROC OPTIONS (MAIN);
          GET LIST (AB,BC,CD,DE,EA,AD,BD);
          AREA_1 =TR_AREA(AD,DE,EA);
          AREA_2 =TR_AREA(AB,BD,AD);
          AREA_3 =TR_AREA(BC,CD,BD);
```

```
AREA =AREA_1 + AREA_2 + AREA_3;
PUT LIST (AREA);
END PENTA2;
```

which is simpler than the previous one. The only catch is that there is no built-in function TR_AREA(X,Y,Z). However, we can write a program for such a function ourselves. Such a function is a "user-defined function" and is named a *function procedure*. A program for such a function reads

```
TR_AREA:   PROCEDURE(X,Y,Z);
           S=(X+Y+Z)/2;
           A=SQRT(S*(S−X)*(S−Y)*(S−Z));
           RETURN(A);
           END TR_AREA;
```

This program has two new features. First, the procedure statement is different from the usual one. Second, the statement

```
RETURN(A);
```

is a new statement, not encountered until now. There is still the question of what to do with the TR_AREA program—how to give it to the computer. We will describe these new features and answer the posed question presently.

To describe what takes place, let us go back to the PENTA2 program. In the third statement, the compiler encountered the expression

```
TR_AREA(AD,DE,EA)
```

and interpreted it as a transfer to the function procedure named TR_AREA. Consequently, a jump to the procedure statement

```
TR_AREA: PROCEDURE(X,Y,Z);
```

takes place. The arguments AD, DE, EA are transferred to the procedure so that the first argument AD becomes the identifier X in the procedure, the second argument DE becomes the identifier Y in the procedure, and the third argument EA becomes the identifier Z in the procedure. The TR_AREA program is then carried out, and the desired result is calculated as A. The fourth statement of the TR_AREA procedure, that is,

```
RETURN(A);
```

is encountered and means that:

1. A return to the original program is to take place.
2. The value of A (that is, the contents of the location assigned to A) replaces the expression TR_AREA(AD,DE,EA).

We have just described the compiler action to the function procedure statement [that is, to TR_AREA: PROCEDURE (X,Y,Z);] and to the RETURN statement. It remains to show how the TR_AREA program is given to the computer.

The TR_AREA program can be inserted anywhere within the PENTA2 program after the statement

PENTA2: PROC OPTIONS(MAIN);

For the time being, we will assume that the TR_AREA program is inserted before the END PENTA2; statement. It is also possible to insert the program after the END PENTA2; statement, as we will discuss in Sec. 22.6. The complete program then reads

```
PENTA2:  PROC OPTIONS(MAIN);
         GET LIST(AB,BC,CD,DE,EA,AD,BD);
         AREA_1 = TR_AREA(AD,DE,EA);
         AREA_2 = TR_AREA(AB,BD,AD);
         AREA_3 = TR_AREA(BC,CD,BD);
         AREA   = AREA_1 + AREA_2 + AREA_3;
         TR_AREA: PROCEDURE(X,Y,Z);
                  S = (X+Y+Z)/2;
                  A = SQRT(S*(S-X)*(S-Y)*(S-Z));
                  RETURN(A);
                  END TR_AREA;
         PUT LIST(AREA);
         END PENTA2;
```

Observe that the TR_AREA procedure is entered only when needed for the calculation of the TR_AREA function. Therefore, after the statement

AREA = AREA_1 + AREA_2 + AREA_3;

we execute the statement

PUT LIST (AREA);

and the TR_AREA procedure is ignored. Hence the program is executed in the same way for any placement of the TR_AREA procedure, and it does not matter where we place this procedure in the PENTA2 program, as asserted.

Let us now introduce some of the terms used by programmers. In the PENTA2 program, the statement

AREA_1 = TR_AREA(AD,DE,EA);

made reference to the function TR_AREA(AD,DE,EA). The appearance of a function name is named a *function reference*. The parenthesized list of variables, that is,

(AD,DE,EA)

is named an *argument list*. The statement

TR_AREA: PROCEDURE(X,Y,Z);

is the procedure statement of the *function procedure*. The parenthesized list of variables, that is,

(X,Y,Z)

Name in
PENTA2

Name in
TR_AREA

AD | Storage location | X

Figure 22.2 Different names for same storage location.

is named a *parameter list*. When the function procedure is executed, the compiler assigns to the first parameter X the same storage location which has been assigned to the first argument AD. This situation is portrayed in Fig. 22.2. Similarly, the compiler assigns to the parameters Y and Z storage locations which have been reserved for the arguments DE and EA. Thus the association between each parameter and argument is according to their respective positions. In general, for any function reference

$$function\_name(arg1,arg2, . . . ,argn)$$

there will be a procedure statement

$$function\_name:PROCEDURE(par1,par2, . . . ,parn);$$

During the execution of the function, *par1* in the *function_name* procedure will describe the same storage location as does *arg1* in the main procedure, *par2* will designate the same location as *arg2*, and so on.

When the compiler identifies a function reference, it transfers the program execution to the function procedure. In computer jargon, this start of the function procedure is named *invocation* of the function procedure, that is, the function procedure is *invoked*.

A function procedure always returns a single value with its RETURN statement. However, there can be several return statements, as in

```
EXAMPLE:  PROCEDURE(X,Y);
          Z = 2*X + Y;
          IF Z > 5 THEN RETURN(Z);
                  ELSE RETURN(Y);
          END EXAMPLE;
```

with each returning a single value.

The keyword PROCEDURE can be abbreviated to PROC as before. It also is allowed to have an expression in the parentheses following RETURN, as in

```
EXAMPLE:  PROC(A,B,C);
          RETURN(A*B/C);
          END EXAMPLE;
```

In all situations where expressions are allowed, functions are allowed too. Thus it is legal to use the function FUNC, for example, as an operand in

$$X = X + A*FUNC(A,B);$$

or as a subscript in

$$C(FUNC(A,B),3) = 7;$$

or as an argument in another function GUNC, as in

$$Y = B*GUNC(FUNC(A,B),X);$$

Incidentally, in the statement

$$C = (FUNC(A))*D;$$

the parentheses around FUNC(A) are redundant; hence

$$C = FUNC(A)*D;$$

suffices. The compiler interprets the expression from left to right; thus

$$FUNC(A)$$

is obtained first, and the result is multiplied by D.

There is a little more that can be said about function procedures. We will do so after we describe the subroutine procedures.

22.2 SUBROUTINE PROCEDURES

There are problems for which function procedures are inconvenient. A function procedure cannot be used, for example, for the return to the point of invocation of the solution of two equations in two unknowns. Such equations yield two values, but a function procedure can return only a single value. Even though this problem can be handled with a function procedure, it is more convenient to do so with a subroutine procedure.

A subroutine procedure is *invoked* with the statement

$$CALL \; subroutine\_name(arg1,arg2, \ldots ,argn);$$

which causes a transfer to the subroutine procedure. The procedure statement of the subroutine procedure has the same form as the procedure statement of the function procedure, that is,

$$subroutine\_name: \; PROC(par1,par2, \ldots ,parn);$$

where the association among the parameters and arguments is as in a function procedure.

To illustrate the use of a subroutine procedure, consider the following example.

Given

Ten sets of equations. Each set consists of two equations in two unknowns.

Find

The solutions for each set.

Solution Assume that for each set the values of a_1, b_1, c_1, a_2, b_2, and c_2 are given, where

$$a_1 x + b_1 y = c_1$$
$$a_2 x + b_2 y = c_2$$

Solving for x and y gives

$$x = \frac{b_2 c_1 - b_1 c_2}{a_1 b_2 - a_2 b_1} \qquad y = \frac{a_1 c_2 - a_2 c_1}{a_1 b_2 - a_2 b_1}$$

Let us name the subroutine procedure for calculaton of x and y as EQUA-TION. If we assume that $a_1 b_2 - a_2 b_1 \neq 0$, a program for this procedure is

```
EQUATION:   PROC(A1,B1,C1,A2,B2,C2);
            DET = A1*B2 - A2*B1;
            X = (B2*C1 - B1*C2)/DET;
            Y = (A1*C2 - A2*C1)/DET;
            RETURN;
            END EQUATION;
```

Observe that the above return statement is different from the return statement of the function procedure—now there is no identifier or expression following RETURN. The RETURN statement here merely signifies a command to return to the invoking program (that is, the program which invoked the subroutine procedure with the CALL statement).

The complete program with the above subroutine procedure can be written as

```
EXAMPLE: PROC OPTIONS(MAIN);
         DO I=1 TO 10;
             GET LIST(A,B,C,D,E,F);
             CALL EQUATION(A,B,C,D,E,F);
             PUT SKIP DATA(X,Y);
             EQUATION: PROC(A1,B1,C1,A2,B2,C2);
                       DET = A1*B2 - A2*B1;
                       X = (B2*C1 - B1*C2)/DET;
                       Y = (A1*C2 - A2*C1)/DET;
                       RETURN;
                       END EQUATION;
         END;
         END EXAMPLE;
```

The subroutine procedure EQUATION can be entered only with a CALL statement. Hence the CALL statement results in a jump to the subroutine procedure. Upon the completion of the subroutine, the program execution proceeds with the statement following the CALL statement, that is, with PUT SKIP DATA(X,Y);. The next statement is the procedure statement of the subroutine procedure—but this statement and the rest of the procedure are omitted, because a subroutine procedure is not entered sequentially but only when invoked with the CALL statement. Hence the END; statement is executed after the PUT SKIP DATA(X,Y); statement.

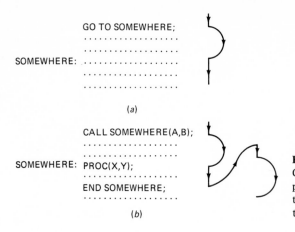

Figure 22.3 Program executions with the GO TO statement and with the subroutine procedure: (*a*) program execution with the GO TO statement; (*b*) program execution with the subroutine procedure.

Recall that the appearance of a function name is named *function reference*. Similarly, the appearance of a subroutine name in the CALL statement is named *subroutine reference*. Observe that the CALL statement functions similarly to the GO TO statement. However, after the completion of the program segment following the GO TO statement, the program is executed sequentially. The CALL statement transfers just like the GO TO statement, but after the completion of the subroutine procedure, the statement after the CALL statement is executed next. These situations are portrayed in Fig. 22.3, with curved lines indicating a jump. There are still other features which make a procedure different from just a program segment, especially in the compilation; these will be described later in this chapter.

Consider again the subroutine EQUATION in the program EXAMPLE. Upon encountering the statement RETURN; the program execution returns to the main program. If the statement RETURN; is omitted, the statement END EQUATION; will also cause a return to the main program. Hence in this subroutine procedure the RETURN statement is redundant. It is also possible to have a subroutine procedure with several RETURN statements, as, for example,

```
JOE:   PROC(A,B);
       IF A > B THEN RETURN;
       C = A + B;
       IF C > 5 THEN RETURN;
       C = 5;
       RETURN;
       END JOE;
```

In the above, if A > B, nothing is done and we return to the main program. If A ≯ B, then C is calculated as A+B, and if C > 5 we return to the main program. If C ≯ 5, then C is set for 5 and again we return to the main program.

We can rewrite the above procedure JOE without the three RETURN statements, as in

```
JOE2:  PROC(A,B);
          IF A ¬> B THEN DO;
                          C = A + B;
                             IF C  ¬> 5 THEN C = 5;
                       END;
          END JOE2;
```

because the END statement also provides a return to the main program. Thus in the procedure JOE the RETURN statement was used as an alternate exit from the procedure. In the procedure JOE2 we leave the procedure just at the END JOE2; statement.

22.3 EXITS AND ENTRIES FOR FUNCTION AND SUBROUTINE PROCEDURES

The exits and entries for a function procedure and for a subroutine procedure are identical. We will describe these here.

A Exits from a Procedure

There are three ways of leaving a procedure:

1. Exit through a GO TO statement
2. Exit through an END statement
3. Exit through a RETURN statement

As an example, consider the following program illustrating all three types of exits:

```
EXIT:     PROC OPTIONS(MAIN);
          GET LIST(A,B)COPY;
AGAIN:    A = A + 1;
          B = B + 1;
          CALL SUB(A,B);
          PUT LIST(C);
          SUB: PROC(X,Y);
              IF X<1 THEN GO TO AGAIN;
              C = X*Y/3;
              IF C>5 THEN RETURN;
              C = C + 1;
              END SUB;
          END EXIT;
```

Observe that A in the main procedure becomes X in the SUB procedure. For

X < 1, we exit from the subroutine procedure with a GO TO statement. For X ≮ 1, we calculate C. For C > 5, we exit from the subroutine procedure with a RETURN statement. And finally, for C ≯ 5, we calculate C and exit from the subroutine procedure with an END SUB; statement.

*B Alternate Entries

A procedure is usually entered with its PROCEDURE statement. It is sometimes desired to enter a procedure at another point. We will introduce the use of such an alternate entry with an example.

We wish to calculate average velocities in miles per hour. We are given distance in either miles or kilometers and time in hours. Let us assume that the input is in the forms such as

$$55 \quad 'MILES' \quad 3.5$$

or

$$113.7 \quad 'KM' \quad 5.3$$

where the second number designates time in hours.

A program for calculating the velocities can be written as

```
VEL1:    PROC OPTIONS(MAIN);
         DCL UNITS CHAR(5) VAR;
         DO WHILE(1);
            GET LIST(DIST,UNITS,TIME);
            IF UNITS='KM' THEN DIST = DIST*0.6214;
            VELOCITY = FUNC(DIST,TIME);
            PUT LIST(VELOCITY);
         END;
         FUNC: PROC(A,B);
               C = A/B;
               RETURN(C);
               END FUNC;
         END VEL1;
```

The same can be accomplished with the program

```
VEL2:    PROC OPTIONS(MAIN);
         DCL UNITS CHAR(5) VAR;
         DO WHILE(1);
            GET LIST(DIST,UNITS,TIME);
            IF UNITS='KM' THEN VELOCITY = FUNC1(DIST,TIME);
                         ELSE VELOCITY = FUNC2(DIST,TIME);
            PUT LIST(VELOCITY);
         END;
```

*If time does not permit the coverage of the entire chapter, the starred sections can be omitted without any loss of continuity.

```
FUNC1: PROC(A,B);
       A = A*0.6214;
FUNC2: ENTRY(A,B);
       C = A/B;
       RETURN(C);
       END FUNC1;
  END VEL2;
```

The second program contains a new statement, not encountered as yet, in

FUNC2: ENTRY(A,B);

which we will explain together with the rest of the program. In the program the following actions take place:

1. The appearance of the function reference

FUNC1(DIST,TIME)

invokes the function procedure FUNC1. As before, the function procedure is entered at the

FUNC1: PROC(A,B);

statement. The execution begins with the first executable statement, that is, with

A = A*0.6214;

2. The appearance of the function reference

FUNC2(DIST,TIME);

invokes the function procedure in which FUNC2 appears. Thus the function procedure FUNC1 is activated. However the control is transferred to the

FUNC2: ENTRY(A,B);

statement. The execution starts with the first executable statement, that is, with

C = A/B;

The statement

FUNC2: ENTRY(A,B);

is named a *secondary entry point*. The statement

FUNC1: PROC(A,B);

is named the *primary entry point* of the procedure.
3. In execution of the procedure FUNC1, the entry statement

FUNC2: ENTRY(A,B);

is ignored. Thus, after the execution of the statement

$$A = A*0.6214;$$

the computer executes next the statement

$$C = A/B;$$

When we enter a procedure at a secondary entry point, we execute only that part of the procedure following the entrance. However, the declarations above the entrance are "known." For example, in the program

```
EXAMPLE:    PROC OPTIONS(MAIN);
            ......................

            IF X > Y THEN Z = U*FUNC1(X,Y);
                     ELSE Z = V*FUNC2(X,Y);

                     .........................

            FUNC1: PROC(A,B);
                   DCL(A,B) FIXED(3,1);
                   ...................

            FUNC2: ENTRY(A,B);
                   ............

                   END FUNC1;
                   ...........

END EXAMPLE;
```

the declaration for A and B following the FUNC1 procedure statement is also known to the compiler when we enter the procedure at the FUNC2 secondary entry point.

C Multiple Closure

As before, the closing of the main procedure provides closure to all program segments requiring an END; statement. Thus closing of the main procedure also closes all other procedures. For example, both program segments

```
A: PROC OPTIONS(MAIN);      A: PROC OPTIONS(MAIN);
   ....................         ....................

   B: PROC(X,Y);               B: PROC(X,Y);
      ...........                 ...........

      END B;                      END A;
   END A;
```

are equivalent, because END A; also closes the B procedure. Because the program on the left (with a separate closing for the B procedure) is clearer, it is preferable.

22.4 ARGUMENTS AND PARAMETERS

Recall that in the CALL statement

$$CALL \; JOE(A,B,C);$$

A, B, and C are named *arguments,* while in the procedure statement

JOE: PROC(X,Y,Z);

X, Y, and Z are named *parameters.* Recall further that there is the association

$$(A,B,C)$$
$$\downarrow \downarrow \downarrow$$
$$(X,Y,Z)$$

in that the parameter X in the subroutine procedure JOE describes the same storage location as the argument A in the main procedure. Similarly, Y and Z are the names in the subroutine procedure for the storage locations known by the names B and C in the main procedure.

If A and X describe the same storage location, then A and X stand for the same number, or for the same bit or character string. Hence there has to be a match in attributes of A and X. We must ensure such a match. We will now show how to do so.

A Use of the DECLARE Statements for Matching of Attributes

If an argument variable has certain attributes declared in the main procedure, then a matching declaration in the subroutine or function procedure will provide the desired uniformity of attributes with the corresponding parameter. Consider, for example, the program

```
EX_1:     PROC OPTIONS(MAIN);
          DCL A FIXED DEC(6,3);
          GET LIST(A,B);
          C = B + FUNC(A);
          PUT LIST(C);
          FUNC:  PROC(N);
                 DCL N FIXED DEC(6,3);
                 RETURN(5 + 3*N);
                 END FUNC;
          END EX_1;
```

where the DECLARE statements for A (in the main procedure) and for N (in the function procedure FUNC) provide the uniformity of attributes.

In the above case we needed the DECLARE statements in the main and FUNC procedures. If the default attributes are satisfactory, one or both DECLARE statements can be omitted. In

```
EX_2:     PROC OPTIONS(MAIN);
          GET LIST(A,B);
          C = B + FUNC(A);
          PUT LIST(C);
          FUNC: PROC(N);
                DCL N FLOAT;
                RETURN(5 + 3*N);
                END FUNC;
          END EX_2;
```

A is REAL FLOAT DEC(6) by default. By the rules of Sec. 5.3, the partial declaration for N makes it also REAL FLOAT DEC(6), thus providing the desired match. Hence just the DECLARE statement in the procedure FUNC suffices. Similarly, in

```
EX_3:    PROC OPTIONS(MAIN);
         DCL A FIXED BIN;
         GET LIST(A,B);
         C = B + FUNC(A);
         PUT LIST(C);
         FUNC: PROC(N);
               RETURN(5 + 3*N);
               END FUNC;
         END EX_3;
```

just a declaration in the main procedure is needed, because N is FIXED BIN by default. In

```
EX_4:    PROC OPTIONS(MAIN);
         GET LIST(A,B);
         C = B + FUNC(A);
         PUT LIST(C);
         FUNC: PROC(X);
               RETURN(5 + 3*X);
               END FUNC;
         END EX_4;
```

the attributes of the argument A are the same as those of the parameter X by default, and no declaration for either A or X is necessary.

B Declaration of ENTRY Attributes and Creation of Dummy Variables

In general, the argument list in

$$\text{CALL } Procedure\_name(arg1,arg2,argn);$$

can contain expressions and constants. For example,

$$\text{CALL JOE } (A, 5.32, 1.5E-2*(A+B));$$

is a legal statement. However, the parameter list in

$$Procedure\_name: (par1,par2, \ldots ,parn);$$

can contain only names of variables—no constants or expressions are allowed—because it is not the argument's value but its location that is passed to a function or subroutine procedure. The parameter is the name given to the location in the procedure. In view of this restriction let us consider what happens when the statement

$$\text{CALL JOE } (A, 5.32, 1.5E-2*(A+B));$$

invokes the procedure JOE with the procedure statement

JOE: PROC(X,Y,Z);

1. X is associated with A as before, with X in the procedure JOE describing the same storage location as does A in the main procedure.
2. A storage location is created to hold 5.32, and Y is associated with this location. But now Y is not associated with any variable in the main procedure. At the end of the procedure JOE, the storage assigned to Y is released and the content of Y is not available any longer to the main procedure (we will say more about it later in Sec. 22.4F, when we discuss the so-called *scope rules*).
3. 1.5E-2*(A+B) is calculated and stored in a location identified as Z in the procedure. Again, as above, at the end of the procedure JOE, this storage location is released, and the value of Z is lost.

In the last two cases, the PL/I compiler created argument variables that were not there. It interpreted the CALL statement as

```
ARG_2 = 5.32;
ARG_3 = 1.5−2*(A+B);
CALL JOE (A, ARG_2, ARG_3);
```

and then associated the parameters X, Y, and Z with the arguments A, ARG_2, and ARG_3. Hence it created the argument variables ARG_2, ARG_3, whose storage locations are known only to the compiler, not to the programmer. Consequently these are named *dummy variables,* and the process just described is known as *dummy creation.*

It is still necessary to ensure that the items on the argument list have the same attributes as the corresponding items on the parameter list. Consider again the CALL statement

CALL JOE(A, 5.32, 1.5−2*(A+B));

and the procedure statement

JOE: PROC(X,Y,Z);

Evidently, 5.32 is by its appearance FIXED DEC(3,2). If Y is FLOAT DEC(6), we must convert 5.32 to FLOAT DEC(6). We can do so either by writing 5.32 as

5.32000E0

or through the use of the built-in function FLOAT (see Sec. 21.3), as in

FLOAT(5.32)

If we apply the built-in function FLOAT to the constant 5.32 and to the expression 1.5E-2*(A+B), then the CALL statement

CALL JOE(A,FLOAT(5.32), FLOAT(1.5−2*(A+B)));

will provide the needed match of attributes with the procedure statement

JOE: PROC(X,Y,Z);

There is still another way to provide the identity of attributes in the corresponding arguments and parameters. We do so with a DECLARE statement for ENTRY attributes. Such a statement has the form

DCL *Entry_name* ENTRY (*attribute1,attribute2, . . . ,attributen*);

and declares the attributes of the parameters of the procedure. Here *attribute1* is the set of attributes of the first parameter, *attribute2* is the set of attributes of the second parameter, and so on. For the preceding example, we will write

DCL JOE ENTRY(FLOAT,FLOAT,FLOAT);

The number of items on the list of attributes must be the same as the number on the list of parameters. In the above example, no conversion of attributes was needed for the first parameter, because the first parameter X already had the same attributes as the first argument A. In such a case, we can include a *null specification,* this being just a comma, as in

DCL JOE ENTRY(,FLOAT,FLOAT);

However, a redundant specification, as before [that is, (FLOAT, FLOAT, FLOAT)], is legal and is often included for better documentation. Other examples of such ENTRY declarations are

DCL SUE ENTRY(FIXED(6,2), BIN FIXED(3,1));
DCL JOSE ENTRY(FLOAT(3), FIXED(4,1), FLOAT(5));
DCL JUNK ENTRY(FIXED(2), , ,FIXED(3,−1));

Factoring of ENTRY attributes is not allowed. For example,

DCL DON ENTRY ((FIXED(3,2),FIXED(2,1))COMPLEX);

is illegal.

We create a dummy variable if the argument is a constant or an expression. We also create a dummy variable if an argument has different attributes from its associated parameter. For example, in

```
JOE:   PROC OPTIONS(MAIN);
       DCL MOE ENTRY (FLOAT,FLOAT);
       GET LIST (M,N);
       CALL MOE (M,N);
       MOE: PROC(A,B);
             . . . . . . . . . .
            END MOE;
             . . . . . . . . . .
       END JOE;
```

we matched the attributes of the arguments with the attributes of the parameters through the ENTRY declaration. However, M and N in the main procedure are by default FIXED BINARY (15,0) numbers. A and B are by default FLOAT DECIMAL (6) numbers. Clearly, M and A cannot occupy the same storage location. Hence a new location is assigned to A, and changes in A do not affect M at all. In computer jargon, we created a dummy variable for the argument M. Similarly, we create a dummy variable for the argument N whose attributes are different from its associated parameter B.

We can also create a dummy variable by enclosing the argument in parentheses. For example, in

$$\text{CALL EVE(X,(Y),Z);}$$

a dummy variable will be created for Y. As an illustration consider the following two program segments:

```
X,Y,Z = 1;            X,Y,Z = 1;
CALL EVE (X,(Y),Z);   CALL EVE (X,Y,Z);
EVE: PROC (A,B,C);    EVE: PROC (A,B,C);
      B = A + C + 1;        B = A + C + 1;
      END EVE:              END EVE;
PUT LIST (Y);         PUT LIST (Y);
```

In the program segment on the left, Y remains unchanged and the output is 1.00000E+00. In the program segment on the right, Y changes with B and the output is 3.00000E+00.

C Array Arguments

If an argument of a procedure is an array, special handling is needed to ensure a match in dimensions between the array argument and the corresponding array parameter.

One method for ensuring such a match is to provide a declaration in the procedure, as in

```
EX_1:     PROC OPTIONS(MAIN);
          DCL A(5,10), B(2:6,7:13);
          CALL JOE (A,B);
          . . . . . . . . . . . . . .

          JOE: PROC(X,Y);
              DCL X(5,10), Y(2:6,7:13);

              . . . . . . . . . . . . . . . . . . . . . . .

          END JOE;
          . . . . . . . . . . . . . .

          END EX_1;
```

In this example we assumed that whoever wrote the procedure JOE knew the bounds of the array parameters. If the procedure was written in terms of general bounds, N1, N2, N3, N4, N5, N6 we can pass the values for N1, N2, N3, N4, N5, and N6 to the procedure. In such an event the preceding example modifies to

```
EX_2:     PROC OPTIONS(MAIN);
          DCL A(5,10), B(2:6, 7:13);
          N1=5; N2=10; N3=2; N4=6; N5=7; N6=13;
          CALL JOE(A,B,N1,N2,N3,N4,N5,N6);

          . . . . . . . . . . . . . . . . . . . . . . . . . . . . . . . .

          JOE: PROC(X,Y,N1,N2,N3,N4,N5,N6);
               DCL X(N1,N2), Y(N3:N4, N5:N6);


               END JOE;
          . . . . . . . . . . . . .

     END EX_2;
```

Still another (and better) way is to make use of the asterisk notation. With this notation the above program becomes

```
EX_3:     PROC OPTIONS(MAIN);
          DCL A(5,10), B(2:6, 7:13);
          CALL JOE (A,B);

          . . . . . . . . . . . . . . . .
          JOE: PROC (X,Y);
               DCL X(*,*), Y(*,*);

               . . . . . . . . . . . . . . . .
               END JOE;
          . . . . . . . . . . .
          END EX__3;
```

where the asterisks signify that X has the same subscripts as A and that Y has the same subscripts as B.

Should we need any of the subscripts of X and Y in the procedure JOE, we can make use of the LBOUND, HBOUND, or DIM built-in functions described in Sec. 21.4. For example, if we wish to add 25 to the elements of the first row of the array Y, we can rewrite the procedure JOE as

```
JOE:      PROC(X,Y);
          DCL X(*,*), Y(*,*);
          . . . . . . . . . . . . . . . .

          DO I=LBOUND(Y,2) TO HBOUND(Y,2);
               Y(LBOUND(Y,1),I) = Y(LBOUND(Y,1),I) + 25;
          END;
          . . . . .

          END JOE;
```

Note that

LBOUND(Y,2)	= Lowbound of the second dimension of Y
	= Lowbound of the second dimension of B = 7
HBOUND(Y,2)	= Highbound of the second dimension of Y
	= Highbound of the second dimension of B = 13
LBOUND(Y,1)	= Lowbound of the first dimension of Y
	= Lowbound of the first dimension of B = 2

Thus the DO loop is interpreted as

```
DO I = 7 TO 13;
    Y(2,I) = Y(2,I) + 25;
END;
```

which is equivalent to

```
Y(2,7) = Y(2,7) + 25;
Y(2,8) = Y(2,8) + 25;
. . . . . . . . . . . . . . . . . .
Y(2,13) = Y(2,13) + 25;
```

and results in the addition of 25 to the elements of the first row of Y, as desired.

Recall that in Sec. 19.7 the asterisk was used to represent all subscripts in an array dimension. For example, in

$$A(3,*)$$

the asterisk represents all subscripts of the second dimension of A; hence $A(3,*)$ represents the entire third row of A. Thus $A(3,*)$ is a one-dimensional array, and the program

```
EXAMPLE: PROC OPTIONS(MAIN);
         DCL A(3,3);
         GET LIST(A);
         CALL JOE(A(3,*));
         PUT DATA(A);
         JOE: PROC(X);
              DCL X(*);
              X = X+2;
              END JOE;
         END EXAMPLE;
```

is a valid one. Here the one-dimensional array argument $A(3,*)$ becomes the one-dimensional array parameter X, with the subscripts of X being the same as those represented by the asterisk in $A(3,*)$. The result is that the elements of the third row of A are increased by 2.

We can also employ the asterisk notation in ENTRY declarations for array arguments. Consider, for example, the program

```
EX_1:     PROC OPTIONS(MAIN);
          DCL A(3,4:7) FIXED(3,2),
              JOE ENTRY((3,4:7) FLOAT,FLOAT);
          GET LIST(A);
          X = 3*A(2,5);
          CALL JOE(A,X);
          JOE: PROC(B,Y);
               DCL B(3,4:7);
               B = B - Y;
               PUT LIST(B);
               END JOE;
          END EX_1;
```

where the ENTRY declaration signifies that the attributes of the first parameter B of the procedure JOE are

$$(3,4:7) \text{ FLOAT}$$

The ENTRY declaration is necessary here because the argument A and the associated parameter B have different attributes. Using the asterisk notation, the program becomes

```
EX_2:     PROC OPTIONS(MAIN);
          DCL A(3,4:7) FIXED(3,2),
              JOE ENTRY((*,*) FLOAT,FLOAT);
          GET LIST(A);
          X = 3*A(2,5);
          CALL JOE(A,X);
          JOE: PROC(B,Y);
               DCL B(*,*);
               B = B - Y;
               PUT LIST(B);
               END JOE;
          END EX_2;
```

D Structure Arguments

If an argument of a procedure is a structure, the associated parameter must be declared as a structure. The usual way is to declare the parameter just like the argument, as in the following program:

```
EX_1:     PROC OPTIONS(MAIN);
          DCL 1 A,
                2 B FIXED(2,1),
                2 C,
                  3 D CHAR(2),
                  3 E CHAR(5) VAR;
          GET LIST(A);
          CALL JOE(A);
          JOE: PROC(X);
               DCL 1 X,
                     2 Y FIXED(2,1),
```

```
            2 Z,
              3 U CHAR(2),
              3 V CHAR(5) VAR;
         V = V||U;
         END JOE;
     PUT LIST(A);
     END EX_1;
```

In this example, both the argument A and the parameter X were major structure names. An argument may also be a minor structure name. The associated parameter, however, must be a major structure name (that is, a level 1 item), as in the following example:

```
EX_2:    PROC OPTIONS(MAIN);
         DCL 1 A,
               2 B FIXED(2,1),
               2 C,
                 3 D CHAR(2),
                 3 E CHAR(5) VAR;
         GET LIST(A);
         CALL JOE(C);
         JOE: PROC(JACK);
              DCL 1 JACK,
                    2 JILL CHAR(2),
                    2 MOE CHAR(5) VAR;
              MOE = MOE||JILL;
              END JOE;
         PUT LIST(A);
         END EX_2;
```

It is legal to assign to the parameter structure level numbers different from those of the argument structure, provided that the organization of the structure (that is, structuring) remains the same. For example, the declaration for JACK in the last program may read

```
         DCL 1 JACK,
               13 JILL CHAR(2),
                7 MOE CHAR(5) VAR;
```

When an ENTRY declaration is made (for specifying the attributes of parameters) for a structure, there is no need to list the names in the structure—just the level numbers suffice. As an example, for the program labeled EX_1, a declaration for JOE will read

```
         DCL JOE ENTRY(1,2 FIXED(2,1),2,3 CHAR(2), 3 CHAR(5)VAR);
```

E String Arguments

If an argument of a procedure is a character string or a bit string, we must declare it as such in the procedure, as, for example,

```
EX_1:      PROC OPTIONS(MAIN);
           DCL A CHAR(5), B CHAR(6) VAR, C BIT(7);
           CALL JOE(A,B,C);
           . . . . . . . . . . . . . . . .
           JOE: PROC(X,Y,Z);
                DCL X CHAR(5), Y CHAR(6) VAR, Z BIT(7);
                . . . . . . . . . . . . . . . . . . . . . . . . . . . . . . . . . . . .
                END JOE;
           . . . . . . . . . . . . . .
           END EX_1;
```

We can employ asterisks, as we did for array subscripts. An asterisk signifies that the length of the character or bit string is to match the argument. Using the asterisk notation, the DCL statement in the procedure reads

```
DCL X CHAR(*), Y CHAR(*) VAR, Z BIT(*);
```

while the rest of the program remains unchanged.

F Scope of Names

The mechanism of argument-parameter association allows variables of the main procedure to be *passed* on to the subroutine or function procedure. Such variables are then "known" to both the procedures. This brings up the following questions:

1. Which variables are known to the entire program?
2. Which variables are known just within one or more procedures?

These two questions are answered by the *scope* rules, that is, by the rules describing the extent or *scope* of the variables. These rules are:

1. If a variable is declared in the main procedure (that is, through a DECLARE statement), then such a variable is known within the main procedure and within all procedures contained in the main procedure.
2. If a variable is declared in a subroutine or function procedure A, then such a variable is known only within the procedure A.
3. If a name appears in a parameter list of a subroutine or function procedure A, then such a parameter is known only within the procedure A.
4. If a variable is introduced in a context of a statement anywhere in the program, then such a variable is known within the entire program.

In computer jargon we name the first three declarations as *explicit declarations*. The introduction of a variable in a statement (for example, in an assignment statement) is named a *contextual declaration*. Since names in a program are given to either variables or labels, let us now list the rule for the scope of labels.

5. A label contained in procedure A is known only to procedure A and to the procedures contained within A.

The appearance of a label is recognized by the compiler by the : symbol (following a label) and is as such a *explicit declaration* of a label.

We will give now three examples illustrating the scopes of names in a program.

Example 22.4.1

```
P1:   PROC OPTIONS(MAIN);
      DCL A FIXED(3,2);
      GET LIST(A,B);
      C = A + B;
      D = C*P2(A);
      PUT LIST(D);
      P2: PROC(X);
          DCL X FIXED(3,2);
          E = X + 3;
          CALL P3(E);
          P3: PROC(Y);
              DCL Z;
              Z = 1;
              Y = Y + Z;
              RETURN;
              END P3;
          F = E*B;
          RETURN(F+2);
          END P2;
      END P1;
```

P1	P1 is contained within the main procedure; hence the scope of P1 is the entire program. In fact, P1 being an external name is even known to the program supervising the operations of the computer (and named the operating system).
A	A is declared in the main procedure; hence its scope is the entire program.
B,C,D	These are contextually declared; hence their scope is the entire program.
P2	P2 appears within P1; hence its scope is the entire program.
X	X appears in the parameter list of procedure P2; hence the scope of X is the procedure P2. X is, of course, the same variable as A.
E	E is contextually declared; hence its scope is the entire program.
P3	P3 appears within P2; hence its scope is the procedure P2.
Y	Y appears in the parameter list of P3; hence its scope is the procedure P3. Y is the same variable as E.

Z   Z is declared in the procedure P3; hence its scope is the procedure P3.

F   F is contextually declared in P2; hence its scope is the entire program.

We indicated the scope of the names by the lines on the right side of the program.

Example 22.4.2

```
P1:  PROC OPTIONS(MAIN);
     GET LIST(A,B);
     CALL P2(A);
     X = A + 2;
     PUT LIST(X);
     P2: PROC(B);
         DCL A;
         A,C = 1;
         B = B + 2*C + A;
         RETURN;
         END P2;
     END P1;
```

P1   The scope of P1 is the entire program (and the operating system).

A,B   The scope of A and B should be the entire program. However, the procedure P2 contains variables A and B whose scope is specifically restricted to the scope of P2. Thus the A and B in P2 must be different from the A and B declared contextually (through the GET LIST statement) in P1. In fact, B in P2 is the same variable as A in P1. Consequently, the scope of A and B is the entire program except the procedure P2.

P2   P2 is contained within P1. Its scope is the entire program.

C   C is contextually declared in P2. Its scope is the entire program.

X   X is contextually declared. Its scope is the entire program.

B'   Since the B in P2 is different from the B in P1, we denote here the B in P2 as B'. Because B' appears in the parameter list of P2, its scope is the procedure P2.

A'   Again we denote the A in P2 as A'. Because of the explicit declaration, its scope is just the procedure P2.

As before, we indicated the scope of the names by the lines adjacent to the program.

Example 22.4.3 The scopes of all variables and labels are as indicated. Note that the scope of the label L1 is the entire program, while the scope of the label L2 is just the procedure P2. Observe that the statement

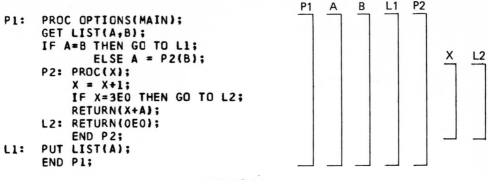

```
P1:    PROC OPTIONS(MAIN);
       GET LIST(A,B);
       IF A=B THEN GO TO L1;
            ELSE A = P2(B);
       P2: PROC(X);
           X = X+1;
           IF X=3E0 THEN GO TO L2;
           RETURN(X+A);
       L2: RETURN(0E0);
           END P2;
L1:    PUT LIST(A);
       END P1;
```

GO TO L2;

would not be legal in the main program, because the main program does not know of the existence of L2. It is a legal statement in the procedure P2, because the scope of L2 encompasses the procedure P2.

Consider now the program

```
P1:    PROC OPTIONS(MAIN);
       DCL SIN;
       GET LIST(A);
       SIN = A + 1;
       B = P2(SIN);
       PUT LIST(B);
       P2: PROC(X);
           DCL SIN BUILTIN;
           Y = SIN(X);
           RETURN(Y);
           END P2;
       END P1;
```

The statement

DCL SIN;

informed the compiler that SIN is a name of a variable and not of a built-in function. In P2, the statement

DCL SIN BUILTIN;

informed the compiler that SIN is a built-in function within P2 and overruled the previous command to the compiler. Hence, within P2, SIN is the built-in function, but in the remainder of the program SIN is the name of a variable.

Consider next the program

```
P1:    PROC OPTIONS(MAIN);
       GET LIST(A,B);
       C = P2;
       CALL P3;
       PUT LIST(E);
```

```
P2: PROC;
    D = A + B;
    RETURN(D);
    END P2;
P3: PROC;
    E = C + 1;
    RETURN;
    END P3;
END P1;
```

Observe that P2 is a function procedure and that P3 is a subroutine procedure. Note further that we have listed neither arguments nor parameters. Such an omission is legal. Consider first the function procedure P2. Since the scopes of A and B encompass the entire program, D is obtained and returned in place of P2. Similarly, in execution of the subroutine procedure P3, E is obtained. Since the scope of E is the entire program, E is printed out in the PUT LIST(E); statement. Consequently, it is not essential to list any arguments or parameters, as the above example illustrated.

*G Label Arguments

The arguments of a subroutine or function procedure can be variables, constants, and expressions. They can also be labels. Consider first the following program:

```
EX_1:    PROC OPTIONS(MAIN);
REPEAT:  GET LIST(A);
         CALL SQUARE(A);
         SQUARE: PROC(X);
                 IF X=0 THEN RETURN;
                 IF X>0 THEN PUT SKIP LIST(X,X*X);
                 GO TO REPEAT;
                 END SQUARE;
         END EX_1;
```

In this program, we acquire a number A. Through the CALL statement A becomes X, and if $X = 0$, we return to the END EX_1; statement, thus ending the program. If $X > 0$, we print X and X^2 and return to the process the following number. If $X < 0$, we just return to the GET LIST (A); statement.

An alternate version of this program is

```
EX_2:    PROC OPTIONS(MAIN);
REPEAT:  GET LIST(A);
         CALL SQUARE(A,REPEAT);
         SQUARE: PROC(X,Y);
                 DCL Y LABEL;
                 IF X=0 THEN RETURN;
                 IF X>0 THEN PUT SKIP LIST(X,X*X);
                 GO TO Y;
                 END SQUARE;
         END EX_2;
```

Here the argument REPEAT and the corresponding parameter Y are labels. Observe that the procedure SQUARE must be informed that Y is a label, and we do so with the statement

DCL Y LABEL;

There is no need for an explicit declaration in the main procedure of REPEAT as label. REPEAT is known to be a label because of its appearance as label.

The use of the label argument as in the EX_2 program was of no particular advantage here. However, this use made it possible for different programmers to write the main program and the SQUARE procedure. For example, the programmer who wrote the procedure SQUARE did not have to know that the GET LIST(A); statement was labeled REPEAT. Since large programs are usually broken up into procedures written by different programmers, it is convenient to make the names in the subroutine and function procedures independent of names in the main procedure.

Incidentally, in the last two programs the procedure SQUARE has the parameter X in the data list of the list-directed statement (that is, in the PUT LIST statement), which is allowed. Parameters cannot appear, however, in a data list of a data-directed statement. Thus in the last program the statement

PUT DATA(X);

is illegal in the procedure SQUARE and meaningless outside this procedure (because the scope of the parameter X is limited to the procedure SQUARE).

*H ENTRY Arguments

We have just seen that a label can be an argument of a subroutine or of a function procedure. Even more generally, an argument can be the name of a built-in function, of a function procedure, or of a subroutine procedure. In such a case, we say that the argument is an ENTRY *name*. We will illustrate with examples several uses of such ENTRY arguments.

We can differentiate between two situations.

Situation 1. The ENTRY argument is either a built-in function or a function procedure, which is invoked and replaced by its return. This replacement takes place in the following four instances:

1. The ENTRY argument is accompanied by its own argument list, as, for example,

CALL JOE (ZOE(X), Y, SQRT(Z));

The compiler interprets ZOE(X) as a function procedure. The procedure is invoked, and the returned value replaces ZOE(X) in the argument list. Similarly, SQRT(Z) is interpreted as a built-in function. This function is invoked, and the result (that is, the value of $\sqrt{Z}$) replaces SQRT(Z) in the argument list. As an example, a program with this CALL statement may read

```
EX_1:      PROC OPTIONS(MAIN);
           X,Y,Z = 36;
           CALL JOE(ZOE(X),Y,SQRT(Z));
           PUT DATA(U,V);
           JOE: PROC(SUE,B,AAA);
                U = (SUE + B)*AAA;
                V = (SUE - B)*AAA;
                END JOE;
           ZOE: PROC(D);
                RETURN(D-32);
                END ZOE;
           END EX_1;
```

Observe the following:

a In the statement

CALL JOE(ZOE(X), Y, SQRT(Z));

(1) ZOE(X) is invoked, and the return (that is, $D - 32 = X - 32$ or 4 in FLOAT) replaces ZOE(X) in the argument list.
(2) SQRT(Z) is invoked and the return (that is, $\sqrt{36}$ or 6 in FLOAT) replaces SQRT(Z) in the argument list.
(3) Dummy variables are created to store the returns of ZOE(X) and SQRT(Z).

b Because the returns of ZOE(X) and SQRT(Z) have the FLOAT attributes, there is an agreement with the parameters SUE and AAA which are FLOAT by default. The attribute of the argument Y similarly agrees with the attribute of the parameter B.

c U and V are calculated as

$$U = (4+36)*6 = 240 \text{ in FLOAT}$$
$$V = (4-36)*6 = -192 \text{ in FLOAT}$$

and in fact, the printout is

```
U= 2.40000E+02          V=-1.92000E+02;
```

2. The ENTRY argument is without an argument list but is enclosed in parentheses, as in

CALL JOE((ZOE), Y);

Here the compiler interprets ZOE as a function procedure without arguments. The procedure is invoked, and the return replaces ZOE in the argument list. An example of a program with such a statement is

```
EX_2:      PROC OPTIONS(MAIN);
           X,Y = 10;
           CALL JOE((ZOE),Y);
           PUT DATA(U,V);
           JOE: PROC(SUE,B);
                U = B*SUE;
```

```
            V = (X+B)*SUE;
            END JOE;
      ZOE: PROC;
            RETURN(X-5);
            END ZOE;
      END EX_2;
```

As before, the return of ZOE, this being $X-5$ or 5 in FLOAT, replaces ZOE in the CALL statement. Consequently a dummy variable is created to store this return. U and V are calculated as

$$U = 10*5 = 50 \text{ in FLOAT}$$
$$V = 20*5 = 100 \text{ in FLOAT}$$

and in fact the printout is

```
U= 5.00000E+01              V= 1.00000E+02;
```

Incidentally, recall that by enclosing an argument in parentheses we create a dummy variable. Hence by writing (ZOE) we requested a creation of a dummy variable for the procedure ZOE. Since such a request will make sense only for the return of a function procedure, the compiler indeed makes such an interpretation.

3. The ENTRY argument appears in an expression, as, for example,

$$\text{CALL JOE(ZOE*X + MOE(Y), Y);}$$

Here the compiler interprets both ZOE and MOE(Y) as function procedures. Both functions are invoked for the calculation of the expression. Again, this is the only logical interpretation (a subroutine procedure cannot appear in an expression). An example of a program having this CALL statement is

```
EX_3:     PROC OPTIONS(MAIN);
          X,Y = 10;
          CALL JOE(ZOE*X+MOE(Y),Y);
          JOE: PROC(SUE,B);
               U = B*SUE;
               V = (X+B)*SUE;
               PUT DATA(U,V);
               END JOE;
          ZOE: PROC;
               RETURN(X-5);
               END;
          MOE: PROC(Z);
               RETURN(2*Z);
               END;
          END EX_3;
```

Here ZOE is invoked and the return $X-5$ or 5 in FLOAT replaces ZOE. Similarly MOE(Y) is invoked and is replaced by its return of 20. Consequently, the first argument is evaluated as $5*10+20=70$. Thus

$$U = 10*70 = 700 \text{ in FLOAT}$$
$$V = 20*70 = 1400 \text{ in FLOAT}$$

and in fact the output of this program is

```
U= 7.00000E+02              V= 1.40000E+03;
```

4. The ENTRY argument is associated with a non-ENTRY attribute, as illustrated in the following program

```
EX_4:    PROC OPTIONS(MAIN);
         DCL JOE ENTRY(FLOAT,FLOAT);
         X,Y = 10;
         CALL JOE(ZOE,X);
         PUT DATA(U,V);
         JOE: PROC(SUE,B);
              U = B*SUE;
              V = (X+B)*SUE;
              END JOE;
         ZOE: PROC;
              RETURN(X-5);
              END ZOE;
         END EX_4;
```

Here the declaration

DCL JOE ENTRY(FLOAT, FLOAT);

tells the compiler that the first parameter has the FLOAT attribute. This means that just a FLOAT number is passed to the procedure, and it identifies ZOE as representing the return of a function procedure.

In summary:

1. A built-in function or a function procedure with arguments is replaced by its return if the ENTRY argument is accompanied by its own argument list.
2. A function procedure without arguments is replaced by its return whenever it is made clear to the compiler that this is our intention. We can do so in the following three ways:
   a By enclosing the function name in parentheses
   b By using the function name in an expression
   c By specifying non-ENTRY attributes (for example, FLOAT) for this function name in the associated declaration

Situation 2. The ENTRY argument is either a built-in function, a function procedure, or a subroutine procedure, and the ENTRY name itself is passed to the invoked procedure. To let the compiler know that this is our intent, we must observe the following rules:

1. The ENTRY argument may not have its own argument list.
2. We must declare in the invoking procedure that the ENTRY parameter has the ENTRY *attribute*.
3. We must declare in the invoked procedure that the associated parameter has the ENTRY *attribute*.

As an example, consider the program

```
EX_5:      PROC OPTIONS(MAIN);
           DCL JOE ENTRY (ENTRY,FLOAT,FLOAT);
           X = 20;
           Y = 10;
           CALL JOE(MOE,X,Y);
           PUT DATA(X,Y,C,D);
           CALL JOE(MOE,Y,X);
           PUT DATA(X,Y,C,D) SKIP;
           JOE: PROC(SUE,A,B);
                DCL SUE ENTRY;
                IF A>B THEN CALL SUE(A);
                     ELSE CALL SUE(A+B);
                END JOE;
           MOE: PROC(Z);
                C = Z/4;
                D = 10*Z;
                END MOE;
           END EX_5;
```

Note the following:

1. The ENTRY argument MOE has no argument list (as required in rule 1 above).
2. The DECLARE statement

DCL JOE ENTRY(ENTRY, FLOAT, FLOAT);

   tells the compiler that
   a JOE is an ENTRY name.
   b The first parameter of JOE is an ENTRY name (that is, has the ENTRY *attribute*, as required in rule 2 above).
3. In the statement

CALL JOE(MOE,X,Y);

   MOE is interpreted as a name of ENTRY (that is, a name of procedure here), because the DECLARE statement above tells the compiler that the first argument of JOE is an ENTRY name.
4. The statement

JOE: PROC(SUE,A,B);

   associates the name SUE with the procedure name MOE, and the parameters A, B, with the arguments X,Y.

5. The statement

DCL SUE ENTRY;

informs the compiler that SUE is an ENTRY name (and not FLOAT variable, which is the default interpretation of the name SUE), as required in rule 3 above.

6. The statement

IF A > B THEN CALL SUE(A);

invokes the procedure SUE, which is named MOE in the main program. Consequently, the procedure MOE is invoked and C and D are calculated.

7. The output of this program follows from

$$X = 20$$
$$Y = 10$$
$$A = X = 20$$
$$B = Y = 10$$

Because A > B we execute CALL SUE(A);

$$Z = A = 20$$
$$C = Z/4 = 5$$
$$D = 10*Z = 200$$

The PUT DATA statement causes the printout in FLOAT form

X = 20   Y = 10   C = 5   D = 200;

We now execute CALL JOE(MOE,Y,X);

$$A = Y = 10$$
$$B = X = 20$$

Because A $\not>$ B we execute CALL SUE(A+B);

$$Z = A+B = 30$$
$$C = Z/4 = 7.5$$
$$D = 10*Z = 300$$

The PUT DATA statement produces the printout in FLOAT form

X = 20   Y = 10   C = 7.5   D = 300;

and indeed the actual printout is

```
X= 2.00000E+01        Y= 1.00000E+01      C= 5.00000E+00      D= 2.00000E+02;
X= 2.00000E+01        Y= 1.00000E+01      C= 7.50000E+00      D= 3.00000E+02;
```

In the program EX_5, the ENTRY name was the name of a subroutine procedure. In the next example, the ENTRY name is the name of a function procedure.

```
EX_6:     PROC OPTIONS(MAIN);
          DCL JOE ENTRY(ENTRY,FLOAT,FLOAT);
          X,Y = 30;
          CALL JOE(TOM,X,Y);
          PUT LIST(Z);
          JOE: PROC(AAA,A,B);
               DCL AAA ENTRY;
               Z = (A+B)*AAA(A);
               END JOE;
          TOM: PROC(U);
               RETURN(U+20);
               END TOM;
          END EX_6;
```

Observe that:

1. The first argument of JOE is an ENTRY name, as declared in

   DCL JOE ENTRY(ENTRY, FLOAT, FLOAT);

2. Because of the above declaration, in the statement

   CALL JOE(TOM,X,Y);

   TOM is identified as an ENTRY name.
3. The statement

   JOE: PROC(AAA,A,B);

   associates TOM with AAA, X with A, and Y with B.
4. The statement

   DCL AAA ENTRY;

   informs the compiler that AAA is an ENTRY name. This is necessary to prevent conversion of an ENTRY name to a FLOAT number (which is not possible and will result in a program-stopping error).
5. The output of the program follows from

   $$X = Y = 30$$
   $$A = X = 30$$
   $$B = Y = 30$$
   $$AAA(A) = TOM(U) = TOM(30) = U + 20 = 50$$
   $$Z = (A+B)*AAA(A) = 60*50 = 3000$$

The PUT LIST(Z); statement causes the printout of 3000 in FLOAT. Indeed the actual printout is

3.00000E+03

as asserted.

An example of usage of the name of a built-in function as an argument is

```
EX_7:    PROC OPTIONS(MAIN);
         DCL JOE ENTRY(ENTRY,FLOAT,FLOAT);
         X,Y = 30;
         CALL JOE(SIND,X,Y);
         PUT LIST(Z);
         JOE: PROC(AAA,A,B);
              DCL AAA ENTRY;
              Z = (A+B)*AAA(A);
              END JOE;
         END EX_7;
```

The output of this procedure is Z, where

$$Z = (A+B)*AAA(A) = 60*SIND(30) = 30 \text{ in FLOAT}$$

and in fact, the printout of this program is

2.99999E+01

which is sufficiently close to the asserted value.

Recall that the argument-parameter association allows different names for the same storage location. The argument gives the name in the invoking procedure, the parameter the name in the invoked procedure. For all ENTRY arguments, the association is a similar one. As illustrated in Fig. 22.4, the procedure AAA in the procedure JOE is identified as being the same as the procedure TOM in the procedure EX_6.

We just described the use of ENTRY arguments. We may ask: When do these arguments have applications? We can give examples of two applications: (1) These arguments allow writing programs with a uniform formula, and (2) they allow the use of built-in functions and procedures outside their scopes. We will now illustrate these two applications.

The program

```
EX_8:    PROC OPTIONS(MAIN);
         DCL JOE ENTRY(ENTRY,FLOAT,FIXED);
         X = 16;
         CALL JOE(SQRT,X,1);    /* THE LAST ARGUMENT TELLS    */
         PUT SKIP DATA(Z);      /* WHETHER THE ENTRY IS A     */
         CALL JOE(MOE,2*X,2);   /* FUNCTION OR A SUBROUTINE.  */
         PUT SKIP DATA(Z);      /* 1 MEANS FUNCTION, AND 2    */
         CALL JOE(ZOE,X,1);     /* MEANS SUBROUTINE           */
         PUT SKIP DATA(Z);
         CALL JOE(SUE,X+4,2);
```

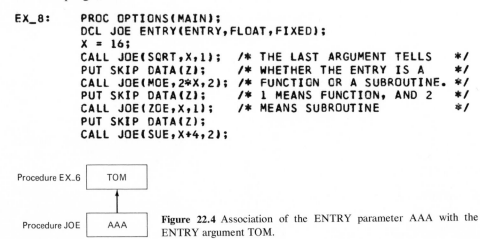

Figure 22.4 Association of the ENTRY parameter AAA with the ENTRY argument TOM.

```
      PUT SKIP DATA(Z);
JOE:  PROC(A,B,C);
         DCL A ENTRY,C FIXED;
         IF C=1 THEN Z=A(B);
                  ELSE CALL A(B);
         END JOE;
SUE:  PROC(W);
         Z = 3*W + 2;
         END SUE;
MOE:  PROC(U);
         Z = U + 4;
         END MOE;
ZOE:  PROC(V);
         RETURN(10*V);
         END ZOE;
      END EX_8;
```

illustrates an application where Z is obtained (in the procedure JOE) in a uniform
way either from CALL A(B), where A is a subroutine procedure, or from Z = A(B),
where A is either a built-in function or a function procedure. Here A is made to
represent any entry parameter passed on from the invoking procedure. Observe
that:

1. In the first invocation of procedure JOE,

$$Z = A(B) = SQRT(16) = 4 \text{ in FLOAT}$$

2. In the second invocation of procedure JOE, we invoke

$$A(B) = MOE(2*X)$$

hence

$$Z = U+4 = 2*X + 4 = 32 + 4 = 36 \text{ in FLOAT}$$

3. In the third invocation of procedure JOE,

$$Z = A(B) = ZOE(X)$$

giving the return of $10*V = 10*X = 160$; thus

$$Z = 160 \text{ in FLOAT}$$

4. In the fourth invocation of procedure JOE, we invoke SUE(X+4); hence

$$Z = 3*W + 2 = 3*(X+4) + 2 = 3*(16+4) + 2 = 62 \text{ in FLOAT}$$

and the printout is

```
Z= 4.00000E+00;
Z= 3.60000E+01;
Z= 1.60000E+02;
Z= 6.20000E+01;
```

The program

```
EX_9:     PROC OPTIONS(MAIN);
          DCL JOE ENTRY(ENTRY,ENTRY);
          CALL JOE(SQRT,SUE);
          JOE: PROC(A,B);
               DCL(SQRT,SUE) FLOAT,
                  (A,B) ENTRY;
               SQRT,SUE = 4;
               Z = A(SQRT) + B(SUE);
               PUT LIST(Z);
               END JOE;
          SUE: PROC(X);
               RETURN(5*X);
               END SUE;
          END EX_9;
```

illustrates the use of the built-in function SQRT and of the function procedure SUE outside their scopes. In the procedure JOE note that SQRT and SUE are names of FLOAT variables. Hence we use the entry parameters as shown in the program EX_9 to employ these functions in the procedure JOE. Incidentally, note that Z is calculated as

$$Z = A(SQRT) + B(SUE) = SQRT(4) + SUE(4) = 2+20 = 22 \text{ in FLOAT}$$

giving the printout

```
2.20000E+01
```

I Results as Arguments

In our previous use of arguments in the CALL statement, the arguments constituted the inputs to the procedure. The procedure used these inputs to calculate the desired results, which were then available to the main or other procedures through the scope rules.

It is also possible to include these results in the argument list. As an example, recall the program named EXAMPLE in Sec. 22.2 for the solution of 10 sets of equations. In this program the arguments were A, B, C, D, E, F, and the results were X, Y. If we rewrite the program with X and Y in the argument list and call the associated parameters X1 and Y1, the CALL statement changes to

$$CALL EQUATION(A,B,C,D,E,F,X,Y);$$

and the procedure statement changes to

$$EQUATION: PROC(A1,B1,C1,A2,B2,C2,X1,Y1);$$

This changes the names of X and Y in the procedure EQUATION to X1 and Y1 while all the other statements remain as before. Again this feature allows the writing of the subroutine EQUATION without knowledge of the names given to the results in the main procedure.

*J Arguments and Parameters with Different Precisions

Recall from Sec. 14.2 that there are only two precisions available internally for FLOAT numbers, these precisions being FLOAT(6) and FLOAT(16). For example, whether we specify FLOAT(3) or FLOAT(4), we have within the computer the same number, this being one of precision (6). Similarly, only two precisions are available internally for FIXED BIN numbers, these precisions being either 15 binary digits or 31 binary digits. For example, whether we specify FIXED BIN(10) or FIXED BIN(11), we still have within the computer the same number, this being one of precision (15). Because there is no difference internally between such different precisions, the following program works.

```
EX_1:    PROC OPTIONS(MAIN);
         DCL A1 FLOAT(3), B1 FIXED BIN(10);
         A1 = 12.3;
         B1 = 12.1;
         CALL JOE(A1,B1,C1);
         PUT DATA(A1,B1,C1);
         JOE: PROC(A,B,C);
              DCL A FLOAT(4), B FIXED BIN(11);
              C = A + B;
              END JOE;
         END EX_1;
```

As far as the compiler is concerned there is no discrepancy in the precisions of either the argument A1 and the parameter A, or the argument B1 and the parameter B.

22.5 THE RETURNS OPTION FOR FUNCTION PROCEDURES

We will now describe the attributes of the return from a function procedure. Let us start with the default attributes. As in the case of identifiers these attributes depend upon the first letter of the name of the function procedure. For example, in

```
N=JOE(A,B);
. . . . . . . . . . . .
JOE: PROC(X,Y);
. . . . . . . . . . . . . . . .
        RETURN(C);
        END JOE;
```

the return has the attributes associated with the name JOE, or FIXED BIN REAL(15,0). Similarly, a function procedure named SUE gives a return associated with the name SUE, or FLOAT DEC REAL(6).

If we attach two labels to a function procedure, we can have returns with different attributes. For example, in

```
                              K=MOE(A,B);

                              . . . . . . . . . . . . . .
                              C=D*DOLLY(A,B);

                              . . . . . . . . . . . . . . . .
                              MOE: DOLLY: PROC(X,Y);

                                       . . . . . . . . . . . . . . . . . .
                                                RETURN (Z);
                                                END MOE;
```

we attached two labels MOE and DOLLY to the function procedure. When we invoke the function with

$$K=MOE(A,B);$$

the return has FIXD BIN REAL(15,0) attributes. When we invoke the function with

$$C=D*DOLLY(A,B);$$

the return has FLOAT DEC REAL(6) attributes. If we have several labels, we can terminate the procedure with either label following the END keyword.

Sometimes we wish the return from a function to have specific, nondefault attributes. This is achieved with the use of the keyword RETURNS followed by a parenthesized list of attributes for the return. This keyword is included in the PROCEDURE statement, as in

$$JOE: PROC(A,B) RETURNS (FLOAT);$$

and in the ENTRY declaration as in

$$DCL JOE ENTRY(FLOAT, FIXED DEC(3,2))RETURNS (FLOAT);$$

The above use of the keyword RETURNS is known as the *RETURNS* option of the PROCEDURE or ENTRY statements.

We will illustrate the use of this option by the following example.

```
P1:   PROC OPTIONS(MAIN);
      DCL JOE ENTRY(FIXED(3,1),FIXED(3,1)) RETURNS(FIXED(4,1)),
         (A,B)FIXED(3,1),C FIXED(4,1);
      A = 67.8;
      B = 78.9;
      C = JOE(A,B);
      PUT LIST(C);
      JOE: PROC(X,Y) RETURNS(FIXED(4,1));
         DCL(X,Y)FIXED(3,1);
         RETURN(X+Y);
         END JOE;
      END P1;
```

Observe that we used the RETURNS options in both the ENTRY declaration and in the procedure statement for JOE, as required. In this example, we specified the attributes of the entry JOE (that is, an attribute list). If we have no list of attributes, the DCL statement reduces to

DCL JOE ENTRY RETURNS (FIXED(4,1));

In fact, because of the keyword RETURNS, the compiler identifies JOE as a function name, and the keyword ENTRY can be omitted, as in

DCL JOE RETURNS (FIXED(4,1));

22.6 INTERNAL AND EXTERNAL PROCEDURES

The subroutine and function procedures described so far have been contained within the main procedure. If a procedure B is contained within another procedure, then B is named an *internal procedure*. A procedure which is not contained within another procedure is named an *external procedure*. The main procedure is one example of an external procedure, since it is never contained within another procedure.

A Internal Procedures

Internal procedures can be nested within other procedures, as, for example,

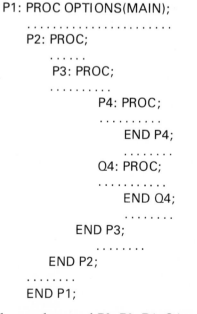

```
P1: PROC OPTIONS(MAIN);
        . . . . . . . . . . . . . . . . . . . .
    P2: PROC;
            . . . . . .
        P3: PROC;
            . . . . . . . . . .
            P4: PROC;
                    . . . . . . . . . .
                END P4;
                    . . . . . . . .
            Q4: PROC;
                    . . . . . . . . . .
                END Q4;
                    . . . . . . . .
            END P3;
                . . . . . . . .
        END P2;
            . . . . . . . .
    END P1;
```

Here P1 is an external procedure, and P2, P3, P4, Q4 are internal procedures. Observe that P4 and Q4 are nested in P3, P3 is nested in P2, and P2 is nested in P1. In this example, we have three *levels of nesting* relative to the main procedure, with

P2 at the first level of nesting, P3 at the second level of nesting, and P4 and Q4 at the third level of nesting. In the F compiler implementation of the PL/I language on the System/360 or System/370, there can be up to 50 levels of nesting. The actual allowable number of nestings is usually smaller, because it depends upon other factors (the number of active IF statements, the number of unmatched left parentheses, and so on), but this writer knows of no problem where not enough levels of nestings were available.

In passing, note that because of the scope rules P2 can be activated anywhere in the program, since the scope of P2 is the entire program. P3 can be activated only within P2; P4 and Q4 can be activated only within P3. Hence a statement such as

CALL Q4;

can only be placed within the body of P3. It can be placed within P4, or within Q4 (in which case the procedure calls itself), or anywhere else within P3.

B External Procedures

A procedure which is not contained within another procedure is an external procedure.

The function and subroutine procedures in the previous examples were given as internal procedures. It is just as possible to place these procedures outside the main procedure, that is, after the END statement of the main procedure. However, for external procedures the scope rules are different.

An internal procedure shares its variables with other procedures. In external procedures this sharing of variables is more closely controlled. Only variables which have been declared as EXTERNAL are shared among procedures.

As an example, consider the program

```
P1:   PROC OPTIONS(MAIN);
      DCL A FIXED(2,1) EXTERNAL;
      A,B = 1;
      CALL P2;
      PUT LIST(A,B);
      END P1;
P2:   PROC;
      DCL(A,B)FIXED(2,1)EXTERNAL;
      A,B = 7;
      END P2;
```

Here P1 and P2 are external procedures. A is declared as an external variable in both P1 and P2; hence the variable A in P1 is the same as the variable A in P2. In other words, through the declaration of A as EXTERNAL, we have made the scope of A to extend over both procedures P1 and P2.

The variable B is declared as an EXTERNAL variable only in the procedure P2. This is not a sufficient declaration. For the scope of B to extend over both procedures P1 and P2, B must be declared as EXTERNAL in both procedures.

Hence, these two B's are different variables with different attributes. The B in P1 is 1 in DEC FLOAT(6) by default, while the B in P2 is 7.0. Thus the printout is

```
7.0                    1.00000E+00
```

Variables which are shared by being declared as EXTERNAL must have the same attributes. Also names of labels can be shared among external procedures, with declarations, for example, such as

```
DCL JOE LABEL EXTERNAL;
```

in all procedures within the scope of the label named JOE.

The name of an external procedure cannot exceed seven characters in the System 360 or System/370 implementations. The keyword EXTERNAL can be abbreviated to EXT.

22.7 RECURSIVE PROCEDURES

Consider the problem of finding 7! Obviously, we can do so with the program

```
EX_1:     PROC OPTIONS(MAIN);
          DCL FACT FIXED BIN;
          FACT = 1;
          DO I=2 TO 7;
             FACT = FACT*I;
          END;
          PUT LIST(FACT);
          END EX_1;
```

A different way to program this problem is to employ a function procedure which calls upon itself. Such a procedure is named *RECURSIVE*. Using such a procedure, the program reads

```
EX_2:     PROC OPTIONS(MAIN);
          DCL FACT ENTRY(FIXED BIN) RETURNS(FIXED BIN);
          PUT LIST(FACT(7));
          FACT: PROC(N) RECURSIVE RETURNS(FIXED BIN);
              IF N=0|N=1 THEN RETURN(1);
                      ELSE RETURN(N*FACT(N-1));
              END FACT;
          END EX_2;
```

Let us describe how this program works. The main program invokes the function procedure FACT with the parameter N = 7. The procedure FACT then invokes itself with the parameter being N − 1, or 6. This is named a *second invocation* of the procedure FACT. The successive invocations of the procedure FACT continue, with the third invocation having 5 as a parameter, the fourth invocation having 4 as a parameter, and so on. The seventh invocation of FACT has 1 as a parameter. This parameter results in the return of 1, and the RETURN terminates the seventh invocation. The control returns to the sixth invocation, and in particular to the statement ELSE RETURN (N*FACT (N−1));. But now N = 2, and the returned value for function FACT(1) is 1. Thus 2*1 is evaluated and returned to the fifth invocation, with the corresponding termination of the sixth invocation. This process continues, and as we return the control and the function value to the kth invocation, we terminate the $(k + 1)$st invocation. Finally the desired function value of FACT(7) is obtained in the first invocation and returned to the PUT LIST statement, with the attendant termination of the first invocation.

Observe from the above that:

1. A procedure which invokes itself is identified by the keyword RECURSIVE. This is known as the *recursive option*. Examples of procedure statements with this option are

   ```
   JOE:  PROC (X,Y,Z) RECURSIVE;
   MOE: PROC  RECURSIVE;
   SUE: PROCEDURE  RECURSIVE RETURNS (FIXED(3,2));
   ```

2. As we invoke the procedure for the second time, both the first and the second invocations are active. As we invoke it for the nth time, all the n invocations are active. The compiler distinguishes the different invocations and treats them like separate procedures.
3. As we terminate the nth invocation of a recursive procedure, the control returns to the $(n−1)$st invocation.

In the above example, the recursive procedure was a function procedure. It is just as possible to have a recursive subroutine procedure.

22.8 THE BEGIN BLOCK

Consider the following problem:

Given

Two N*N arrays, A(N,N) and B(N,N).

Find

The sum C = A+B for arrays of any N.

As a possible solution consider the program with the value of N preceding the arrays:

```
EX_1:   PROC OPTIONS (MAIN);
        GET LIST (N);
        DCL (A,B,C)(N,N);
        GET LIST (A,B);
        C = A+B;
```

```
        PUT LIST (C);
        END EX_1;
```

which unfortunately does not work. It does not work because the declaration

$$DCL(A,B,C)(N,N);$$

is processed by the compiler before the executable statements, and at that time the value of N is not known. Consequently, we wish to execute the GET LIST(N); statement first, prior to processing of the DECLARE statement.

A solution to our problem is to use a procedure, as in

```
EX_2:   PROC OPTIONS(MAIN);
        GET LIST(N);
        CALL ADD(N);
        ADD: PROC(M);
            DCL (A,B,C)(M,M);
            GET LIST(A,B);
            C = A + B;
            PUT LIST(C);
            END ADD;
        END EX_2;
```

When we invoke the procedure ADD we already know M, and the DCL statement is processed correctly. There is another way to handle this problem, and this is through the use of the BEGIN statement. This statement has the form

$$BEGIN;$$

and is followed by other statements and an eventual terminating END; statement. The statements following the BEGIN; and terminated by END; constitute in the computer jargon a *block*. Hence the BEGIN block has the form

```
        BEGIN;
            statement1;
            . . . . . . . . . . .
            statementn;
        END;
```

and notifies the compiler that the processing of the statements within the BEGIN block is to *begin* after the BEGIN; statement. This processing includes storage allocation; hence storage is allocated to the variables within the BEGIN block after the BEGIN; statement.

Using the BEGIN; statement, we can rewrite the last program as

```
EX_3:   PROC OPTIONS(MAIN);
        GET LIST(N);
        BEGIN;
          DCL (A,B,C)(N,N);
          GET LIST(A,B);
          C = A + B;
          PUT LIST(C);
        END;
        END EX_3;
```

The END; statement can be omitted, because END EX_3; terminates the BEGIN block also.

The BEGIN block is similar to a procedure. In a BEGIN block, just like in a procedure, the storage allocation to the variables declared in the block takes place after the *activation* of the block. Similarly, the scope rules of the procedure apply to a BEGIN block. For example, in

```
B:   PROC OPTIONS(MAIN);
     A = 1;
     BEGIN;
       DCL A;
       A = 2;
       PUT LIST(A);
     END;
     PUT LIST(A);
     END B;
```

the A within the BEGIN block is different from the A outside the BEGIN block, because the DCL A; statement limits the scope A to the BEGIN block. Just like in a procedure, the storage for A in the BEGIN block is released after the termination of the block. Hence the printout is

```
2.00000E+00            1.00000E+00
```

There can be one or more labels in front of the BEGIN; statement, as, for example,

```
JOE: BEGIN;
```

or

```
JOE: DESK: BEGIN;
```

If there is a label in front of the BEGIN; statement, such as JOE, for example, then the terminating statement is either

```
END;
```

or

```
END JOE;
```

If there are several labels in front of the BEGIN; statement, then any one of the labels can follow the END keyword.

The BEGIN block must be internal to the main procedure. BEGIN blocks can be nested, just like DO groups. The statement BEGIN; can appear at any place in the program where any other statement is legal. For example, the statements

```
If A>B THEN BEGIN;
```

and

ELSE BEGIN;

are valid.

A BEGIN block is *activated* (note that a procedure is *invoked*) through the normal sequence (where a procedure requires a function reference or a CALL statement) or through a GO TO statement, as in

IF X>Y THEN GO TO JOE;

. . . .

JOE: BEGIN;

. . . .

END JOE;

. . . .

With the above GO TO statement the BEGIN block is entered at the "top," that is, with the statement

JOE: BEGIN;

It is illegal to enter a BEGIN block at any other point. Thus, for example, the program segment

IF A>B THEN GO TO MOE;

. . . .

JOE: BEGIN;

. . . .

MOE: B=C;

. . . . .

END JOE;

is an illegal one.

22.9 FLOWCHART SYMBOLS FOR PROCEDURES

Consider the program

```
EXAMPLE: PROC OPTIONS(MAIN);
         GET LIST(A);
         B = SQUARE(A);
         CALL CALC(A,C,D);
         PUT LIST(A,B,C,D);
         SQUARE: PROC(X);
                 RETURN(X*X);
                 END SQUARE;
         CALC: PROC(X,Y,Z);
               Y = X*X*X;
               Z = 1.5*X + 3.2*Y;
               END CALC;
         END EXAMPLE;
```

which calculates A^2, A^3, and $1.5A + 3.2A^3$. What is the flowchart for this program?

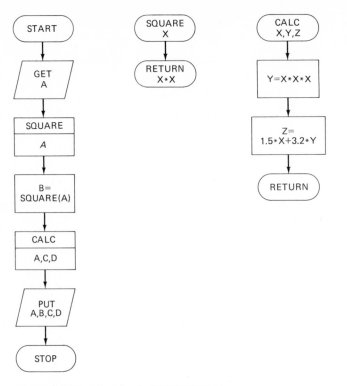

Figure 22.5 Flowchart for the EXAMPLE program.

The flowchart is shown in Fig. 22.5. This flowchart exhibits the following features:

1. There is a new symbol—the box with the horizontal line—to designate a procedure. In such a box, we place the name of the procedure above the line and the arguments below the line.
2. We use separate flowcharts for the procedures.
3. In the flowchart for the function procedure SQUARE, we use the start symbol (that is, the oval) but place there the name of the procedure and the parameter, rather than the word START. We also use the stop symbol (that is, the oval) but place in it the word RETURN and the expression being returned (that is, $X*X$ here).
4. In the flowchart for the subroutine procedure CALC, we identify the start with the oval containing the name of the subroutine procedure and its parameters (that is, just like for a function procedure). The end of the subroutine procedure is identified again by the oval containing the word RETURN.

22.10 EXAMPLES

Example 22.10.1 There are a number of character strings on data cards. No string exceeds 10 characters, and the last string is the null string. Write a

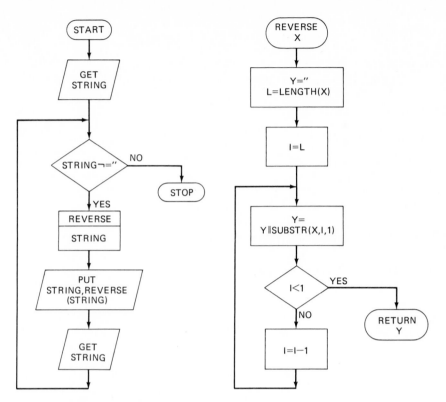

Figure 22.6 Flowchart for Example 22.10.1.

program using a function procedure to print out each string and its reverse (for example, the reverse of 'ABCD' is 'DCBA').

The flowchart for this problem is shown in Fig. 22.6. This problem is similar to the one introduced in Example 17.6.1, but now we will program it with a procedure. The resulting program is

```
EX_1:   PROC OPTIONS(MAIN);
        DCL STRING CHAR(10)VAR,
            REVERSE ENTRY(CHAR(10)VAR) RETURNS(CHAR(10)VAR);
        GET LIST(STRING);
        DO WHILE(STRING¬='');
           PUT LIST(STRING,REVERSE(STRING))SKIP;
           GET LIST(STRING);
        END;
        REVERSE: PROC(X) RETURNS(CHAR(10)VAR);
                 DCL (X,Y) CHAR(10)VAR;
                 Y = '';
                 L = LENGTH(X);
                 DO I=L TO 1 BY -1;
                     Y = Y||SUBSTR(X,I,1);
                 END;
                 RETURN(Y);
                 END REVERSE;
        END EX_1;
```

Observe the use of the RETURNS option in both the ENTRY declaration and in the procedure statement for REVERSE, as necessary.

Example 22.10.2 There is a stack of data cards which comprise several data sets. Each set contains information on either an array A or two arrays A and B. Each array is a two-dimensional square array, with the lowbound being 1 and the highbound being N. The data are listed in the following order:

1. The number N.
2. The operations to be performed. The operations are given as the following character strings:

   'AB'   meaning the matrix multiplication AB
   'BA'   meaning the matrix multiplication BA
   'AA'   meaning A^2, that is, A is multiplied by itself
3. The N×N elements of the array A.
4. For 'AB' and 'BA', the N×N elements of the array B. If the character string describing the operation was 'AA', there would be no further data in this data set.

The arrays in each set are neither 2×2 or 3×3 or 4×4. The results of the operation are stored in an array C. C is to be printed out so that each row of C appears on a separate line. The results of the operations on the first set are to be headed by

RESULTS OF THE OPERATIONS ON SET #1

The second and the remaining sets are to be identified by similar headings. The program is to end upon finding the value of zero for N.

We will first draw a flowchart (shown in Fig. 22.7) and write a program to accomplish the above. We will follow the program with an explanation.

```
EX_2:  PROC OPTIONS(MAIN);
       M = 1;                /* NUMBER FOR THE FIRST SET */
       GET LIST(N);
       DO WHILE(N);
         BEGIN;
           DCL(A,B,C)(N,N), OP CHAR(2);
           GET LIST(OP);
           IF OP='AA' THEN   DO;
                                   GET LIST(A);
                                   B = A;
                             END;
                       ELSE IF OP='AB' THEN GET LIST(A,B);
                                       ELSE GET LIST(B,A);
           CALL MUL(A,B);
           PUT LIST('RESULTS OF THE OPERATIONS ON SET #'||M);
           PUT SKIP(2);
           CALL PRINT;
           PUT SKIP(3);
           M = M + 1;      /* NUMBER FOR THE NEXT SET  */
           GET LIST(N);
```

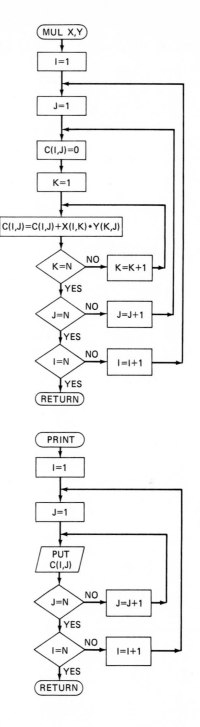

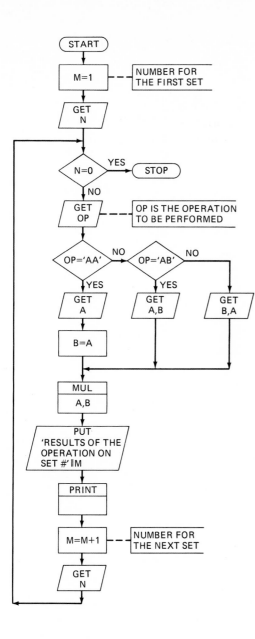

Figure 22.7 Flowchart for Example 22.10.2.

```
MUL: PROC(X,Y);
      DCL(X,Y)(*,*);
      DO I=1 TO N;
         DO J=1 TO N;
            C(I,J) = 0;
            DO K=1 TO N;
               C(I,J) = C(I,J) + X(I,K)*Y(K,J);
      END MUL;
PRINT: PROC;
        DO I=1 TO N;
           DO J=1 TO N;
              PUT LIST(C(I,J));
           END;
           PUT SKIP;
        END;
        END PRINT;
   END;
END;
END EX_2;
```

Explanation of the program:

1. We acquire N in the main program. The DCL statement is in the BEGIN block; hence N is known when the DCL statement is read by the compiler.
2. For the operation 'AA', 'AB', and 'BA' we arrange the arguments to obtain the desired operation when we call the procedure MUL.
3. The program for matrix multiplication has been written earlier (see Example 19.11.2). Consequently, the procedure MUL is a slight modification of this earlier program.
4. The procedure PRINT has no arguments. Since C is declared in the BEGIN block, its scope is the entire BEGIN block, and it is thus known within the procedure PRINT. With the DO loops we print out the elements of C in the desired format.
5. The END MUL; statement closes the three DO loops as well as the procedure MUL.

Observe that DO WHILE(N); is equivalent to DO WHILE(N $\neg$ =0); as discussed on page 262.

Example 22.10.3 There are a number of first- or second-degree equations in one unknown to be solved. Each first-degree equation is specified by the number 1 (giving the degree) and by the values of the coefficients a_1 and a_0, where

$$a_1 x + a_0 = 0$$

Thus, for example, the equation

$$5x + 10 = 0$$

will be given by the numbers

$$1, 5, 10$$

Each second-degree equation is specified by the number 2 (giving the degree) and by the values of the coefficients a_2, a_1, and a_0, where

$$a_2x^2 + a_1x + a_0 = 0.$$

Hence, for example, the equation

$$5x^2 - 3.7x + 18 = 0$$

will be described by the four numbers

$$2, 5, -3.7, 18$$

Write a program which will print out the coefficients and the root or roots of each equation.

Solution To obtain the solution we must do the following:

1. Read in the degree N.
2. Read in the coefficients. It is convenient to form an array for the coefficients.
3. Use one formula for a linear equation (that is, when N=1), and another for a quadratic equation (that is, when N=2).

One possible way to accomplish this is shown in the flowchart of Fig. 22.8 and in the following program:

```
EX_3:   PROC OPTIONS(MAIN);
        DO WHILE(1);
            GET LIST(N);
            BEGIN;
              DCL A(0:N);
              /* THE COEFFICIENTS ON DATA CARDS ARE  */
              /* IN THE ORDER A(N),...,A(0). WE WISH */
              /* TO PLACE THEM INTO THE ARRAY        */
              GET LIST((A(I) DO I=N TO 0 BY -1));
              IF N=1 THEN CALL LINEAR;
                     ELSE CALL QUAD;
              LINEAR: PROC;
                      X = -A(0)/A(1);
                      PUT SKIP LIST(A,
                        'THE SOLUTION OF THIS LINEAR EQUATION IS',X);
                      END LINEAR;
              QUAD: PROC;
                    DCL(X1,X2,C,D) CPLX;
                    C = A(1)*A(1) - 4*A(2)*A(0);
                    D = SQRT(C);
                    X1 = (-A(1)+D)/(2*A(2));
                    X2 = (-A(1)-D)/(2*A(2));
                    PUT SKIP LIST(A,
                      'THE ROOTS OF THIS QUADRATIC EQUATION ARE',X1,X2);
                    END QUAD;
            END;
        END;
        END EX_3;
```

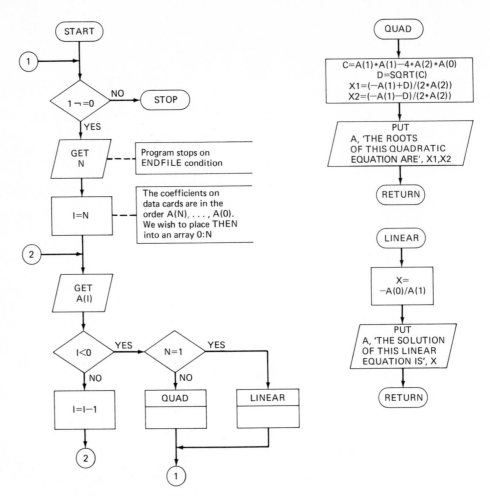

Figure 22.8 Flowchart for Example 22.10.3.

Note that C is declared to be complex. If C is a positive number, X1 and X2 are real but will be given in a complex form, that is, with zero imaginary parts. If C is negative, X1 and X2 have nonzero imaginary parts. For example, for A(0) = 3, A(1) = 4, and A(2) = 1, we obtained

$$-1.00000E+00+0.00000E+00I$$

and

$$-3.00000E+00+0.00000E+00I$$

as the results for X1 and X2 (which can be identified as -1 and -3). Similarly, for A(0) = 1, A(1) = 1, and A(2) = 1, we obtained

$$-5.00000E-01+8.66025E-01I$$

and

$$-5.00000E-01-8.66025E-01I$$

as the results for X1 and X2.

Observe that we used procedures without arguments. It is possible to eliminate the BEGIN block and to use a function procedure for the solution of the linear equation. With these two changes, the program reads

```
EX_4:   PROC OPTIONS(MAIN);
        DO WHILE(1);
           GET LIST(N);
           IF N=1 THEN PUT LIST(FIRST);
                 ELSE CALL QUAD;
           FIRST:   PROC;
                    DCL A(0:1);
                    GET LIST(A(1),A(0)); /* AN ALTERNATIVE TO
                                            THE DO LOOP OF EX_3 */
                    PUT SKIP LIST(A,
                     'THE SOLUTION OF THIS LINEAR EQUATION IS');
                    RETURN(-A(0)/A(1));
                    END FIRST;
           QUAD: PROC;
                    DCL A(0:2),(X1,X2,C,D) CPLX;
                    GET LIST(A(2),A(1),A(0));
                    C = A(1)*A(1) - 4*A(2)*A(0);
                    D = SQRT(C);
                    X1 = (-A(1)+D)/(2*A(2));
                    X2 = (-A(1)-D)/(2*A(2));
                    PUT SKIP LIST(A,
                     'THE ROOTS OF THIS QUADRATIC EQUATION ARE',X1,X2);
                    END QUAD;
           END;
           END EX_4;
```

22.11 SUMMARY

We described here the topic of procedures (also known as subprograms). The following main features were discussed:

1. There are two types of procedures, namely, function and subroutine procedures (or functions and subroutines for short).
2. A function procedure *returns* a single result to the point in the program where the name of the function appears. The subroutine procedure takes over the control of the program, and upon the completion of its task *returns* this control.
3. It is usual to enter a procedure at the PROCEDURE statement, this being the primary entry point. It is also possible to enter a procedure at other secondary entry points.
4. The variables on the list of the CALL or function reference statement are named arguments. The variables on the list of the associated procedure state-

ment are named parameters. For example, in the CALL statement

$$\text{CALL JOE}(arg1, arg2);$$

or in the function reference statement

$$\text{X} = \text{MOE}(arg1, arg2);$$

variables *arg1* and *arg2* are arguments. In the procedure statements

$$\text{JOE: PROC}(par1, par2);$$
$$\text{MOE: PROC}(par1, par2);$$

the variables *par1* and *par2* are parameters.

5. The attributes of an argument must be the same as the attributes of the associated parameter. Such identity of paramenters is achieved with the declaration

$$\text{DCL } Entry\_name \text{ ENTRY } (attribute1, attribute2, \dots attributen);$$

6. An array argument requires declaration of array dimensions in both the invoking and the invoked procedures.
7. Structure and string (that is, character or bit) arguments require declarations in both the invoking and the invoked procedures.
8. The rules on scopes of names determine whether or not a variable is "known" within a segment of a program.
9. A label can be an argument of a procedure. Also, the name of a procedure or a built-in function can be an argument of a procedure.
10. The argument list can contain the variables giving the results of calculations (that is, the solutions or outputs) as arguments.
11. The procedures can be either internal or external. An internal procedure is contained within another procedure. A procedure not contained within another procedure is an external procedure. In external procedures only variables declared as EXTERNAL are shared among the procedures.
12. A RECURSIVE procedure is a procedure which invokes itself.
13. The BEGIN block is activated when the BEGIN; statement is processed. A BEGIN block is an additional tool for subdividing a complex program into smaller parts.

PROBLEMS

22.1 Write a function procedure named AREA which has the parameters C and ALPHA. C is the hypothenuse and ALPHA the angle (in degrees), as shown in Fig. P22.1. The function returns the area of the right triangle.

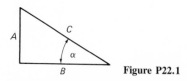

Figure P22.1

Figure P22.2

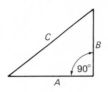

Figure P22.3

22.2 The program

```
P2: PROC OPTIONS(MAIN);
    GET LIST(A,C);
    CALL TRIANGLE(A,C);
    PUT LIST(A,B,C,RADIUS);
    END P2;
```

uses the subroutine procedure TRIANGLE to calculate the side B and the radius of the circle containing the right triangle with the sides A,B,C shown in Fig. P22.2. Write the procedure TRIANGLE.

22.3 The program

```
P3: PROC OPTIONS(MAIN);
    GET LIST(A,C);
    PUT LIST(SQUARE(A,C));
    END P3;
```

uses the function procedure SQUARE to calculate the square of the minimal side, where C is the hypothenuse and A one side of a right triangle, as shown in Fig. P22.3 (that is, SQUARE returns A^2 if $A<B$, and B^2 otherwise). Write the procedure SQUARE. (You can assume that A and C are nonnegative.)

22.4 Write a function subprogram which has a single parameter X. X is a two-dimensional array whose bounds are known only at execution time. The function is called SUMUP and returns a floating-point value which is the sum of all the elements of the array.

22.5 Write a function procedure which evaluates polynomials of the form

$$a_0 + a_1 x + a_2 x^2 + \cdots + a_N x^N$$

The function is invoked by the use of POLYNOM(A,X). Here A is the array of coefficients with zero lowbound and a highbound (corresponding to N in the equation above) known only at execution time. X corresponds to x in the polynomial.

22.6 The first number gives the dimension N of an N×N array. N is at most 5. Obtain this array and print it out as a square (for example, a 3 × 3 array is to be printed with three numbers on each line).

22.7 Write a program which takes two numbers A and B from the data cards. The program uses a function procedure named DEC to determine whether A>B. If A>B, the function procedure returns 1, and 0 otherwise. The main program should print "ONE" if the return is 1, and "ZERO" if the return is 0.

22.8 Write procedures accomplishing the same thing as the SIGN and FIXED built-in functions.

22.9 Write a program for a function procedure named SUMDIAG, which has one parameter called A. A is a two-dimensional square array, with the lowbounds being 1 for both dimensions. The procedure returns the sum of the elements on the array's main diagonal, that is,

$$a_{11} + a_{22} + a_{33} + \cdots$$

22.10 The statement

$$\text{CALL CORNERS(X,Y);}$$

invokes the subroutine procedure CORNERS. X is a two-dimensional array, and Y is the sum of the elements on the four corners of the array. Y is calculated in CORNERS. Write the procedure CORNERS.

22.11 Write a program that reads in a value N and creates an N×N array B by using a BEGIN block. It then reads in the elements of B (from data cards) and prints out the sum of all elements of the B array.

22.12 Write a program that will find the transpose of a square matrix. The data cards contain the values of the elements of the matrix. The dimensions of the matrix are not known at the time the program is written, but it is known that the matrix is at most a 10×10 one. Print out the elements of the transpose matrix.

22.13 The data cards contain data for 3 two-dimensional square arrays A,B, and C. The last number of each array is followed by a zero. There are no zero elements in the arrays. Write a program which will print out the arrays A, 2∗A, B, 2∗B, C, and 2∗C. No array is larger than 20∗20.

22.14 The data cards contain data on pythagorean triangles in the data-directed form. Each triangle is described by two sides (see Fig. P22.14). Using procedures, print out all three sides and the area of each triangle.

Note: The input has either the form

$$\begin{array}{ll} & \text{AB} = \textit{value} \quad \text{CA} = \textit{value;} \\ \text{or} & \text{AB} = \textit{value} \quad \text{BC} = \textit{value;} \\ \text{or} & \text{BC} = \textit{value} \quad \text{CA} = \textit{value;} \end{array}$$

with each set of data terminated with a semicolon. The last card is also in data-directed form and has zeros for values.

22.15 It is desired to perform operations on several N×N arrays. The data on cards contain the following:

(*a*) The number N, giving the number of rows (or columns) of the array.

(*b*) The N×N numbers comprising the elements of the array.

(*c*) One character describing the operation to be performed on the array. 'A' stands for addition and 'S' for subtraction.

(*d*) A number that is either added to or subtracted from the elements of the array.

(*e*) The program is to stop if N=0.

22.16 There are 20 data cards. Each card contains a character string (enclosed in quotes) and two numbers. If the character string is 'AB', the two numbers give the values for the sides A and B. If the character string is 'AC', the two numbers give the values for A and C. And if the string is 'AH', the two numbers give the values for A and H. Write a program which will acquire the data and use three function procedures to obtain and print out the area of the right triangle *xyz* (Fig. P22.16).

Note: For the last case,

$$Q^2 = A^2 - H^2 \qquad \frac{H}{Q} = \frac{B}{A}$$

22.17 A subroutine procedure is invoked by the CALL statement

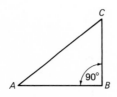

Figure P22.14

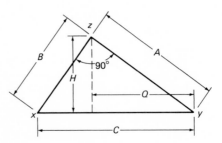

Figure P22.16

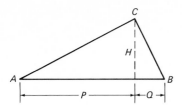

Figure P22.18

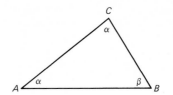

Figure P22.22

CALL PRINT(A);

where A is a two-dimensional array declared in the calling (for example, main) procedure.

The subroutine is to print out the array without the outer shell (for example, without the first and last rows, first and last columns). Write the subroutine.

22.18 In the right triangle of Fig. P22.18, where angle ACB = 90°, it is known that P × Q = H².

(*a*) Write a function procedure HEIGHT which has P and Q as parameters and which returns the height H of the right triangle.

(*b*) The data cards contain P and Q. Write a program which uses the function procedure HEIGHT and the return H to calculate (and print) the area of the right triangle.

22.19 Write a function procedure called ZERO which accepts a single parameter. The parameter is to be a one-dimensional array of unknown bounds containing integers only. The purpose of the function is to determine how many elements of the array are equal to zero. The integer value of this count is to be returned by the function.

22.20 A two-dimensional square array X, with identical subscripts in both dimensions having floating-point numbers of default precision as elements, is declared in the main program. The main program contains the statement

CALL CENTER(X);

which invokes the subroutine CENTER. This subroutine prints the center element if the array has an odd number of elements, and the four center elements otherwise. Write the subroutine.

22.21 Write a program that:

(*a*) Reads in the integer number N (up to three digits).

(*b*) Reads in the school phone directory consisting of N names and extension numbers (four digits). Names are given in a form 'last name, first name' (up to 20 characters) and are separated from extension numbers with the space.

(*c*) Reads in a name of the person given in a form 'first name a few blanks last name' (up to 25 characters).

(*d*) Prints out the person's name and his or her extension number. If there is more than one person in a directory with the same name, it should print the extension of the first one only; if no person with the given name is listed, it should print out the message NOT FOUND.

22.22 In the triangle ABC (Fig. P22.22) it is desired to know the sides and the area. The triangle is described by either:

1. One side and any two angles
2. Two sides and the angle between the sides
3. Three sides (here just the area has to be found)

The input is given in the data-directed form, with a semicolon terminating the data for each triangle. The angles are given in degrees. Print out the desired output with a heading, in the data-directed form, as, for example,

TRIANGLE #1
AB = *value*   BC = *value*   CA = *value*   AREA = *value;*

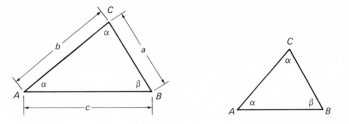

Figure P22.23   **Figure P22.25**

Use a function procedure to calculate the area, and use a subroutine procedure to calculate the sides. Also print out a message if the input is such that no triangle can be constructed. Use your program to calculate the triangles from

AB = 5	BC = 8	CA = 7;
ALPHA = 37	BETA = 84.5	AB = 7;
AB = 7	CA = 3.8	ALPHA = 43;
AB = −3	BC = 4	CA = 2;
ALPHA = 183	BETA = 30	BC = 5

22.23 Write the following subroutine procedures for the triangle in Fig. P22.23:

Procedure	Given parameters	Desired results
TR1	c, a, β	α, b
TR2	c, a, α	$\alpha\, b$ (if no solution, print out NO SOLUTION; if two solutions, print out both sets)
TR3	c, a, b	α, γ
TR4	c, α, β	a, b

Write a main program which uses these procedures and solves Prob. 21.19.

22.24 Write four subroutine procedures

$$TR1(A,B,C)$$
$$TR2(A,B,ALPHA)$$
$$TR3(A,B,GAMMA)$$
$$TR4(A,ALPHA,BETA)$$

for the calculation of the missing sides and angles of a triangle. Write also a function procedure

$$VOL(X,Y,H)$$

for the calculation of the volume of a parallelepiped with sides X, Y, H. Redo Prob. 21.20 using these procedures.

22.25 It is desired to know the three sides, the three angles, and the area of triangles ABC (Fig. P22.25).

The information about each triangle is on a separate card in data-directed form, preceded by a character string in the following three possible forms:

'THREE SIDES'	Three values for three sides
'TWOᵇSIDES'	Two values for two sides, one value for angle
'ONEᵇSIDE'	One value for one side, two values for angles

The angles are given in degrees.

Write a program using subroutine procedures to calculate the missing information and a function procedure to calculate the area. Print out the total required information for each triangle (for example, all sides and angles as well as the area). The given data are:

'ONEᵇSIDE',	A=3.7,	ALPHA=38,	GAMMA=14;
'ONEᵇSIDE',	C=14.3,	ALPHA=18,	BETA=93.2;
'TWOᵇSIDES',	A=12.3,	B=16.4	ALPHA=64;
'TWOᵇSIDES',	A=12.3,	C=14.8	BETA=44.3;
'ONEᵇSIDE',	C=7.3,	BETA=13.5,	ALPHA=59.7;
'THREEᵇSIDES',	A=5.2	C=8.2	B=7.5;

22.26 It is desired to solve the equation F(X) = 0 with a quadratic interpolation by passing a quadratic polynomial through three points. We are given the values X1 and X3 (on data cards) such that

$$F(X1)>0 \quad \text{and} \quad F(X3)<0$$

The quadratic is to intersect F(X) at X1, at X3, and at the midpoint X2 between X1 and X3, as shown in Fig. P22.26. The solution is the zero of the quadratic. Write a main procedure to do so. Assume that we have a function procedure F(X) and a subroutine procedure named QUAD (these do not have to be written). QUAD is invoked by the CALL statement

$$\text{CALL QUAD (X1,X2,X3,A,B,C);}$$

and calculates the coefficients A, B, C of the quadratic

$$AX^2 + BX + C$$

passing through the points (X1, F(X1)), (X2, F(X2)), (X3, F(X3)). Print out the zero of the quadratic.

22.27 Each data card contains eight numbers, which are the x, y coordinates of four points. The first number gives the x coordinate of the first point, the second number the y coordinate of the first point, the third number the x coordinate of the second point, and so on. The last card contains only zeros.

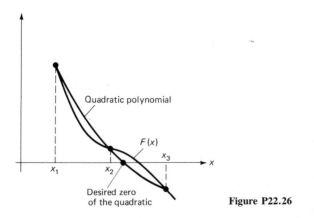

Quadratic polynomial

F(x)

x_1 x_2 x_3

Desired zero
of the quadratic

Figure P22.26

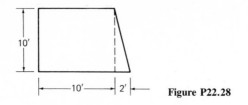

Figure P22.28

Write a program using procedures to determine whether or not these four points can be the corner points of a square. If so, print out the points and the message THESE POINTS FORM A SQUARE. If not, print out the points and the message NO SQUARE. The points are

0,0	4,3	7,−1	3,4
2,3	4,3.5	7,5	−1,5
0,0	0,1	1,1	1,0
4,8	7,2	9,3	−2,3
1,0	8,−1	4,3	5,3
0,0	0,0	0,0	0,0

22.28 The Three Dollar Bill Company sells real estate lots of different shapes. The cost of each lot is determined by the size and the regularity of the lot. The following applies:

    1. The basic cost is 50 cents/ft².

    2. A rectangular-shaped lot is sold at the basic price.

    3. A lot which consists of two rectangles (for example, ⊟) has a 5 percent reduction in cost.

    4. A lot which consists of three rectangles has a 10 percent reduction in cost.

    5. A lot which contains one or more triangles has a 20 percent reduction. Furthermore, a triangle having an angle under 20° has an additional reduction of 10 percent on the cost of the triangular part of the lot. For example, the lot shown in Fig. P22.28 costs

$$(100 \times 0.8 + 10 \times 0.7) \times 0.5 \text{ dollars}$$

    6. No lot consists of more than three shapes.

The input has the following form:

    1. Three characters designating the figures constructing the lot, followed by the sides of the figures. A rectangle is described by its diagonal and one of its sides. For example,

        'R', 'R', 'T', 63, 11, 19, 8, 12, 18, 22

describes a lot consisting of two rectangles and a triangle. The first two numbers (that is, 63 and 11) describe the diagonal and one side of the first rectangle in feet. The next two numbers (that is, 19 and 8) give the diagonal and one side of the second rectangle in feet. The triangle has 12, 18, and 22 ft as its sides.

    2. If a lot requires less than three figures for its construction, zeros appear instead of characters. For example,

        'R', '0', '0', 104, 84

describes a lot consisting of a single rectangle (with 104 ft being its diagonal and 84 ft one of its sides), while

        'R', 'T', '0', 93, 78, 14, 23, 17

describes a lot containing a rectangle and a triangle.

The rectangles are listed before triangles; thus listings such as 'R', 'T', 'R', will never occur.

    Write a program which will calculate the size and the cost of a lot. The program is to terminate when there is no more input.

    The input to your program is

```
'R'  '0'  '0'  200   82
'R'  'T'  'T'  162   35   75  83   92  111  110  12
'T'  '0'  '0'  183  112  84
'T'  'T'  '0'   75   86   95  73   82   14
'R'  'R'  'R'   44   28   77  83   95   32
'R'  'R'  '0'   47   36   81  28
'R'  'T'  '0'   83   28   14  48   60
'R'  'R'  'T'   92   28   67  32  110   22  101
'T'  'T'  'T'   14   17   30  62   58   63   73  53  77
```

23 STRUCTURED PROGRAMMING IN LARGE TASKS

A large programming task requires the production of more than just a program. It requires diagrams, manuals, the necessary documentation, description of tests, and various additional papers, tapes, or cards. This entire set is named *software* (as differentiated from *hardware,* which refers to the "hard" parts of the computer). The PL/I compiler is an example of a software. Another example of software is the programming performed for the Apollo mission project.

The accomplishment of large programming tasks requires the effort of many programmers. The coordination of their work calls for organizational and management techniques not necessary for small, single-programmer jobs. We will describe here such techniques.

23.1 BOTTOM-UP PROGRAMMING

A technique used exclusively in the 1960s is known as *bottom-up programming.* The name refers to the hierarchical layout of the program and the order in which the parts of the layout are produced. We will illustrate the meaning of the last sentence by an example.

Consider a program to be written named MAIN. The program MAIN has three parts: INPUT (the input-acquiring part), PROCESS (the processing part), and OUTPUT (the output-printing part). In addition there are two subprograms SUB1 and SUB2. The INPUT part uses SUB1, the OUTPUT part uses SUB2, and the PROCESS part uses both SUB1 and SUB2. Then the hierarchical layout of the program—known also as the modular program because of the division of the program into modules—is as portrayed in Fig. 23.1.

In bottom-up programming, the program is produced from the bottom to the top. Thus the programs SUB1 and SUB2 are the first ones to be written. However, to test SUB1 and SUB2, we need programs that simulate the conditions which will exist when SUB1 is called by either INPUT or PROCESS and when SUB2 is called by either OUTPUT or PROCESS. Such programs are named *driver programs,* or just *drivers.* Thus we must write a driver for SUB1 and then test SUB1 together

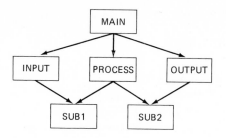

Figure 23.1 Hierarchical layout of the program MAIN.

with its driver. Similarly, we must write a driver for SUB2 and test SUB2 together with its driver. If the driver for program X is named DX, then the order of activities is as shown in Fig. 23.2, with boxes on the same horizontal position describing the activity at the same time period. As can be seen the modules of the program shown in Fig. 23.1 are produced in a bottom-up order, and that is why this technique is named bottom-up programming.

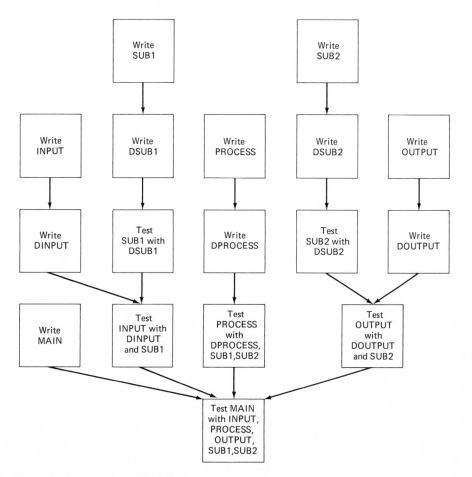

Figure 23.2 Order of activities in bottom-up programming.

There are several advantages to bottom-up programming. The two main ones are:

1. The modules can be designed and tested individually. For example, difficulties in the design of INPUT do not slow down the work on SUB1.
2. Errors are discovered in a small module, which makes their debugging easier.

There are also several disadvantages, with the main ones being:

1. When all the modules are integrated and the test of the entire program takes place, the inevitable errors are discovered. These are named interface or integration errors and are difficult to debug, because we work now with the entire large program. Hence the most difficult debugging task is at the very end of the project, usually causing delays in completion.
2. Extensive rewriting of modules is often needed, especially of the higher, untested ones (for example, MAIN).

Because of these two major disadvantages, a technique known as *top-down programming* has been introduced. We will describe this technique next.

23.2 TOP-DOWN PROGRAMMING

To eliminate the integration problems arising in the bottom-up programming, a technique known as *top-down programming* has been introduced. Here again we start with the hierarchical layout (that is, modular design) of the program as in the bottom-up programming. But now we produce the modules by starting from the top and continuing downward. We will illustrate the top-down technique with the previous example.

Again consider the program MAIN having the hierarchical (modular) layout as shown in Fig. 23.1. In a top-down construction, the first program to be written is MAIN. Next we wish to test MAIN but cannot do so because the programs INPUT, PROCESS, and OUTPUT have not yet been written. So we write short programs to replace the actual INPUT, PROCESS, and OUTPUT programs. Such programs are named *program stubs,* or simply *stubs.* The stubs are designed to meet interface requirements, that is, to accept the input and to return the output.

We will illustrate the design of a stub. Let us assume that PROCESS is a procedure which solves 10 equations in 10 unknowns. If the equations have the form

$$A(1,1)*X(1)+A(1,2)*X(2)+ \ldots +A(1,10)*X(10)=A(1,11)$$
$$A(2,1)*X(1)+A(2,1)*X(2)+ \ldots +A(2,10)*X(10)=A(2,11)$$
$$\ldots\ldots\ldots\ldots\ldots\ldots\ldots\ldots\ldots\ldots\ldots \qquad \ldots\ldots\ldots\ldots\ldots\ldots$$
$$A(10,1)*X(1)+A(10,2)*X(2)+ \ldots +A(10,10)*X(10)=A(10,11)$$

then PROCESS accepts the array A(10,11) and returns the array X(10). Because in the test of the program MAIN it might not matter whether PROCESS supplies the correct values for the array X, and any numbers may do, a possible program stub for PROCESS is

```
PROCESS:   PROC(A,X);
           DCL A(10,11),X(10);
           X=1;
           END PROCESS;
```

Hence if MAIN calls the stub for PROCESS, the stub delivers the expected 10 values for X.

Returning to the top-down construction, if the stub for program Y is S_Y, then the order of activities is as shown in Fig. 23.3, and as before the boxes on the same horizontal position describe the activity at the same time period. As can be seen, the modules are produced from the top on downward and are tested immediately upon their completion. Consequently, continuous integration takes place, because the

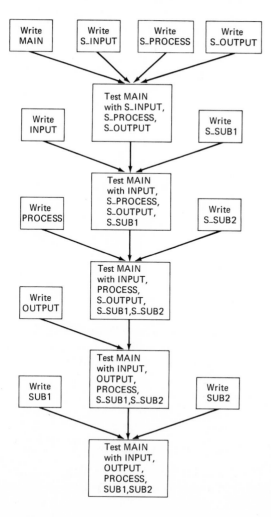

Figure 23.3 Order of activities in top-down programming.

entire program is tested initially with stubs and then with actual code as it becomes available. The top-down design clearly has the following advantages:

1. With the continuous integration there is no need for a separate integration phase.
2. Integration errors are discovered relatively early. In the initial test, errors are easy to debug, because the program stubs reduce the size of the program. As each component is completed a new test is undertaken. An error discovered in the test can be credited to the added component. This localization of errors makes debugging easier.
3. The continuous testing leads to fewer unpleasant surprises at the end of the project (as is the case in the bottom-up design).
4. It is usually easier to design stubs than drivers. Because both stubs and drivers are eventually discarded, in top-down programming we discard easily produced short programs.

For these reasons top-down programming is the recommended technique for production of programs. Evidently the management of a top-down programming task is different from the management of a bottom-up job. We will describe next the IBM Chief Programmer Team approach, which, as said earlier, was applied with great success to the *New York Times* information retrieval project. In the next section we will also describe the top-down approach to the development of programs of any size.

23.3 CHIEF PROGRAMMER TEAM

The Chief Programmer Team concept has been described by Baker[1] and Baker and Mills.[2] The factors which have so greatly increased productivity are:

1. Top-down design
2. Structured programming
3. Development support library
4. The team and its procedures

We already described the top-down design techniques and structured programming. The development support library allows the separation of the clerical work from the more creative tasks of the project. The library is maintained by a librarian and contains the obtained programs and the documentation describing the chronological development as well as the current status of the project.

The librarian collects and files all the significant information obtained from the team and ensures that this information is in a standard form. The librarian also

[1]F. T. Baker, Chief Programmer Team Management of Production Programming, *IBM Syst. J.,* vol. 11, no. 1, pp. 56–73, 1972.

[2]F. T. Baker and H. D. Mills, Chief Programmer Teams, *Datamation,* pp. 58–61, December 1973.

performs various clerical duties, such as bringing and picking up programs and maintaining control cards. Because all results are available in a single place (that is, the library) accessible to the team, there is no need for conferences, memos, telephone calls. This reduction in the need for communication among team members, and the elimination of clerical work, results in an increase in programming productivity.

The team has at least three permanent members, these being the *chief programmer,* the *backup programmer,* and the *librarian.* The chief programmer is a senior-level programmer, responsible for the programming task, who performs the modular design and personally writes the critical and difficult parts of the program.

The organization is analogous to that of a surgical team, which has a single doctor performing the surgery. The rest of the team is solely for the surgeon's support. Similarly, the chief programmer writes the main code, and the rest of the personnel performs only the supporting tasks. This organization differs from the traditional organization in programming groups, where the leader manages the group (with all the attendant administrative tasks) and supervises the work performed by other programmers.

The backup programmer is also a senior-level programmer who can assume the leadership of the team if necessary. The backup programmer develops alternate designs as backups should the original designs prove no good, provides technical and managerial support to the chief programmer, plans and performs tests independently of the chief programmer, and writes large segments of the program.

Obviously, both the chief programmer and the backup programmer must be experienced and skilled programmers of broad scope, with high technical and managerial abilities. The duties of the librarian we discussed already, but they call for either a secretary with some programming training or a junior programmer with some administrative training. Baker[1] recommends employing a secretary as a librarian because of bad experiences with the use of overqualified personnel. The remaining team members are programmers assigned to the team, and they perform design and coding duties as specified by the chief programmer.

The procedures that help in program development are HIPO diagrams and "structured walk-throughs." The HIPO (acronym for Hierarchy plus Input-Process-Output) is a set of charts which defines functional interfaces. Structured walk-throughs are reviews by the team of programs developed by team members. They are a learning experience for the team, while contributing to the detection of errors and to the evolution of test strategies.

23.4 SUMMARY

We described two methods for producing large software, the bottom-up and the top-down methods. We illustrated why the top-down approach is preferrable. We described the organization of the Chief Programmer Team.

[1]F. T. Baker, Structured Programming in a Production Programming Environment, *IEEE Trans. Software Eng.,* vol. SE-1, no. 2, pp. 241–252, June 1975.

23.5 FURTHER READING

Aron, J. D.: "The Program Development Process," pt. 1, Addison-Wesley, Reading, MA, 1974.

Horowitz, E. (ed.): "Practical Strategies for Developing Large Software Systems," Addison-Wesley, Reading, MA, 1975.

Hughes, J. K., and J. I. Michtom: "A Structured Approach to Programming," Prentice-Hall, Englewood Cliffs, NJ, 1977.

McClure, C. L.: Top-Down, Bottom-Up and Structured Programming, *Proc. First Natl. Conf. Software Eng.,* pp. 89–94, September 1975.

Mills, H.: Top-Down Programming in Large Systems, in "Debugging Techniques in Large Systems," R. Rustin (ed.), Prentice-Hall, Englewood Cliffs, NJ, 1971, pp. 41–55.

Weinberg, G. M.: "The Psychology of Computer Programming," Van Nostrand Reinhold, New York, 1971.

Yohe, J. M.: An Overview of Programming Practices, *Comput. Surv.,* vol. 6, no. 4, pp. 221–245, December 1974.

PROBLEMS

23.1 Construct a hierarchy chart for processing a purchase order, which entails checking the account for the outstanding debt. If such a debt is overdue (say, more than 90 days outstanding) and large (say, more than $200), the purchase order is rejected. If the debt is overdue and small, the purchase order is processed with a warning message (for example, that no future purchase orders will be honored).

23.2 Modify the chart of Prob. 23.1 to include inventory control. If an ordered item is not available, generate a rush order to the manufacturing division and process the partial order. If inventory reaches a certain limit, generate a normal request to the manufacturing division. Make all reasonable assumptions and try to construct a fairly complete chart.

23.3 Construct a top-down design chart (similar to the one of Fig. 23.3) for Prob. 23.1.

23.4 Construct a hierarchy chart and a top-down design chart for calculating a payroll and generating checks.

23.5 Construct a hierarchy chart and a top-down design chart for handling a mortgage application. This requires an inspection report to ascertain the value of the property and a check on adequacy of insurance and the credit rating of the applicant. Make the charts as complete as you possibly can.

EDIT-DIRECTED INPUT-OUTPUT

24

We shall now describe a new form for handling input and output data, the edit-directed form.

With the edit-directed input we exercise complete control over the punched card. We can tell the compiler which specific columns of the card are to be read and what interpretation is to be given to the data listed there. With the edit-directed output we exercise complete control over the display of our output. We can tell the compiler in which specific columns of the page we wish the output to be printed and the attributes that this output should have.

24.1. EDIT-DIRECTED INPUT

The edit-directed input statement has the appearance

GET EDIT (*data list*) (*format list*);

The data list is the same as in the GET LIST or GET DATA statements. It is, as before, a listing of variable names. An example of a data list is

(JOE, L, SUE, AAA)

which lists the names of variables for which data is to be acquired.

The format list tells where the data appears on the card and the interpretation to be given to this data. An example of data format is

(F(3,2), F(5,1), F(2,0), F(6,3))

which together with the previous data list results in the GET EDIT statement

GET EDIT(JOE, L, SUE, AAA) (F(3,2), F(5,1), F(2,0), F(6,3));

and tells the compiler the following:

1. The first item on the data list is the variable named JOE. This variable is associated with the first item on the format list, this being F(3,2). The letter F

tells the compiler that the data for JOE are in a fixed form. The numbers (3,2) reveal that the data for JOE are in the first three columns of the data card (that is, columns 1–3) and that the data are to be interpreted as a fixed number of the form x.xx. This specification of the form for JOE is the same as the one for the precision of a fixed number, where the first number denotes the total number of digits and the second number denotes the number of digits to the right of the decimal point.

2. The variable named L is the second item on the data list. F(5,1) is the second item on the format list, and it ''belongs'' to L. This means that the next five columns of the data card (that is, columns 4–8) contain data for L, with the interpretation as a fixed number of the form xxxx.x.

3. The variable named SUE is associated with F(2,0). Thus the next two columns of the data card (that is, columns 9 and 10) contain data for SUE, in the form xx (this being an integer, since there are zero digits to the right of the decimal point).

4. The variable AAA is associated with F(6,3). Thus the input for AAA appears in the next six columns of the data card (that is, columns 11–16), and this input is to be interpreted as being in the form xxx.xxx.

As an example, the preceding statement

    GET EDIT(JOE, L, SUE, AAA) (F(3,2), F(5,1), F(2,0), F(6,3));

with the data card

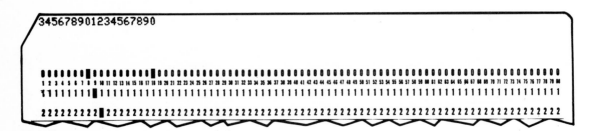

interprets the input as

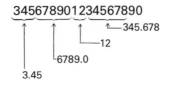

thus causing the assignment of

    3.45   to JOE
    6789.0   to L

```
12          to SUE
345.678     to AAA
```

Observe that the data beyond column 16 are ignored.

Incidentally, the preceding GET EDIT statement is equivalent to the GET LIST statement

GET LIST(JOE,L,SUE,AAA);

with the data card

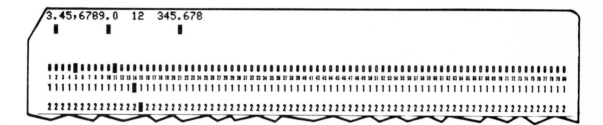

Note the compactness of data achieved with the GET EDIT statement. There is neither any need to separate individual data items with spaces or commas nor to specify on the data card the location of the decimal point. The format item takes care of both of these.

We will summarize briefly the introduced concepts. As described in Sec. 15.1, the data on the input device are viewed as a continuous stream of characters. The reading of the data for the first variable on the data list starts in column 1 of the data card. The first variable is paired with the first specification on the format list. The specification tells in how many columns the data appears and the interpretation to be given to this data. If this specification is $F(w,d)$, then:

1. The data for the first variable appears in columns 1 through w of the first data card.
2. The specification $F(w,d)$ assigns to the first variable the number having the w characters appearing in columns 1 through w, with d digits to the right of the decimal point.
3. The leftmost digit or character of the data for the next variable is in column $w + 1$ of the first data card. The specification associated with the next variable tells how the data are to be interpreted.

We just described how to specify fixed-point data. There is still more to be said about the fixed-point data (and we will do so in Sec. 24.3). It is also possible to specify other types of data, such as floating-point numbers or character strings. We will describe next the edit-directed output, and then we will tell (in Sec. 24.3) how to specify various types of data for the input and for the output.

24.2 EDIT-DIRECTED OUTPUT

The edit-directed output statement has the form

PUT EDIT (*data list*) (*format list*);

The data list is the same as in the PUT LIST statement. It is a listing of variable names, constants, or expressions. An example of a data list is

(JOE, JACK*K+3, A, 3.1E0)

The format list tells where and in what form the output is to appear on the printed page. An example of a data format is

(F(4,2), F(5,1), F(2,0), F(6,3))

which together with the previous data list results in the PUT EDIT statement

PUT EDIT(JOE, JACK*K+3, A, 3.1E0) (F(4,2), F(5,1), F(2,0), F(6,3));

and tells the compiler the following:

1. The first item on the data list is associated with the first item on the format list. F(4,2) means that JOE is to be printed out in the form x.xx (total "width" is 4 and there are two digits to the right of the decimal point) in the first four columns of the current line.
2. The second item on the data list is the expression JACK*K +3. This expression is evaluated and printed in the form xxx.x in the next five columns (that is, columns 5–9) of the current line.
3. A is associated with F(2,0) and hence printed in the form xx in the next two columns (columns 10 and 11) of the current line.
4. The constant 3.1E0 is associated with F(6,3) and thus printed in the form xx.xxx in the next six columns (columns 12–17). As usual, zeros in front (that is, the leading zeros) are replaced by blanks. As an example, the program

```
EXAMPLE: PROC OPTIONS(MAIN);
         DCL JOE FIXED(4,3);
         JOE = 3.432;
         JACK = 2;
         K = 3;
         A = 6.2E1;
         PUT EDIT(JOE,JACK*K+3,A,3.1E0)
               (F(4,2),F(5,1),F(2,0),F(6,3));
         END EXAMPLE;
```

gives the output

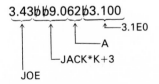

We just illustrated the PUT EDIT statement with data having the F or fixed specification on the format list. There is still a little more to be said about the F specification, and we will do so in the next section. There are also other specifications available with both the GET EDIT and the PUT EDIT statements. These specifications will also be described in the following section.

24.3 FORMAT ITEMS

We have seen that in both the edit-directed input and the edit-directed output, the data list is accompanied by a format list. We also described the fixed or F specification. There are other specifications, thus the format list may contain different format items.

It is usual to group the format items into three categories:

A   Data format items, of which the F specification was an example
B   Control format items, telling about the layout of the data
C   Remote format item, telling where the format list is

A Data Format Items

We will now describe the data format items, these being,

A.1   The F format item for fixed-point numbers
A.2   The E format item for floating-point numbers
A.3   The C format item for complex numbers
A.4   The A format item for character strings
A.5   The B format item for bit strings

A.1 The F format item. The F format item

$$F(w,d)$$

tells that the associated data item has w characters (that is, has the "width" of w), with d digits to the right of the decimal point. If $d = 0$ we can write either

$$F(w,0) \text{ or } F(w)$$

a The F format item on input

a.1 Interpretation by the compiler of data containing plus or minus signs and decimal points. Consider the program

```
F_TEST:   PROC OPTICNS(MAIN);
          DCL A FIXED(6,3),B FIXED(5,2), C FIXED(3);
          GET EDIT(A,B,C)(F(4,2),F(5,2),F(3));
          PUT DATA(A,B,C);
          END F_TEST;
```

with the data card

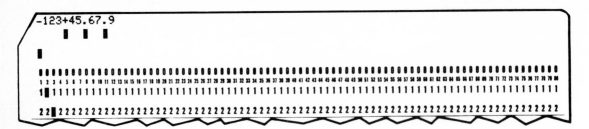

What is the resulting output?

1. The specification F(4,2) assigns to A the first four characters of the data, with two digits to the right of the decimal point. Hence −1.23 is assigned to A.
2. The specification F(5,2) assigns to B the next five characters of the data, that is,

$$+45.6$$

with the plus sign and the decimal point each being counted as one character. The data here contains a decimal point, with one digit to the right of it. This data conflicts with the decimal point implied by the specification (the specification tells that there should be two digits to the right of the decimal point). When such a conflict occurs, *the decimal point given by the data card prevails;* hence 45.6 is assigned to B.
3. The specification F(3) assigns to C the next three characters. Again, the decimal point on the data card overrides the decimal point implied by the specification, and 7.9 is assigned to C.

As a result of the declaration for A, B, and C, A and B acquire extra zeros, and C is truncated to 7. Consequently, the expected output is

$$A=\not b\not b\not b-1.230 \qquad B=\not b\not b\not b45.60 \qquad C=\not b\not b\not b\not b\not b7;$$

which agrees with the actual printout obtained with the F_TEST program.

a.2 The input data must be unambiguous. The data for a variable must be unambiguous. Thus blanks can appear before or after the number, but double signs or a blank between the sign and the number are not allowed. For example, the program

```
TEST:   PROC OPTIONS(MAIN);
        DCL A FIXED(5,2);
        GET EDIT(A)(F(4,2));
        PUT LIST(A);
        END TEST;
```

with the data card

$$+-12$$

will result in an error, stopping the program. Here the compiler expects the plus sign to be followed by a digit and tries to convert the minus sign to such a digit. This attempted conversion results in a *conversion error*. Similarly, if the data card for the program is either

$$++12 \quad \text{or} \quad --12 \quad \text{or} \quad +\!\!/\!\!b12 \quad \text{or} \quad -\!\!/\!\!b12$$

we also have a conversion error.

b The F format item on output

b.1 Examples of the F format item on output. F(5,2) means that the associated data items are to be printed out as

$$\overset{\displaystyle \ulcorner 2 \text{ digits to right of decimal point}}{\underset{\displaystyle \uparrow\!\!\_\_ 5 \text{ characters, counting decimal point as a character}}{\underline{XX.XX}}}$$

Specifically, the program segment

```
A=-1.343;
PUT EDIT(A)(F(5,2));
```

will cause the printout

$$\overset{\displaystyle \swarrow d = 2}{\underset{\displaystyle \uparrow\!\!\_\_ w=5, \text{ with both the minus sign and the decimal point counted as characters}}{-1.\underline{34}}}$$

If d is larger than necessary to display the number, extra zeros are added on the right. For example, the statements

```
A=1.26;
PUT EDIT(A)(F(6,4);
```

will give the output

$$\overset{\displaystyle \swarrow d=4}{\underset{\displaystyle \uparrow\!\!\_\_ w=6}{\underline{1.2600}}}$$

with two zeros added on the right to satisfy the $d = 4$ requirement.

If d is such that fractional digits are lost, a roundoff takes place. This means that if the most significant digit lost is 5 or larger, 1 is added to the digit on the left of the lost digit. For example,

```
A=1.68;
PUT EDIT(A)(F(3,1));
```

gives the printout

$$1.7$$

If w is larger than necessary, extra blanks will precede the output. For example,

A=1.68;
PUT EDIT(A)(F(5,1));

results in the output

ᵇᵇ1.7

b.2 The SIZE condition. In the F specification, the requirement on d is satisfied first. In computer jargon, we say that the number is "right-adjusted," meaning that we satisfy the specifications from right to left. Consequently, if w is too small, a loss in the most significant digits occurs. If the number is negative, the negative sign vanishes. This type of error is named the SIZE condition. For example, the statements

DCL JOE FIXED(4,3);
JOE = −3.456;
PUT EDIT (JOE) (F(3,2));

yield the printout

.46

Here the SIZE condition has occurred. In the compiler diagnostics enclosed with the printout, there would be a warning to this effect. If we wish, we can stop the program execution whenever the SIZE condition occurs. We will discuss in Chap. 26 how this is done.

c An alternate form of the F format item An alternate form of the F format item has three numbers, that is,

F(w,d,p)

w and d have the same meaning as before. The third number p is named a scaling factor, because it means that the associated data item is to be multiplied by 10^p. We will illustrate this alternate form by examples.

The statement

GET EDIT(A)(F(3,1,2));

with the data card

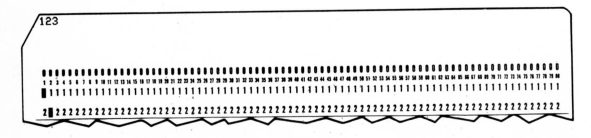

causes the assignment of 12.3×10^2, or 1230, to A. Thus the data is interpreted as

F(3,1), this being 12.3, and then multiplied by 10^2. As a further example, the statement

$$\text{GET EDIT(B)(F(5,2,}-3));$$

and the data card

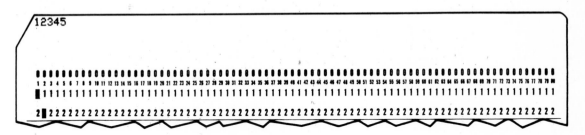

result in the assignment of 123.45×10^{-3}, or 0.12345, to B.

As an output example, the statements

$$C=1.35;$$
$$\text{PUT EDIT(C)(F(6,3,1));}$$

result in the printout of 1.35×10^1, or 13.5, in the specification F(6,3). Consequently, the printout is

$$\underbrace{13.\overbrace{500}^{d\,=\,3}}_{w\,=\,6}$$

A.2 The E format item.

The E format item

$$E(w,d)$$

tells that the associated data item is a floating-point number of w characters, with d digits to the right of the decimal point.

a Examples of the E format item on input

1. The statement

$$\text{GET EDIT(A,B,C)(E(4,1),E(4,2),E(4,2));}$$

with the data card

$$\underbrace{12E2}_{A}\underbrace{12E2}_{B}\underbrace{1234}_{C}$$

causes the assignment of

1.2E2	to A ($d = 1$ here)
.12E2	to B ($d = 2$ here)
12.34E0	to C ($d = 2$ here)

Observe that the input for C is a fixed-point number. In such a case an exponent of zero is assumed, giving the indicated assignment.

2. As in the case of the fixed-point specification, a decimal point in the input data overrides the decimal point implied by the d specification. For example, the statement

$$\text{GET EDIT(A)(E(6,1));}$$

with the data

$$1.23E1$$

results in the assignment of 1.23E1 to A, and the decimal point implied by the value of d is ignored.

b Examples of the E format item on output

1. The statements

$$A = 1.23;$$
$$\text{PUT EDIT(A)(E(8,1))}$$

result in the printout

$$\overset{\displaystyle \overset{d=1}{\downarrow}}{\underset{\underset{w=8}{\smile}}{\underline{\text{b}1.2E+00}}}$$

Note that the period is also counted as a character. As before, the number is "right-adjusted"; hence the specification on d is satisfied first, and then the correct w is achieved through the addition of extra blanks.

2. The statements

$$A=-1.23;$$
$$B=-127;$$
$$\text{PUT EDIT(A,B)(E(8,1),E(8,1));}$$

will result in the printout

$$\underset{A}{\underline{-1.2E+00}}\,\underset{B}{\underline{-1.3E+02}}$$

Note that the specification for A resulted in the truncation to -1.2, while the specification for B resulted in the roundoff to -130. As we said before, whenever the digit lost on the right is 5 or greater, 1 is added to the digit on the left of the lost digit.

c An alternate form of the E format item
An alternate form of the E format item on output is

$$E(w,d,s)$$

where s specifies the number of significant digits in the mantissa. With this specification, the item is printed out as

$$\underbrace{\not b\not b\not b\underbrace{xx.}_{s-d}\underbrace{xxx}_{d}E+yy}_{w}$$

thus $s - d$ digits precede the decimal point (rather than a single digit) and d digits follow the decimal point. The width is then adjusted with leading blanks. For example, 14.53 with E(13,3,5) will be printed as

$$\underbrace{\not b\not b\not b\underbrace{14.}_{\uparrow\ s-d=2}\overset{d=3}{\overline{530}}E+00}_{w=13}$$

Observe that the exponent part occupies four characters. Thus, to print out a negative number of just a single digit, a w of at least 6 is necessary. To print out all digits and the decimal point of a number such as 123.4, we require a w of at least 9. If we specify a w which is too small to display a number with the required d digits on the right of the decimal point, there is a loss in the most significant digits, or in the sign, or in both. This is so because the number is "right-adjusted," with the specification on d satisfied first. In such a case, as in the case of the fixed-point specification, the SIZE condition occurs.

A.3 The C format item. The C format item

C(F or E specifications, F or E specification)

tells the compiler the following about the associated data item:

1. It is complex.
2. Its first specification describes the real part.
3. Its second specification describes the imaginary part.

As an example, the statements

```
DCL A CPLX;
GET EDIT(A)(C(F(3,1),E(7,2)));
```

with the data card

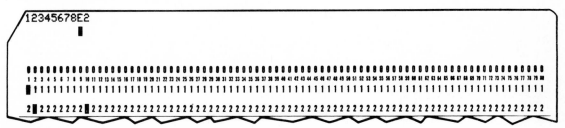

will result in the assignment of

$$12.3+456.78E2I$$

to A.

In the printout the letter I is not shown. The sign between the real and imaginary is only shown if it is minus. For example,

```
DCL(A,B) CPLX;
A=1.23 + 4.56I;
B=-1.36 - 4.567I;
PUT EDIT(A,B)(C(F(3,1),E(7,1)),C(F(4,1),E(10,2)));
```

results in the printout[1]

1.24.6E+00−1.4♭−4.57E+00

with annotations: Real part of A, Imaginary part of A, Real part of B, Imaginary part of B

If the specification for the real and imaginary parts are the same, just a single specification needs to be shown. For example, the statements

```
GET EDIT(A)(C(F(6,3)));
PUT EDIT(B)(C(E(7,1)));
```

accomplish the same thing as

```
GET EDIT(A)(C(F(6,3),F(6,3)));
PUT EDIT(B)(C(E(7,1),E(7,1)));
```

A.4 The A format item. The A format item

$$A(w)$$

tells the compiler that the associated data item is a character string of w characters.
As an example, the statements

```
DCL X CHAR(10)VAR;
GET EDIT(X)(A(7));
```

with the data card

SO IT IS

result in the assignment of

SO♭IT♭I

to X (that is, the first seven characters of SO♭IT♭IS).

---

[1]To obtain a separation between the real and the imaginary parts of A, we must use a larger w in the E specification for the imaginary part of A. For example, E(9,1) will provide two spaces of separation.

If quotation marks appear on the data card, they are interpreted as characters. For example, the previous statements with the data card

'SO IT IS'

assign 'SO∅IT∅ to X.
The statements

DCL(X,Y) CHAR(10)VAR;
X,Y='SO IT IS';
PUT EDIT (X,Y,X)(A(8),A(10),A(5));

will result in the output

SO∅IT∅ISSO∅IT∅IS∅∅ SO∅IT
X in A(8)   Y in A(10)   X in A(5)

Hence the following rules apply:

1. If w is too large, extra blanks are added on the right.
2. If w is too small, characters are truncated on the right.

Thus the string is "left-adjusted," meaning that it is placed correctly on the left end, with the right end either elongated or truncated to satisfy the given width w.

3. If $w \le 0$, the item is skipped. For example,

DCL R CHAR(4)VAR;
R='JOE';
X=3.1;
PUT EDIT(2*X,R,X)(F(3,1),A(0),E(8,1));

will give the output

6.2∅3.1E+00
2*X in F(3,1)   X in E(8,1)

Hence the character string is ignored, as asserted.
4. If w is not given (that is, just A is shown), it is assumed to be equal to the current length of the associated character string. For example,

DCL X CHAR(6)VAR;
X='SUE';
PUT EDIT('JOHN',X)(A,A);

will print out

JOHNSUE

Note that w must always be given with the GET EDIT statement because the length of the string on the data card is not known. It is only on output that w may be omitted.

A.5 The B format item. The B format item

$$B(w)$$

tells the compiler that the associated data item is a bit string.
The following rules apply:

1. The data card for the bit string must contain bit-string characters that are either 0s or 1s. Blanks may precede or follow the bit string.
2. On the output, the bit string is left-adjusted, meaning that to satisfy the given w, either bits are truncated or zeros are added on the right.
3. If $w \leq 0$, the item is ignored.
4. If w is not given (that is, just B is written), the bit string is assumed to be equal to the current length of the associated bit string. As previously, w can be omitted only with the output (that is, PUT EDIT) statement.
5. Neither the quotation marks nor the letter B is printed out.

As examples note the following:

1. The statements

```
DCL X BIT(10)VAR;
GET EDIT(X)(B(7));
```

with the data card

result in the assignment to X of the bit string

$$'1010111'B$$

2. The statements

```
DCL A BIT(10)VAR;
GET EDIT(A)(B(6));
```

with the data card

result in the assignment to A of the bit string

'101'B

3. For the statements

DCL P BIT(4);
GET EDIT(P)(B(4));

the data cards

or

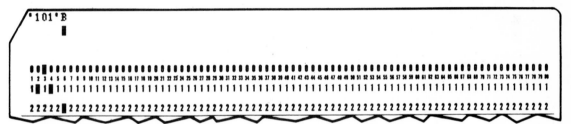

are all illegal, because they contain characters other than 0s and 1s.

4. The statements

DCL A BIT(3);
A='10'B;
PUT EDIT(A)(B);

will result in the output

100

because the declared length extended A to '100'B.

A.6 General rules for data format items. The following rules apply to data format items:

1. The numerical data is right-adjusted; the string data is left-adjusted.
2. If w is too small in the F or E specification, there is a loss of characters on the left. In such an event, a minus sign or the most significant digits are lost. The compiler is aware of this loss, which is named SIZE condition. The printout of compiler diagnostics informs us when the SIZE condition occurs. We will discuss in Chapter 26 how to activate a system action (for example, stop the program execution) when the SIZE condition occurs.

3. *w, d,* and *s* can be expressions. For example, the last two statements in

```
A=3.23;
GET EDIT(X)(F(3*A,A−1));
PUT EDIT(X)(E(4+A,A−2));
```

are equivalent to

```
GET EDIT(X)(F(9,2));
PUT EDIT(X)(E(7,1));
```

with the usual truncation to integers taking place. If the data card in the last example is

then

$$1234567.89$$

is assigned to X. In the E(7,1) form there is room for only three characters in the mantissa. Hence the output is 1.2E+06.

B Control Format Items

The format list can contain control format items in addition to the data format items just described. The following control format items exist:

B.1   The spacing or X format item
B.2   The COLUMN format item
B.3   The SKIP format item
B.4   The LINE format item
B.5   The PAGE format item

B.1 The X format item. Up to now the GET EDIT statement caused the reading of data in all columns of the data card. With the spacing format item, we can skip over several columns. We do so with the specification

$$X(w)$$

which tells the compiler that *w* characters are to be skipped over. For example, the statement

GET EDIT(A,J,K)(X(2),F(2,1),X(1),F(2),X(3),F(1));

with the data card

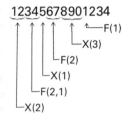

will result in the following interpretation:

12345678901234

1. We will skip over the first two characters.
2. The next two characters are assigned to A with the F(2,1) format. Hence 3.4 is assigned to A.
3. We skip over the next character.
4. 67 is assigned to J.
5. We skip over the next three characters.
6. 1 is assigned to K.

On output, that is, with the PUT EDIT statement,

$$X(w)$$

tells the compiler that w blanks are to be inserted. For example,

```
A=1.23;
PUT EDIT(A,2*A)(F(3,1),X(2),F(4,2));
```

results in

1.2ᵇᵇ2.46

In the item X(w), w stands for the "width," that is, the number of characters to be skipped over. w can be an expression. A noninteger w is truncated to an integer. If $w \leq 0$, the compiler interprets w as zero [X(0) means no skip and is ignored].

B.2 The COLUMN format item. The COLUMN format item

COLUMN (*p*)

tells the compiler that the card reading on input, or the printing on output, is to start at column *p*. For example, the statement

GET EDIT(A,B,C)(COLUMN(2),F(2,1),COLUMN(5),E(2,1),COLUMN(9),F(2));

with the data card

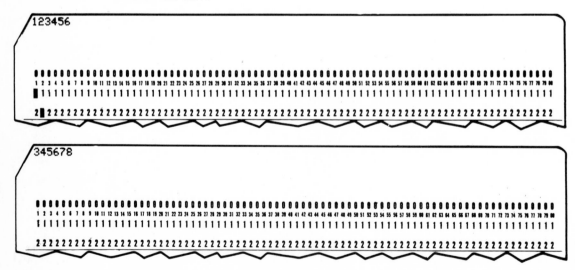

results in the following:

1. The card data is read from column 2.
2. 2.3 is assigned to A.
3. The card data is read from column 5.
4. 5.6E0 is assigned to B.
5. The card data is read from column 9.
6. 90 is assigned to C.

The reading of card data proceeds sequentially; hence if an item has a column number lower than the preceding item, the data will come from the next card. For example, the statement

GET EDIT(A,B) (COLUMN(2), F(2,1), COLUMN(1), F(2,1));

with the data cards

will cause the assignment of 2.3 to A and 3.4 to B (that is, first column of the second card).

The keyword COLUMN can be abbreviated to COL. Hence, a preceding statement, for example, can be written as

GET EDIT(A,B,C)(COL(2),F(2,1),COL(5),E(2,1),COL(9),F(2));

As an example of the use of the COL item on output (that is, with the PUT EDIT statement), consider the program segment

```
DCL A CHAR(5)VAR;
A='JOE';
B=1.23;
PUT EDIT(B,A,2*B+1)(COL(2),F(4,2),COL(7),A,X(3),F(4,2));
```

which results in the output

    Col. 2   Col. 7

b̷1.23b̷JOEb̷b̷b̷3.46

   B   A X(3) 2*B+1

If $p < 1$, then p is assumed to be 1. If $p > 80$ with the GET EDIT statement, the data will come from the next card starting at column 1. If p is larger than the line size (which is usually 120) with the PUT EDIT statement, then p is assumed to be 1.

B.3 The SKIP format item. The format item

SKIP(n)

tells the compiler that the card reader on input, or the printer on output, is to skip n times. For example, the statement

GET EDIT(I,N,C)(F(3),SKIP(2),F(3,1),F(4,2));

with the data cards

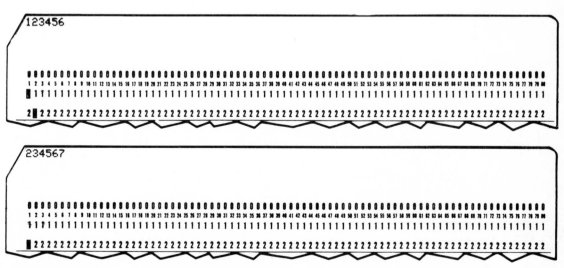

```
3456789
```

will result in

1. The assignment of 123 to I
2. The skip to the contents of third card
3. The assignments of 34.5 to N and 67.89 to C

Recall that in the list- and data-directed statements the SKIP option appeared either after the word GET or at the end of the statement. With the edit-directed statement it is still permissible to place the SKIP option there. Hence the above statement is equivalent to

```
GET EDIT(I)(F(3));
GET SKIP(2)EDIT(N,C)(F(3,1),F(4,2));
```

with two statements required now. The placement of the SKIP as a format item is more flexible, because we can skip with it before obtaining the data for a specific variable (for example, before obtaining the data for N), rather than before obtaining the data for all the variables on the list.

The use of the SKIP item on the output is illustrated by the statements

```
I,J,K,L=2;
PUT EDIT(I,J,K,L) (SKIP(2),F(1),SKIP,F(1),
                    SKIP(3),F(1),X(1),F(1));
```

If the printer is on the first line, prior to the execution of the PUT EDIT statement, then the following takes place:

1. The skip to the third line
2. The printout of 2 (in the first column of the third line)
3. The skip to the fourth line
4. The printout of 2 (in the first column of the fourth line)
5. The skip to the seventh line
6. The printout of 2 (in the first column of the seventh line)
7. The single space
8. The printout of 2 (in the third column of the seventh line)

Hence the printout has the appearance

2	third line
2	fourth line
2 2	seventh line

As before, SKIP is the same as SKIP(1) on either input or output. On output, if $n \leq 0$, the carriage of the printer will return to the first column of the current line. We can use such an n for underlining or overprinting. For example,

```
I = 1;
PUT EDIT(1,'_')(F(1),SKIP(0),A);
```

will give the output

<u>1</u>

If the SKIP item causes an advance to the next page, we print on the first line of the new page. For example,

```
J=2;
PUT LINE(40)DATA(J);
PUT EDIT(J)(SKIP(35),F(1));
```

will cause the printouts of

J=2;	on line 40
2	on the first line of the next page

B.4 The LINE format item. The format item

LINE(n)

tells the printer to print the next item on the nth line. For example, the statements

```
I,J,K=3;
PUT EDIT(I,J,K)(LINE(2),F(1),LINE(4),F(1),X(1),F(1));
```

will cause the following:

1. The positioning of the carriage of the printer on the first column of the second line
2. The printout of 3 (that is, the value of I) in the first column (of the second line)
3. The positioning of the carriage of the printer on the first column of the fourth line
4. The printout of 3 (that is, the value of J) in the first column (of the fourth line)
5. The single space
6. The printout of 3 (that is, the value of K) in the third column (of the fourth line)

If the printer carriage is positioned somewhere on the nth line, a statement with the item LINE(n) will position the carriage at the first column of the nth line. This allows overprinting, as, for example,

PUT EDIT('VVV','III')(LINE(10),A,LINE(10),A);

which results in the output

V V V

If the line number has already been passed, we print on the first line of the next page. Similarly, if the line number exceeds the number of allowable lines on the page, we print on the first line of the next page. For example,

PUT EDIT('1')(LINE(20),A);
PUT EDIT('2')(LINE(8),A);
PUT EDIT('3')(LINE(80),A);

causes the printout of 1 on line 20 of the first page, the printout of 2 on line 1 of second page, and the printout of 3 on line 1 of the third page.

B.5 The PAGE format item. The format item

PAGE

tells the printer to print the next item on the first line of a new page. For example,

I,J,K=4;
PUT EDIT(I,J,K)(F(1),PAGE,F(1),PAGE,F(1));

causes the printout of

    4   (that is, the value of I) in the first column of the first page
    4   (that is, the value of J) in the first column of the second page
    4   (that is, the value of K) in the first column of the third page

B.6 General rules for control format items. Several control format items may precede a data format item, as, for example,

N=1;
M=2;
PUT EDIT(N,M)(PAGE,LINE(10),F(1),PAGE, LINE(6),F(1));
PUT EDIT(M,N)(PAGE,SKIP(2),F(1),PAGE,F(1));

which causes the printout of

    1   (that is, the value of N) on the tenth line of the first page
    2   (that is, the value of M) on the sixth line of the second page
    2   (that is, the value of M) on the third line of the third page [the SKIP(2) item advanced the carriage to the third line]
    1   (that is, the value of N) on the first line of the fourth page

In the format items

$$X(w)$$
$$COL(p) \text{ or } COLUMN(p)$$
$$SKIP(n)$$
$$LINE(n)$$

w, p, and n can be expressions, which are evaluated and converted to integers (by truncation). For example,

```
A=3.23;
GET EDIT(B)(X(2*A),F(2));
PUT EDIT(B+2,2*B)(LINE(A+1),F(A-1),SKIP(A+2),
        X(B/(8*A)),E(B/10,A-2));
```

with the data card

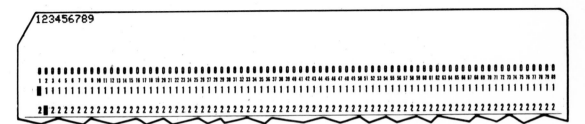

causes the following:

1. Since $2*A = 6.46$, $X(2*A)$ is the same as $X(6)$. Hence 78 is obtained for B.
2. The format with the PUT EDIT is equivalent to

$$(LINE(4), F(2), SKIP(5), X(3), \quad E(7,1))$$

with the values $3.23+1$, $3.23-1$, $3.23+2$, $78/25.84$, $78/10$, $3.23-2$ underneath.

3. The resulting output is

80   (that is, the value of B+2) is printed in columns 1 and 2 on line 4
156   (that is, the value of 2*B) is printed in the E(7,1) format (that is, as 1.6E+02 because of the roundoff) on the ninth line, starting in column 4

Thus the printout is

80   on line 4
↑
Col. 1

1.6E+02   on line 9
↑
Col. 4

The control format items are only executed if they are needed for actual acquiring or printout of data. If no data follows, the control items are ignored. For example,

$$\text{GET EDIT(A)(F(3,2),X(2));}$$
$$\text{GET EDIT(B)(F(2));}$$

with the data card

acquires 1.23 for A and 45 for B. Here X(2) was ignored, because there is no more data to be obtained for the first GET EDIT statement. If we wish to skip two spaces, we must write either

$$\text{GET EDIT(A)(F(3,2));}$$
$$\text{GET EDIT(B)(X(2),F(2));}$$

that is, placing X(2) before the F(2) specification, or the single statement

$$\text{GET EDIT(A,B)(F(3,2),X(2),F(2));}$$

which obtains now 1.23 for A and 67 for B.

Similarly, the statements

$$\text{PUT EDIT(N)(X(1),F(1),PAGE,LINE(3));}$$
$$\text{GET EDIT(A,B)(COL(2),E(7,1),COL(15),F(2),COL(25));}$$
$$\text{PUT EDIT(A+B)(LINE(10),COL(3),F(3),SKIP(2));}$$

are equivalent to

$$\text{PUT EDIT(N)(X(1),F(1));}$$
$$\text{GET EDIT(A,B)(COL(2),E(7,1),COL(15),F(2));}$$
$$\text{PUT EDIT(A+B)(LINE(10),COL(3),F(3));}$$

with the control format items at the end of the format list ignored.

C The Remote Format Item

Consider the program segment

$$\text{GET EDIT (A,B)(X(2),F(3,1),SKIP(2),COL(3),E(9,1));}$$
$$\text{PUT EDIT (A+B,A-B)(COL(2),LINE(3),F(4,2),X(1),E(8,1));}$$

```
GET EDIT (C,D)(X(2),F(3,1),SKIP(2),COL(3),E(9,1));
PUT EDIT (Y,C)(X(2),F(3,1),SKIP(2),COL(3),E(9,1));
PUT EDIT (D−C,2*C)(COL(2),LINE(3),F(4,2),X(1),E(8,1));
```

Note the repeated presence of the same format lists. In such an occurrence it is convenient to use the so-called "remote" format item, or the R format item, having the form

R(*label1*)

with the format list appearing in a statement labeled *label1,* as in

label1: FORMAT(*format list*);

Observe that the word FORMAT precedes the format list. For our program segment we can write

```
GET EDIT(A,B)(R(L1));
PUT EDIT(A+B,A−B)(R(L2));
GET EDIT(C,D)(R(L1));
PUT EDIT(Y,C)(R(L1));
PUT EDIT(D−C,2*C)(R(L2));
L1:   FORMAT(X(2),F(3,1),SKIP(2),COL(3),E(9,1));
L2:   FORMAT(COL(2),LINE(3),F(4,2),X(1),E(8,1));
```

The R format item and the associated FORMAT statement must be internal to the same block. Within a block, the FORMAT statement may be placed anywhere. The FORMAT statement is not executable and is only entered through the R format item.

In the above example, the format list contains just the R format item. This is not required, and the statement

```
PUT EDIT(A,B,C)(X(2),F(3,1),R(JOE),COL(25),A(15));
```
with
```
JOE: FORMAT(COL(10),F(5,2));
```

is legal.

A FORMAT statement may not contain a recursive R format item which leads back to itself. For example, the FORMAT statement

```
SUE: FORMAT(X(2),F(3),R(SUE),X(2),F(4,1));
```

is illegal, because it contains an R format item, which leads back to itself. Similarly, the FORMAT statements

```
JACK: FORMAT(X(4),F(3,1),R(JILL),F(7,2));
JILL:   FORMAT(R(JACK),F(4,1),X(2),E(7,1));
```

are illegal because of the recursion from JACK to JILL and back to JACK.

It is legal to have nonrecursive R format items in a format statement. For example, the program segment

```
                        A=3.23;
                        PUT EDIT(A,2*A)(R(JOE));
        JOE:    FORMAT(COL(10),F(4,2),R(MOE));
        MOE:    FORMAT(COL(20),F(4,2));
```

is a valid one.

24.4 MORE ON FORMAT LISTS

There is still more to be said about format lists. We will do so now.

A Format List with Excessive Format Items

Consider the program segment

    GET EDIT(A,B)(F(3,2),X(1),F(5,1),X(3),F(3,1));

Clearly, just the portion of the format list

    F(3,2),X(1),F(5,1)

is sufficient for A and B. Consequently the extra format items

    X(3),F(3,1)

are ignored. Thus the above statement is equivalent to

    GET EDIT(A,B)(F(3,2),X(1),F(5,1));

In general, all excess format items in a GET or PUT EDIT statement are ignored.

B Data List with Excessive Data Items

Consider now the program segment

    PUT EDIT(A,B,C,D)(F(3,1),X(1),E(7,1));

where the data items exceed the format items. In such a case, the format list is reused. Hence the above statement is equivalent to

    PUT EDIT(A,B,C,D)(F(3,1),X(1),E(7,1),F(3,1),X(1),E(7,1));

Similarly,

    PUT EDIT(A,B,C)(F(3,1),X(2),F(5,2),COL(15));

is equivalent to

    PUT EDIT(A,B,C)(F(3,1),X(2),F(5,2),COL(15),F(3,1));

Here, the COL(15) item at the end of the format list is executed, because the data list is not yet exhausted.

An array or structure in a data list requires as many format items as there are elements in the array or in the structure. For example,

```
DCL A(2,2);
B=2;
A=3;
PUT EDIT(B,A)(F(3,1),X(1),F(4,1));
```

is equivalent to

```
PUT EDIT(B,A(1,1),A(1,2),A(2,1),A(2,2))
    (F(3,1),X(1), F(4,1),F(3,1),X(1),F(4,1),F(3,1));
```

and results in the output

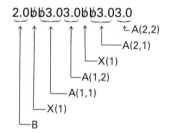

C The Iteration Factor

Consider the program segment

```
GET EDIT(A,B,C,D)(F(3,1),F(4,1),F(4,1),F(4,1));
```

It is possible to simplify the writing of the format list by replacing it by

```
(F(3,1),3 F(4,1))
```

The number 3 preceding F(4,1) is named an "iteration factor." It means that F(4,1) is to be used three times. The following rules govern the use of the iteration factor:

1. The iteration factor may be an expression. The expression must be enclosed in parentheses, as, for example,

```
PUT EDIT(A,B,C)((3*I+A) F(3,1));
```

Iteration factor

The expression is evaluated and truncated to an integer. If the result is either zero or negative, then the format item is not used. For example, in the program segment

```
I=3;
GET EDIT(A,B,C)((3*I−10)F(3,1),X(1),F(2,1));
```

the iteration factor is −1; thus the format item is ignored, and the program segment is equivalent to

```
I=3;
GET EDIT(A,B,C)(X(1),F(2,1));
```

2. If the iteration factor is an unsigned decimal integer, parentheses are not necessary (although legal), but there must be a space between the integer and the format item. For example,

```
PUT EDIT(A,B,C)(F(2,1),2F(3,1));
```

is illegal, because there is no space between 2 and F(3,1).

3. The iteration factor may precede several format items. For example,

```
I=1.35;
PUT EDIT(A,2*B+A,C,D+B,E+D)(2(F(3,1),X(2)),(I+2)(E(7,1),X(1)));
```

is legal and is equivalent to

```
PUT EDIT (A,2*B+A,C,D+B,E+D)
         (F(3,1),X(2),F(3,1),X(2),E(7,1),X(1),E(7,1),X(1),E(7,1),X(1));
```

$$\underbrace{(F(3,1),X(2),F(3,1),X(2),}_{2(F(3,1),X(2))}\underbrace{E(7,1),X(1),E(7,1),X(1),E(7,1),X(1));}_{3(E(7,1),X(1))}$$

4. There can be a nesting[1] of iteration factors, as in

```
DCL A(5,2);
PUT EDIT(A)(2(F(4,1),2(X(2),2 F(3,1))));
```

which is equivalent to

```
DCL A(5,2);
PUT EDIT(A) (F(4,1),X(2),F(3,1),F(3,1),X(2),F(3,1),F(3,1),
             F(4,1),X(2),F(3,1),F(3,1),X(2),F(3,1),F(3,1));
```

D Multiple Data and Format Lists

A somewhat different form of the edit-directed statement is

$$\begin{array}{l} \text{GET} \\ \text{PUT} \end{array} \text{EDIT } (\textit{data list}) (\textit{format list})$$

```
        data list) (format list)
       . . . . . . . . . . . . . . . . . .
       (data list) (format list);
```

which features several data and format lists.

As an example, the statement

```
PUT EDIT(A,B)(F(3,1),X(2),F(2))(2*A,C)(F(1),F(2,1));
```

is equivalent to either

---

[1] In the F compiler there can be up to 20 nested iteration factors.

PUT EDIT(A,B,2*A,C)(F(3,1),X(2),F(2),F(1),F(2,1));

or

PUT EDIT(A,B)(F(3,1),X(2),F(2));
PUT EDIT(2*A,C)(F(1),F(2,1));

24.5 OPTIONS WITH THE EDIT-DIRECTED STATEMENTS

In Chaps. 15 and 16 we introduced several options with the list- and data-directed statements. These options can also be used with the edit-directed statements. We will review these options and also introduce an additional option, the STRING option.

A Input Options

The statement

GET FILE(JUNK)EDIT(A,B)(F(1),SKIP(2),E(10,3))SKIP(2*I/3)COPY;

illustrates the use of the input options. It requires the following:

1. The input for A and B is to come from the file named JUNK.
2. The input reader is to skip 2*I/3 cards from the present position.
3. The values acquired for A and B are to be copied.

B Output Options

The statements

PUT EDIT(A,B)(F(3), SKIP(3), X(2), E(7,1))SKIP(2*J+K);
PUT SKIP(3*K/J)EDIT(A) (F(3));
PUT PAGE LINE (4*K−J) EDIT(B)(COL(3), E(7,1));
PUT EDIT(X,Y)(COL(4),F(2,1),SKIP,X(3),F(3,1)) PAGE LINE (A/B);

illustrate the use of the output options. As before, the options are executed first and then the printout takes place.

C The STRING Option

Assume that we have a character string named CUSTOMER which we wish to separate into three strings. Let us further assume that these three strings are named NAME, ADDRESS, and TEL. We wish to assign to NAME the first 20 characters, to ADDRESS the next 40 characters, and to TEL the last 12 characters of the string CUSTOMER. The program segment to do so may read

NAME = SUBSTR(CUSTOMER,1,20);
ADDRESS = SUBSTR(CUSTOMER,21,40);
TEL = SUBSTR(CUSTOMER,61,12);

An alternate way accomplishes the same thing with the STRING option. The statement

```
GET STRING(CUSTOMER)EDIT(NAME,ADDRESS,TEL)(A(20),A(40),A(12));
```

tells the compiler that the first 20 characters of the string CUSTOMER are to be assigned to the string NAME, the next 40 characters to the string ADDRESS, and the following 12 characters to the string TEL. In the above statement, there is no reading of data from an external input device, but only an internal assignment of data.

Observe that the STRING option offers a more compact way of separating a string than the SUBSTR function. With the STRING option, just one statement suffices instead of the three statements needed with the SUBSTR function.

Consider next the inverse problem: Given three strings named NAME, ADDRESS, and TEL, having the lengths as before, we wish to join them into a single string named CUSTOMER.

Clearly, concatenation yields the desired joining with the statement

$$\text{CUSTOMER} = \text{NAME}|\text{ADDRESS}|\text{TEL};$$

Alternately we can utilize the PUT STRING option, as in

```
PUT STRING(CUSTOMER)EDIT(NAME,ADDRESS,TEL)(A(20),A(40),A(12));
```

to do the same thing. Here the PUT statement causes no printout but just the indicated assignment to the string CUSTOMER.

24.6 APPLICATION TO PLOTTING OF FUNCTIONS

In many problems we wish to plot a function rather than merely tabulate the function values. The edit-directed output provides a convenient way for obtaining such a plot. To illustrate this application consider the following example.

Example 24.6.1 Plot

$$y = 0.43x^3 + 1.34x^2 + 1.73x + 1.27 \qquad \text{for } 0 \leq x \leq 5 \text{ in steps of } 0.1$$

Solution Observe that for $x = 0$, $y = 1.27$ and for $x = 5$, $y < 100$. Let the lines of the page correspond to the x axis, with each line representing 0.1 of the x scale. Thus the x axis is running vertically downward. Let the columns of the page be the y axis, with each column representing 1 on the y scale. Thus the y axis is running horizontally. A program which plots the given function and lists the y values vertically (that is, along the x axis) is

```
EX_1:  PROC OPTIONS(MAIN);
       DO X=0 TO 5 BY 0.1;
          Y = 1.27+X*(1.73+X*(1.34+X*0.43));
          PUT EDIT(Y,'*')(COL(1),F(5,2),COL(5+Y),A);
       END EX_1;
```

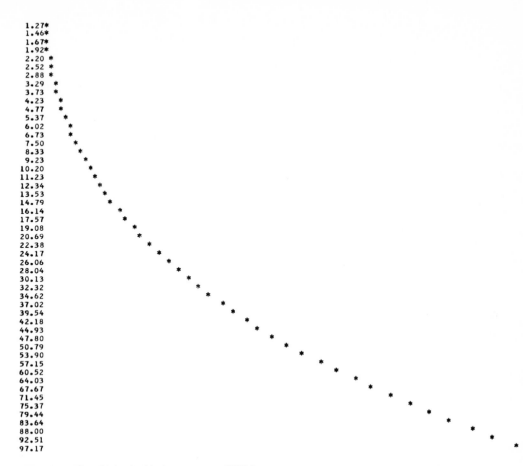

Figure 24.1 Plot obtained with the program of EX_1.

and places the asterisk in the $(y + 5)$th column. The 5 is added to y to prevent the placement of the asterisk within the vertically tabulated values. The resulting plot is shown in Fig. 24.1. The plot appears bumpy, because the points are plotted in column $5 + y$, and the value of $5 + y$ is truncated to the integer. Note, for example, that the y values of 1.27, 1.46, 1.67, 1.92 are all interpreted as 1 and are plotted in the sixth column.

It is often desired to show the y axis with a scale. We do so with the statements

```
DO I=0 TO 100 BY 5;
    PUT EDIT(I)(COL(2+I),F(LOG10(I+1)+1));
END;
PUT EDIT('0',(101)'_',(20)'bbbb','|')
    (COL(1), 2 A,SKIP(0), COL(2), 2 A);
```

The DO loop with the first PUT EDIT statement places the scale, with each multiple of 5 identified. Observe that F(LOG10(I+1)+1) is F(1) for the one-digit values of I (that is, for 0 and 5), F(2) for the two-digit values of I, and F(3) for I=100.

The second PUT EDIT statement places a zero in the corner of the coordinate system, and then the y axis. The $'|'$ marks emphasize the scale. We can similarly place the x scale and the x axis. A program with both the x and y axes is

```
EX_2:   PROC OPTIONS(MAIN);
        DCL X FIXED(2,1);
        /*PLACING THE Y-SCALE */
        DO I=0 TO 100 BY 5;
           PUT EDIT(I)(COL(2+I),F(LOG10(I+1)+1));
        END;
        /*PLACING THE Y-AXIS */
        PUT EDIT('0',(101)'_',(20)'|      ','|')(COL(1),2 A,SKIP(0),
                                                 COL(2),2 A);
        DO X=0.1 TO 5 BY 0.1;
           Y=1.27+X*(1.73+X*(1.34+X*0.43));
          /*PLACING THE X-SCALE AND THE X-AXIS */
          N = X;
          IF N=X THEN PUT EDIT
             (X,'+')(COL(1),F(1),A);
                 ELSE PUT EDIT
             ('|')(COL(2),A);
             PUT EDIT('*')(COL(2+Y),A);
        END EX_2;
```

The resulting plot is portrayed in Fig. 24.2.

In the plots of the preceding examples we chose the x axis to run vertically and the y axis to run horizontally. With this choice of axes, the plotted function monotonically decreased, and once we plotted on the nth line, the next point was never plotted on a line above the nth line. Observe that with the programs just constructed we are able to plot only monotonic functions. We will now describe a method for the plotting of any function (that is, monotonic or nonmonotonic), and the axes will be placed in the familiar places, that is, the x axis horizontally and the y axis vertically. To this end consider the following example.

Example 24.6.2 Plot

$$y=1.3 - 7.6e^{-0.8x}\sin x \qquad \text{for } 0 \leqslant x \leqslant 10$$

with the x axis drawn horizontally and the y axis vertically.

Solution We will now choose the lines as the scale for y and the columns as the scale for x. Note that for $x=0$ and for $x \approx 3.14$ (that is, for $x = \pi$), $y = 1.3$. Furthermore, after plotting the point $y = 1.3$ for $x = 0$, we must move to a line above this point for $x = 4$, which is not possible. To avoid this predicament, we will construct an array of characters that will contain asterisks for the x, y points satisfying the given relationship, and blanks for all other points of the xy plane.

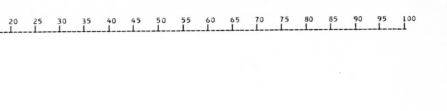

Figure 24.2 Plot obtained with the program EX_2.

To display the plot on the major part of the page, we should know the minimum and maximum values of x and y. With such information, we can scale the plot to the available space. From the given range of x we know that x has a minimum of 0 and a maximum of 10. We could calculate the extremes of y, but this is not necessary. With some simple calculations we can see that $y_{max} < 2$ and $y_{min} > -2$; thus let us choose -2 and 2 as the range for y. Let us then choose 41 lines for y, with the twenty-first line corresponding to $y = 0$, the first line to $y = 2$, and the last (that is, the forty-first line) to $y = -2$. Let us choose 101 columns for x, where again the first column corresponds to $x = 0$, and each 10 columns correspond to one unit of the x scale. With such a choice, we can define an array

$$GRAPH(0{:}100, \ -20{:}20)$$

whose elements are either blanks, asterisks, or dots. The asterisks will form the curve to be plotted, while the dots are used to form x and y axes. The program reads

```
EX_3:      PROC OPTIONS(MAIN);
           DCL GRAPH(0:100,-20:20) CHAR(1);
           GRAPH = ' '; /* INITIAL LOADING WITH BLANKS */
           /* PLACING OF AXES */
           GRAPH(0,*) = '.'; /* THE Y-AXIS */
           GRAPH(*,0) = '.'; /* THE X-AXIS */
           DO X=0 TO 10 BY 0.1;
               Y=F(X);
               IX = 10*X; /* X SCALING */
               IY = 10*Y; /* Y SCALING */
               GRAPH(IX,IY) = '*';
           END;
           F: PROC(X);
               Y = 1.3 - 7.6*EXP(-0.8*X)*SIN(X);
               RETURN(Y);
               END F;
           DO IY = 20 TO -20 BY -1;
               DO IX = 0 TO 100;
                   PUT EDIT(GRAPH(IX,IY))(COL(IX+1),A);
           END EX_3;
```

The resulting plot is shown in Fig. 24.3.

We can also put scales on the x and y axes. To place the x scale, we will display all integer values of x and replace at such points the dot by |. The statements

```
DCL A FIXED(2,1);
DO A = 1 TO 9;
    GRAPH (10*A,0) = '|';
    GRAPH (10*A,1) = SUBSTR(A,3,1);
END;
GRAPH (100,0) = '|';
GRAPH (99,1) = '1';
GRAPH (100,1) = '0';
```

will place the x scale. Observe the use of the SUBSTR function to eliminate the leading blanks and the special treatment for placing the two digits 10 on the scale. A was chosen as FIXED(2,1) rather than an integer, because such a number is needed for the y scale to be described below.

On the y scale we will display the multiples of 0.5; that is, a value will be shown on each fifth line. Because we need four characters to display the y scale (for example, -2.0), it is convenient to use a separate array for this scale. The statements

```
DCL Y SCALE(-20:20)CHAR(4);
Y_SCALE = 'bbbb';
DO A = -2.0 TO 2.0 BY 0.5;
    Y_SCALE(10*A) = SUBSTR(A,2);
END;
```

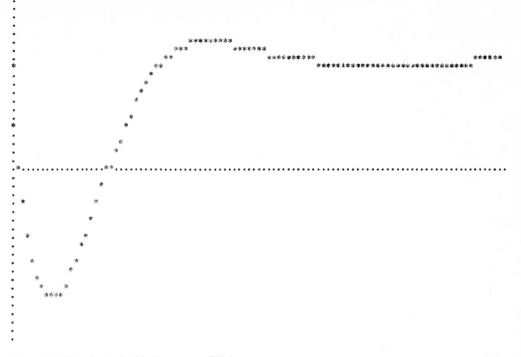

Figure 24.3 Plot obtained with the program EX_3.

will place the *y* scale. Observe that with the *y* scale the program labeled EX_3 will need a PUT EDIT statement which starts the plot in column 5 (rather than in column 1), because the first four columns are now occupied by the *y* scale. With such additions and changes we obtain the program named EX_4, which results in the plot portrayed in Fig. 24.4.

```
EX_4:     PROC OPTIONS(MAIN);
          DCL GRAPH(0:100,-20:20) CHAR(1),
              Y_SCALE(-20:20) CHAR(4),
              A FIXED(2,1);
          GRAPH = ' '; /*INITIAL LOADING WITH BLANKS */
          /* PLACING OF AXES */
          GRAPH(0,*) = '.';
          GRAPH(*,0) = '.';
          DO X=0 TO 10 BY 0.1;
              Y=F(X);
              IX = 10*X; /* X SCALING */
              IY = 10*Y; /* Y SCALING */
              GRAPH(IX,IY) = '*';
          END;
          F: PROC(X);
              Y = 1.3 - 7.6*EXP(-0.8*X)*SIN(X);
              RETURN(Y);
          END F;
          DO A=1 TO 9;
```

```
        GRAPH(10*A,0) = '|';
        GRAPH(10*A,1) = SUBSTR(A,3,1);
    END;
    GRAPH(100,0) = '|';
    GRAPH(99,1)  = '1';
    GRAPH(100,1) = '0';
    Y_SCALE = '      ';
    DO A=-2.0 TO 2.0 BY 0.5;
        Y_SCALE(10*A) = SUBSTR(A,2);
    END;
    DO IY = 20 TO -20 BY -1;
        PUT EDIT(Y_SCALE(IY))(COL(1),A);
        DO IX = 0 TO 100;
            PUT EDIT(GRAPH(IX,IY))(COL(5+IX),A);
    END EX_4;
```

In program EX_3 we determined the range of y by hand calculations to display the y axis on the major part of the page. In practice it may be difficult to do so. We can then either determine the range by obtaining one or more preliminary plots, or with a program. In fact, a program can be written that will do the entire scaling automatically.

Let us assume that we wish to display the plot on a page consisting of M lines and N columns. Generally we know the range of X of interest; thus XMIN and XMAX, the minimum and maximum values of X, are known. With reference to Fig. 24.5, it is evident that XMAX − XMIN corresponds to N − 1 columns and XINCR, the smallest increment of X, where

$$XINCR = (XMAX - XMIN)/(N - 1)$$

corresponds to a single column.

To convert X to columns, we write

$$X = XMIN + X - XMIN$$

We know that XMIN corresponds to the first column. Evidently X − XMIN corresponds to (X−XMIN)/XINCR columns. Hence the scaling factor XS multiplying X − XMIN is 1/XINCR, or alternatively

$$XS = (N-1)/(XMAX-XMIN);$$

To find the maximum and the minimum values of y we can use

```
YMIN, YMAX = F(XMIN);
DO X=XMIN TO XMAX BY XINCR;
    Y=F(Y);
    IF Y > YMAX THEN YMAX = Y;
    IF Y < YMIN THEN YMIN = Y;
END;
```

With YMIN and YMAX we can write the scaling formula as

$$YS = (M-1)/(YMAX-YMIN);$$

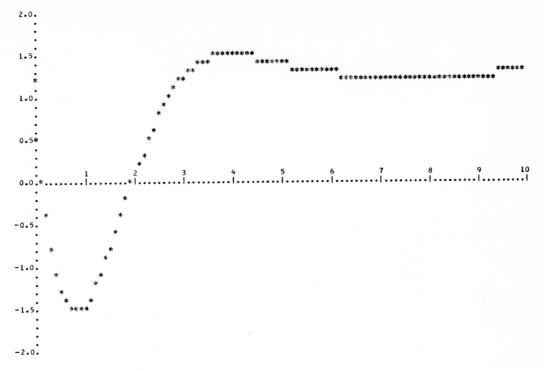

Figure 24.4 Plot obtained with the program EX_4.

We are now ready to write a complete program with automatic scaling and a display of the *x* and *y* scales. For M = 61 (that is, 61 lines) and N = 101 (that is, 101 columns), such a program is

```
EX_5:    PROC OPTIONS(MAIN);
         DCL GRAPH(0:100,-30:30) CHAR(1),
             Y_SCALE(-30:30) CHAR(5),
             A FIXED(4,2);
         OPEN FILE(SYSPRINT) PAGESIZE(61);
         /* FINDING THE RANGE OF Y */
         XMIN = 0;
         XMAX = 10;
         XINCR = (XMAX - XMIN)/100;
         YMIN,YMAX = F(XMIN);
         DO X=XMIN TO XMAX BY XINCR;
             Y = F(X);
             IF Y>YMAX THEN YMAX=Y;
             IF Y<YMIN THEN YMIN=Y;
         END;
```

XMIN XMAX

├────────┤

COL(1) COL(N)   **Figure 24.5** Correspondence between the range of X and the columns of a line.

```
/* SCALING FORMULAS */
XS = 100/(XMAX-XMIN);
YS =  60/(YMAX-YMIN);
/* LOCATING THE Y=0 LINE FROM THE FORMULA */
/* (YMAX-YMIN)/YMAX = 60/(I0-1)            */
/* SOLVING FOR I0                          */
I0 = YMAX*YS + 1;
/* THE ARRAY SUBSCRIPT FOR THE Y=0 LINE    */
/* IY0 - 1 = 30 - I0                       */
IY0 = 31 - I0;
Y_SCALE = '     ';
GRAPH = ' ';
/* PLACING OF AXES */
GRAPH(0,*) = '.';
GRAPH(*,IY0) = '.';
/* PLACING OF X-SCALE */
DO A=1 TO 9;
    GRAPH(10*A,IY0) = '|';
    GRAPH(10*A,IY0+1) = SUBSTR(A,4,1);
END;
GRAPH(100,IY0) = '|';
GRAPH(99,IY0+1)  = '1';
GRAPH(100,IY0+1) = '0';
/* PLACING THE Y-SCALE */
DO K= IY0 TO 30 BY 5,IY0-5 TO -30 BY -5;
    A = (K - IY0)/YS;
    Y_SCALE(K) = SUBSTR(A,3);
    GRAPH(0,K) = '+';
END;
/* CONSTRUCTING THE PLOT     */
DO X=XMIN TO XMAX BY XINCR;
    IX = XS*(X-XMIN) + 0.5*SIGN(X);
    Y = F(X);
    IY = YS*(Y-YMIN) -30 + 0.5*SIGN(Y);
    GRAPH(IX,IY) = '*';
END;
F: PROC(X);
    Y = 1.3 - 7.6*EXP(-0.8*X)*SIN(X);
    RETURN(Y);
END F;
/* PRINT-OUT OF THE PLOT     */
DO IY = 30 TO -30 BY -1;
    PUT EDIT(Y_SCALE(IY))(COL(1),A);
    DO IX=0 TO 100;
        PUT EDIT(GRAPH(IX,IY))(COL(6+IX),A);
END EX_5;
```

Observe several features of this program:

1. We use the PAGESIZE option to display 61 lines on the page.
2. We automatically find the minimum and maximum values of Y.
3. We no longer place the *x* axis (that is, the $Y = 0$ line) in the center of the page but calculate its placement. With reference to Fig. 24.6, showing the correspondences between YMAX and line 1, $Y = 0$ and line I0, YMIN and line 61, we obtain

YMAX   LINE 1

Y=0   LINE I0

YMIN   LINE 61   **Figure 24.6** Correspondence between values of Y and lines.

$$(YMAX - YMIN)/(YMAX - 0) = (1 - 61)(1 - I0)$$

or

$$I0 = 60*YMAX/(YMAX - YMIN) + 1$$
$$= YMAX*YS + 1$$

The I0th line results in the array subscript

$$IY0 = 31 - I0 \text{ (if } I0 = 31, \text{ the array subscript is zero).}$$

4. To reduce the truncation error we round off IX and IY by the additions of 0.5*SIGN(X) to IX and 0.5*SIGN(Y) to IY.

The resulting plot is portrayed in Fig. 24.7.

In closing, note that there are 6 lines per inch and 10 columns per inch. Consequently, the x and y scales are not uniform. In the plot of Fig. 24.7 we allowed 10 columns, or 1 inch, to a unit of x but around 19 lines, hence over 3 inches, to a unit of y. If uniformity of scale is desired, we must either multiply the y axis by 0.6 or the x axis by 1/0.6.

24.7 EXAMPLES

Example 24.7.1 Print out the first 50 integers, their squares, cubes, square roots, cube roots, and logarithms to base 2 and e, properly identified.

Solution The desired program is

```
EX_1:      PROC OPTIONS(MAIN);
           /* HEADING IN CENTER */
           PUT EDIT('TABLE OF FIRST 50 NUMBERS, THEIR SQUARES,CUBES,SQUAR
E ROOTS, CUBE ROOTS, BASE 2, AND NATURAL LOGARITHMS')(COL(8),A);
           /* HEADINGS FOR TABLE */
           PUT SKIP(2) EDIT('N','N**2','N**3','SQRT(N)','CUBERT(N)',
                           'LOG2(N)','LOGE(N)')(R(L1));
           PUT SKIP(0) EDIT('_','____','____', (7)'_',(9)'_',(7)'_',
                           (7)'_')(R(L1));
           /* THE TABLE */
           DO X=1E0 TO 5E1;
              PUT EDIT(X,X*X,X*X*X,SQRT(X),X**(1/3),LOG2(X),LOG(X))
                      (COL(3),F(2),COL(20),F(4),COL(36),F(6),COL(55),
                       F(8,6),COL(73),F(8,6),COL(90),F(8,6),COL(108),
                       F(8,6))SKIP;
           END;
L1:        FORMAT(COL(4),A,COL(21),A,COL(39),A,COL(55),A,COL(72),A,
                  COL(91),A,COL(109),A);
           END EX_1;
```

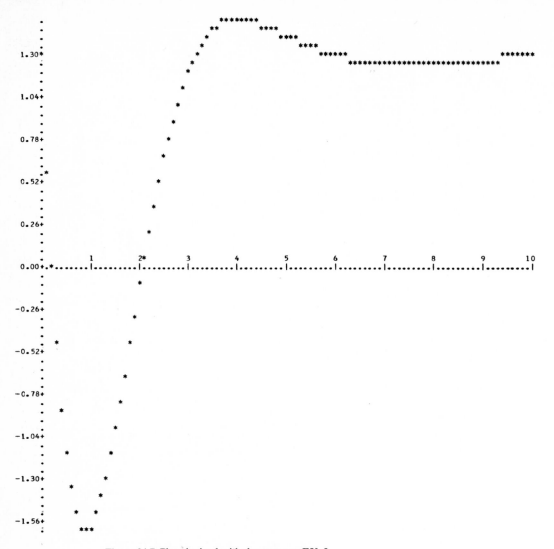

Figure 24.7 Plot obtained with the program EX_5.

The resulting output is shown in Fig. 24.8.

Example 24.7.2 Print out a 2×2 inch square in the center of the page.

Solution There are 6 lines per inch and 10 columns per inch. Thus the square will occupy 20 columns and 12 lines. Let us use I for the vertical lines and _ for the horizontal lines. If we center the square (the page has room for 66 lines and 132 columns), the horizontal lines must appear on lines 28 through 39. Hence the top horizontal line of the square must appear on line 27. But the first line of

TABLE OF FIRST 50 NUMBERS, THEIR SQUARES,CUBES,SQUARE ROOTS, CUBE ROOTS, BASE 2, AND NATURAL LOGARITHMS

N	N**2	N**3	SQRT(N)	CUBERT(N)	LOG2(N)	LOGE(N)
1	1	1	1.000000	1.000000	0.000000	0.000000
2	4	8	1.414213	1.259921	1.000000	0.693147
3	9	27	1.732051	1.442250	1.584962	1.098612
4	16	64	2.000000	1.587401	2.000000	1.386294
5	25	125	2.236068	1.709976	2.321929	1.609438
6	36	216	2.449490	1.817121	2.584963	1.791759
7	49	343	2.645751	1.912931	2.807355	1.945910
8	64	512	2.828427	2.000000	3.000000	2.079441
9	81	729	3.000000	2.080084	3.169926	2.197225
10	100	1000	3.162277	2.154435	3.321928	2.302585
11	121	1331	3.316625	2.223980	3.459432	2.397895
12	144	1728	3.464102	2.289428	3.584963	2.484906
13	169	2197	3.605552	2.351335	3.700440	2.564949
14	196	2744	3.741657	2.410142	3.807356	2.639057
15	225	3375	3.872983	2.466212	3.906891	2.708050
16	256	4096	4.000000	2.519842	4.000001	2.772589
17	289	4913	4.123106	2.571282	4.087463	2.833213
18	324	5832	4.242640	2.620741	4.169926	2.890371
19	361	6859	4.358899	2.668402	4.247929	2.944439
20	400	8000	4.472136	2.714418	4.321929	2.995732
21	441	9261	4.582576	2.758924	4.392319	3.044522
22	484	10648	4.690415	2.802039	4.459433	3.091043
23	529	12167	4.795832	2.843867	4.523563	3.135494
24	576	13824	4.898979	2.884499	4.584964	3.178054
25	625	15625	5.000000	2.924018	4.643858	3.218876
26	676	17576	5.099020	2.962496	4.700441	3.258097
27	729	19683	5.196153	3.000000	4.754889	3.295836
28	784	21952	5.291503	3.036589	4.807356	3.332204
29	841	24389	5.385165	3.072317	4.857982	3.367295
30	900	27000	5.477225	3.107233	4.906892	3.401197
31	961	29791	5.567764	3.141381	4.954197	3.433987
32	1024	32768	5.656855	3.174802	5.000000	3.465735
33	1089	35937	5.744563	3.207534	5.044395	3.496508
34	1156	39304	5.830952	3.239612	5.087464	3.526361
35	1225	42875	5.916080	3.271066	5.129285	3.555348
36	1296	46656	6.000000	3.301927	5.169927	3.583519
37	1369	50653	6.082763	3.332222	5.209455	3.610918
38	1444	54872	6.164414	3.361975	5.247929	3.637586
39	1521	59319	6.244998	3.391211	5.285404	3.663562
40	1600	64000	6.324555	3.419952	5.321929	3.688879
41	1681	68921	6.403124	3.448217	5.357553	3.713572
42	1764	74088	6.480741	3.476027	5.392318	3.737669
43	1849	79507	6.557439	3.503398	5.426267	3.761200
44	1936	85184	6.633249	3.530348	5.459433	3.784189
45	2025	91125	6.708204	3.556893	5.491855	3.806663
46	2116	97336	6.782330	3.583048	5.523563	3.828641
47	2209	103823	6.855655	3.608826	5.554590	3.850147
48	2304	110592	6.928204	3.634241	5.584964	3.871201
49	2401	117649	7.000000	3.659306	5.614711	3.891820
50	2500	125000	7.071068	3.684031	5.643857	3.912023

Figure 24.8 Table obtained with the program of Example 24.7.1.

print appears usually on line 4 of the page. Thus, if the top horizontal line is specified on line 24, it will actually be printed on line 27. With such a specification, the program reads

```
EX_2:    PROC OPTIONS(MAIN);
         PUT EDIT((18)'_')(LINE(24),COL(58),A);
         DO I = 1 TO 12;
             PUT EDIT('|','|')(LINE(24+I),COL(57),A,COL(76),A);
         END;
         PUT EDIT((18)'_')(LINE(36),COL(58),A);
         END EX_2;
```

The square is shown in Fig. 24.9. On the printout the square is centered as required.

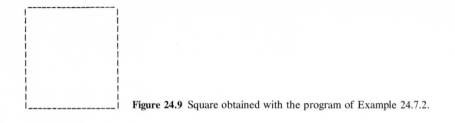

Figure 24.9 Square obtained with the program of Example 24.7.2.

24.8 SUMMARY

We described the edit-directed input and output. With the edit-directed input we can exercise complete control over the data card and read the data in specific columns of the card. With the edit-directed output we can print in specific columns of the page. The input and output options, discussed in Chap. 15 and 16, can also be used with edit-directed statements. As we illustrated, the edit-directed output is very useful for the printout of tables and plots.

PROBLEMS

24.1 Write statements to obtain five fixed-point numbers from each of 20 cards. The numbers are in columns 1–20 and are to be interpreted as (4,2), (7,1), (2,0), (3,1), (4,1). Print these numbers out, allowing at least two blanks of separation.

24.2 The data card contains

> 12345678912302

What values are assigned to A and B by the statement

> GET EDIT (A,B)(F(6,2,3),F(8,3,2));

24.3 Write a program to print out

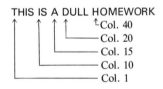

THIS IS A DULL HOMEWORK

24.4 Print out the square roots of the first 10 integers:
    (*a*) On the second line with three decimal places
    (*b*) On the sixth line in the float form X.XXE+YY

24.5 The first 20 data cards contain students' last names in columns 1–20. The following 20 data cards contain students' grades in column 2. Using the STRING option, associate the first name with the first grade, and so on, and print out the list of students and their grades. Provide your own input.

24.6 Write a program which will print out each of the elements of a 7×7 array of integers in a seven-column format. The elements of the array are formed as follows:
    1. The elements on the main diagonal (that is, a_{ii}, $i = 1,2, \ldots, 7$) are read in from data cards.
    2. The value of each off-diagonal element equals the sum of its subscripts, with a negative sign if the sum is odd. For example,

$$a_{42} = 6 \qquad \text{because } 2 + 4 = 6, \text{ even}$$
$$a_{43} = -7 \qquad \text{because } 4 + 3 = 7, \text{ odd}$$

24.7 Write a program to produce a table of values for x and t for the function

$$x = Ae^{-(Bt + C)} \sin(DT + E) + Ft + G$$

The program should

(a) Read in values for A,B,C,D,E,F, and G.

(b) Calculate x for $t = 0.0, 0.2, 0.4, \ldots, 9.8, 10.0, 10.5, 11.0, \ldots, 13$.

(c) Print out a table of x and t using the format

Col. 5 Col. 10   Col. 25 Col. 30

$X = \underbrace{\underbrace{nnnn}_{4}.\underbrace{nnn}_{3}}_{\text{Value}}$ $T = \underbrace{\underbrace{nn}_{2}.\underbrace{n}_{1}}_{\substack{\text{Value} \\ \text{of } t}}$

24.8 The data cards are filled with 40 character strings starting from column 1 of the first card. Each character string has no blanks and is at most 10 characters long. The data on cards are treated like a continuous stream, with column 80 being followed by column 1 of the next card. The character strings are separated by one blank.

The first 20 character strings are elements of a one-dimensional array. Similarly, the subsequent 20 character strings are the elements of a one-dimensional array. There are no quotes anywhere on the data cards.

Write a program to calculate and print out the elements of a new array of integers. The array element is 0 if the corresponding elements in the two arrays of characters are the same. The array element is 1 if the corresponding elements in the arrays of characters are reverses of one another (for example, such strings as PEN and NEP). The array element is 2 if the corresponding elements in the arrays of characters are neither the same nor reverses of one another.

24.9 Write a program with a subroutine which converts the last observed time into the correct time by adding the increase in time. The subroutine has four parameters:

NHOUR	the hours of the last observed time
NMIN	the minutes of the last observed time
IHOUR	the hours of the increase
IMIN	the minutes of the increase

The procedure should print

    THE LAST OBSERVED TIME WAS NHOUR:NMIN
    THE CORRECT TIME IS NN:MM

For example, the data

        NHOUR = 11
        NMIN   = 15
        IHOUR = 7
        IMIN   = 50

will give the output

    THE LAST OBSERVED TIME WAS 11:15
    THE CORRECT TIME IS 7:05

24.10 The data cards contain the elements of a one-dimensional array A. A has the bounds (0:N), and the value of N precedes the elements. Print out the polynomial

$$\overset{N}{A(N)X} + \overset{N-1}{A(N-1)X} + \ldots + A(1)X + A(0)$$

where the exponents are to be above the coefficients and X's and the values of A's are to be printed with three decimal places. It is known that $|A(K)|<1000$ for $0 \leqslant K \leqslant N$. For example, if N=2, the printout should have the form

$$\overset{2}{12.345X} - 163.483X + 0.835$$

24.11 The data cards contain a 6×8 array of positive integers. No integer exceeds 100. Print them out on six lines, with each line having eight integers.

24.12 Print out the array of Prob. 24.11 in the data-directed form.

24.13 The data cards contain the elements of three arrays. Each array is two-dimensional, has a lowbound of 1, and is preceded by two numbers giving its highbounds (for example, the elements of a 3×5 array are preceded by 3,5). No highbound exceeds 10. The last number is 20 and is to be used to terminate the execution. Print out each array properly titled. Display the elements in a suitable way (for example, a 3×8 array on three lines, with each line having eight numbers).

24.14 Print out a table listing

N	N**2	N**3	N**4	N**(1/2)	N**(1/3)	N**(1/4)
XX.X	XXXX.XX	X.XXXXE+YY	X.XXXXE+YY	X.XXXX	X.XXXX	X.XXXX

for N in the range 50.0 to 51.0 in steps of 0.1. Observe that N**3 and N**4 are to be printed in floating-point form, and the other values in fixed-point form as indicated. Your table should have a uniform spacing and be headed by the title

<u>TABLE</u> OF <u>POWERS</u> AND <u>ROOTS</u>

centered above your table.

24.15 Punch three cards giving your name, address, telephone number (with area code), department, standing, and section. Do this in the form as shown in the example below:

```
              Col. 1
               ↓
First card:   SMITH, JOHN A.
              Col. 1
               ↓
Second card: 1420 FOX AVENUE, BROOKLYN, N.Y. 11232
Third card:  212-643-2263 PHYSICS FRESHMAN SEC A
             ↑            ↑        ↑         ↑
             Col. 1       Col. 15  Col. 35   Col. 55
```

(*a*) Write a program which will print out a listing of all this information on a single line. Have a running number in the extreme left.

(*b*) The cards in the deck comprise several sections, each separated by a single blank card. Write a program to list each section on top of a new page, with its own running numbers.

24.16 Each data card contains a letter in column 1 and two positive numbers in columns 10–15 and 20–25. If the letter is S, print out

- - -First number- - -Second number- - -

If the letter is P, print out

```
    - -First number  - -
- -               - -
    - -Second number- -
```

(These are to portray series and parallel connections of electric elements.)

24.17 Print out the triangle shown in Fig. P24.17, where

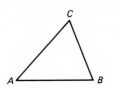

Figure P24.17

Figure P24.18

$$AB = 52$$
$$BC = 42$$
$$CA = 46$$

using a suitable scale.

24.18 (a) Plot the function

$$0.1x^2 - 4x + 50$$

for values of x from 0 to 50.

Your plot should portray the x axis vertically downward and the y axis horizontally, as shown in Fig. P24.18. Use the * or some other suitable symbol to identify the plot.

(b) Plot on a separate page the same plot as in (a) but list the values of y corresponding to each of the points plotted.

(c) Plot on a separate page the same plot as in (a) but show the x and y axes with suitable scales.

(d) Plot on a separate page the same plot as in (a) but display the x axis horizontally and the y axis vertically, that is, in the usual way.

24.19 Plot the functions

(a) $y = x \sin(1.3x)$ for $0 \leqslant x \leqslant 10$

(b) $y = (x + \sqrt{x}) \cos(1.6x + \sin 1.3x)$ for $0 \leqslant x \leqslant 10$

24.20 Plot the circle

$$(x-1)^2 + (y+2)^2 = 5^2$$

(a) Choose your scales to portray the entire circle on the major part of the page. Show the x and y axes and indicate the scales. Use the columns for the x scale and the lines for the y scale.

(b) Choose scales to make the circle symmetrical and plot it on a separate page.

25 RECORD-ORIENTED INPUT-OUTPUT

In the transmission of data from an input device (such as the card reader) to the computer storage and from the computer storage to an external device (such as the line printer), conversions of data take place. These conversions are needed because the numbers and characters as we like to see them are different from their internal representation in the computer.

For many applications a collection of data is for computer use only. In such a case if we modify the data we do not wish to accompany the modifications with the costly conversions. Record-oriented transmission, to be discussed here, allows such a conversion-free processing.

25.1 INTRODUCTION

A collection of data outside the computer is named a *data set*. Thus input is the transmission of data from a data set to a program. Similarly, output is the transmission of data from a program to a data set.

The data sets are stored on various external storage devices. The most common are punched cards, magnetic tape, and magnetic disks. Up to now we considered just punched cards as the input. We also described the stream-oriented transmission only, in which data are treated as a continuous stream of individual items. For data sets on magnetic tape and magnetic disks it is convenient to move a group of data rather than an individual item.

The transmission of a group of data is called *record-oriented* transmission. The portion of data transmitted as a unit is called a *block*. The block itself contains one or more logical subdivisions called *records*. A collection of related blocks is named a *file*.

Whenever we have problems involving extensive input-output operations, we should consider using record-oriented transmission. Such a transmission is more efficient than stream-oriented transmission because there are no time-consuming conversions. Record-oriented transmission requires the organization of data into files. The files require special handling, and there are special PL/I statements for files. We will describe the files next.

25.2 FILES

We have defined a file as a collection of related records. As an example of a file, consider the collection of subscribers to the XYZ magazine. The name of one subscriber is an *item,* the complete information on one subscriber is a *record,* and the collection of complete information on all subscribers is a *file*.

Before any processing can be undertaken, a file must be named and described. The file name is limited to seven characters and is described by a declaration. The declaration may include the files attributes, which tell of the files function. The attribute

STREAM   or   RECORD

tells how the data in the file are to be treated. STREAM is the transmission of a continuous stream of characters, while RECORD defines a transmission of a series of separate records, each consisting usually of many data items. The attribute

INPUT   or   OUTPUT

tells whether the file is to be read (INPUT) or is to hold the results of the program (OUTPUT). Examples of declarations include:

1. DCL PAYROLL FILE;
2. DCL CUSTMER FILE INPUT;
3. DCL (OVER50, UNDER50) FILE OUTPUT;
4. DCL LATE FILE RECORD,
       ONTIME FILE STREAM;
5. DCL INVNTRY FILE RECORD OUTPUT;
6. DCL TEMP RECORD OUTPUT;

Declaration 1 declares PAYROLL as a file name. Because the default attributes are STREAM and INPUT, the declaration is equivalent to

DCL PAYROLL FILE STREAM INPUT;

Declaration 2 defines CUSTMER as a stream input file. In declaration 3 both OVER50 and UNDER50 are stream output files. In declaration 4 LATE is a record input file and ONTIME a stream input file. In declaration 5 INVNTRY is a record output file. In declaration 6 the FILE attribute is omitted. This is legal, because the other attributes already define TEMP as a record output file.

Observe that a file corresponds to secondary storage. The association between the file name and the device providing the secondary storage (for example, tape) must also be specified on the job control cards (that is, JCL cards).

25.3 THE OPEN AND CLOSE STATEMENTS

Before a file can be used, the correct device associated with the file must be made available. The allocation is provided with the OPEN statement which "opens" the file for our use. This statement has the form

OPEN FILE (name) attributes;

as, for example,

```
OPEN FILE (LATE);
OPEN FILE (INVNTRY) OUTPUT;
OPEN FILE (PAYROLL) OUTPUT;
```

The OPEN statement opens *explicitly* a file. The GET LIST statement results in an *implicit* opening of the SYSIN (that is, SYStem INput, usually the card reader's contents) file. Similarly, the CLOSE statement

CLOSE FILE (PAYROLL);

closes *explicitly* the PAYROLL file. The result of the CLOSE statement is that if the file is reopened we will again read the file from the beginning.

If a file has been declared as an INPUT or an OUTPUT one, the OPEN statement must be consistent with the declaration. Thus it is illegal to have a declaration

DCL BALANCE FILE INPUT;

and the OPEN statement

OPEN FILE (BALANCE) OUTPUT;

If, however, the declaration has no INPUT or OUTPUT attribute, as in

DCL PAYROLL FILE;

it is legal to open this file as either INPUT or OUTPUT, that is, as either

OPEN FILE (PAYROLL) INPUT;

or

OPEN FILE (PAYROLL) OUTPUT;

In fact, with the CLOSE statement, the file can be alternatively INPUT or OUTPUT, as in

```
DCL PAYROLL FILE;
OPEN FILE (PAYROLL) INPUT;
CLOSE FILE (PAYROLL);
OPEN FILE (PAYROLL) OUTPUT;
```

25.4 THE READ AND WRITE STATEMENTS

The input statement for records has the form

READ FILE (*file name*) INTO (*variable name*);

as, for example,

READ FILE (PAYROLL) INTO (CASH);

where CASH is either a scalar variable, an array, or a structure.

The READ statement causes a single record to be moved into the location assigned to CASH, that is, from the file to the internal memory used by the program. The READ statement can be used with any input file.

The output statement for records has the form

WRITE FILE (*file name*) FROM (*variable name*);

as, for example,

WRITE FILE (BANK1) FROM (DEPOSIT);

where DEPOSIT is again either a scalar variable, an array, or a structure.

The WRITE statement moves the record from the internal memory to the file. This statement can be used with any output file.

25.5 SEQUENTIAL AND DIRECT FILES

There are two types of files: sequential and direct access.

In a sequential file, records are placed in an ordered sequence. To reach a certain record, we must start at the beginning and traverse all records up to the desired one. A magnetic tape results in a sequential file. To reach the center of the tape, we must start at the beginning and move the tape to the desired position. There is no way of accessing the center of the tape directly.

In a direct-access file, records can be reached directly. A magnetic disk may be used as a direct-access file. An area of such a disk can be reached directly without passing through preceding records.

A sequential file is useful for tasks such as calculating a payroll. The payroll is calculated in alphabetical order, which corresponds to sequential processing. A direct-access file is useful for accessing the file in an arbitrary manner. To obtain information on a publication in a library we do not wish go through all the records. We would rather reference the publication by some keyword. In fact, in every direct-access file the location of a desired record is specified by a character string. This string is called a *key,* and the direct-access file has a KEYED attribute.

If the type of access is not specified, the file is sequential by default. Hence

DCL PAYROLL RECORD OUTPUT;

and

DCL PAYROLL RECORD OUTPUT SEQUENTIAL;

are equivalent. The attribute SEQUENTIAL can be abbreviated to SEQL.

To declare the file LIBRARY as a direct-access one, we write

DCL LIBRARY RECORD DIRECT;

The INPUT, the OUTPUT, and the KEYED attributes may also be included in the declaration, as in

DCL LIBRARY RECORD DIRECT KEYED OUTPUT;

The KEY identifies a specific record. It can be used in the READ statement, as, for example,

READ FILE (LIBRARY) INTO (CARD) KEY (LIBKEY);

which requests that the record identified by LIBKEY be assigned to the variable CARD.

The WRITE statement for direct-access files uses the KEYFROM attribute, as in

WRITE FILE (LIBRARY) FROM (CARD) KEYFROM (LIBKEY);

which requests that the value of CARD be written in the file LIBRARY, with the value of LIBKEY being the key.

25.6 THE ENVIRONMENT ATTRIBUTE

The ENVIRONMENT attribute tells about the length of a record in the file and which type of input or output equipment is to be used for the file. It also tells how the file is organized. We will describe here the *regional* organization.

In REGIONAL(1) organization, the file consists of *regions*. Each region contains a single record, accompanied by the *region number*.

In REGIONAL(2) organization, a key is stored with each record. The key is a character string of at most 255 characters.

In REGIONAL(3) organization, a region may contain more than one record but is otherwise similar to REGIONAL(2) organization.

The ENVIRONMENT attribute may be abbreviated to ENV. As an illustration, the declaration

DCL PAYROLL RECORD DIRECT ENV (REGIONAL(1));

defines PAYROLL as a direct-access file in a REGIONAL(1) organization.

The details of this and other file organizations are beyond the scope of this book. The regional organization provides a means minimizing the access time to a device. For further discussion of this topic the reader is referred to the IBM literature.[1]

25.7 THE UPDATE ATTRIBUTE AND THE REWRITE STATEMENT

The UPDATE attribute is used for a file whose items are to be changed (that is, updated). This attribute allows the insertion and deletion of records in a file. An UPDATE file is first declared with

DCL name FILE UPDATE;

Such a file can be used for both input and output.

The REWRITE statement is used to replace a record in an update file. For sequential files, the last record read from the file is rewritten. For direct-access files, any record can be rewritten. For the sequential file SEQ, the statement

REWRITE FILE (SEQ) FROM (TEMP);

writes the contents of TEMP into the same location where the last READ statement read the data from the file SEQ. Thus a record must be read before it can be rewritten. For example, the statements

```
DCL FILE (PAYROLL) UPDATE;
READ FILE (PAYROLL) INTO (OLD);
REWRITE FILE (PAYROLL) FROM (NEW);
```

illustrate the updating of the sequential file PAYROLL.

To update a direct-access file we write

REWRITE FILE (name) FROM (variable) KEY (expression);

as, for example

REWRITE FILE (LIBRARY) FROM (CARD) KEY (LIBKEY);

The rewriting does not require prior reading, just the declaration. To illustrate this pair of statements, consider

```
DCL LIBRARY FILE UPDATE RECORD DIRECT ENV (REGIONAL(1));
REWRITE FILE (LIBRARY) FROM (CARD) KEY (LIBKEY);
```

where the declaration opens the file LIBRARY as an UPDATE file, and the REWRITE statement performs the desired replacement of a record.

---

[1]IBM System/360 Operating System PL/I(F) "Language Reference Manual," IBM Systems Reference Library, order no. GC28-8201, pp. 125–142; and IBM System/360 Operating System PL/I(F) "Programmers Guide," IBM Systems Reference Library, order no. GC28-6594, pp. 124–149.

25.8 EXAMPLES

Example 25.8.1 Load 20 cards into a sequential file named PAYROLL. After loading, open the file for update and change the contents of the tenth card by replacing SMITH, which is in columns 1–5, with SMYTHE. Print out the new file.

Solution The program is named EX1 and is shown below together with its output. Observe the following:

1. PAYROLL is declared as RECORD. Hence this file can be opened as either INPUT, OUTPUT, or UPDATE.
2. We write the card data into the file PAYROLL. We close the file, so when we reopen, we start at the beginning.
3. The tenth card (containing the name SMITH) is in TEMP after the second DO loop. Hence we change SMITH to SMYTHE as desired and rewrite this record into file.
4. We close the file in order to reopen at the beginning.
5. We print the contents of the file, and as the printout shows the desired change has been made.

```
EX1: PROC OPTIONS(MAIN);
     DCL TEMP CHAR(80),
         PAYROLL RECORD;
     OPEN FILE(PAYROLL) OUTPUT;
     DO I=1 TO 20;
         GET EDIT(TEMP)(A(80))COPY;
         WRITE FILE(PAYROLL) FROM (TEMP);
     END;
     CLOSE FILE(PAYROLL);
     OPEN FILE(PAYROLL) UPDATE;
     DO I=1 TO 10;
         READ FILE(PAYROLL) INTO (TEMP);
     END;
     SUBSTR(TEMP,1,6) = 'SMYTHE';
     REWRITE FILE(PAYROLL) FROM (TEMP);
     CLOSE FILE(PAYROLL);
     OPEN FILE(PAYROLL) INPUT;
     PUT EDIT('NEW FILE',(8)'_')(SKIP(2),A,SKIP(0),A);
     DO I=1 TO 20;
         READ FILE(PAYROLL) INTO (TEMP);
         PUT EDIT(TEMP)(COL(1),A);
     END;
     END EX1;
```

```
COOK              1001
ABLE              1003
FOX               1005
MORGAN            1007
```

GAUSS	1009
EULER	1011
JONES	1013
JOHNS	1015
STAR	1017
SMITH	1019
SUR	1002
SOR	1004
WONG	1006
WOLF	1008
JUNG	1010
NYE	1012
NEW	1014
OLD	1016
DOL	1018
LOD	1020

NEW_FILE

COOK	1001
ABLE	1003
FOX	1005
MORGAN	1007
GAUSS	1009
EULER	1011
JONES	1013
JOHNS	1015
STAR	1017
SMYTHE	1019
SUR	1002
SOR	1004
WONG	1006
WOLF	1008
JUNG	1010
NYE	1012
NEW	1014
OLD	1016
DOL	1018
LOD	1020

Example 25.8.2 Redo Example 25.8.1 but now PAYROLL is a direct-access file. Each record is identified by a three-digit number named PAY_NO, which is punched in columns 41–43 of each of the first 20 cards. Change the record identified by the PAY_NO on the twenty-first card by replacing 'SMITH' by 'SMYTHE' as previously. Print out all records identified by the numbers 101–120.

Solution The program is named EX2 and is shown below together with its output. Incidentally, the twenty-first card contains '119', as it must. Observe the following:

1. PAYROLL is declared as DIRECT RECORD organized in ENV (REGIONAL(1)) manner.
2. Since the records are accessed directly, there is no need to open or close files.
3. Note that the printout lists records in order of keys 101 to 120 even though the records were not written in such order.

```
EX2: PROC OPTIONS(MAIN);
     DCL TEMP CHAR(80), PAY_NO CHAR(3),
         PAYROLL RECORD DIRECT ENV(REGIONAL(1));
     DO I=1 TO 20;
         GET EDIT(TEMP)(A(80))COPY;
         PAY_NO = SUBSTR(TEMP,41,3);
         WRITE FILE(PAYROLL) FROM (TEMP) KEYFROM(PAY_NO);
     END;
     GET LIST(PAY_NO);
     READ FILE(PAYROLL) INTO(TEMP) KEY(PAY_NO);
     SUBSTR(TEMP,1,6) = 'SMYTHE';
     REWRITE FILE(PAYROLL) FROM (TEMP) KEY(PAY_NO);
     PUT EDIT('NEW FILE',(8)'_')(SKIP(2),A,SKIP(0),A);
     DO I=101 TO 120;
         READ FILE(PAYROLL) INTO(TEMP) KEY(I);
         PUT EDIT(TEMP)(COL(1),A);
     END;
     END EX2;
```

```
COOK                                    101
ABLE                                    103
FOX                                     105
MORGAN                                  107
GAUSS                                   109
EULER                                   111
JONES                                   113
JOHNS                                   115
STAR                                    117
SMITH                                   119
SUR                                     102
SOR                                     104
WONG                                    106
WOLF                                    108
WONG                                    110
NYE                                     112
NEW                                     114
OLD                                     116
DOL                                     118
LOD                                     120


NEW_FILE
COOK                                    101
SUR                                     102
```

ABLE	103
SOR	104
FOX	105
WONG	106
MORGAN	107
WOLF	108
GAUSS	109
WONG	110
EULER	111
NYE	112
JONES	113
NEW	114
JOHNS	115
OLD	116
STAR	117
DOL	118
SMYTHE	119
LOD	120

25.9 SUMMARY

We described the record-oriented transmission, which is useful for transferring large blocks of data from a secondary storage (for example, tape) to the computer, and vice versa. We described the READ and WRITE statements, which are the counterparts of the GET and PUT. We also described the sequential and direct-access files and gave examples of their use.

PROBLEMS

25.1 Write declarations defining the file CHECKS as a
(*a*) Stream output file
(*b*) Record output file
(*c*) File which can be either input or output

25.2 Write declarations and the OPEN and CLOSE statements for the file CHECKS which is to be used
(*a*) As an input file
(*b*) As an output file
(*c*) First as an output file and then as an input file

25.3 Write statements to
(*a*) Define the file BANK as sequential
(*b*) Define the file CUSTMER as direct
(*c*) Assign the record identified by the key NUMBER in the direct file CUSTMER to the variable INVOICE
(*d*) Write in the file CUSTMER the value of the variable INVOICE with the key being the value of NUMBER

25.4 Write statements to
(*a*) Declare the file SUBS as an update file
(*b*) Replace the presently available record of the sequential file SUBS with the contents of the variable NEW

(*c*) Declare the file SUBS2 as a direct-access update file having REGIONAL(2) organization

(*d*) Replace the record in the file SUBS2 identified by the key NUMBER with the contents of the variable NEW2.

25.5 Load the 20 names with the numbers of Example 25.8.1 into a sequential file named PAYROLL.

(*a*) Create and print out a new file PAY1, with all names in alphabetical order

(*b*) Create and print out a new file PAY2, with all numbers in ascending order

(*c*) Create a new file from PAY1, with salaries in columns 30–40 being 200 for EULER and GAUSS, 250 for MORGAN, and 300 for everyone else. Name this file PAY3.

(*d*) Increase the salary of MORGAN to 300, leave the salaries of JUNG and STAR unchanged, and increase everyone else's salary by 10 percent in the PAY3 file. Print the PAY3 file after these changes.

25.6 Load the 20 names with the numbers of Example 25.8.2 into a direct-access file named PAYROLL.

(*a*) Print out this file in the descending order of the numbers.

(*b*) Create a new direct-access file named PAY_A, with all names in alphabetical order.

(*c*) Create a new direct-access file named PAY_B, with names in alphabetical order and all numbers consecutive from 101 to 120 with the alphabetical names (for example, ABLE is 101).

(*d*) Create a new direct-access file named PAY_C from PAY_B, with salaries in columns 30–40 being 200 for EULER and GAUSS, 250 for MORGAN, and 300 for everyone else. Name this file PAY_D.

(*e*) Increase the salary of MORGAN to 300, leave the salaries of JUNG and STAR unchanged, and increase everyone else's salary by 10 percent in the PAY_D file. Print the PAY_D file.

PROGRAM INTERRUPTS

In Sec. 15.1 we described what happens when we have a GET LIST statement but no data. We said that such lack of data is named the ENDFILE condition and results in the termination of the program.

We will now tell in more detail how the computer handles the ENDFILE condition. We will then describe other exceptional conditions and the resulting computer actions. We will also tell how we can change these computer actions to others more to our liking.

26.1 THE FINISH, ERROR, AND ENDFILE CONDITIONS

The operations of a computer are supervised by a program named the *operating system*. This program includes the PL/I compiler, as well as compilers for other computer languages. It provides the services that are needed in executing programming jobs and various management functions, such as billing for the use of computer time. It also monitors the current programming job and, if necessary, interrupts its execution. If an interrupt occurs, the operating system takes over, and what it does depends upon the cause of the interrupt, as we will see presently.

A The FINISH Condition

When the programming job is finished, as, for example, through an execution of an END or a STOP statement, the operating system interrupts the program execution. In computer jargon we say that the FINISH *condition* is "raised" (that is, has occurred). As a result of this condition the operating system terminates the programming job.

B The ERROR Condition

When there is an error in the programming job (as, for example, in a statement such as A = 2 + 'HI';), an interrupt takes place. Now we say that the ERROR condition is raised. This results in two steps:

1. The printing of a message telling us about the error
2. The raising of the FINISH condition (which terminates the job)

C The ENDFILE Condition

In Sec. 15.1 we considered the statement

GET LIST (A);

with no data for the variable A. Again, the execution of the program is interrupted, and we say that the ENDFILE condition is raised. This results in two steps:

1. The printing of a message telling us that the ENDFILE condition has occurred
2. The raising of the ERROR condition (which in turn causes the printout of an error message and program termination)

Note how the raising of one condition (such as ENDFILE) causes the subsequent raising of the ERROR and FINISH conditions, each of which has a specific task.

As an illustration consider the program

```
TEST1: PROC OPTIONS(MAIN);
       GET LIST(A,B);
       END TEST1;
```

with the data card containing just one number. The result of the program is the message

IHE140I FILE SYSIN — END OF FILE ENCOUNTERED IN STATEMENT 00002 AT OFFSET +0006A FROM ENTRY POINT TEST1

Diagnostic
message
code[1]

26.2 ENABLED AND DISABLED CONDITIONS

We just described three conditions to which the operating system responds. The resulting interruption in program execution required nothing on our part—the operating system acted on its own. When such an interrupt occurs, without any requests from us to do so, we say that the condition which caused the interrupt is "enabled." Thus the conditions FINISH, ERROR, and ENDFILE are *enabled* conditions.

[1]A listing and explanation of all diagnostic messages is to be found in IBM System/360 Operating System PL/I (F) "Programmer's Guide," IBM Systems Reference Library, order no. GC28-6594, app. K.

Some conditions are always enabled, while some other conditions can be *disabled*. We will tell how to do such a disabling. There are still other conditions which are disabled but can be enabled through appropriate instructions.

We will first describe the enabled conditions which can be disabled.

A Enabled Conditions Which Can Be Disabled

The conditions

> CONVERSION
> FIXEDOVERFLOW
> OVERFLOW
> UNDERFLOW
> ZERODIVIDE

are enabled. We will first explain when these conditions occur, and the resulting action by the operating system.

A.1 The CONVERSION condition. The CONVERSION condition results (that is, is raised) whenever the program or data calls for an illegal conversion of a character string.

For example, the last statement in the program segment

> DCL X CHAR(3);
> X = 'CAT';
> B = 1;
> A = B+X;

will raise the CONVERSION condition. As a second example, the statements

> DCL (A,B) FLOAT;
> GET LIST (A,B);

with the data card

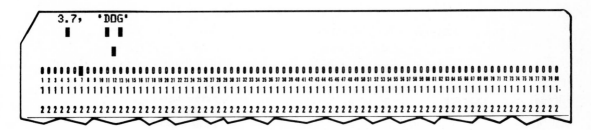

will raise the CONVERSION condition. In both cases the compiler attempts to convert character strings to numbers and finds such a conversion to be illegal.

When the CONVERSION condition occurs, the result is undefined. The value of A in A = B + X; in the first example and the value of B in GET LIST (A,B); in the second example are undefined. The system action causes the printing of a message and the raising of the ERROR condition.

A.2 The FIXEDOVERFLOW condition. The FIXEDOVERFLOW condition occurs when the result of arithmetic operations, performed on fixed-point numbers, exceeds the maximum allowable number of digits. For System/360 or System/370 the maxima are 15 digits for FIXED DECIMAL numbers and 31 for FIXED BINARY numbers. As an example, consider the program

```
TEST2: PROC OPTIONS(MAIN);
       DCL(I,J,K) FIXED BIN(31);
       I,J = 1E6;
       K = I*J;
       END TEST2;
```

To express 10^6 in binary form requires 20 binary digits. Hence I*J requires more than 31 digits, and the FIXEDOVERFLOW condition will be raised during the computation of I*J.

When the FIXEDOVERFLOW condition is raised, the result is undefined. Thus, in the above example, the value of I*J is undefined. The system action causes the printing of a message and the raising of the ERROR condition. In fact, the output of this program is

IHE320I FIXEDOVERFLOW IN STATEMENT 00004 AT OFFSET +00060 FROM ENTRY POINT TEST2

A.3 The OVERFLOW condition. Recall that the exponent of a floating-point number cannot exceed 75 (see Sec. 4.5). If the result of a calculation calls for a larger exponent, the OVERFLOW condition is raised. For example, in the program segment

$$A,B = 1E40;$$
$$C = A*B;$$

the calculation of A*B raises the OVERFLOW condition.

When the OVERFLOW condition occurs, the result is undefined. Thus, in the above example, the value of A*B is undefined. As before, the system causes the printing of a message and the raising of the ERROR condition. In fact, the output is

IHE300I OVERFLOW IN STATEMENT 00003 AT OFFSET +0005C FROM ENTRY POINT EXAMPLE

A.4 The UNDERFLOW condition. The just-described OVERFLOW condition is raised when the exponent of a floating-point number is too large. Similarly, the UNDERFLOW condition occurs when the exponent of a floating-point number is too small. Recall that such an exponent cannot be smaller than -78 (see Sec. 4.5). If the result of a calculation demands an exponent smaller than -78, the UNDERFLOW condition is raised. For example, in

$$A,B = 1E{-}40;$$
$$C = A*B;$$

the UNDERFLOW condition is raised in the calculation of $A*B$.

When the UNDERFLOW condition occurs, the result is set to zero. In the example, $A*B$ is replaced by zero. The system causes the printing of a message and returns to the program, proceeding with its execution. For example, in

```
TEST3: PROC OPTIONS(MAIN);
       A,B = 1E-40;
       D = 2*A + A*B;
       PUT DATA(D);
       END TEST3;
```

the calculation of $A*B$ will raise the UNDERFLOW condition. $A*B$ is replaced by zero, and the program execution continues with

$$D = 2*A + 0;$$

Thus assigning the value $2E{-}40$ to D. The resulting printout consists of a message that UNDERFLOW has occurred, and the value of D. In fact, the actual output is

```
IHE340I UNDERFLOW IN STATEMENT 00003 AT OFFSET +00064 FROM ENTRY POINT TEST3
D= 1.99999E-40;
```

A.5 The ZERODIVIDE condition. The ZERODIVIDE condition occurs whenever an attempt is made to divide by zero. For example, in

$$A = 0;$$
$$B = 1;$$
$$C = B/A;$$

the ZERODIVIDE condition is raised in the calculation of B/A.

When the ZERODIVIDE occurs, the result is undefined; thus, in the above example B/A is undefined. The system causes the printing of a message and the raising of the ERROR condition.

In summary, in the four conditions

CONVERSION, FIXEDOVERFLOW, OVERFLOW, ZERODIVIDE

the result of the operation that gave rise to the condition is undefined. The system prints a message and raises the ERROR condition (which raises the FINISH condition, thus stopping the program execution). If the UNDERFLOW condition occurs, zero is substituted for the small number (that is, for the number with an exponent smaller than -78), and the program execution continues. Note further that OVERFLOW and UNDERFLOW occur in the operations on floating-point numbers, while FIXEDOVERFLOW occurs in the operations on fixed-point numbers.

B Disabling of Conditions

To disable a condition, say, the OVERFLOW condition, we must precede the statement to which the disabling is to apply by

(NOOVERFLOW):

In general, we prefix the statement by the word NO followed by the name of the condition. Note that there are no spaces between NO and the condition name. Also note that the prefix is enclosed in parentheses and followed by a colon. In fact, the above disabling is known in computer jargon as disabling through a *condition prefix*. Let us now illustrate the results of the disabling of the conditions.

In the program segment

```
                    DCL (A,B) FLOAT, X CHAR(3);
                    A = 1E0;
                    X = 'CAT;
(NOCONVERSION):     B = A + X;
                    PUT DATA (B);
```

no CONVERSION condition is raised, since it is disabled. Consequently, a meaningless number is assigned to B, and the program continues its execution without interruption and without a diagnostic message. Similarly, in

```
                        DCL(I,J,K) FIXED BIN (31);
                        I, J = 1E6;
(NOFIXEDOVERFLOW):      K = I*J;
                        A,B = 1E40;
(NOOVERFLOW):           C = A*B;
                        D,E = 1E−40;
(NOUNDERFLOW):          F = D*E;
                        G = 0;
(NOZERODIVIDE):         H = A/G;
                        PUT DATA (K,C,F,H);
```

there is no interruption in program execution, no diagnostic messages, and meaningless numbers are assigned to K, C, and H. Zero is assigned to F, as with no disabling of the UNDERFLOW condition.

C Enabled Conditions That Cannot Be Disabled

The conditions

ENDFILE
ERROR
FINISH

are always enabled and cannot be disabled through a condition prefix.

D Disabled Conditions That Can Be Enabled

The conditions

SIZE
STRINGRANGE
SUBSCRIPTRANGE

are disabled. We will explain and illustrate these three conditions.

D.1 The SIZE condition. The SIZE condition occurs whenever there is a loss of most significant digits caused by an insufficient size specification for the number. We gave an example of the SIZE condition in Sec. 24.3A.1 (subsection b.2). A further illustration is

```
TEST4: PROC OPTIONS(MAIN);
       DCL (A,B) FIXED(5,2);
       A = 123.45;
       B = 10*A;
       PUT DATA(B);
       END TEST4;
```

Here we calculate 10*A as 1234.5 and assign it to B. But B is specified as having the precision (5,2), which is an insufficient size for the value of B. Consequently, the most significant digit (that is, the leftmost digit) is lost and just 234.50 is assigned to B, giving the printout

```
B=   234.50;
```

D.2 The STRINGRANGE condition. Recall that the SUBSTR built-in function has the form

SUBSTR ($String, I, L$)

where I = place of starting character of the substring
L = number of characters in the substring
    Clearly, if the original string has K characters, then for correct formation of the SUBSTR function the following inequalities must be satisfied:

$$1 \leqslant I \leqslant K$$
$$0 \leqslant L \leqslant K - I + 1$$

As an illustration of these two inequalities, consider the statements

DCL (X,Y) CHAR(8) VAR;
X = 'ELEPHANT';

Then in

Y = SUBSTR (X, I, L);

I must be a number between 1 and 8 and L a number between 0 (which gives the null string) and $8 - I + 1$. If these inequalities are not satisfied, as in

$$Y = \text{SUBSTR (X,9,2)};$$
or
$$Y = \text{SUBSTR (X,1,15)};$$
or
$$Y = \text{SUBSTR (X,}-3,-2);$$

the STRINGRANGE condition occurs, meaning that the specifications are outside the range of the string. In such a case the compiler calculates new values of I and L that are within the range, following certain formulas[1] (for $I > K$, the return is the null string). Usually we do not obtain what we want, and the result is in error.

D.3 The SUBSCRIPTRANGE condition. The SUBSCRIPTRANGE condition occurs if the subscripts of an array do not lie within the specified range. For example, if the subscripts of the array TABLE are specified by

$$\text{DCL TABLE }(-2:5,4:7);$$

and if

$$I = 3;$$

then either of these statements

$$\text{TABLE }(-4,5) = 7;$$
$$\text{TABLE }(4,2) = 4;$$
$$\text{TABLE }(1,5) = 2*\text{TABLE }(3,9);$$
$$\text{TABLE }(-3,2) = 5;$$
$$\text{TABLE }(2*I,I+5) = 0;$$

raises the SUBSCRIPTRANGE condition, because the subscripts do not conform to the declared range. Note that in the last two examples, both subscripts are outside the allowable range. Here the SUBSCRIPTRANGE condition is raised twice, first when the first subscript is found to be outside the range and then again when the second subscript is checked.

The array elements with the illegal subscripts are generally undefined. Since the SUBSCRIPTRANGE condition is disabled, the program execution continues after its occurrence, and the effect is just that the illegal elements are undefined.

In summary, the three conditions

$$\text{SIZE, STRINGRANGE, SUBSCRIPTRANGE}$$

give rise to undefined results. Because program execution continues, there can be errors in the output of the program. We can avoid such errors by enabling these conditions.

---

[1]These are described in IBM System/360 Operating System PL/I (F) "Language Reference Manual," IBM Systems Reference Library, order no. GC28-8201, p. 319.

E Enabling of Conditions

To enable a condition, say, the SIZE condition, we must precede the statement to which the enabling is to apply by

(SIZE):

Thus the enabling is done by a condition prefix. Through enabling, we are made aware that the SIZE condition has occurred, because the system prints a message and raises the ERROR condition. For example, in

```
TEST5:   PROC OPTIONS(MAIN);
         DCL (A,B) FIXED(5,2);
         A = 123.45;
(SIZE):  B = 10*A;
         PUT DATA(B);
         END TEST5;
```

the output is

```
IHE310I SIZE IN STATEMENT 00004 AT OFFSET +0007A FROM ENTRY POINT TEST5
```

thus telling us that the SIZE condition has occurred.

If we enable the STRINGRANGE condition, the system prints a message and continues with the execution. For example, the program

```
TEST6:  PROC OPTIONS(MAIN);
        DCL (X,Y) CHAR(8) VAR;
        X = 'ELEPHANT';
        I = 3;
(STRINGRANGE):
        Y = SUBSTR(X,3*I,I+4);
        PUT DATA(Y);
        END TEST6;
```

yields the output

```
IHE350I STRINGRANGE IN STATEMENT 00005 AT OFFSET +000DA FROM ENTRY POINT TEST6
Y='';
```

Note that the second argument evaluates as 9 and there are only eight characters in the string. Hence the return from the SUBSTR function is the null string (see Sec. 26.2D.2). If we enable the SUBSCRIPTRANGE condition, the system prints a message and raises the ERROR condition. For example, the program

```
TEST7:  PROC OPTIONS(MAIN);
        DCL TABLE(-2:5,4:7);
(SUBSCRIPTRANGE):
        TABLE(-4,5) = 3;
        PUT LIST(TABLE(-4,5));
        END TEST7;
```

gives the printout

```
IHE500I SUBSCRIPTRANGE IN STATEMENT 00003 AT OFFSET +00082 FROM ENTRY POINT TEST7
```

26.3 CONDITION PREFIXES

We just described the condition prefixes for enabling or disabling of conditions. There is a little more that we can say about their use.

A Multiple Prefixes

It is possible to have several condition prefixes attached to a single statement, as in

$$\text{(SIZE): (NOOVERFLOW): A = 7*B;}$$

The order of these prefixes is of no consequence. Thus this statement is equivalent to

$$\text{(NOOVERFLOW): (SIZE): A = 7*B;}$$

Alternately, several condition prefixes can be listed within a single pair of parentheses, as in

$$\text{(SIZE, NOOVERFLOW): A = 7*B;}$$

which is equivalent to the previous statement.

B Prefixes and Labels

If the condition prefix is applied to a statement with a label, the condition prefix must be written first. The label must be adjacent to the statement itself, as, for example,

$$\text{(NOCONVERSION, STRINGRANGE):(NOZERODIVIDE):JOE: A = B/A;}$$

C Abbreviations

The following abbreviations apply:

CONV	for CONVERSION
FOFL	for FIXEDOVERFLOW
OFL	for OVERFLOW
UFL	for UNDERFLOW
ZDIV	for ZERODIVIDE
STRG	for STRINGRANGE
SUBRG	for SUBSCRIPTRANGE

The statement above can, for example, be written more conveniently as

$$\text{(NOCONV, STRG):(NOZDIV):JOE: A = B/A;}$$

26.4 THE ON STATEMENT

A The On-Unit

Up to now we described how to enable or disable a condition. It is possible to do more—we can specify what is to take place when a condition occurs. This is done with the so-called "ON statement" which has the form

ON *condition statement1;*

as, for example,

ON ZERODIVIDE Y = X + 1;

In PL/I jargon the *statement1*, following the *condition*, is named an *on-unit*. This tells what we want the computer to do when the condition occurs. Unlike a condition prefix which applies to a single statement only, the ON statement applies to the program following the ON statement. The ON statement is like a procedure —it is bypassed and entered only when the condition occurs. It is then that the on-unit action replaces the standard interrupt action.

As an example of the on-unit, consider the program

```
TEST8: PROC OPTIONS(MAIN );
       N = 1;
       ON ZDIV N=3;
       M = 5/(N-1);
       PUT DATA(N);
       END TEST8;
```

The ON statement establishes an on-unit (that is, the programmer specified action) for the ZERODIVIDE condition. When the condition occurs in the $M = 5/(N-1)$; statement, the on-unit sets N to 3 and the program execution returns to the point immediately following the interrupt, thus to the PUT DATA(N); statement, giving the output

```
N=         3;
```

As a second example, consider the program

```
TEST9: PROC OPTIONS(MAIN);
       N = 1;
       ON ZDIV N=N+1;
       M = 2/(N-1) + 3/(N-2);
       PUT DATA(N);
       END TEST9;
```

where the following take place:

1. The calculation of $2/(N-1)$ raises the ZDIV condition. Consequently $N = N + 1$ is executed and N is set to 2.

2. The program execution continues from the point immediately following the interrupt. Now $3/(N-2)$ is calculated, which raises again the ZDIV condition.
3. Again $N = N + 1$ is executed and N is set to 3. The execution continues now with the PUT DATA (N); statement, yielding

```
N=          3;
```

as output.

The on-unit in the above examples was an assignment statement. In general it can be either any simple statement or a BEGIN block. It cannot be another ON statement, or an IF statement, or a DO group; that is, it cannot be a compound statement. It also cannot be an END statement or a DECLARE statement. As a further restriction, the on-unit cannot be labeled. Examples of ON statements are

```
ON OFL GO TO LOOP1;
ON CONV STRING = 'DOG';
ON STRG BEGIN;
          X=Y;
          Y=Y+2;
     END;
ON ENDFILE (SYSIN) PUT DATA (A,B);
ON UFL GET LIST (NAME, GRADE);
```

A question can be asked: After the termination of the on-unit, to which point of the program do we return? We will answer this question next.

In the previous example, with the ON statement for the ZDIV condition, upon the termination of the on-unit (that is, after the execution of $N=N+1$;) the control returned to the point immediately following the interrupt. The same is true for the conditions

```
FIXEDOVERFLOW
OVERFLOW
UNDERFLOW
SIZE
SUBSCRIPTRANGE
```

that is, the control is returned to the point immediately following the interrupt. Incidentally, because the SIZE (or the SUBSCRIPTRANGE) condition is normally disabled, it must be first enabled before an on-unit is effective, as, for example,

```
TEST10:  PROC OPTIONS(MAIN);
         DCL N FIXED(3,0);
         ON SIZE I=I-1;
         M,N = 2;
         DO I=2 BY 1;
(SIZE):     N = N**I;
            IF M>I THEN STOP;
            M = I + 1;
            PUT SKIP LIST(N);
         END;
         END TEST10;
```

Here N is first calculated as 2^2, or 4. M is set to 3 and we print out N. Next we calculate N as 4^3, or 64. M is set to 4 and again we print out N. When we calculate N as 64^4, the SIZE condition is raised and I is set to 3. We execute next the statement immediately following the interrupt, that is,

$$\text{IF M} > \text{I THEN STOP;}$$

and because M is 4 and I is 3, the program execution stops. Hence the output is

```
4
64
```

If there is an on-unit for the CONVERSION condition, then after the execution of the on-unit the control returns to the beginning of the string (which caused the CONVERSION condition), and the conversion is tried again. It is assumed that the on-unit fixed the cause of the condition.

To correct the CONVERSION condition we use the ONCHAR or the ONSOURCE built-in functions. The ONCHAR function returns the single character that caused the CONVERSION condition. The ONSOURCE function returns the contents of the entire field that caused the CONVERSION condition. To illustrate the use of the ONCHAR function consider the following example:

```
TEST11: PROC OPTIONS(MAIN);
        DCL C CHAR(3);
        C = '1A3';
        ON CONV ONCHAR ='2';
        N = C;
        PUT DATA(N);
        END TEST11;
```

The statement N = C; raises the CONVERSION condition. The condition is raised in the conversion of the second character, that is, in conversion of A to the number needed for C. The ON CONV statement uses the ONCHAR built-in function as a pseudovariable and replaces the character A by 2. We return to the N = C; statement and now convert '123' to 123, giving the output

```
N=       123;
```

As an example of the use of the ONSOURCE function consider the program

```
TEST12: PROC OPTIONS(MAIN);
        DCL C CHAR(3);
        C = 'CAT';
        ON CONV ONSOURCE = '123';
        N = C;
        PUT DATA(N);
        END TEST12;
```

Here the statement N=C; raises the CONVERSION condition. Now the ON statement changes the illegal field from 'CAT' to '123'. Upon the return to the N=C; statement '123' is converted to 123, giving the output

```
N=       123;
```

After the completion of the on-unit for the STRINGRANGE condition, the program control returns to the SUBSTR function that raised the condition. As was the case without the on-unit the compiler supplies new values for the starting position and the length of the substring (see Sec. 26.2D.2).

If there is an on-unit for the ENDFILE condition, then after the completion of the statements comprising the on-unit the control returns to the statement just after the one that caused the condition. For example, in the program

```
TEST13: PROC OPTIONS(MAIN);
        ON ENDFILE(SYSIN) B=3;
        GET LIST(A,B);
        C = A + B;
        PUT DATA(A,B,C);
        END TEST13;
```

with the data card

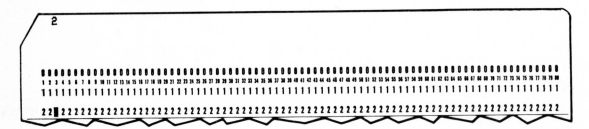

the ENDFILE condition is raised in the GET LIST statement, because there is no data for B. Consequently, the on-unit B=3; is executed and the control returns to the C = A + B; statement. The output is then

A= 2.00000E+00   B= 3.00000E+00   C= 5.00000E+00;

If there is an on-unit for the FINISH condition, the on-unit is executed and then the program is terminated. Similarly, if there is an on-unit for the ERROR condition, after the completion of the on-unit the system responds as without the on-unit, that is, causes (1) the printing of a message and (2) the raising of the FINISH condition (see Sec. 26.1B).

If there are several ON statements for the same condition in a program, then each new ON statement overrides a previous one. For example, in the program

```
TEST14: PROC OPTIONS(MAIN);
        DCL A FIXED(3,2);
        N = 1;
        ON ZDIV N=3;
        M = 5/(N-1);
        PUT DATA(N);
        ON SIZE N=4;
```

```
(SIZE): A = 10*N;
        PUT SKIP DATA(N);
        ON ZDIV N=5;
        M = 5/(N-4);
        PUT SKIP DATA(N);
(SIZE): A = 10*N;
        PUT SKIP DATA(N);
        ON SIZE N=6;
(SIZE): A = 10*N;
        PUT SKIP DATA(N);
        END TEST14;
```

the first ON statement for the ZDIV condition provides N=3; as the on-unit. Because M=5/(N−1); raises the ZDIV condition, N=3, and this value is printed out. The ON statement for the SIZE condition establishes N=4; as the on-unit. Because A=10*N; raises the SIZE condition, N=4, which is printed out. The new ON statement for ZDIV condition has a new on-unit, this being the N=5; statement. Hence, when the ZDIV condition occurs in the next statement, N=5, and this value will be printed out. The SIZE condition occurs next, resulting in the N=4; statement as its on-unit and the subsequent printout. But now, a new ON statement establishes N=6; as the on-unit for the SIZE condition. Thus when this condition is raised, N is set to 6 and subsequently printed out. Therefore the printout is

```
N=        3;
N=        4;
N=        5;
N=        4;
N=        6;
```

Note that if there is no on-unit, the interrupt is handled by so-called "standard system action," that is, by the specified actions of the operating system. If there is an on-unit, and we wish to replace it by the standard system action, we do so with the statement

ON *condition* SYSTEM;

As an example, in the program

```
TEST15: PROC OPTIONS(MAIN);
        ON ZDIV N=3;
        DO WHILE(1);
            N = 1;
            M = 5/(N-1);
            PUT LIST(N);
            ON ZDIV SYSTEM;
        END;
        END TEST15;
```

when the ZDIV condition is raised, N is set to 3, and this number is printed out. The statement

ON ZDIV SYSTEM;

restores standard system action (see Sec. 26.2A.5). In the second execution of the loop, the ZDIV condition is raised, causing the ERROR condition. Consequently the output of this program is

3

```
IHE330I ZERODIVIDE IN STATEMENT 00006 AT CFFSET +00092 FROM ENTRY POINT TEST15
```

B The REVERT Statement

To cancel the ON statement we use the REVERT statement, having the form

$$REVERT \ condition;$$

which cancels the action established by one or more ON statements for the condition. The cancellation only applies to the ON statements within a block. For example, the program

```
TEST16: PROC OPTIONS(MAIN);
        N = 1;
        ON ZDIV N=N+1;
        M = N/(N-1);
        PUT SKIP DATA(N);
        ON ZDIV N=N+2;
        M = N/(N-2);
        PUT SKIP DATA(N);
        N = N - 2;
        REVERT ZDIV;
        M = N/(N-2);
        PUT SKIP DATA(N);
        END TEST16;
```

gives the output

```
N=       2;
N=       4;
```

```
IHE330I ZERODIVIDE IN STATEMENT 00013 AT OFFSET +00160 FROM ENTRY POINT TEST16
```

because the REVERT ZDIV eliminated the actions specified with the ON statements for the ZDIV condition, and thus the ZDIV condition was raised with the last assignment statement for M.

Note that the program

```
TEST17: PROC OPTIONS(MAIN);
        N = 1;
        ON ZDIV N=N+1;
        CALL JOE;
        JOE: PROC;
             M = N/(N-1);
             PUT SKIP DATA(N);
             ON ZDIV N=N+2;
             DO WHILE(N¬=1);
                M = N/(N-2);
```

```
        PUT SKIP DATA(N);
        N = N - 2;
        REVERT ZDIV;
      END;
      END JOE;
   END TEST17;
```

gives the output

```
N=        2;
N=        4;
N=        3;
```

because the REVERT statement only nullifies the ON statements within its block (that is, within the procedure JOE). Hence here the REVERT statement restores the action of the ON statement specified at the entry to the procedure, this being the on-unit N=N+1;.

Incidentally, if there is no on-unit for a condition, then the REVERT statement cancels nothing and is interpreted just like a null statement.

C The Null On-Unit

Since the on-unit can be any simple statement, it can also be the null statement. We speak then of the *null on-unit*. In such a case we ask the computer to do nothing when the condition occurs. The ON statement with the null on-unit has the form

ON condition;

The null on-unit is an alternative to the disabling of a condition. For example, in the two program segments

```
                 N=1;              N=1;
  (NOZDIV): M=3/(N−1);             ON ZDIV;
            PUT LIST (N);          M=3/(N−1);
                                   PUT LIST (N);
```

the disabling of ZDIV condition in the first program segment is alternatively accomplished in the second segment with the null on-unit. Incidentally, the internal operations of the computer are different for the two segments. In the first segment the disabling of ZDIV eliminates the checking for this condition. In the second segment the checking still takes place. Thus the execution of the first segment takes less time.

The null on-unit may be specified for a condition which cannot be disabled with a condition prefix, such as the ENDFILE condition in the program

```
TEST18: PROC OPTIONS(MAIN);
        ON ENDFILE(SYSIN);
        DO I=1 TO 5;
           GET LIST(N);
           PUT SKIP LIST(I,N);
        END;
        END TEST18;
```

with the data card

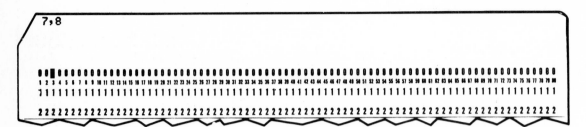

which gives the output

1	7
2	8
3	8
4	8
5	8

Incidentally, the null on-unit will not cause an "infinite" loop with the CONVERSION condition. Recall that after the completion of an on-unit for the CONVERSION condition the control returns to the beginning of the string which raised the CONVERSION condition (see page 483). However, no conversion will be undertaken if the invalid characters were not changed by the on-unit. Since the null on-unit changed nothing, the ERROR condition is raised, thus avoiding the creation of an infinite loop.

26.5 THE CHECK CONDITION

In Sec. 8.3 we described the use of output statements for help in debugging. Thus, for example, the program

```
TEST19: PROC OPTIONS(MAIN);
        ITOTAL = 0;
        GET LIST(M);
        DO WHILE(M>0);
            GET LIST(N);
            ITOTAL = ITOTAL + M*N;
            PUT SKIP DATA(M,N,ITOTAL);
            GET LIST(M);
        END;
        PUT SKIP DATA(ITOTAL);
        END TEST19;
```

with the input

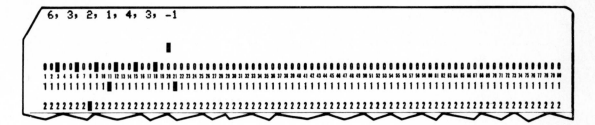

gives the output

```
M=          6           N=          3           ITOTAL=      18;
M=          2           N=          1           ITOTAL=      20;
M=          4           N=          3           ITOTAL=      32;
ITOTAL=         32;
```

which monitors the data and the formation of the output ITOTAL.

Similar monitoring can be achieved conveniently with the CHECK condition, which has the form

CHECK (name list);

The check prefix can only be appended to a procedure or a BEGIN block. The CHECK condition appended to the procedure statement of the preceding example

```
(CHECK(ITOTAL,M,N)):
TEST20: PROC OPTIONS(MAIN);
        ITOTAL = 0;
        GET LIST(M);
        DO WHILE(M>0);
            GET LIST(N);
            ITOTAL = ITOTAL + M*N;
            GET LIST(M);
        END;
        PUT DATA(ITOTAL);
        END TEST20;
```

with the previous input, produces the output

```
ITOTAL=          0;

M=          6;

N=          3;

ITOTAL=         18;

M=          2;

N=          1;
```

```
ITOTAL=          20;

M=          4;

N=          3;

ITOTAL=          32;

M=          -1;
ITOTAL=          32;
```

The order of the variables on the list for the CHECK condition is immaterial—the names of the variables and their values are printed out as they are encountered during the program execution. Thus, in the above example, the prefix

$$(CHECK (M,N, ITOTAL)):$$

will cause an identical output as the prefix

$$(CHECK (ITOTAL,M,N)):$$

The names on the list for the CHECK conditions can be more general than just names of variables. They can also be the names of

1. Labels
2. Entries
3. Arrays
4. Structures

but they cannot be the names of variables having the DEFINED attribute (see Sec. 19.9) or the names of parameters. Whenever a labeled statement is executed, the label is printed out. Thus, for example, the program

```
(CHECK(ITOTAL,M,N,LOOP)):
TEST21: PROC OPTIONS(MAIN);
        ITOTAL = 0;
        GET LIST(M);
LOOP:   GET LIST(N);
        ITOTAL = ITOTAL + M*N;
        GET LIST(M);
        IF M>0 THEN GO TO LOOP;
        PUT DATA(ITOTAL);
        END TEST21;
```

with the previous input has the output

```
ITOTAL=          0;

M=          6;

LOOP

N=          3;
```

```
ITOTAL=          18;

M=          2;

LOOP

N=          1;

ITOTAL=          20;

M=          4;

LOOP

N=          3;

ITOTAL=          32;

M=       -1;
ITOTAL=          32;
```

Similarly, whenever an entry is involved, the entry name is printed out. For an array or structure, we print out all the contained elements.

Usually, the CHECK condition produces a large number of printed values. Hence, after its use for help in debugging we remove the CHECK prefix.

26.6 SCOPE RULES

A Scope of a Condition Prefix

A prefix attached to a procedure statement or to a BEGIN block applies to all statements within the procedure or the BEGIN block. For example, the prefix

$$\text{(NOZDIV): JOE: PROC (X,Y);}$$

applies to all statements within the procedure JOE as well as to all statements in procedures or BEGIN blocks internal to the procedure JOE. The prefix does not apply to any procedures or blocks external to the procedure JOE.

A prefix attached to a statement applies only to the statement itself. A prefix attached to an IF statement applies only to the condition following the IF. For example, in

$$\text{(NOOFL): IF A*B} > \text{1E20 THEN C=(A*B)**3;}$$

the NOOFL prefix applies only to the A*B > 1E20 condition and not to the THEN clause [that is, not to the C=(A*B)**3 assignment]. If desired, the THEN or ELSE clauses may have their own prefixes, as in

$$\text{(NOOFL): IF A*B} > \text{1E20 THEN (NOOFL): C=(A*B)**3;}$$
$$\text{ELSE (NOZDIV): D=A/B;}$$

A prefix attached to a DO statement applies only to the DO statement itself and not to any other statements within the DO group.

A prefix can be attached to any statement with two exceptions. It cannot be attached to a DECLARE statement or to an ENTRY statement.

B Scope of an ON Statement

The ON statement establishes an action for the specified condition. This action will continue until it is replaced by a different action. Such replacement may be performed in three different ways:

1. An ON statement in a procedure A applies as long as the procedure is active. When the procedure is terminated and the control returns to the activating block, all interrupt actions existing before the invocation of A are again reestablished.
2. The execution of a new ON statement for the same condition provides a new on-unit for the condition.
3. The REVERT statement cancels the action specified by the ON statement. If the REVERT statement is in a procedure, the action existing at the entry to the procedure is reestablished (see text in Sec. 26.4B following TEST17 program). Similarly, if the REVERT statement is in the main procedure, the action existing at the start of the main procedure (that is, the standard system action) is again in force.

26.7 EXAMPLES

Example 26.7.1 A set of numbers representing grades is given on data cards. Find the average of the grades.

Solution Apparently the number of grades is unknown and has to be found by programming. We can do so by summing and counting the grades until we raise the ENDFILE condition. With such an approach the program is

```
EX_1:   PROC OPTIONS(MAIN);
        TOTAL = 0;
        DO I = 1 BY 1;
           ON ENDFILE(SYSIN) BEGIN;
                                N = I - 1; /* N IS NUMBER
                                                 OF GRADES */
                                AVE = TOTAL/N;
                                PUT DATA(AVE);
                                STOP;
                           END;
           GET LIST(GRADE);
           TOTAL = TOTAL + GRADE;
        END;
        END EX_1;
```

Observe that if there are no grades on data cards, N becomes zero and the ZERODIVIDE condition is raised.

Example 26.7.2 Tabulate the function

$$y = \begin{cases} -10 & \text{for } x \sin x < -10 \\ x \sin x & \text{for } -10 \leqslant x \sin x \leqslant 10 \\ 10 & \text{for } x \sin x > 10 \end{cases}$$

in the range $0 \leqslant x \leqslant 20$, using steps of 0.5. List y to two decimal places. The units of x are radians.

Solution One possible solution is to establish the value of y through the use of appropriate IF statements. A program with such an approach is

```
EX_2A:  PROC OPTIONS(MAIN);
        DCL X FIXED(3,1), Y FIXED (4,2);
        /* HEADING             */
        PUT EDIT('X','Y')(COL(6),A,COL(30),A);
        PUT EDIT('_','_')(SKIP(0),COL(6),A,COL(30),A);
        PUT SKIP;
        DO X=0 TO 20 BY 0.5;
            Y = X*SIN(X);
            IF Y>10 THEN Y = 10;
            IF Y<-10 THEN Y = -10;
            PUT SKIP LIST(X,Y);
        END;
        END EX_2A;
```

A second solution is to establish the value of y of 10 or -10 with the ON statement, as shown in

```
EX_2B:   PROC OPTIONS(MAIN);
         DCL X FIXED(3,1), Y FIXED(4,2), Y1 FIXED(3,2);
         /* HEADING             */
         PUT EDIT('X','Y')(COL(6),A,COL(30),A);
         PUT EDIT('_','_')(SKIP(0),COL(6),A,COL(30),A);
         PUT SKIP;
         ON SIZE Y = 10*SIGN(Y);
         DO X=0 TO 20 BY 0.5;
(SIZE):      Y,Y1 = X*SIN(X);
             PUT SKIP LIST(X,Y);
         END;
         END EX_2B;
```

Note that Y1 is declared as FIXED (3,2). Hence, whenever the SIZE condition is raised for Y1, we assign the appropriate value to Y.

Example 26.7.3 There are several pairs of nonnegative numbers on data cards. The first number in each pair represents the real part, and the second number the imaginary part of a complex number. For each complex number represented by the pair, print out the polar form, with angles given in degrees. No number exceeds 10, and the results are to be printed with two decimal places.

Solution This example is very similar to the one in Example 21.3.2. It requires the calculation of the magnitude and angle of the complex number by the formulas

$$\text{Magnitude} = \sqrt{A^2 + B^2}$$
$$\text{Angle} \quad = \tan^{-1}\frac{B}{A}$$

where A, B are given as a pair of numbers. Note that since A and B are nonnegative, the angle is between 0 and 90°. We need only a protection from division by zero. Such a protection is achieved with the program

```
EX_3:   PROC OPTIONS(MAIN);
        DCL (MAGNITUDE,ANGLE) FIXED(4,2);
        ON ENDFILE(SYSIN) STOP;
        ON ZDIV ANGLE=90;
        DO WHILE(1);
            GET LIST(A,B);
            MAGNITUDE = SQRT(A*A+B*B);
            ANGLE = ATAND(B,A);
            PUT SKIP DATA(MAGNITUDE,ANGLE);
        END;
        END EX_3;
```

26.8 SUMMARY

We described in this chapter the protective features of the operating system, which interrupts the program execution when unusual condition occur. We described how to enable and how to disable the various conditions. We also told how, when a program interrupt occurred, to substitute the desired action instead of the standard system action.

PROBLEMS

26.1 Write a program to calculate correctly
(*a*) A = 1.49E52 * 1.79E59 + 8.35E42 * 7.82E68;
(*b*) B = 1.49E−52 * 1.79E−59 + 8.35E−42 * 7.82E−68;

26.2 Given that

$$y = \frac{(x - a)(x - b)}{(x - c)(x - d)}$$

Write a program to calculate y for

a	b	c	d	x
1	2	3	4	4
1	2	1	4	6
2.8	3.7	4.2	3.7	3.7
7.3	3.7	−8.3	7.3	−8.3
8.2	8.2	8.2	8.2	8.2

26.3 Write a program which protects against obtaining undefined results because of either SIZE, STRINGRANGE, or SUBSCRIPTRANGE conditions, and give operations where these conditions may occur.

26.4 The input consists of a character string of 20 characters. The string has several blanks separating individual numbers. In some of these numbers the letters A, B, and C were accidentally punched. Replace A by 1, B by 2, and C by 3, and print out the sum of the numbers. The input is

$$'123A2\not b5BC1\not b2CBB4\not b147'$$

26.5 The data cards contain the elements of one-dimensional array A, followed by the elements of one-dimensional array B. Both arrays have the same bounds. Print out the elements of the array C, where

$$C = A + B;$$

It is known that the lowbound for all three arrays is 3, and there are no more than 100 numbers on the cards.

26.6 You are given the following program:

```
P_6: PROC OPTIONS(MAIN);
     GET LIST(N);
     M = N/2;
     BEGIN;
       DCL ARRAY(-M:M)FIXED, N FLOAT;
       GET LIST(ARRAY);
       AVERAGE = SUM(ARRAY)/N;
       PUT DATA(AVERAGE);
     END;
     END P_6;
```

The data card contains

$$7 \quad 3 \quad -2 \quad 5 \quad 8 \quad -9 \quad 17 \quad 6$$

Upon running this program, the ZERODIVIDE message has been printed. Why? What mistake did the programmer make?

26.7 An unknown number of English words is punched on data cards in the format shown. No word exceeds 15 characters. Your program is to compute the average length of a word. The result is to be printed as a decimal fraction with two digits after the decimal point. In addition, each word read in should be printed out. For example, if the data card contained

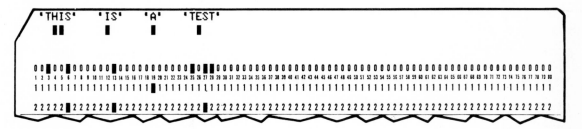

the average word length would be

$$\frac{4 + 2 + 1 + 4}{4} = \frac{11}{4} = 2.75$$

Note that you have no access to the data and do not know what the last word is.

26.8 A list of numerical data items (that is, numbers) is punched onto data cards. The total number of data items is not known. Write a program which will separate the data into the three sets:

Set #1 of data items which are < 10
Set #2 of data items which are ≥ 10, but < 20
Set #3 of data items which are ≥ 20

The required output for each set is N(J) and AVE(J),
where J = 1, 2, or 3   N(J) = the number of data items in the set
AVE(J) = the mean of the data items in the set, that is,

$$AVE(J) = \frac{\text{the sum of the data items in the set}}{N(J)}$$

Note: You should "protect" your program against the possibility that a set might be empty [that is, N(J) = 0]. For example, in such a case, print a zero rather than attempt to calculate the mean, which would result in a ZERODIVIDE condition.

26.9 The equations of two lines are given in the form

$$y = m_1 x + k_1$$
$$y = m_2 x + k_2$$

The lines intersect if $m_1 \neq m_2$. If $m_1 = m_2$ and $k_2 \neq k_2$, the lines are parallel. If $m_1 = m_2$ and $k_1 = k_2$, both equations represent the same line.

The data cards contain eight sets of four numbers. Each set of four numbers consists of the values for m_1, k_1, m_2, and k_2. Using the ZERODIVIDE condition, print out for each set the type of lines that the set represents (for example, INTERSECTING LINES, PARALLEL LINES, SAME LINE). The data are

1.43	4.83	-2.75	14.2
20.83	13.7	20.83	15.2
1.87	-12.3	2.4	4.7
2.83	12.1	2.83	12.1
14.2	13.2	14.2	1.82
-2.7	2.8	2.75	7.3
8.3	-9.5	8.3	-9.5
7.8	-12.7	13.2	7.2

26.10 The data cards contain the elements of an N×N array A (N is not given) in the usual row order. Write a program to print out A in the column order (that is, $a_{11}, a_{21}, \ldots, a_{n1}, a_{12}, a_{22}, \ldots, a_{nn}$). It is known that A has fewer than 1000 elements.

APPENDIX 1

NUMBERS AND THEIR REPRESENTATION IN SYSTEM/360 AND SYSTEM/370

We will now describe how numbers are represented internally. This information is needed to explain certain curious results, such as obtaining a negative number for the product of two positive numbers.

Positive Binary Integers

Positive binary integers are represented in the usual form. As the result of the assignment statement, for example,

$$I = 81;$$

the value for I being by default a FIXED BIN (15) number is stored as

$$0000\ 0000\ 0101\ 0001$$

Negative Binary Integers

Negative binary integers are represented in 2's complement. To obtain the 2's complement of a binary number:

1. Change each 0 to 1 and each 1 to 0 (this gives the so-called logical complement or 1's complement).
2. Add 1.

For example, to represent -81 in 2's complement, do the following:

1. Represent 81 in binary form, that is,

$$81_{10} = 0000\ 0000\ 0101\ 0001_2$$

2. Obtain the logical complement, that is,

Logical complement = 1111 1111 1010 1110

3. Add 1 to the result:

$$
\begin{array}{r}
1111\ 1111\ 1010\ 1110 \\
+\ \underline{\hspace{4.5cm}1} \\
\text{2's complement} = \quad 1111\ 1111\ 1010\ 1111
\end{array}
$$

In general, the leftmost digit tells whether the number is positive or negative. If this digit is 0, the number is positive in binary representation. If this digit is 1, the number is negative in 2's complement representation. Hence, the largest positive binary integer representable with 16 binary digits is

0111 1111 1111 1111 $(= 2^{15} - 1 = 32,767)$
↑
Sign digit

The negative numbers are representable in 2's complement up to

1000 0000 0000 0000
↑
Sign digit

Incidentally, to convert the 2's complement to the more familiar base 10 form:

1. Replace the number by its logical complement.
2. Add 1.
3. Convert to base 10 form (this gives the magnitude of the number).
4. Append a minus sign.

As an example, to convert to decimal form:

$$
\begin{array}{rl}
1111\ 1111\ 1010\ 1111 =& \text{number to be converted} \\
0000\ 0000\ 0101\ 0000 =& \text{logical complement} \\
0000\ 0000\ 0101\ 0001 =& \text{logical complement} + 1 \\
81 =& \text{base 10 magnitude} \\
-81 =& \text{desired result}
\end{array}
$$

Similarly,

$$
\begin{array}{rl}
1000\ 0000\ 0000\ 0000 =& \text{number to be converted} \\
0111\ 1111\ 1111\ 1111 =& \text{logical complement} \\
1000\ 0000\ 0000\ 0000 =& \text{logical complement} + 1
\end{array}
$$

$$32{,}768 = \text{base 10 magnitude}$$
$$-32{,}768 = \text{result}$$

With 2's complements representing negative numbers, there is no need for the operation of subtraction, because

$$A - B = A + (2\text{'s complement of } B)$$

and this is the reason for the use of 2's complements.

Example A1.1

$$
\begin{aligned}
17_{10} - 3_{10} &= 0000\ 0000\ 0001\ 0001_2 - 0000\ 0000\ 0000\ 0011_2 \\
&= 0000\ 0000\ 0001\ 0001_2 + 1111\ 1111\ 1111\ 1101_2 \\
&= 0000\ 0000\ 0000\ 1110_2 \\
&= 14_{10} \quad \text{(the leading seventeenth digit is ignored)}
\end{aligned}
$$

The UNSPEC Function

PL/I provides a built-in function

$$\text{UNSPEC (X)}$$

which returns a bit string giving the internal representation of the argument X. As an example, the program segment

```
N=2;
PUT LIST (UNSPEC(N));
```

gives the output

```
'0000000000000010'B
```

this being the internal representation for the value of N.

The UNSPEC function is useful for obtaining the internal representation needed to explain unexpected results. We will illustrate such a case in the following example.

Example A1.2 As an example of a program with an unexpected output, consider

```
TEST:  PROC OPTIONS(MAIN);
       N = 1;
       DO I=1 TO 20;
          N = 2*N;
          PUT SKIP LIST(I,N,UNSPEC(N));
       END;
       END TEST;
```

which gives the output

1	2	'0000000000000010'B
2	4	'0000000000000100'B
3	8	'0000000000001000'B
4	16	'0000000000010000'B
5	32	'0000000000100000'B
6	64	'0000000001000000'B
7	128	'0000000010000000'B
8	256	'0000000100000000'B
9	512	'0000001000000000'B
10	1024	'0000010000000000'B
11	2048	'0000100000000000'B
12	4096	'0001000000000000'B
13	8192	'0010000000000000'B
14	16364	'0100000000000000'B
15	−32768	'1000000000000000'B
16	0	'0000000000000000'B
17	0	'0000000000000000'B
18	0	'0000000000000000'B
19	0	'0000000000000000'B
20	0	'0000000000000000'B

The UNSPEC function has been included to help explain the unexpected results of −32768 for 2^{15} and zeros for 2^{16}, 2^{17}, 2^{18}, 2^{19}, 2^{20}.

To understand the reason for these results, observe that the internal representation for 2^{15} is

$$1000\ 0000\ 0000\ 0000$$

which is interpreted as 2's complement because of the 1 in the sign digit portion. Now

$$\underbrace{1000\ 0000\ 0000\ 0000}_{\text{2's complement}} = -\underbrace{(0111\ 1111\ 1111\ 1111 + 1)_2}_{\text{logical complement}}$$
$$= -1000\ 0000\ 0000\ 0000_2$$
$$= -2^{15} = -32{,}768$$

Similarly, 2^{16} is calculated as

$$\underbrace{1000\ 0000\ 0000\ 0000}_{\text{Representation of N}} * 10_2 = 1\underset{\text{ignored}}{0000\ 0000\ 0000\ 0000}$$
$$= 0000\ 0000\ 0000\ 0000_2$$
$$= 0_{10}$$

Obviously 2^{17}, 2^{18}, 2^{19}, 2^{20} are then also zero.

The Hexadecimal Number System

The hexadecimal or base 16 number system uses the letters A through F for 10 through 15. Several examples of correspondence between decimal and hexadecimal numbers are

$$15_{10} = F_{16} \qquad 42_{10} = 2A_{16}$$
$$16_{10} = 10_{16} \qquad 65_{10} = 41_{16}$$

Observe that an eight-digit binary number

$$B_7B_6B_5B_4B_3B_2B_1B_0 = \underbrace{(B_7*2^3 + B_6*2^2 + B_5*2^1 + B_4)}_{H_1}* 16 + \underbrace{(B_3*2^3 + B_2*2^2 + B_1*2^1 + B_0)}_{H_0}$$

$$= H_1H_0 \quad \text{in hexadecimal}$$

Thus the hexadecimal system provides a convenient notation for binary numbers. In hexadecimal notation only one-fourth the digits are needed. The conversion from binary to hexadecimal is illustrated by

$$\underset{9}{\underline{1001}} \ \underset{14}{\underline{1110}} \ \underset{13}{\underline{1101}} \ \underset{1}{\underline{0010}}_2 = 9ED2_{16}$$

$$\underset{5}{\underline{0101}} \ \underset{15}{\underline{1111}} \ \underset{1}{\underline{0001}} \ \underset{8}{\underline{1000}}_2 = 5F18_{16}$$

and from hexadecimal to binary by

$$1FA2_{16} = \underset{1}{\underline{0001}} \ \underset{F}{\underline{1111}} \ \underset{A}{\underline{1010}} \ \underset{2}{\underline{0010}}_2$$

$$EB7C_{16} = \underset{E}{\underline{1110}} \ \underset{B}{\underline{1011}} \ \underset{7}{\underline{0111}} \ \underset{C}{\underline{1100}}_2$$

These examples show the ease of both conversions.

Fixed-decimal Numbers

A fixed-decimal number is represented internally during operations in the form

Digit	Digit	Digit		Sign

where each digit is represented by 4 bits. The sign is represented also by 4 bits, where

1100 or 1111 (that is, hexadecimal C or F)   means +
1101 (that is, dexadecimal D)   means −

Examples A1.3

2.43 is represented by $\underset{2}{\underline{0010}} \ \underset{4}{\underline{0100}} \ \underset{3}{\underline{0011}} \ \underset{C}{\underline{1100}}$

-1.75 is represented by $\underset{1}{\underline{0001}} \ \underset{7}{\underline{0111}} \ \underset{5}{\underline{0101}} \ \underset{D}{\underline{1101}}$

24.3 is represented by $\underset{2}{\underline{0010}} \ \underset{4}{\underline{0100}} \ \underset{3}{\underline{0011}} \ \underset{C}{\underline{1100}}$

Note that 2.43 and 24.3 are represented the same way. Since each variable and number have the precision attribute associated with them, the correct decimal point is inserted when calculations are performed.

In Examples A1.3 we represented the three-digit decimal numbers with 16 bits. In computer jargon 8 bits are named a *byte*, 16 bits a *half-word*, 32 bits a *full word*, and 64 bits a *double word*. A fixed-decimal number is always represented by an integer number of bytes, with zeros filling in the unneeded digit positions. As an example, 21.73 is represented with 3 bytes as

$$\underbrace{0000\ 0010}_{2}\ \underbrace{0001}_{1}\ \underbrace{0111}_{7}\ \underbrace{0011}_{3}\ \underbrace{1100}_{C}$$

But in

DCL A FIXED (6,2);
A = 21.73;

A is represented as

$$0000\ 0000\ 0000\ \underbrace{0010}_{2}\ \underbrace{0001}_{1}\ \underbrace{0111}_{7}\ \underbrace{0011}_{3}\ \underbrace{1100}_{C}$$

to provide the required precision and integer number of bytes.

The just-described representation of fixed-decimal numbers is called the *packed-decimal* format.

Floating-point Numbers

Floating-point numbers are represented internally in the form

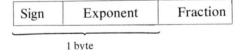

Sign	Exponent	Fraction

1 byte

where the sign is a single bit, with 0 designating a positive number and 1 a negative number; the fraction occupies either 3 bytes [for FLOAT(6)] or 7 bytes [for FLOAT(16)]; the exponent is a 7-bit number. Its difference from 64 gives the exponent of 16.

We will illustrate the representation of floating-point numbers by examples.

Example A1.4 What number is represented by

0100 0001 1100 0100 1100 1100 1100 1100

Solution The number is positive and hexadecimal: 41C4CCCC. The exponent is

$$41_{16} - 64_{10} = 65_{10} - 64_{10} = 1$$

The number is then

$$16^1(0.C4CCCC_{16}) = C.4CCCC_{16}$$
$$= 12 + \frac{4}{16} + \frac{12}{16^2} + \frac{12}{16^3} + \frac{12}{16^4} + \frac{12}{16^5}$$
$$= 12 + 0.25 + 0.046875 + 0.0029296 + 0.0001831 + 0.0000114$$
$$= 12.299998 = 12.3$$

Example A1.5 Convert the floating-point representation

$$1100\ 0000\ 0001\ 1111\ 0111\ 1100\ 1110\ 1101$$

to the decimal representation.

Solution The number is negative and hexadecimal: $-401F7CED$. The exponent is

$$40_{16} - 64_{10} = 64_{10} - 64_{10} = 0$$

The number is then

$$-0.1F7CED_{16} = -\left(\frac{1}{16} + \frac{15}{16^2} + \frac{7}{16^3} + \frac{12}{16^4} + \frac{14}{16^5} + \frac{13}{16^6}\right)$$
$$= -(.0625 + 0.0585937 + 0.0017089 + 0.0001831 + 0.0000133 + 0.0000114)$$
$$= -0.122997 = -0.123$$

Example A1.6 How is $1.6128E-2$ represented?

Solution

$$1.6128 * 10^{-2} = 16^{-1} * 16 * 1.6128 * 10^{-2} = 16^{-1}(0.258048)$$

Now

$$0.258048 * 16 = 4.128768$$
$$0.128768 * 16 = 2.060288$$
$$0.060288 * 16 = 0.964608$$
$$0.964608 * 16 = 15.433728$$
$$0.433728 * 16 = 6.939648$$
$$0.939648 * 16 = 15.034368$$

Taking the integer parts of the multiplications, we obtain

$$0.258048_{10} = 0.420F6F_{16}$$

Hence the sign is 0, the exponent is $63_{10} = 3F_{16}$, and the number is represented by $3F420F6F_{16}$.

Observe that exponents of less than 40_{16} represent negative exponents.

APPENDIX 2
THE
PL/C COMPILER

The PL/C compiler was constructed at Cornell University for processing students' programs. Such programs have the following characteristics:

1. They are much shorter than commercial programs, and usually have short execution time relative to compilation time.
2. They are written by inexperienced programmers, who require additional debugging help.

The PL/C compiler was designed for these characteristics by providing:

1. Very fast compilation time without regard to fast execution time
2. Debugging aids exceeding those of the F compiler

We will first describe these debugging aids, and then the differences between PL/C and PL/I.

PL/C DEBUGGING AIDS

PL/C provides three kinds of debugging aids:

1. Diagnostic messages
2. Repair of errors
3. Statements and counts for finding errors

Diagnostic Messages

As in PL/I two types of errors are detected, namely,

1. Syntax errors found during compilation
2. Requests for illegal actions, detected during program execution

All errors detected are reported in the form of error messages. Each error message is accompanied by a two-letter code (indicating in which phase the error occurred) and a message number. The two-letter codes are:

SY   for errors detected in syntactic analysis (for example, missing semicolon)

SM   for errors detected in semantic analysis (for example, mismatched dimensionality)

XR   for errors detected in cross reference (for example, improper statement found by cross reference)

CG   for errors detected in code generation (for example, no file specified)

EX   for errors detected in execution (for example, fixed decimal overflow)

The error message is similar to the one of PL/I(F). As an example, the PL/I(F) message

IEM0096I 2 SEMI-COLON NOT FOUND WHEN EXPECTED IN STATEMENT NUMBER 2. ONE HAS BEEN INSERTED.

becomes in PL/C

ERROR IN STMT 2 MISSING SEMI-COLON (OR MISUSE OF RESERVED WORD) (SY08)

Contrast the PL/I(F) wording with the simpler MISSING SEMI-COLON. As another example, the PL/I(F) message

IEM0003I 6 RIGHT PARENTHESIS INSERTED IN STATEMENT NUMBER 6

becomes in PL/C

ERROR IN STMT 6 MISSING) IN COLUMN 24 (SY04)

which is more graphical and pinpoints the exact place where the parenthesis is inserted. As these two examples show, the PL/C messages are simpler. Because there are approximately five times as many PL/I messages as PL/C messages, there is more "hairsplitting" in the PL/I messages. There are, for example, several PL/I messages relating to the right parenthesis. The by-product of these extra messages is extra confusion to the beginning programmer. Also the PL/C message occurs immediately after the offending statement, thus displaying the incorrect statement and the diagnostic message together. In PL/I the diagnostic message is placed less conveniently on a separate listing, requiring the program debugger to look from one sheet to another.

In summary, the PL/C diagnostic messages are preferrable to those of PL/I(F) for beginning programmers because they are simpler and better displayed.

Repair of Errors

The second debugging aid of PL/C is its error-repair feature. PL/C attempts to execute programs with errors, subscribing to the philosophy that such programs will reduce the number of runs required otherwise. The repaired PL/C programs will indicate many errors, thus eliminating the one-at-a-time error correction followed by some inexperienced programmers.

The error and its correction are communicated through a diagnostic message as described previously, followed by a description of the repair. As an example, let the tenth statement of a program be

$$A=B-(C-D;$$

PL/C will follow this statement with

ERROR IN STMT 10 MISSING) IN COLUMN 19(SY04)
FOR STMT 10 PL/C USES A=B−(C−D);

which shows the repair. If a statement has several errors, it is followed by diagnostic messages (one for each error) and the description of the repair. For example, the eleventh statement

LOOP; GET LIST (A B);

is followed by

ERROR IN STMT 11 IMPROPER ELEMENT IN COLUMN 15 (SY16)
ERROR IN STMT 11 MISSING: (SY09)
ERROR IN STMT 11 MISSING COMMA IN COLUMN 27 (SY06)
FOR STMT 11 PL/C USES LOOP: GET LIST(A,B);

indicating the repair of the eleventh statement.

If we are lucky, the repair is the correct one. If PL/C is completely confused as to the meaning of a statement, a null statement is substituted.

It is possible to stop execution if too many errors are to be repaired. PL/C provides an option

$$ERRORS=(c,e) \quad \text{or} \quad E=(c,e)$$

where c limits the number of errors in compilation and e the number of errors in execution. If this option is not specified, $c = 50$ and $e = 50$ are assumed, meaning that 50 compile-time errors will inhibit execution and 50 execute-time errors will stop execution. Note that ERRORS(1,1) will result in no error repair. The ERRORS option is specified on PL/C control cards (see App. 6).

Statements and Counts for Finding Errors

The third debugging aid of PL/C consists of additional statements and statistics for finding errors.

The CHECK and NOCHECK statements. The statement

NOCHECK;

eliminates the printing occurring with the CHECK condition but does not disable the condition. The statement

CHECK;

cancels the action of the NOCHECK; statement. Thus in PL/C we can control a little better the large amount of output resulting from the CHECK condition.

Another version of the CHECK statement is

CHECK(*expression*);

which limits the number of printouts resulting from raising the CHECK condition. For example,

CHECK(6);

allows at most six CHECK printouts.

The FLOW and NOFLOW statements. The FLOW and NOFLOW statements are used to print statement numbers in the execution of the IF statement and whenever the program execution is not in sequence (that is, whenever statement number n is not followed by statement number $n + 1$). The printout is in the form

$$k*(x->y)$$

meaning that statement number y was executed k times after statement number x. If $k = 1$ the printout is

$$x->y$$

To obtain the indicated printout, we prefix the procedure statement with (FLOW):, as, for example,

```
(FLOW):
EXAMPLE: PROC OPTIONS(MAIN);
```

and then place the statement

FLOW;

prior to the segment to be traced. Similarly, the statement

NOFLOW;

inhibits the printout of the following segment. Finally, the prefix

(NOFLOW):

excludes an internal procedure or block from the (FLOW): action. As an example, the PL/C program

```
STMT
  1     (FLOW):
        EXAMPLE: PROC OPTIONS(MAIN);
  2              GET LIST(M);
  3              DO WHILE(M>0);
  4                  FLOW;
  5                  IF M>5 THEN N=0;
```

```
7                    ELSE N=1;
8                    DO I=1 TO 2 WHILE(N=0);
9                        PUT SKIP LIST(I);
10                   END;
11                   DO I=1 TO 2 WHILE(N=1);
12                   END;
13                   PUT SKIP LIST(I);
14                   NOFLOW;
15                   GET LIST(M);
16             END;
17             END EXAMPLE:
```

with the data

$$10,2,-1$$

gives the output

```
*FLOW*   0005->0006
   1
*FLOW*   0010->0008
   2
*FLOW*   0010->0008   0008->0011   0011->0013
   1
*FLOW*   0005->0007   0008->0011   2*(0012->0011)   0011->0013
   3
```

As with the CHECK statement, the number of the FLOW messages can be limited. For example, FLOW(10); means that at most 10 FLOW messages are to be printed. Unlike the CHECK prefix, the (FLOW): and (NOFLOW): prefixes can be specified on any executable statement.

The postmortem dump. After printing the program output, the PL/C compiler provides final values of variables and various counts which are helpful in tracing errors. It gives the final values of scalar variables and, if requested, final values of array elements. (The printout of ??? for a variable means that no value was assigned to this variable.) It also gives the number of times each label and procedure name was passed in program execution. Additionally, we can request the listing of statements for the last 18 nonsequential executions.

The final lines tell how much core was used as well as the compile and execution times. All these listings after the execution printout are named the *postmortem dump*.

DIFFERENCES BETWEEN PL/I AND PL/C

Several of the differences between PL/I and PL/C were described previously. These are:

1. PL/C compiles faster than PL/I.
2. PL/I executes faster than PL/C.
3. PL/C diagnostic messages are fewer but simpler.
4. PL/C replaces invalid statements by valid ones (although not always by correct ones). PL/C attempts to execute programs with errors.
5. PL/C provides diagnostic aids with the CHECK condition, the CHECK and FLOW statements, and the postmortem dump.

Other differences are:

6. In PL/I, keywords can be used for identifiers. In PL/C, the following 39 keywords cannot be used as identifiers:

ALLOCATE	END	NO	RETURN
BEGIN	ENTRY	NOCHECK	REVERT
BY	EXIT	NOFLOW	SIGNAL
CALL	FLOW	NOSOURCE	SOURCE
CHECK	FORMAT	ON	STOP
CLOSE	FREE	OPEN	THEN
DCL	GET	PROC	TO
DECLARE	GO	PROCEDURE	WHILE
DO	GOTO	PUT	WRITE
ELSE	IF	READ	

7. PL/C allows certain comments to be treated as statements. Such comments must have either a colon or an integer from 1 through 6 as the first character. For example,

/*: CHECK */

and all other comments with a colon will be treated as statements if the control card contains the option COMMENTS.

Similarly, the option COMMENTS=(5) on the control card will result in interpreting as statements all comments having either a colon or a 5 as the first character. This feature provides compatibility between PL/I and PL/C by allowing certain PL/C statements to be treated as PL/I comments.

In PL/C each comment is limited to a single line. This restriction is easily met by giving to each comment line its own set of comment symbols (that is, /* and */). It is even possible to eliminate this restriction through an option on the control card.

8. There is no conversion between string and arithmetic data (that is, no arithmetic operations allowed with strings).
9. String constants cannot have repetition factors,
10. The PAGESIZE and LINESIZE default attributes cannot be changed by the programmer.
11. PL/C contains the built-in function RAND(X), which returns a pseudorandom number. The argument X must be in the range $0 < X < 1$.

12. When a PL/C program contains features not compatible with PL/I, a warning message is printed.
13. There are internal differences between PL/I and PL/C in the representation of data. Also the order of evaluation in DCL statements is different in both compilers.
14. The allowable maximum nestings of IFs, procedures, factors in DCL statements, and parentheses are smaller in PL/C than in PL/I.
15. There is no POLY function.
16. There are no ALLOCATE, FREE, or REWRITE statements.
17. There are no DEFINED, CONTROLLED, ENVIRONMENT, UPDATE, or LIKE attributes.
18. The conditions SIZE, STRINGRANGE, and SUBSCRIPTRANGE are enabled by default.
19. A constant may not extend beyond a single card without a control card option.
20. PL/C allows the statement

$$\text{PUT } option1, option2, \dots, optionk$$

where one of the options can be FLOW. (There are several other options that were not discussed here.)
21. There are no direct-access files.
22. If a DO, PROCEDURE, or BEGIN is preceded by several labels, as, for example,

$$label1:label2:label3:\text{BEGIN};$$

then the terminating END statement must contain the first label, that is,

$$\text{END } label1;$$

(in PL/I END can contain any one of these three labels).
23. In the declaration of array, structure, or string parameters of a procedure, asterisks must be used. Thus, for example,

$$\begin{array}{l}\text{QUAD: PROC(A,B)};\\ \quad\text{DCL A(10,5),B CHAR(5)};\end{array}$$

is illegal, but

$$\begin{array}{l}\text{QUAD: PROC(A,B)};\\ \quad\text{DCL A(*,*),B CHAR(*)};\end{array}$$

is legal.

PL/I has many features (not described in this book) not found in PL/C, but future additions are planned for PL/C (for example, the ALLOCATE statement). For additional information on PL/C, consult the following:

"User's Guide to PL/C," release 7.6, Department of Computer Science, Cornell University, Ithaca, NY 14853, May 1977.

APPENDIX 3
THE PLAGO INTERPRETER

An interpreter performs the same function as a compiler but employs a different translating strategy. A compiler translates the entire source program into an object program before the start of execution. An interpreter translates a segment of the program and executes that segment immediately. Thus an interpreter varies translation with execution.

The PLAGO (Polytechnic Load And GO) interpreter was developed by the faculty and students at the Polytechnic Institute of New York (H. W. Lawson, Jr., performed the original design in 1968). Similar to PL/C described in App. 2, PLAGO was designed for processing students' programs. It has clear diagnostic messages, an extra diagnostic aid, and fast translation from source code to object code. Unlike PL/C, PLAGO repairs no errors.

We will first describe and give examples of PLAGO error messages. Afterwards, we will describe the diagnostic aid and then discuss the differences between PLAGO and PL/I.

DIAGNOSTIC MESSAGES IN PLAGO

The syntax errors are located when PLAGO first scans the source program. The message for such an error immediately follows the incorrect statement, as, for example,

```
        8     A=(B+C;
  **ERROR**          $ 6 – RIGHT PAREN MISSING
```

Here the eighth statement is incorrect. It is followed by the diagnostic message. The $ sign appears under the column where the error was detected, 6 is the error number, and the text is the message.

Program construction errors are located in the second pass through the source program. Messages for such errors appear at the end of the program text. Messages for execution errors are mixed with the output. These messages have the format

ERROR *error number* IN STATEMENT *statement number*

The listing of messages corresponding to error numbers is given in the "PLAGO User's Handbook" (see reference listed at end of this appendix).

THE TRACE SUBROUTINE PROCEDURE

PLAGO contains a built-in subroutine procedure named TRACE for use as a diagnostic aid in debugging programs. The subroutine is invoked with

CALL TRACE(number);

where the number ranges from 1 to 15. The number represents the following features:

1 statement trace; prints a message for each statement after TRACE
2 procedure invocation trace; prints a message for each procedure invoked after TRACE
4 procedure return trace; prints a message for each return from procedure after TRACE
8 statement count trace; prints a table showing how many times each statement was executed

By adding the numbers, we can obtain several tracing features at once. For example,

CALL TRACE(3);   results in features given by numbers 1 and 2
CALL TRACE(15);   results in all features

To remove a tracing feature, request TRACE with a zero in the binary bit position where this feature occurs. For example, if

CALL TRACE(2);

which requests the feature given by the number 2 [that is, binary (0010)], is followed by

CALL TRACE(9);

then the features given by 8 and 1 are enabled but the features given by 4 and 2 are disabled, because $9_{10} = 1001_2$ and thus has the zeros in the indicated positions. Since 2 was previously enabled, it is now disabled.

Note that

CALL TRACE(0);

removes all tracing features.

The TRACE should not be overused because it gives rise to a large output.

DIFFERENCES BETWEEN PL/I AND PLAGO

PLAGO is a subset of PL/I, much smaller than the one implemented by the D compiler and somewhat smaller than PL/C. This subset is more than sufficient for science-oriented student jobs. PLAGO contains almost none of the PL/I features omitted from discussion in this book. In the following we will describe most of the features of PLAGO which differ from PL/I.

1. The only files supported by PLAGO are SYSIN and SYSPRINT. Thus there are no READ, WRITE, OPEN, or CLOSE statements.
2. In the DCL statement, FIXED implies FIXED BIN(31). All integer constants are FIXED BIN(31), and all variables having I through N as a first letter are by default FIXED BIN(31).
3. Noninteger constants are either FLOAT DEC(6) or FLOAT DEC(16), depending upon their precision.
4. Observe from features 2 and 3 that the only number types available in PLAGO are FIXED BIN(31), FLOAT DEC(6), and FLOAT DEC(16). Hence there is no complex mode and no precision other than the available may be declared. For example,

    DCL A FIXED BIN(31);

    is legal, but

    DCL B FIXED DEC(5,4);

    is illegal.
5. All procedures are recursive even without any declaration. There are no external procedures.
6. Array and structures (and even labels) may be returned by a function procedure.
7. Various limits are smaller in PLAGO than in PL/I. A character string, for example, cannot be longer than 255 characters [32,767 in PL/I (F)]. An identifier may be 31 characters long (as in PL/I), but only the first 8 characters are read.
8. The repetition factor may be an expression (it must be a nonnegative integer in PL/I).
9. In the remote format item

    R(*label*)

    label may be a function procedure returning a label (see feature 6 above).
10. The main procedure statement may read as in PL/I or simply

    name: PROCEDURE;

    where PROCEDURE may be abbreviated to PROC, as in PL/I.
11. There are no CHECK or SIZE conditions and no condition prefixes.

12. The *on-unit* for the ON condition can only be a
    a. Null statement
    b. GO TO statement
    c. STOP;
    d. SYSTEM;

13. There are no ONCHAR, ONSOURCE, BOOL, ROUND, or POLY built-in functions. The name SUM is reserved and cannot be used for the name of a variable without a declaration. There are no functions for operations on complex numbers. The MAX and MIN functions may have array arguments. Except for these two functions and ABS, PROD, and SUM, all other built-in functions must have scalar arguments.

14. Besides TRACE, PLAGO contains five built-in functions not in PL/I. These are:

    a. CPUTIME   returns elapsed CPU time (no arguments)

    b. LINESIZE(X)   changes line size to X (X ranges from 1 to 132) and returns the previous line size. For example, in

    $$N=LINESIZE(130);$$

    N is now the previous line size, and the present line size has been set to 130 columns.

    c. NARGS   used in an internal procedure, NARGS returns the number of arguments passed into the procedure. NARGS has no arguments.

    d. RANDOM(X)   returns a pseudorandom FLOAT(6) number in the range 0 to 1.

    e. TABSIZE(X)   changes to X the width of the field for list- and data-directed outputs and returns the previous width. For example, in

    $$M=TABSIZE(20);$$

    M is the previous field width (whose default value is 24), and the present width has been set to 20.

15. There are no bit-string variables.

16. There is no dynamic storage allocation and hence no ALLOCATE or FREE statements.

17. There are no INITIAL, DEFINED, CONTROLLED, or LIKE attributes. There is no BY NAME option.

18. Comments must be placed only before or after a statement (except in the DCL statement, where they can be placed whenever blanks are allowed).

For further information on PLAGO, see the following:

"PLAGO User's Handbook" (for PLAGO version 3.1), Polytechnic Institute of New York, Brooklyn, N.Y.

APPENDIX 4

THE PL/I(D) COMPILER

The PL/I(F) compiler requires at least 64,000 bytes of core and a computer at least as large as the IBM System/360 Model 30. For IBM computers not meeting these requirements, IBM offers the PL/I(D) compiler which needs only 16,000 bytes of core.

The part of PL/I implemented by the D compiler is called *basic* PL/I or *subset*. A program written for the D compiler will also run on the F compiler, but the reverse does not hold. The core-storage savings in the D compiler are achieved at the cost of restrictions in the statements as well as fewer built-in functions, attributes, abbreviations, and modes.

Many of these restrictions apply to PL/I features not described in this book. We will now describe the restrictions applying to the material in the book.

Restrictions in Statements

1. The DECLARE statement must immediately follow the PROCEDURE statement.
2. No multiple assignments.
3. No multiple closure.

Restrictions in Options

1. No COPY option.
2. In SKIP(w), w is either 0, 1, 2, or 3.
3. In LINE(w), w is an unsigned integer constant of less than 256.
4. No LINESIZE option.
5. No BY NAME option.

Restrictions in Arrays

1. No arrays of structures.
2. Arrays have at most three subscripts (that is, three dimensions).

3. Lowbounds of arrays may not be specified and are always 1.
4. No cross sections of arrays.

Restrictions in Built-in Functions

1. No DIM, LBOUND, or HBOUND function
2. No LENGTH function
3. No POLY function
4. No ONCHAR or ONSOURCE functions

Restrictions in Mode

No complex mode. All numerical data are assumed to be real. Hence there is no C format with the edit-directed statements and no built-in functions associated with complex values (that is, REAL, IMAG, CONJG, and COMPLEX).

Restrictions in Attributes

1. No VARYING attribute.
2. In the DEFINED attribute both arrays must have the same bounds. Also the *i*SUB correspondence cannot be used.
3. No LIKE attribute.

Restrictions in Dynamic Storage Allocation

1. No ALLOCATE or FREE statements
2. No CONTROLLED attribute

Restrictions in Conditions

1. The on-unit associated with the ON statement may only be either a GO TO or a null statement.
2. No CHECK, STRINGRANGE, or SUBSCRIPTRANGE conditions.

Restrictions on Abbreviations

The keywords

BINARY	FIXEDOVERFLOW
COLUMN	OVERFLOW
CONVERSION	DEFINED

may not be abbreviated.

Restriction on Conversions

No conversions between character strings and numerical data are allowed.

Restrictions on Qualified Names

1. Qualified names may not include major structure names.
2. Subscripts must appear at the extreme right of a qualified name [for example, A.B.C(2,2,1) is legal, but A(2).B(2).C(1) is illegal].

Restriction on Procedures

No recursive procedures are allowed.

Restrictions on Names

1. An external name may have at most six characters.
2. The name SYSIN may not be used for a file name without an explicit declaration

Other Restrictions

There are other restrictions concerning the maximum permissible nestings of IFs, parentheses, procedures, BEGIN blocks, and DOs. The maximums for the D compiler are smaller than for the F compiler. For these and other details, see:

"IBM System/360 Disk and Tape Operating Systems, PL/I Subset Reference Manual," IBM Systems Reference Library, form C28-8202.
"IBM System/360 Disk and Tape Operating Systems PL/I Programmer's Guide," IBM Systems Reference Library, form C24-9005.

APPENDIX 5
PL/I CHECKOUT
AND OPTIMIZING
COMPILERS

The checkout and optimizing compilers were introduced by IBM. The checkout compiler is principally for debugging. Once the debugging is completed, the optimizing compiler can be used to produce an efficient code for either fast compilation or fast execution.

THE CHECKOUT COMPILER

The checkout compiler meets three objectives:

1. To check the program thoroughly
2. To print detailed diagnostic messages
3. To translate quickly

The checking is divided into two phases. In the first phase, syntax and semantic errors are checked. In the syntax-error check each individual statement as well as a group of several statements are scanned. An individual statement is checked for syntax correctness, while a group of several statements is scanned for complementing statements (for example, a BEGIN statement needs a complementing END statement).

In the semantic check (also known as *global* check) the compiler looks for errors caused by conflicting specifications in different places. An example of such an error is two declarations of conflicting attributes for the same variable.

After the global check the program is subjected to the second phase of checking, the so-called *interpretation checking*. In this phase variables and their storage assignment are checked as well as the legality of various transfers. An illegal transfer into an iterative DO group is one example of an error detected in this phase.

If the operating system of the computer contains the timesharing facilities, the checkout compiler can be used in a so-called *conversational mode*. In such a mode the program can be checked as it is being written (at a terminal), with attendant conveniences to the programmer.

For debugging there is first the CHECK condition prefix. Just like PL/C, the checkout compiler has the CHECK, NOCHECK, FLOW, and NOFLOW statements. The compiler also has the COUNT option for counting the number of executions of each statement. It is possible to obtain the printout of the contents of the storage (named the *dump*) and various storage addresses, helpful in detecting difficult program bugs.

THE OPTIMIZING COMPILER

The optimizing compiler aims at producing programs to run quickly and occupy little storage. The compiler operates with or without an optimizing option. With the option, execution time is reduced; without the option, compilation time is reduced. Even without the option, an efficient program ensues.

The execution of scientific programs runs approximately half as long with the optimizing compiler as it does with the F compiler. On business-oriented programs, it takes 30 percent less time with the optimizing compiler than with the F compiler. Such fast execution usually requires 25 percent more compilation time as the price paid for the optimizing option.[1]

How does the optimizing compiler achieve faster execution? It does so by following good programming techniques. This means that the optimizing compiler improves a badly written program more than a well-written program. We will now describe three such improvements by examples.

1. *Elimination of common expressions*. In

$$
\begin{array}{l}
\text{X1}=\text{A}+3; \\
\text{X2}=\text{A}+3; \\
\text{.........} \\
\text{Xn}=\text{A}+3;
\end{array}
$$

A+3 is evaluated just once and its value substituted whenever needed.

2. *Transfer of statements from DO loops*. In

---

[1]"OS PL/I Optimizing Compiler: General Information," p. 3, IBM, order no. GC33-0001-2, p. 3.

$$DO\ I=1\ to\ 100;$$

. . . .

$$X=10;$$

. . . . . .

$$END;$$

99 executions will be saved by placing $X=10;$ outside the loop.

3. *Simplification of expressions.* In

$$X=Y**2;$$
$$Z=Y**3+3;$$

simplification results in the faster version

$$X=Y*Y;$$
$$Z=X*Y+3;$$

These examples illustrate the ways in which the optimizing compiler improves the program. The compiler also does other things. It quickly initializes arrays and structures, it eliminates redundant expressions, it performs more involved simplifications than the ones illustrated, and it converts quickly. For a description of these and other such techniques, references are listed at the end of this appendix.

THE CHECKOUT AND OPTIMIZING COMPILERS

The checkout and optimizing compilers provide a complementing pair of compilers for both debugging and fast execution. Both these compilers are compatible with one another, and also with PL/I(F) except for minor differences. The differences are that the checkout and optimizing compilers contain extra features. We will list three such features.

1. Procedures written in Cobol, Fortran, or assembly languages may be used.
2. Floating-point numbers have the maximum precisions
   109 for FLOAT BIN   (53 in PL/I(F))
   33 for FLOAT DEC   (16 in PL/I(F))
3. There are additional mathematical built-in functions ASIN(X) and ACOS(X) for computing arcsin x and arccos x. The returned angle is in radians, and only real arguments are allowed.

There are several other extensions. For a description of these and additional details on these two compilers, see the following IBM publications:

"OS PL/I Checkout Compiler: General Information," order no. GC33-0003.
"OS PL/I Optimizing Compiler: General Information," order no. GC33-0001.

"OS PL/I Checkout and Optimizing Compilers: Language Reference Manual," order no. SC33-0009.
"OS PL/I Checkout Compiler: Programmer's Guide," order no. SC33-0007.
"OS PL/I Optimizing Compiler: Programmer's Guide," order no. SC33-0006.

For use in the timesharing mode, see:

"OS PL/I Checkout Compiler: TSO User's Guide," order no. SC33-0033.
"OS PL/I Optimizing Compiler: TSO User's Guide," order no. SC33-0029.

APPENDIX 6
JOB CONTROL
LANGUAGE

Job control language, abbreviated to *JCL,* is a set of statements directing the operating system to execute the program.

The operating system contains *processing programs* consisting of *language translators* and *service programs.* The higher-level language translators are named *compilers.* The compiler translates a *source deck* or *source module* into an *object module.* One useful service program is the *linkage editor* for linking object modules (for example, obtained from the compiler and subroutine libraries) into a so-called *load module.* The load module is suitable for loading into core storage and subsequent execution. Another service program is the *loader* which combines both link editing and loading. Each processing program has a name. We use the desired processing programs by providing the JCL with their names.

The JCL also tells the operating system which input and output devices are to be allocated to the program. In computer jargon each program to be executed by the operating system is named a *job.* A typical job has three parts: compilaton, link editing, and execution. These parts are named *job steps,* or just *steps.*

JCL Statements

Typical JCL statements are:

1. The JOB statement at the beginning of the job. It has the form

    //name JOB parameters comments

2. The EXEC (execute) statement of the form

    //name EXEC parameters comments

3. The DD (data definition) statement describing the data set. It has the form

    //name DD parameters comments

4. The delimiter statement indicating the end of the data set. It has the form

/* comments

5. The null statement at the end of the job. It has the form

/ /

In all instances the slashes start in column 1 of the JCL card. The name in the first three statements comprises one to eight characters. The first character is a letter; the other characters are either digits or letters. As in PL/I, #, @, and $ may be used for letters.

JCL for PL/I(F)

As an example, the JCL cards to run a PL/I program with the PL/I(F) compiler are

```
/ / POLY7562  JOB parameters
/ / HRSTP EXEC PL1FCG
/ / PL1L.SYSIN DD *
   [The PL/I program
/ *
/ / GO.SYSIN DD *
   [data
/ *
/ /
```

We will now explain these cards.

The JOB statement. POLY7562 is the job name and identifies the job. The reason that such an awkward name is chosen here is that in our computer center (and others) a job card is supplied with the name prepunched. The name starts in column 3.

At least one blank separates JOB from the name. There is at least one blank to separate JOB from the parameters.

The parameters are divided into two types: *positional* and *keyword*. The positional parameters are coded first and consist of accounting information and the programmer's name, in that order. The keyword parameters tell (1) whether or not to list all JCL cards (MSGLEVEL), (2) job priority (PRTY), (3) time limit on the job (TIME), (4) core storage requested (REGION), and so on.

The accounting information is in the form

(account number, additional accounting information)

If the *account number* is omitted, a comma must be shown. If there is no *additional accounting information,* the parentheses may be omitted.

The programmer's name may have from 1 to 20 characters and may contain a period. If it contains special characters (for example, a blank), it must be enclosed in single quotes. Examples include

```
//POLY7542 JOB (1642,53), RUSTON
//TRIANGLE JOB 1053, 'HENRY RUSTON'
//ALPHA JOB  , RUSTON, TIME=(,29)
```

The TIME parameter is in the form (*minutes, seconds*); hence we request 29 seconds. If the programmer's name contains a quote, it must be expressed as a double quote (for example, 'O"HARA' for O'Hara).

The EXEC statement. HRSTP is the name of the step. At least one blank separates EXEC from both HRSTP and PL1FCG.

PL1FCG is the name of a *cataloged procedure*. A cataloged procedure is a set of job control statements which the operating system substitutes for the name (for example, for PL1FCG). This procedure can be used to compile and load-and-execute a PL/I(F) program. Another catalog procedure for the PL/I(F) compiler is PL1LFCLG, which compiles, link edits, and executes. Other cataloged procedures only compile, or only link edit and execute.

The DD statement. This statement describes the input and output devices needed. Here PL1L.SYSIN tells us that the data needed to execute the cataloged procedure will use SYSIN, that is, the system input (usually the card reader). The asterisk after DD tells us that data for the cataloged procedure will follow immediately. Here the PL/I program following the DD statement is the data for the cataloged procedure.

The delimiter statement. The delimiter statement (the /* statement) indicates the end of the PL/I source program. (This card can be omitted on many installations).

The DD statement. The statement

```
//GO.SYSIN DD *
```

tells us that the input data will follow.

The delimiter statement. This statement identifies the end of the data deck.

The null statement. This statement marks the end of the job. (This statement affords an extra protection from strange cards but is in practice unnecessary.)

If the program has no data, there is no need for the //GO.SYSIN DD * control card. In such a case follow the PL/I program by just the /* and // cards.

JCL for the D, Checkout, and Optimizing Compilers

To use any of these PL/I compilers we must call the correct cataloged procedure (shown on the EXEC card).

For the D compiler: No cataloged procedure
For the checkout compiler:

        PLICKR   (translate, interpret)

or

        PLICKCLG   (translate, link edit, interpret)

or

        PLICKCG   (translate, link edit, interpret)

For the optimizing compiler:

        PLIXCG   (compile, load-and-execute)

or

        PLIXCLG   (compile, link edit, and execute)

Examples of control cards include the following:

For the D compiler (used under the *Disk Operating System*):

```
// JOB PENTA PROGRAM
// OPTION LINK
// EXEC PL/I
   PENTA: PROCEDURE OPTIONS (MAIN):
   [The remainder of the PL/I(D) program
/*
// EXEC LNKEDT
// EXEC
   [data
/*
/&
```

For the checkout compiler:

```
// TABLE JOB (1234, 126), 'H RUSTON'
// HRSTEP EXEC PLICKR
// GO.SYSCIN DD *
   [ The PL/I program
 * DATA      (omit if no data)
   [data
/*
```

For the optimizing compiler:

```
// SQUARE JOB 16835, RUSTON
// HR EXEC PLIXCLG
// PLI. SYSIN DD *
```

```
                        [ The PL/I program
            /*
            // GO.SYSIN DD *
               [data
            /*
```

Information on JCL for a specific compiler can be found in that compiler's "Programmer's Guide." Additional information on JCL for the IBM System/360 and System/370 can be found in the following references:

"IBM System/360 Operating System: Job Control Language Reference," IBM Systems Reference Library, Order No. GC28-6704

Ashby, G. P., and R. L. Heilman: "Introduction to I/O Concepts and Job Control Language for the Operating System 360," Dickenson, Encino, CA, 1971.

Brown, G. D.: "System/360 Job Control Language," Wiley, NY, 1970.

Shelly, G. B., and T. J. Cashman: "OS Job Control Language," Anaheim Publishing, Fullerton, CA, 1972.

JCL for PL/C

The control cards for PL/C have an asterisk in column 1, a keyword in column 2, and have the form

```
* PL/C   ID = 'programmer's name' options
  [ The PL/C program
* DATA      (omit if no data)
  [ data
```

Examples of *options* are

$$ERRORS = (c,r)$$

which means suppress execution if there are c or more compilation errors, terminate execution if there are r or more runtime errors

$$PAGES = n$$

where n is the maximum number of pages to be printed

$$TIME = (m,s)$$

which means time limit (compilation + execution) = m minutes and s seconds

An example of PL/C control cards is

```
* PL/C   ID = 'HENRY RUSTON', ERRORS = (25,1 0), TIME= (,20)
  [The PL/C program
* DATA
  [data
```

Note that the requested maximum time is 20 seconds.

There are more options, and their names can be abbreviated. It is also possible to run independent programs as a single job. For these and additional details see the "PL/C User's Guide" referenced at the end of App. 2.

JCL for PLAGO

The control cards for PLAGO have a $ in column 1, a keyword in column 2, and have the form

```
$BEGIN     account no.  name, options
 [The PLAGO program
$DATA      (must be present even if the program has no data)
 [data
$END
```

There is at least one blank separating the *account no.* from BEGIN and *name*. The *account no.* consists of eight characters. The *options* may be omitted, but if present they are separated from the *name* by a comma with no intervening blanks. The different *options* are separated from one another also by a comma, with no spaces in between. Examples of the first control card are

```
$BEGIN     EE231231    RUSTON,TIME=20,LINES=50
```

(limits the time to 20 seconds and prints 50 lines per page) and

```
$BEGIN     EE530530    RUSTON-H,NOATR,SM(1,80)
```

(the table of attributes is not printed, and the entire card is scanned for source statements, that is, columns 1–80 rather than 2–72).

There are more options. For further details see the "PLAGO Users Handbook" referenced at the end of App. 3.

INDEX

A format item, 426–427
Abbreviations:
  for character strings, 228
  for conditions, 480
  in declaration, 47
  for statements, 88
ABS built-in function, 335
ACOS built-in function in checkout and optimizing
    compilers, 520
Activation of a block, 391
Algol, 2
Algorithm, 5
ALLOCATE statement, 289
AND operator, 67–68, 253
  symbol for, 67
Annotation symbol, 29
Argument, 230, 348, 358–383
  array, 363–366
  constant, 360–363
  ENTRY, 373–381
  expression, 360–363
  label, 372–373
  list, 326, 350
  string, 367–368
  structure, 366–367
Arithmetic attributes, 40–44
  base, 40
    BINARY (BIN), 40
    DECIMAL (DEC), 40
  default, 42
  factoring of, 47–48
  mode, 41
    COMPLEX (CPLX), 41
    REAL, 41

Arithmetic attributes:
  partial declaration of, 48
  precision, 41–42
  scale, 41
    FIXED, 41
    FLOAT, 41
Arithmetic conversions, 185–189
  of base, 185–189
  precision in, 187–189
Arithmetic expressions (*see* Expressions)
Aron, Joel D., 161, 414
Array, 274–294
  arguments, 363–366
  assignment, 280–281
  asterisk notation for, 285, 364–366
  cross-section of, 286
  declaration of, 276–279
  dimensions, 275
    attribute, 279
    limits on, 276
  dynamic storage allocation for, 289–291
  elements, 275
  in input, 279–280
  operations on, 281–282
  in output, 279–280
  parameters, 363–366
  of structures, 312–315
  subscripts, 275
    limits on, 276
  type, 274–294
Ashby, Gordon P., 526
ASIN built-in function in checkout and optimizing
    compilers, 520
Assembler, 1